GOVERNMENT PUBLICATIONS
AND THEIR USE

LAURENCE F. SCHMECKEBIER
ROY B. EASTIN

GOVERNMENT PUBLICATIONS
and their use

SECOND REVISED EDITION

THE BROOKINGS INSTITUTION
Washington, D.C.

THE BROOKINGS INSTITUTION is an independent organization devoted to nonpartisan research, education, and publication in economics, government, foreign policy, and the social sciences generally. Its principal purposes are to aid in the development of sound public policies and to promote public understanding of issues of national importance.

The Institution was founded on December 8, 1927, to merge the activities of the Institute for Government Research, founded in 1916, the Institute of Economics, founded in 1922, and the Robert Brookings Graduate School of Economics and Government, founded in 1924.

The general administration of the Institution is the responsibility of a self-perpetuating Board of Trustees. The trustees are likewise charged with maintaining the independence of the staff and fostering the most favorable conditions for creative research and education. The immediate direction of the policies, program, and staff of the Institution is vested in the President, assisted by an advisory council chosen from the staff of the Institution.

In publishing a study, the Institution presents it as a competent treatment of a subject worthy of public consideration. The interpretations and conclusions in such publications are those of the author or authors and do not purport to represent the views of the other staff members, officers, or trustees of the Brookings Institution.

FOREWORD

THE FIRST EDITION of *Government Publications and Their Use,* by Laurence F. Schmeckebier, was published by the Brookings Institution in 1936. In 1939, having attained the status of a reference classic, it was thoroughly revised and re-issued. In the 1950s another revision was undertaken by Schmeckebier with the assistance of Roy B. Eastin, then Executive Officer of the Government Printing Office, and published in 1961, not long after Schmeckebier's death.

Since then, government publications have continued to grow in number and significance. They have become increasingly important tools for educators, researchers, and policy makers. Some titles have established impressive sales and distribution records, reflecting public recognition of their helpfulness. With the need apparent for another revision of *Government Publications and Their Use,* Dr. Eastin, who is now Professor of Business Administration at George Washington University, undertook to make the work current to December 1968.

Users of government publications find it difficult to keep themselves informed of new publications. Lack of uniformity in the classification of government documents complicates locating all material available on a particular subject. The purpose of this volume is to describe the basic guides to government publications, to indicate the uses and limitations of available indexes, catalogs, and bibliographies, to explain the systems of numbering and methods of titling, to call attention to certain outstanding compilations or series of publications, and to indicate how the publications may be obtained. It is thus a guide to the acquisition and use of government publications and not—even though it cites many publications by title—a catalog, a bibliography, or a checklist.

Dr. Eastin and the Brookings Institution wish to record their indebtedness to all those who reviewed the manuscript of the original edition and the later revisions and made constructive suggestions. Particularly helpful ideas and advice were contributed by Carper W. Buckley, S. Preston Hipsley, Helen L. Phelps, Mary E. Poole, and Margaret B. Wilson.

KERMIT GORDON
President

October 1969
Washington, D.C.

CONTENTS

CHAPTER ONE

INTRODUCTION

IN NUMBER AND VARIETY the publications of the government of the United States probably exceed those of any other government or of any commercial publisher. In size they range from pamphlets to ponderous volumes, and in content they vary from articles with a popular appeal to technical treatises of value mostly to the trained scientist. Taken as a whole, they constitute a great library covering almost every field of human knowledge and endeavor.

Many of the publications are transcripts of original records and constitute primary source material in the history of government administration and activities. Others, such as the annual reports, contain accounts by executive officers of the work under their direction. Voluminous series published by different agencies present statistical pictures of conditions and afford bases for measuring social and economic change. An ever-increasing group gives the results of extensive research in both the social and physical sciences.

These books and pamphlets are not mere dry statistical records but touch all facets of human life. Government documents, as they are often called, are the living record of the efforts of a people to govern themselves. The scope of the federal government has broadened throughout its history, and citizens now look more and more to the federal agencies for information outside the traditional concepts of governmental activities.

Some persons, of course, make greater use of government documents than others. The teacher, student, researcher, farmer, war veteran, lawyer, and businessman regularly need and use government publications. Bibliographers in most fields of study would include them. No matter what vocation a person may follow or activity he may pursue, it is safe to say there exists a government publication which he would find helpful or interesting.

It is difficult to imagine a modern general library without a large number of government documents. Most libraries have on their staffs specialists in unlocking for readers the great storehouse of information to be found in government pamphlets and books. Why should specialists be necessary to assist persons interested in the information in government issuances and why are special books needed to guide readers in this field? Why should government publications be treated in a different manner from privately printed works? The staggering number of government publications printed each year, added to the accumulations of past years, is sufficient answer. During the fiscal year 1968, the number of government publications distributed by the Superintendent of Documents to depository libraries was in excess of 16,000.

Few general libraries which receive substantial numbers of government publications attempt to catalog and shelve them in the same manner as they do privately published books and pamphlets. The most popular practice is to depend largely, or entirely, on printed catalogs and indexes and to place government publications together in a separate collection. In these libraries a search of the card catalog for information on a particular subject would reveal only privately published works, although the library would in all likelihood also have government publications on the subject. A reader looking over a shelf of books on postage stamps and stamp collecting would not find *Postage Stamps of the United States, 1847–1967,* although the library would almost surely have this volume. However, it would be found in the public documents collection on a shelf with other publications of the Post Office Department. Similarly, a reader browsing through a collection of books on arboriculture would not find the Department of Agriculture's yearbook entitled *Trees,* for it would usually be shelved with the

Department's other publications in the documents collection.

The reader who regularly peruses the book-review pages of newspapers and magazines will find few government publications mentioned. Such excellent guides as *Publishers' Weekly* and the *Library Journal* contain a limited number of references to government works. Articles from only a very few of the government's many periodicals are listed in the various indexes to periodicals. The Vertical File Index of the H. W. Wilson Company lists only a small number of the thousands of government pamphlets which would be suitable for inclusion. The editor once explained that the indexing service would grow beyond practical size if an attempt were made to include government items regularly. The Library of Congress issues printed catalog cards for only a small number of the many new government publications which appear each month.

The failure to catalog, index, list, and publicize government publications on the same basis as nongovernment works raises a formidable although not insurmountable barrier for the potential reader. He must become acquainted with the guides to government publications which exist and must understand the past and present publishing practices of governmental agencies. A detailed knowledge of the organization of the government is also an invaluable asset. Of course, there is no substitute for day-to-day experience in the use of government documents, and the inexperienced reader usually can obtain valuable assistance from reference librarians and from experienced researchers.

The difficulties described above are enough to discourage most casual readers, but there are many persons who must keep abreast of all developments in a particular field or all governmental statements on a given subject. These specialists will find valuable information in the periodicals issued by government agencies whose activities cover their subjects. Many of these periodicals are something akin to house organs found in business enterprises and give useful facts concerning the publishing practices of the issuing government agency. A list of typical periodicals is included in Chapter 18.

Learning of the existence of a desired government publication then leads to the problem of gaining access to a copy. There is no centralized source from which all government documents may be obtained. Many documents are considered ephemeral in nature and only a few copies are mimeographed. To a person carrying on research, one of these documents may be of vital interest. Other publications are considered to be limited to the internal operations of the government, and no copies are made available to the public. However, these publications are often listed in catalogs and bibliographies, and a demand for copies arises. How to obtain one of these "official use only" documents is a distinct art which many persons find it necessary to master. Some classes of publications are so difficult to acquire on a regular basis that a group of large libraries have underwritten a Documents Expediting Project to serve as a Washington procurement office for fugitive publications.

Not all public documents are placed on sale, and those which are sold are not kept in print perpetually. Documents are reprinted for sale only when the sales record demonstrates a substantial public interest. Chapters 5 and 19 outline methods of procuring photocopies or microfilm copies of publications. There are some documents that are so highly specialized that no copies are printed for public distribution. In this case photocopies of the original are the only source for the researcher.

Within the over-all area of government publishing, there are some classes of publications which follow special rules, practices, and traditions. The publications of the Congress fall into this category and are treated in Chapter 6. Maps are another example and are described in Chapter 16.

Commercial book stores are of limited value to persons interested in obtaining government publications. The law limits the discount to book stores to twenty-five percent, and most book sellers consider this inadequate as there is no return privilege for unsold copies. Book stores seldom maintain stocks of any government works and make little or no effort to keep informed of new documents available for sale. A book store will, however, usually order a government publication upon request of a regular customer who knows the title of the work he is seeking.

Special problems arise in searching for information to be found in older government publications. Titles of series vary, publishing agencies have been transferred from one department to another, new agencies have been created, and others have passed out of existence. Some early indexes and bibliographies were not as inclusive as might be desired.

The chapters that follow are designed to provide an understanding of government publishing practices past and present, to indicate sources of information concerning the existence of publications, and to describe how copies may be obtained. Some publications and series of publications of outstanding importance are listed, particularly in the field of administration and public law, as these publications fall into well-defined classes. This same approach is not possible in the cases of publications giving the results of research. As pointed out in Chapter 17, this group includes such a wide variety of subjects that an adequate presentation would require a history of research by the government or a voluminous cataloging. Chapters 2 to 5 and 17 contain information that applies to almost all classes of publications, while the remaining chapters deal with classes that are of major interest to specialists working in particular fields.

Most persons who use this volume will be experienced researchers who desire a reference volume. Persons new to the field of government publishing should not become discouraged by the apparent complexity, for, after a relatively brief exploration and exposure to the guides available, they will become proficient in availing themselves of the wealth of information to be found in no other sources.

CHAPTER TWO

CATALOGS AND INDEXES

THE VARIETY IN SUBJECT MATTER of government publications, as well as the overlapping functions of many government agencies, make adequate guides to government publications essential. For almost a hundred years practically no comprehensive cataloging and indexing was undertaken. With the enactment in 1895 of the general printing law, which established the Office of the Superintendent of Documents, a systematic program was begun.

The catalogs and indexes which are frequently referred to throughout this book may be classified into three groups: (1) comprehensive general, covering all subjects and a series of years; (2) periodic, covering a definite period and issued regularly; and (3) special, covering a limited group of publications. Each of these groups includes some catalogs and indexes which cover both congressional and executive branch publications, commonly called "departmental" publications.

The bibliographies of government and other publications described in Chapter 3 serve as guides in a number of fields.

Comprehensive General Catalogs and Indexes

Works falling into this category will be discussed approximately in the order of the date of publication rather than by the period covered.

Poore's Descriptive Catalogue, 1774–1881

The first and only attempt to make a complete list of all government publications—executive, legislative, and judicial—resulted in Ben Perley Poore's *Descriptive Catalogue of the Government Publications of the United States, September 5, 1774–March 4, 1881*[1] (1,392 pages), issued also as Senate Miscellaneous Document 67, 48th Congress, 2d session. Some of the problems which confronted the compiler are set forth in the preface:

When the members of the Joint Committee on Printing of the 47th Congress commenced the direction of the work thus entrusted to them, they were in the position of Christopher Columbus when he steered westward on his voyage of discovery, confident that a new world existed, but having no knowledge of its distance or the direction in which it lay. No one could estimate how many publications were to be catalogued, where they were to be found, how long it would take to perform the work, or what would be the probable cost. A plan for the work was adopted by which there was to be obtained in each case: I, the title of the book, pamphlet, or document; II, the name of its author; III, the date of its publication; IV, where it was to be found; and V, a brief abstract of its contents. These were to be chronologically arranged, and accompanied by a copious alphabetical and analytical index for convenience of reference. Work was commenced in accordance with this plan under the superintendence of two gentlemen, each one independent of the other; but when Congress met the ensuing winter it was found that slow progress had been made at a heavy cost, which had consumed a large share of the appropriation.

On the first of March, 1883, the work was placed under the superintendence of the subscriber, with directions to follow the plan approved by the committee, and to employ fourteen gentlemen, who were designated. They at once commenced work in the Libraries of Congress, of the Senate, of the House of Representatives, of the seven executive departments and their respective bureaus, of the Department of Agriculture, of the Smithsonian Institution, of the Coast and Geodetic Survey, of the various exploring and scientific surveys, and in the public library of the city of Boston, which possesses an excellent collection of congressional documents. The valuable collections of political pamphlets in the Congressional Library and several private collections of historical material were also carefully examined. Unfortunately, not one of the clerks employed possessed any experience in the performance of such work, and some proved to be so entirely incompetent that no use could be made of what they did; but by the patient and diligent application of the others, 63,063 books, pamphlets, and documents were found and catalogued.

When the work was so far advanced that an estimate could be made of

[1] Hereafter referred to as *Poore's Catalogue.*

its probable size, it was found that if completed as it had been commenced it would make two bulky volumes. This was not desirable, and by direction of the Joint Committee on Printing those titles which had been completed were rewritten in a more condensed form, subsequently followed. This diminished the size, but impaired the fidelity of description in each individual title. Further appropriations were made by Congress for the prosecution of the work, and its scope was enlarged by including "publications of public interest purchased by the United States for use or distribution."

The Index, that indispensable key to the *Catalogue,* was made as full as possible, without an unnecessary multiplication of titles, and many affiliated topics have been gathered together. The attempt to classify the separate topics was the more difficult because the reconstructed abstracts often failed to give a clear idea of the document to be indexed.

It was found, as the work progressed, that quite a number of executive documents had been printed by each of the printers of the two houses of Congress. In most instances they were duplicates, but some of them varied, not only in the titles, but in the omission of paragraphs or sentences from one or the other copy. To have collated them would have required years of time, and the Joint Committee on Printing directed that each separate publication should be catalogued, without paying any regard to the existence of other editions. Some of the publications catalogued by different clerks working in different libraries were found to be in duplicate, but it was impossible to decide which copy should be retained and which omitted, so each one was given.

This work made a quarto volume of 1,241 pages of catalog and 151 pages of index. The entries in the catalog are arranged chronologically, the executive and judicial publications being given at the beginning of the portion relating to each year and the congressional publications being arranged by the date on which the printing was ordered. Most of the entries are for congressional publications, and many of the departmental reports were missed entirely. Each entry is annotated.

Among the early issues listed are some that are publications of the states and some that appear to be neither state nor federal. For many early entries the citations are to the journals of Congress or to the *Annals of Congress.*[2] It is evident that these entries do not represent separate publications but are index entries to the volumes cited. Many entries for executive

[2] See pp. 136–37 for description.

publications do not indicate the publishing office but give instead the name of the library where the publication was found.

Some of the citations to the numbered publications of the early congresses may prove baffling. The term "State Papers" means at times Gales and Seaton's *American State Papers,* but generally it indicates a House or Senate report or document, as the name "State Papers" appears on the back title of some of the volumes containing these publications. In general when "State Papers" is followed by the name of one of the subdivisions and its volume number in Gales and Seaton's reprint, the citation is to that series. If "State Papers" is followed by a number higher than eight, the citation is to a separate document or report. Thus the citation (on page 47) "State Papers, Naval Affairs, Vol. I, pp. 84–102, 7th Cong., 1st sess." refers to Gales and Seaton's reprint. But on page 132 "State Papers, No. 56, 15th Cong. 2d sess., Vol. I," refers to Senate Document 56 of the session mentioned.

For these early congresses the citations in Poore, in addition to those to "Senate Documents," "House Documents," and "State Papers," include "Senate Papers," "Executive Papers," "Executive Documents," "Documents," and "House Executive Documents." All these refer to the documents or reports, generally to the documents. The best way to locate these publications in the proper series is to compare the citations with the tables at the beginning of the *Checklist of United States Public Documents, 1789–1909* (see pages 12–15), select the volumes which include the publication cited, and then examine the volumes to determine which one contains the desired report. Thus on page 162 of *Poore's Catalogue* a report of December 24, 1823, on distributing post offices is cited as "Ex. Papers, No. 10, 18th Cong. 1st sess., Vol. I." The table in the *Checklist* shows that for this session there is a Volume I of *Senate Documents* and a Volume I of *House Documents.* It shows also that Volume I of *Senate Documents* contains Documents 1–30 and that Volume I of *House Documents* contains Documents 1–16. Therefore "Ex. Papers No. 10, Vol. I" may be either a House or a Senate document. Examination of the books shows that the publication is a House document.

The citations are also incomplete for the years after 1847, when the documents of the two houses were in four series—*Senate Executive Documents, Senate Miscellaneous Documents, House Executive Documents,* and *House Miscellaneous Documents.* For this period there are many references to Senate or House documents without indication whether the publication is a miscellaneous or an executive document. During this period there were no series with the titles *Senate Documents* and *House Documents.* In other cases the citation is to an executive document without indication as to whether it is a House or Senate document. There has never been any series bearing the title *Executive Documents* except in the congressional set.

At times the proper series designation may be found by referring to the tables at the beginning of the *Checklist.* Thus on page 719 of *Poore's Catalogue* is a reference to "Ex. Docs. No. 91, 35th Cong. 1st sess., Vol. XI." The table in the *Checklist* shows that the last Senate executive document for that session was No. 73, and that Volume XI of *Senate Executive Documents* contains No. 30, Part 4. Therefore the publication cannot be a Senate executive document. The table also shows that the last number of the *House Executive Documents* is No. 140, and that Volume XI of *House Executive Documents* contains Nos. 89–96. It is therefore evident that the publication cited is a House executive document.

If the series number of the publication cited occurs in both series and in the same numbered volume in each series, this method yields no results, and it is necessary to consult the books.

The index, though voluminous, is not complete and therefore cannot be relied upon to give references to all the reports. If specific publications are desired, in most cases the index will indicate the page on which they are listed; but if the search is for all the reports on a subject, an examination must be made of all the entries. As the catalog is arranged chronologically, the search is not difficult if it is confined to a limited period. The most unsatisfactory feature of the index is the lack of differentiation. Thus, under the entry "Indian affairs, reports on," there are 187 citations to separate pages of the catalog with no indication regarding the period or subject covered by each citation. As each page of the catalog contains about sixty entries, the loss of time in locating titles is material.

With all its defects, *Poore's Catalogue* is a monumental publication, especially when consideration is given to the fact that there was no assembled collection of the volumes listed and that the work was done by an untrained force. Good or bad, it is the only catalog and index available for much of the material, as the *Tables and Index, 1817–93,* issued by the Superintendent of Documents, covers only selected publications (see pages 33–34).

The Ames Comprehensive Index, 1881–93

John G. Ames, chief of the Division of Documents in the Department of the Interior, supervised the preparation of the *Comprehensive Index to the Publications of the United States Government, 1881–93,* in two quarto volumes of 1,590 pages.[3] This was also issued as House Document 754, 58th Congress, 2d session. It is not a dictionary catalog, each publication being listed only once under the subject entry. It is analytical, however, in that important subordinate sections of a book are indexed separately. There are no entries under the names of personal authors, but some of the publishing agencies are given as major entries, the publications being listed thereunder. The name of the personal author is given in each case in the margin.

At the end of Volume 2 is an index of personal names of authors, the reference being to the pages of the index proper. As the names of authors in the margin are not in alphabetical order it is necessary to scan the entire list on the page cited.

[3] Hereafter referred to as the *Ames Index.* The first edition of this work covered only the years 1889–93.

The only differentiation between the entries in the personal index is in the case of senators and representatives who presented reports on behalf of more than one committee. In such cases there is a classification by committee, but even this often leaves a long list of page references opposite one entry.

The introduction to the *Checklist* contains the following comment on the *Ames Index:*

> Experience has taught that this two-volumed edition of the "Comprehensive index" is not so "comprehensive" as it ought by rights to be. It does not by any means include all the public documents which were issued during the twelve years from 1881 to 1893, the period of the 47th to the 52nd Congresses, inclusive. Like its predecessor, *Poore's Catalogue,* it lacks entries for a very large number of departmental publications.

Examples of incomplete indexing in Ames have been noted:

> In Ames "Results of a Biological Reconnaissance of South-Central Idaho, and Descriptions of a New Genus and Two New Species of North American Mammals" is indexed under "Biological Reconnaissance . . ." and under "Idaho, South Central, Biological Reconnaissance of," but not under "Mammals." However, "Perforated Stones from California" is entered under subject "Stones," but not under place "California." "Use of Gold and Other Metals among the Ancient Inhabitants of Chiriqui, Isthmus of Darien," is indexed under place, "Chiriqui" but not under the subject, "Gold." Incomplete indexing is seen in "Tertiary and Cretaceous Strata of the Tuscaloosa, Tombigbee, and Alabama Rivers," which is entered under "Tuscaloosa" but not under "Tombigbee" nor "Alabama."[4]

The *Ames Index* was succeeded by the biennial *Document Catalog,* which was discontinued in 1947 (see pages 22–26).

Checklist of United States Public Documents, 1789–1909

The latest general compilation of government publications is the third edition of the *Checklist of United States Public Documents, 1789–1909*[5] (1,707 pages), issued by the Office of the Superintendent of Documents in 1911.[6] This work was planned

[4] Marian A. Youngs, "Document Cataloging in Depository Libraries," *The Library Journal,* Vol. 63, Dec. 1, 1938, p. 914.
[5] Hereafter referred to as the *Checklist.*
[6] The first edition of the *Checklist* was compiled under the direction of John G. Ames of the Department of the Interior, and was issued in 1892 by that Department under the title *List of Congressional Documents from the*

to be in two volumes, the first to be the list and the second the index. The index volume has never been issued.

The work is divided into three sections: (1) numbered congressional publications; (2) departmental publications; and (3) miscellaneous publications of Congress. The congressional publications extend to the close of the 60th Congress and the departmental publications to the end of the calendar year 1909.

For the congressional documents and reports the listing is entirely by books, the information shown being the serial number, volume number, part number, series title, document or report numbers included in volumes, and notes.[7] There is no listing of individual documents.

Departmental publications are listed by departments or independent establishments and subdivided by subordinate units. In the case of numbered series such as the Bulletins of the Geological Survey, the series number only is given, the title being omitted. If the student is working in a library where the congressional publications are arranged according to the serial numbers, the *Checklist* is invaluable for use in finding the serial number. In the case of executive publications issued also as documents, the serial number is given in brackets after the entry for each publication. Thus the entry (page 408 of the *Checklist*) for Volume I of the Bulletins of the Fish Commission is

---

15th to the 51st Congress, and of Government Publications Containing Debates and Proceedings of Congress from the 1st to the 51st Congress together with Miscellaneous Lists of Public Documents, with Historical and Bibliographical Notes. This made an octavo volume of 120 pages. It was also published as H. Ex. Doc. 74, 52 Cong. 1 sess.

The second edition of the *Checklist* was issued by the Office of the Superintendent of Documents in 1895 under the title *Checklist of Public Documents Containing Debates and Proceedings of Congress, from the 1st to the 53rd Congress Together with Miscellaneous Lists of Documents and Historical and Bibliographical Notes* (222 pp.). This had been started by Ames, who turned his material over to the newly created Office of Superintendent of Documents. Ames had by this time worked out his scheme of serial numbers, which were used for the first time in the second edition of the *Checklist*. In addition to the *Checklist* proper, this book contains a list of explorations and surveys, a list of government catalogs, and lists of principal annual reports and series by years and serial numbers.

[7] For discussion of the method of numbering congressional publications, see pp. 154–56 and 157–66.

"V. I, 1881 [1996–131]." This indicates that this publication was published also as Document 131 in Serial 1996.

The special *Checklist* classification numbers serve also as a guide to the shelving of the publications in the library of the Office of the Superintendent of Documents.[8] For publications in the congressional series,[9] the *Checklist* is a guide to the location in the Library of Congress and other libraries which shelve their congressional publications according to the serial numbers.

The limiting date "1789" on the title page of the *Checklist* is somewhat misleading, as comparatively little congressional material prior to the 15th Congress is listed. The publications of the first 14 congresses listed are the following reprints:

American state papers (Gales and Seaton), 38 vols.
American state papers (Duff Green), 5 vols.
State papers (T. B. Wait and Sons), 1st ed., 8 vols.; 2d ed., 10 vols.; 3d ed., 12 vols.
Congressional register (Thomas Lloyd)
Journals of the Senate (Gales and Seaton's reprint), 5 vols.
Journals of the House of Representatives (Gales and Seaton's reprint), 9 vols.

A list of original prints of the publications of the first 14 congresses is not included. The cards for such a list were prepared in 1909 after an examination of the originals in various libraries. As the material was voluminous, it was decided to publish it later in separate form. The cards are in essentially the same condition as in 1909, as it has never been possible to prepare the material for the printer and have it published.[10]

Papers relating to the period before 1789 (mostly reprints) entered in the *Checklist* are the following:

American archives (Peter Force), 6 vols. of 4th series and 3 vols. of 5th series; other series not published
Elliot's debates on the adoption of the Constitution
Diplomatic correspondence of the American Revolution (Jared Sparks)
Diplomatic correspondence of the United States, 1783–89 (Francis P. Blair and Blair and Rives)

[8] Hereafter referred to as the Public Documents Library; for description, see pp. 132–33.
[9] See pp. 151–54 for description.
[10] For lists of the publications of the first 14 congresses, see pp. 29–30.

Revolutionary diplomatic correspondence (Francis Wharton)
Journals of the Continental Congress (original and reprints)
Secret journals of the Continental Congress (Thomas B. Wait)
Miscellaneous papers of the Continental Congress

The *Checklist* is of greatest value to the librarian and to the student who already has considerable familiarity with government publications. It does not pretend to be a dictionary catalog and cannot be used as such. As the arrangement is by publishing offices, as it does not give the titles of issues in numbered series, and as it has no index, it cannot be used as a quick reference book by persons who have no detailed knowledge of government publications.

For instance, the casual user of government publications cannot be expected to know that the publications of the King Survey of the 40th Parallel appeared as parts of Volume 18 of the *Professional Papers of the Engineer Department of the Army.* Likewise the *Checklist* is of little assistance if a publication originating in an executive department is published only as a document. Thus a bibliography on interoceanic canal and railway routes originated in the Library of Congress but was published only as Senate Document 59, 56th Congress, 1st session. It is therefore not listed under Library of Congress.

For congressional publications the table at the beginning of the book indicates the documents that are assembled in every volume. Thus for the Senate executive documents of the 2d session of the 44th Congress, the table (page 57 of the *Checklist*) shows that Nos. 21–30, 32–36, and 39–46 are assembled in Serial 1719, that Nos. 31 and 38 are in Serial 1720, and that No. 37 is in Serial 1721.

Catalogue of the Library of the United States Senate

This catalog pertains to a particular collection and does not pretend to be a list of all government publications. Nevertheless, it has some features which make it a desirable aid in locating material published by the government.[11]

A convenient feature of the catalog is the listing of practi-

[11] Hereafter referred to as *Senate Catalogue.* It was issued in 1895, 1901, and every two years from 1906 to 1924. It is no longer published.

cally all the annual reports and important departmental series that were also published as documents up to 1920. These lists give the document, volume, and part number but not the serial number. The catalog also has a table of congressional documents and reports by serial, volume, and document number similar to that in the *Checklist* but extending to the end of the 66th Congress.

A particularly useful portion of the 1924 edition is an index to hearings before committees and special commissions. The index to hearings in the catalog extends to March 4, 1923. This portion has been published separately several times; it is described on pages 180–82 of this book.

Periodic Catalogs and Indexes

The periodic publication of general catalogs and indexes dates from the passage of the Printing Act of 1895, which authorized and directed the issuance of the *Monthly Catalog*, the *Document Index*, and the biennial *Document Catalog*. In all these indexes the names of publishing offices are listed under the first significant word. Thus Bureau of Mines is listed as Mines Bureau. In 1928 what is now known as the *Selected List* was added.

Selected List

The *Selected List of United States Government Publications* was first issued as the *Weekly List* on July 11, 1928. It was changed to a semimonthly in 1942 and became a biweekly in 1951. It is a leaflet giving titles and prices of the more important government publications on sale, with annotations showing the scope of each publication. A check-list order form is included. The *Selected List* may be obtained free from the Superintendent of Documents. Over a half million persons avail themselves of this service, and the Superintendent of Documents regards the *Selected List* as his principal advertising medium.

As the *Monthly Catalog* often does not appear until eight weeks after the issuance of some of the publications listed, the *Selected List* is a valuable interim aid. As it is limited to publications with a wide appeal, it does not take the place of the *Monthly Catalog* for persons interested in more specialized fields.

Monthly Catalog of United States Government Publications[12]

Section 69 of the Printing Act of 1895 (28 Stat. 612) provided as follows:

A catalogue of government publications shall be prepared by the Superintendent of Documents on the first day of each month, which shall show the documents printed during the preceding month, where obtainable, and the price thereof. . . .

The *Monthly Catalog* was first issued under date of January 1895. It has been issued continuously since then under the following titles:

Catalogue of publications issued by government of United States (January–March 1895)

Catalogue of United States public documents, issued monthly (April 1895–December 1905)

Catalogue of United States public documents (January 1906–June 1907)

Monthly catalogue[13] United States public documents (July 1907–December 1939)

United States government publications monthly catalog (January 1940–December 1950)

Monthly catalog of United States government publications (January 1951–)

The *Monthly Catalog* is indispensable to the person desiring to keep in touch with government publications. It is also of more than ephemeral value to the student and bibliographer.

[12] Hereafter called *Monthly Catalog*. An earlier private publication generally known as *Hickcox's Monthly Catalogue* bore the full title *United States Government Publications, a Monthly Catalogue*. It was issued irregularly in monthly numbers making ten volumes from 1885 to 1894. The preface to the *Checklist* (p. xi) makes the statement that "many publications issued during the decade from 1885 to 1894 escaped the notice of Mr. Hickcox; still, it frequently happens that *Hickcox's Catalogue* contains entries for publications not listed elsewhere. This catalogue may be relied on for general excellence."

[13] "Catalog" beginning July 1933.

The catalog, which ordinarily appears at the end of the month of issue, contains titles of publications, instructions for obtaining them, and prices. Through 1905, volumes cover calendar years. The next volume includes eighteen months, January 1906 to June 1907. From July 1907 to June 1934 they appear on a federal fiscal-year basis, followed by a volume covering only six months, July to December 1934. Subsequent volumes revert to a calendar-year basis. Three supplementary catalogs listing material omitted from the *Monthly Catalog* were issued for the periods 1941–42, 1943–44, and 1945–46.

A volume index has been issued since the end of the first year, and a volume title page beginning with 1899. The index, now issued monthly as well as annually, includes subject entries, some title entries, the name of the issuing government agency if used in the title, and the series title, if any. The index refers to page number through August 1947 and to entry number since September. Names of personal authors were not used in the index from 1947 through 1962. A *Decennial Cumulative Index to the Monthly Catalog* for the period 1941–50 has been issued and another for the period 1951–60 will be available soon.

The primary arrangement of items in the *Monthly Catalog* is alphabetically by publishing office. Until September 1947, names of government departments and agencies constitute the main listing, with bureau names as subordinate headings. Thereafter, with some exceptions, the primary listing is by bureau names. In January 1948 a "Classified List of Government Authors" was added, which restored some of the advantages of the former arrangement. From 1952 to 1962, periodicals, press releases, and statistical statements were listed semiannually rather than monthly in an appendix to two issues of the *Monthly Catalog*. In 1961, the appendix became an annual feature.

Ordinarily most government publications are printed at the Government Printing Office, and copies are automatically made available to the compilers of the *Monthly Catalog*. During abnormal periods, however, such as those of the world wars, many of the new agencies obtained authority to have reports printed at commercial establishments instead of at the Government Printing Office. As a result of poor organization, ignorance, or indifference on the part of the publishing offices, copies were not always sent to the compilers of the catalog, and omissions in listings occurred.

Publications of field agencies and processed[14] issues constitute two groups for which there is no completely satisfactory listing. Prior to 1933 there were few publications of field agencies, most of them consisting of maps and books issued by the district offices of the Engineer Corps of the Army.

The change of administration in 1933 was followed by a great expansion in field agencies, many of which, particularly those of the Federal Emergency Relief Administration and its successors, the Works Progress Administration and the Work Projects Administration, issued a large number of publications. Unfortunately these were not listed currently or later assembled in any government publication. For the period from March 1933 to the end of 1936 the publications of both the field agencies and Washington offices of the new establishments were listed in four publications by Jerome K. Wilcox, published by the American Library Association. These were as follows:

Guide to the official publications of the New Deal administrations (mimeographed and printed); covers period March 1933–Apr. 15, 1934, 1934, 113 pp.
Same, supplement, Apr. 15, 1934–Dec. 1, 1935, 1936, 184 pp.
Same, second supplement, Dec. 1, 1935–Jan. 1, 1937,[15] 1937, 190 pp.
Unemployment relief documents: guide to the official publications and releases of the F.E.R.A. and 48 state relief agencies, 1936, 95 pp.; covers period to end of 1935 and contains checklist of publications and releases of F.E.R.A., Federal Surplus Relief Corporation, National Youth Administration, and Works Progress Administration

Prior to 1936 the *Monthly Catalog* included practically no processed publications, although many substantial publications of this type had been issued. Beginning with the issue for Jan-

[14] The term "processed" is used for publications reproduced by duplicating methods other than ordinary printing. It includes mimeographing, multigraphing, multilithing, and similar types. In the *Monthly Catalog* the term was used for the first time in the issue for September 1935; in the biennial *Document Catalog* it was used for the first time in the issue for the 73d Congress (Vol. 22, 1933–34).
[15] Includes also some 1937 titles.

uary 1936 the *Monthly Catalog* includes "such current publications of this type as would seem of sufficient importance to the general public to warrant such entry."

Despite strenuous efforts made by its editors, there is no doubt that the *Monthly Catalog* is incomplete because the compilers do not always receive copies from the publishing agencies and because the issuance and distribution of these publications are scattered among so many minor administrative units in the executive agencies. Until there is better organization of and control over this type of publication, a complete listing cannot be expected.[16]

Document Index

The Printing Act of 1895 (28 Stat. 611) provided that the Superintendent of Documents should "prepare and print in one volume a consolidated index of congressional documents." This index therefore covers only publications which are printed as documents and reports of the Senate or House of Representatives. This is indicated by the title pages, which have been as follows:

54th Congress, 1st session, to 59th Congress, 2d session: Index to the subjects of the documents and reports and to the committees, senators, and representatives presenting them

60th Congress, 1st session, and thereafter: Index to the reports and documents

Beginning with the 3d session of the 58th Congress the volumes were numbered serially, the numbering taking account of the earlier issues without numbers. Each issue was also pub-

---

[16] For lists and bibliographies of processed publications in general, see Jerome K. Wilcox in the following:

American Library Association, Committee on Public Documents, *Public Documents . . . 1933, 1934*, pp. 189–93.
Ibid., 1935, 1936, pp. 25–44.

For comments on difficulties in obtaining copies for listing, see Laurence F. Schmeckebier, "Some Problems of Government Publications," in *Public Documents, Papers Presented at the 1936 Conference of the American Library Association*, pp. 21–27.

lished as a House document. This index need not be used if the biennial *Document Catalog* is available.

Ordinarily the *Document Index* was compiled at the end of the regular sessions, a short special session being included in the volume for the next regular session. If, however, the special session was a long one, a separate index was issued. Special sessions of the Senate were always included with the next regular session.

This publication was discontinued with No. 43 for the 2d session of the 72d Congress. For the 73d Congress and thereafter the index to the *Monthly Catalog* and the biennial *Document Catalog* are the only places where congressional publications are completely indexed. Some material, particularly the congressional committee reports, may be located by means of the index to the *Congressional Record*. The *Document Index* was superseded by the *Numerical Lists and Schedule of Volumes* (see page 22).

While the index applies only to congressional documents and reports, it includes every executive annual report and series which has been printed also under a congressional title page, even though but few copies were available for congressional distribution. It is therefore helpful in ascertaining what has been published in certain departmental series.

The index was made from the titles and is not analytical. Committee reports are indexed under the subject entry, the name of the committee, and the name of the member submitting the report. All entries for committee reports give the number of the bill, but the bill number itself is not indexed. Bill numbers may be ascertained from the index to the *Congressional Record*.

As each index covered all documents and reports of a session or two sessions, it was necessary to index some publications in advance of printing if the index were to be issued with reasonable promptness. This at times resulted in errors, as the titles were changed or the publications not issued at all. All such changes were noted in the preface to succeeding editions. Documents or reports not issued when the index was prepared were indicated by an asterisk.

In the index proper the reference to the publications was always to the document or report number. Up to the end of the 67th Congress the volume number was also given. Beginning with the 1st session of the 68th Congress the serial number was substituted for the volume number, as the practice of stamping the volume number on the books sent to depository libraries was abandoned at that time.[17]

The *Document Index* contains several useful appendixes. A schedule of volume numbers showing the documents or reports in each volume has been included since the first issue, and beginning with the 1st session of the 55th Congress the serial number is also given in the schedule. Beginning with the 2d session of the 54th Congress, there is a numerical list of documents and reports, with a reference to the volume number. Beginning with the 2d session of the 60th Congress the serial number was added to this numerical list.

Numerical Lists and Schedule of Volumes

Since the discontinuance of the *Document Index* the documents and reports have been listed numerically in the pamphlet entitled *Numerical Lists and Schedule of Volumes*.[18] The first issue of this publication covered the 73d Congress; later issues have covered a session of Congress, except in the case of the 2d (special) and 3d sessions of the 75th Congress, which are combined.

Document Catalog

Section 62 of the Printing Act of 1895 (28 Stat. 610) made the following provision for the publication of the biennial *Document Catalog:*

The Superintendent of Documents shall, at the close of each regular session of Congress, prepare and publish a comprehensive index of public documents beginning with the 53rd Congress, upon such plan as shall be approved by the Joint Committee on Printing. . . .

The first issue of this publication took up the work where the

[17] For descriptions of volume and serial numbers in congressional sets, see pp. 157–66.
[18] Hereafter referred to as *Numerical Lists.*

Ames Index stopped, the *Ames Index* being in turn the immediate successor of *Poore's Catalogue*. Thus the several volumes of these three sets supplied a complete listing of all government publications, barring, of course, those inadvertently omitted. Maps and charts were listed in the biennial *Document Catalog*, but not in Poore and Ames.

The full title of this publication was *Catalogue*[19] *of Public Documents of the . . . Congress and all Departments of Government of the United States*. A series number was added with the issue of the seventh number for the 58th Congress, allowance being made for the earlier issues. It was also issued as a House document.

The first issue covered the 53d Congress, the second and third issues were for the 1st and 2d sessions of the 54th Congress, respectively, while each of the later issues was for an entire congress. It was discontinued in 1947, the last issue being Volume 25, 76th Congress, 1939–40.

The biennial *Document Catalog* superseded the *Monthly Catalog* and the *Document Index* for the period covered. It was an analytical dictionary catalog with entries under subject matter, individual authors, and governmental authors. Separates were listed independently and notation was made if the publication was issued in signature form. Beginning with the volume for the 56th Congress, if the publication was in the serial number set, the serial number was added in brackets.

This catalog was the only place where there was a complete list of the important series of orders issued by the President known as executive orders. These are now included in the *Code of Federal Regulations* and in *Public Papers of the Presidents*. Proclamations were also listed, and appeared as well in the *Statutes at Large*. Departmental series were listed under the name of the publishing office, with other entries under subject matter and name of author. Under the entry "Congressional Documents Lists," every issue had a schedule of the volumes of congressional publications. The issue for the 65th Congress

[19] "Catalog" beginning with Volume 21. Herein referred to as biennial *Document Catalog*.

contained for the first time a numerical list of House and Senate documents and reports.

With the exception of the 54th Congress, which was covered by a volume for each session, the period covered by each issue of the catalog to and including the one for the 72d Congress was a congress in the case of congressional publications, and two fiscal years ending June 30 of odd-numbered years in the case of departmental publications. For congressional publications the later volumes continued to cover the period of a congress. For departmental publications, Volume 22 for the 73d Congress listed those issued from July 1, 1933, to December 31, 1934, and the volumes for the 74th and later congresses covered those issued during the two calendar years ending with the even-numbered year. This change resulted from the adoption of the Twentieth Amendment to the Constitution (47 Stat. 2569), which makes the period of a congress practically cotermi- nous with two calendar years.[20]

Congressional publications were entered in the biennial *Doc- ument Catalog* for the congress which authorized their issu- ance. For all publications of a given congress printed before the catalog was completed, the catalog contained complete en- tries. For all publications not issued by that time, the catalog contained only skeleton entries, the complete entries being given in a later volume. Thus the volumes entitled *Papers Re- lating to the Foreign Relations of the United States 1920* form House Document 1045, 66th Congress, 3d session (1921), and a skeleton entry was given in Volume 15 of the *Document Catalog* for that congress. They were not published until 1935–36, and the complete entries are given in Volume 22 of the *Document Catalog* for the 73d Congress.

[20] Prior to the adoption of the Twentieth Amendment, the period of a con- gress ran for two years from March 4 of each odd-numbered year. Unless there was a special session, Congress convened in December of each odd- numbered year. No period was fixed for the first session, which ordinarily ended in June. The second regular session expired by limitation on March 4. Therefore the period of a congress corresponded more nearly to two fiscal years ending June 30 than to two calendar years. For this reason departmental publications were reported by fiscal years. The Twentieth Amendment provides that the period of a congress shall be two years from January 3 of each odd- numbered year.

Departmental publications included everything issued during the period covered. Thus the volume for the 65th Congress included congressional material ordered printed in the two years ending March 4, 1919, and departmental publications actually issued in the two years ending June 30, 1919. But if a departmental publication was also issued as a congressional publication, it was inserted according to congress, regardless of date of issue. Thus Geological Survey Bulletin 682 was published also as House Document 1243, 65th Congress, 2d session (1917–19). Although it was not issued until 1920, it was included in the biennial *Document Catalog* for the 65th Congress (1917–19), as one edition is technically a publication of that congress, notwithstanding the fact that the departmental edition was not issued in the period covered by the catalog. This is one of the anomalous situations that result from the inclusion of the same publication in both a departmental and congressional series.

Periodicals which were issued regularly were included in the biennial *Document Catalog* according to the date given on the title page. Thus a June 1919 issue which did not appear until after July 1 was listed in the catalog for the two years ending with June 1919.

The list in the catalog included not only issues printed from type but also processed publications. Some processed material was listed in Volume 16 as early as 1921–23, and, as such material assumed larger proportions, the number of entries increased. Volume 20 for 1929–31 was the first in which an effort was made to include all processed publications. But whether or not an issue was listed depended upon what the compilers considered a publication, and there was ample room for difference of opinion in this respect. Obviously all processed issues were not included, as a material portion was composed of press releases, notices of publications, and other ephemeral matter.

As in the case of the *Monthly Catalog*, some issues were probably omitted because they were not available to the compilers. Such omissions occur more frequently in abnormal times, such as during the world wars. To one familiar with departmental operations during such periods, it seems remarkable that the compilers were able to make the catalog so nearly complete.

At the end of the catalog appeared a list of government authors or offices, which was a guide to governmental organization for the offices which issue publications.

The biennial *Document Catalog* from its inception was always quite late in making its appearance. From the start it did not appear until three years after the close of the congress it covered. The first world war threw it nine years behind, and from that time forward all efforts to place it on a current basis failed. The cost of compiling and printing this massive publication, added to the fact that the *Monthly Catalog* was becoming more and more demanding, caused the Superintendent of Documents to reexamine both programs in 1947. He decided that he could best discharge his responsibilities to the general public by concentrating on only one catalog. He therefore recommended to the Joint Committee on Printing that the *Monthly Catalog* be expanded to include the features of the *Document Catalog* and that the improved *Monthly Catalog* be considered as discharging the legal requirements of Section 62 of the Printing Act of 1895 previously cited as the basis for issuing the biennial *Document Catalog*. The Joint Committee on Printing approved this recommendation, and the biennial *Document Catalog* was discontinued with Volume 25 covering the 76th Congress, 1939–40, published in 1947. Three supplements to the *Monthly Catalog* were issued to cover publications which had been omitted from the *Monthly Catalog* and which would have appeared in the biennial *Document Catalog*.

Session Indexes Prior to 1895

Prior to 1895 each series of congressional documents and reports was usually indexed separately, and each index generally appeared in the front of every volume of the series to which it applied. Thus for the 15th to the 29th Congress (1817–47) there were separate indexes to *House Reports, Senate Reports,*

House Documents, and *Senate Documents*, and for the 30th to the 53d Congress (1847–95) there were separate indexes to *House Reports, Senate Reports, House Miscellaneous Documents, Senate Miscellaneous Documents, House Executive Documents*, and *Senate Executive Documents*. For instance, each volume of *House Reports* for any session contained an index to all the volumes of *House Reports* for that session, and likewise each volume of any other series contained an index to the session volumes in that series. The general practice was as outlined above, but at times the index did not appear in every volume.

Special Lists and Indexes

Catalogs or indexes covering specified classes of publications or topics have been issued from time to time, some constituting a continuing series and some being isolated issues.[21] All the publications enumerated in the special lists are also listed in the comprehensive catalogs, but the special lists are more convenient if references in a limited field are desired. The items cited on the following pages do not include indexes to particular series of publications, such as laws, court decisions, etc., which are referred to in other chapters.

Price Lists

The Superintendent of Documents issues a series of price lists which are revised from time to time. These lists show only

[21] Several publications in this field by nongovernmental agencies should be noted. One of these is *Introduction to the American Official Sources for the Economic and Social History of the World War*, by Waldo G. Leland and Newton D. Mereness, 1926 (532 pp.). The compiler's preface states that the purpose of this volume is "to present a summary account of those records and official publications of the various branches and offices of the federal government which constitute the primary sources for the history of the social and economic activities of the national government during the period of American participation in the World War." Another publication, in three volumes, is Adelaide R. Hasse's *Index to United States Documents Relating to Foreign Affairs, 1828–61* (Carnegie Institution of Washington, Publication No. 185).

the publications for sale by that officer at the time the lists were prepared; consequently they are not complete subject or series lists. The titles of the lists available in 1968 are shown below. Numbers omitted are no longer published.

10. LAWS, RULES, AND REGULATIONS. Federal statutes and compilations of laws on various subjects

11. HOME ECONOMICS. Foods and cooking

15. GEOLOGY

19. ARMY. Field manuals and technical manuals

21. FISH AND WILDLIFE

25. TRANSPORTATION, HIGHWAYS, ROADS, AND POSTAL SERVICE. Railroad and shipping problems, postal service

28 FINANCE. National economy, accounting, insurance, securities

31. EDUCATION

33. LABOR. Personnel management and work simplification, wages and hours of labor

33A. OCCUPATIONS. Professions and job descriptions

35. NATIONAL PARKS, HISTORIC SITES, NATIONAL MONUMENTS

36. GOVERNMENT PERIODICALS AND SUBSCRIPTION SERVICES.

37. TARIFF AND TAXATION. Compilations of acts, decisions, and regulations relating to tariff and taxation

38. ANIMAL INDUSTRY. Farm animals, poultry, dairying

41. INSECTS. Worms and insects harmful to man, animals, and plants

42. IRRIGATION, DRAINAGE, WATER POWER. Federal Power Commission, water resources

43. FORESTRY. Lumber and timber, ranges and grazing, American woods

44. PLANTS. Culture, grading, marketing, and storage of fruits, vegetables, grasses, grain

46. SOILS AND FERTILIZERS. Soil surveys, erosion, conservation

48. WEATHER, ASTRONOMY, AND METEOROLOGY. Climate, precipitation, floods and flood control

50. AMERICAN HISTORY. Constitution of United States, Revolutionary War, Civil War, World Wars I and II

51. HEALTH AND HYGIENE. Drugs and sanitation

51A. DISEASES. Contagious and infectious diseases, sickness, and vital statistics

53. MAPS, ENGINEERING, SURVEYING

54. POLITICAL SCIENCE. Government, crime, District of Columbia

55. SMITHSONIAN INSTITUTION, NATIONAL MUSEUM, AND INDIANS.

58. MINES. Explosives, fuel, gas, gasoline, petroleum, minerals

59. INTERSTATE COMMERCE. Steam railways, motor carriers, carriers by water

62. COMMERCE. Business, patents and trademarks, and foreign trade

63. NAVY, MARINE CORPS, AND COAST GUARD

64. SCIENTIFIC TESTS. Standards, mathematics, physics

65. FOREIGN RELATIONS OF U. S. Publications relating to foreign countries, United Nations

67. IMMIGRATION, NATURALIZATION, AND CITIZENSHIP

68. FARM MANAGEMENT. Rural electrification, foreign agriculture, agricultural marketing

70. CENSUS. Statistics of agriculture, business, governments, housing, manufactures, minerals, population, and maps

71. CHILDREN'S BUREAU, and other publications relating to children and youth

72. HOMES. Construction, maintenance, community development

78. SOCIAL SECURITY. Industrial hazards, health and hygiene, safety for workers, pensions, workmen's compensation and insurance

79. AIR FORCE. Aviation, civil aviation, naval aviation and Federal Aviation Administration

79A. SPACE, MISSILES, THE MOON, NASA, AND SATELLITES. Space education, exploration, research and technology.

81. POSTERS AND CHARTS

82. RADIO AND ELECTRICITY. Electronics, radar, and communications

83. LIBRARY OF CONGRESS

84. ATOMIC ENERGY AND CIVIL DEFENSE

85. DEFENSE. Veterans' affairs

86. CONSUMER INFORMATION. Family finances, appliances, recreation, gardening, health and safety, food, house and home, child care, clothing and fabrics

87. STATES AND TERRITORIES OF THE UNITED STATES AND THEIR RESOURCES. Including beautification, public buildings and lands, and recreational resources

Congressional Lists and Indexes

The greater portion of the special lists of congressional publications covers the early years of the government, although one —the *Tables and Index*—covers the period 1817–93. The term "congressional lists," as here used, indicates lists which pertain to publications of Congress and not necessarily those ordered compiled or printed by Congress. It should be borne in mind that congressional publications are also included in the works described on the preceding pages under the headings "Comprehensive General Catalogs and Indexes" and "Periodic Catalogs and Indexes."

Documents of the early congresses, 1789–1821. A compilation prepared by General A. W. Greely was published in 1900, under the title *Public Documents of the First Fourteen Congresses, 1789–1817—Papers Relating to Early Congressional Documents* (Senate Document 428, 56th Congress, 1st session). It is a chronological catalog of 858 pages followed by a 45-page index of proper names only, not subject matter.

A supplement was published by General Greely in Volume 1 of the *Annual Report of the American Historical Association for 1903*, published also as House Document 745, 58th Congress, 2d session, pages 343–406. An earlier paper by General Greely, with a preliminary list of the papers of the first two congresses, was published in Volume 1 of the *Annual Report of the American Historical Association for 1896*, issued also as House Document 353, 54th Congress, 2d session, pages 1109–1248. Some of the publications of the first 14 congresses are listed in *Poore's Catalogue*.

The *Senate Catalogue* (pages 935–78 of the 1924 edition) contains a list of the documents and reports of the first 14 congresses in the Senate Library. Some of these are in manuscript form. The volume numbers for these publications as given in this catalog do not refer to books published with these numbers, but to the material as bound for the Senate Library.

Many of the documents and reports of the first 16 congresses (1789–1821) are also cited in Ordway's *General Indexes to the Journals of Congress* listed on page 130.

The more important of the earlier publications of this period are reprinted in *American State Papers* (see pages 188–89), each volume of which is indexed separately. As the material in this compilation is classified, the indexing by separate volumes is fairly satisfactory. Many of the documents and reports included are also cited in Ordway's *General Indexes to the Journals of Congress*.

Indexes to publications of the House of Representatives of the 1st to the 25th Congress, 1789–1839. Four separate indexes were published covering the publications of the House of Representatives for the first 25 congresses, but as these were also consolidated and issued as one publication they will be discussed as a unit. The titles and document numbers or serial numbers of the four indexes are given below:

[1.] Index to the executive communications made to the House of Representatives from the commencement of the present government until the end of the 14th Congress, inclusive [1789–1817], 1824, 247 pp. (H. Doc. 163, 18 Cong. 1 sess.). Pts. 1 and 2 of this index apply to the executive communications, with references to both printed and written documents. Pt. 3 is entitled "Index to all the printed reports of committees from the 1st to the 15th Congress which are now extant." Greely says that this index is incomplete.[22]

[2.] Index to the executive communications made to the House of Representatives from Dec. 3, 1817, to Mar. 3, 1823, 15th, 16th, and 17th congresses, 1823, 129 pp. (Serial 85/2; no document number.)

[3.] A digested index to the executive documents and reports of committees of the House of Representatives from the 18th to the 21st Congress, both included [1823–31], 1832. 152 pp. (Serial 209/2; no document number.) The documents and reports of committees are covered by one index.

[4.] Index to the executive documents and reports of committees of the House of Representatives from the 22d to the 25th Congress, both included, commencing December 1831 and ending March 1839, 380 pp. (Serial 305; no document number.) The documents and reports are covered by one index.

The four indexes were later bound to make one volume, which bears the half title *Index to Documents and Reports, House of Representatives, 1789–1839.* This volume has no document number and is not included in the congressional series. Each of the four parts is paged separately, and, if it were not for the fact that the volume has a half title, one might suspect that the copies available are simply job rebindings of the earlier indexes.

The more important of the papers covered by these indexes are reprinted in *American State Papers.*

[22] *Papers Relating to Early Congressional Documents,* S. Doc. 428, 56 Cong. 1 sess., p. 9.

McPherson's consolidated indexes to House publications, 26th to the 40th Congress, 1839–69. The four indexes listed above were succeeded by the works entitled *Consolidated Index of the Executive Documents of the House of Representatives from the 26th to the 40th Congress, Inclusive* [1839–69], prepared under the direction of Edward McPherson, 1870 (393 pages), and *Consolidated Index of the Reports of the Committees of the House of Representatives from the 26th to the 40th Congress, Inclusive,* prepared under the direction of Edward McPherson, 1869 (158 pages). These volumes, issued without document numbers, have been assigned Nos. 1386 and 1387 in the serial number set.

Indexes to McKee's compilation of committee reports, 1815–87. Under the joint resolution of July 26, 1886 (24 Stat. 345), and the concurrent resolution of March 3, 1887, Thomas Hudson McKee collected the reports of the committees of the Senate and House covering the 14th to the 49th Congress (1815–87). There was a separate collection for each committee, there being in all 95 collections in over 500 volumes. These collections are not reprints but are simply assemblages and bindings of copies of the separate reports. Only a few sets were assembled for the use of the committees, and the compilations are not generally available.

A separate index for the reports of each committee appears at the end of each compilation. The indexes were also published separately for sale, the indexes for the Senate committees being in one volume and those for the House committees in another. These books had no volume title page,[23] but each of the 36 indexes in the Senate volume and each of the 59 indexes in the House volume had a title page and was paged separately. Neither the compilations nor the index volumes are numbered in the congressional set of publications.

[23] The back titles probably vary on different copies of the same book. On a copy of the House indexes in the library of the Brookings Institution, in what appears to be the original binding, the upper panel reads *"Indexes—Compilation of House Reports."* A copy of the same volume in the Harvard College Library, also apparently in an original binding, reads *"McKee's Indexes to House Reports."*

Tables and Index, 1817–93. In 1902 the Office of the Superintendent of Documents issued the publication which is generally known as *Tables and Index* but which is entitled *Tables of and Annotated Index to the Congressional Series of United States Public Documents* (quarto, 769 pages). The first part of this book, the "Tables," is a list of publications of the 15th to the 52d Congress (1817–93) arranged by volumes and containing the following information: serial number, volume number, part number, name of series, series numbers of documents or reports in each volume, and notes on contents and omission or duplication of numbers. The same plan was afterward adopted for the *Checklist*.

The second part is the "Index," which gives a reference to the document or report and to the serial number of the volume which contains the publication referred to. This method of reference facilitates the finding of the publication in libraries where the congressional set is arranged by serial numbers. But if merely a citation is desired, it is necessary to refer to the "Tables" or to the volumes themselves in order to ascertain the congress and session.

The Index is a selective one, as it covers only about 50,000 of the 96,875 numbered documents and reports issued from 1817 to 1893. The preface states that an endeavor was made "to extricate the more important documents from the scattered mass of worthless matter which composes nearly one half the congressional set." For example, entries were not made for any document or report (unless of historic character) that might be included under such headings as appropriations, condemned cannon, contested elections, memorials, petitions, private claims, or public buildings.

The index is not analytical, the entry being taken from the title of the publication, but it gives specific references to the several subordinate reports appended to a general report. Thus in *Poore's Catalogue* the references to the reports on the Columbia Hospital for Women are to various special reports, and no mention is made of the annual reports, which, during the period covered by Poore, were appended to the reports of the Secretary of the Interior and the Commissioners of the District of Columbia. In the *Ames Index* under "Columbia Hospital for Women" there is simply a general statement that the hospital reports are in the annual reports of the Commissioners. In the *Tables and Index* each report is given separately, with an indication of the page of the larger report on which the subordinate report begins.

In the *Tables and Index* the reports on state banks made at various times between 1833 and 1863 are given in 27 entries, each one indicating the period covered by the report and the document and serial number. In the index to *Poore's Catalogue,* 95 references to publications on state banks and the United States Bank are intermixed.

It should be borne in mind that the *Tables and Index* covers only congressional publications. But as many executive publications were issued also as congressional publications, the index is to a limited extent a guide to publications of the executive branch of the government. If the student is looking for a particular report, he may find a reference in the *Tables and Index,* in which case his search will be concluded. If he is looking for all publications on a topic he should use Poore and Ames.

Indexes to bills.   Bills on banking, public finance, and regulation of railroads are listed in the following:

An index of bills presented in the House of Representatives from the 1st to the 42d Congress, inclusive [1789–1873], relating to banks, currency, public debt, tariff, and direct taxes, showing the title of the bill, name of person introducing, nature of the report, and disposition of the bill, 1875, 183 pp. (H. Misc. Doc. 92, 43 Cong. 2 sess.)

History of bills and resolutions introduced in Congress respecting federal regulation of interstate commerce by railways, etc., from the 37th Congress to the 62d Congress, inclusive, 1862–1913, by Samuel W. Briggs, 1913, 167 pp. ([Senate] Committee on Interstate Commerce)

Claims.   The lists of private claims presented to Congress constitute the longest series of indexes to a specific class of congressional papers. The lists include those before the House of Representatives from 1789 to 1891 and those before the Senate from 1815 to 1905. The complete list is as follows:

CLAIMS PRESENTED TO THE HOUSE OF REPRESENTATIVES

Digested summary and alphabetical list of private claims which have been presented to the House of Representatives from the 1st to the 31st Congress [1789–1851] exhibiting the action of Congress on each claim, with references to the journals, reports, bills, etc., elucidating its progress, 1853, 3 vols. This is an unnumbered publication of the House of Representatives but it has been given Nos. 653–55 in the serial number set.

Digested summary and alphabetical list of private claims which have been presented to the House of Representatives from the 32d to the 41st Congress, inclusive [1851–71] . . . by Edward McPherson, 1873, 526 pp. (H. Misc. Doc. 109, 42 Cong. 3 sess.)

Digested summary and alphabetical list of private claims presented to the House of Representatives from the 42d to the 46th Congress, inclusive [1871–81] . . . by Edward McPherson, 1882, 744 pp. (H. Misc. Doc. 53, 47 Cong. 1 sess.)

Digested summary and alphabetical list of private claims presented to the House of Representatives from the 47th to the 51st Congress, inclusive [1881-91] . . . by James Kerr, 1896, 749 pp. (H. Misc. Doc. 213, 53 Cong. 2 sess.)

Consolidated index of claims reported by Commissioners of Claims to the House of Representatives from 1871 to 1880, 1892, 262 pp.; compiled under the supervision of J. B. Holloway and Walter H. French

CLAIMS PRESENTED TO THE SENATE

List of private claims brought before the Senate of the United States from the commencement of the 14th Congress to the close of the 46th Congress [1815–81], 1881, 2 vols. (S. Misc. Doc. 14, 46 Cong. 3 sess.). Earlier cumulative editions were as follows: 14th (1815) to 26th Congress (1841), S. Doc. 236, 26 Cong. 2 sess.; to 30th Congress (1849), S. Misc. Doc. 67, 30 Cong. 2 sess.; to 33d Congress (1855), S. Misc. Doc. 27, 33 Cong. 2 sess. (this volume was also printed as an unnumbered publication of the House of Representatives; it has been assigned No. 91 1/2 in the serial number set); to 39th Congress (1867), S. Misc. Doc. 43, 40 Cong. 3 sess.

List of private claims brought before the Senate of the United States from the commencement of the 47th Congress to the close of the 51st Congress [1881–91], 1895, 3 vols. (S. Misc. Doc. 266, 53 Cong. 2 sess.)

Alphabetical list of private claims which were brought before the Senate of the United States . . . from Mar. 4, 1891, to Mar. 4, 1899, 1900, 2 vols. (S. Doc. 449, 56 Cong. 1 sess.)

Same, Dec. 4, 1899, to Mar. 4, 1903, 1903, 197 pp. (S. Doc. 221, 57 Cong. 2 sess.)

Same, Nov. 9, 1903, to Mar. 4, 1905, 1905, 709 pp. (S. Doc. 3, 59 Cong. 1 sess.)

MISCELLANEOUS CLAIMS

Digest of claims referred by Congress to the Court of Claims from the 48th to the 51st Congress, both inclusive [1883–91], for a finding of facts under the provisions of the act approved Mar. 3, 1883, known as the Bowman Act, by J. B. Holloway, 1891, 127 pp.

Reports of House Committee on Judiciary. The reports of the Committee on Judiciary of the House of Representatives from 1895 to 1913 are indexed in *Index to Reports of the Committee on the Judiciary, House of Representatives, 54th . . . [to] 62d Congress,* 1913 (93 pages). This gives the number of the report and the date of the resulting act, if the bill was passed. It also contains page references, which evidently refer to an assembled set of reports and acts filed with the committee. The page citations are of no value to the general student, but the index numbers offer a convenient method of locating reports during the period covered.

Rivers and harbors. Documents and reports on rivers and harbors have been listed and indexed in a series of small pamphlets printed by the Office of Chief of Engineers of the War Department. The period covered begins with the 2d session of the 56th Congress (1900). Prior to the 3d session of the 62d Congress (1912) there were both a list and an index; thereafter only an index was compiled. These were evidently prepared to accompany an assemblage of the separate publications bound especially for office use. It is not likely that they are generally available, but a set is on file in the Public Documents Library (call number W 7.2: R 52). These publications are also listed in the general indexes published by the Superintendent of Documents, but the separate list may be convenient for some workers.

Department Lists and Indexes

Most of the offices issuing a material number of publications publish current lists of those available. Some are compiled regularly once a year, others are published at irregular intervals, and in some cases monthly supplements are issued. Only the outstanding current lists are included in the following pages. Some give only publications available for free distribution, while others include also publications which may be purchased only from the Superintendent of Documents.

An outstanding complete list is that issued by the United States Geological Survey, which contains notations indicating whether the report is available for free distribution, is obtainable only by purchase from the Superintendent of Documents, or is out of print. It also has an index by authors, areas, states, and subjects. The Bureau of Mines has also issued a complete list of publications.

For various reasons, but probably mostly on account of lack of funds, reports resulting from investigations made by government officers are at times published in scientific, technical, and commercial journals or by private institutions. As the cost of printing is not borne by the United States and as the reports do not bear the imprint of any government office, these issues cannot be regarded as government publications. However, in many cases they form the only available tangible product resulting from an investigation conducted under government auspices. In some instances in order to reach a particular group of readers, such articles are published in a journal and present in different form a portion of the material that is also available in government publications.

The Atomic Energy Commission encourages its scientists to publish the results of their unclassified research in professional and technical journals. About one out of every five Atomic Energy Commission unclassified reports appears in the open literature.[24]

[24] United States Atomic Energy Commission, "Utilization of Atomic Energy Scientific and Technical Information," Minutes of the International Conference held in Geneva, Switzerland, May 26–29, 1958, sponsored by the United States Atomic Energy Commission.

Agricultural Library Notes, a mimeographed publication issued monthly from 1926 to 1942 by the library of the Department of Agriculture contained in each issue a list of "Publications by United States Department of Agriculture Workers Appearing Outside the Department."

The Utilization Research and Development Divisions (Eastern, Northern, Southern, and Western), formerly Regional Research Laboratories and Utilization Research Branches, publish biennial lists of publications and patents.

Publication lists by all the forest experiment stations include publications in the open literature as well as their own publications. Journal articles are also included in the *List of Publications* (semiannual) of the Forest Products Laboratory and its special subject lists.

Some other examples of publication in the open literature are listed and/or indexed in the following publications:

List of journal articles by Bureau of Mines authors published July 1, 1910, to January 1, 1960, with subject index, compiled by Mae W. Hardison and Opal V. Weaver. 1960. 295 pp.

Nuclear Science Abstracts, Vol. I, 1948–, identifies AEC reports published in journals. There is a report number index in each issue. Cumulative report number indexes have been issued (Vols. 1–15, revised with public availability citations, 1965, 756 pp., and Vols. 16–20, 1966, 752 pp.)

A noteworthy example of publication of government material by commercial publishers is afforded by the American Guide Series, compiled by the Federal Writers' Project of the Works Progress Administration. This series was developed in order to give employment to writers during the depression of the 1930's. It includes guides to states, cities, and special areas. These are listed in *Catalogue, WPA Writers' Program Publications,* The American Guide Series, The American Life Series, September 1941 (54 pages), Federal Works Agency, Work Projects Administration, 1942.

With the exception of *Washington: City and Capital* and *Intracoastal Waterway,* which were printed at the Government Printing Office and were sold by the Superintendent of Documents, all issues are sold by commercial publishing houses or some sponsoring organization.

The Historical Records Survey of the Works Progress Administration made an inventory of federal archives in the states and of county and town archives and other historical material. Some of the resulting publications were issued by local organizations, but apparently most were published by the field offices of the Historical Records Survey. As the issues are field publications they were not listed in the *Monthly Catalog* or other lists of the Superintendent of Documents. *Check List of Historical Records Survey Publications* was issued by Federal Works Agency, Work Projects Administration, as WPA Technical Series, Research and Records Bibliography No. 7, revised April 1943 (110 pages).

The special publications listed on the following pages as a rule apply to a particular department or other unit and are listed by the names of such unit (under the first significant word of the name regardless of the sequence of wording used in the official designation). Some of the items cover a definite subject regardless of publishing office or series and are listed under the subject heading.

In the case of the Department of Agriculture, the general department lists also cover publications originating in the bureaus, as bureau publications are issued in the department series. In 1939 the Biological Survey was transferred from the Department of Agriculture to the Department of the Interior. Also in 1939, the Bureau of Public Roads was transferred to the Federal Works Agency, later to the Department of Commerce, and more recently to the newly organized Department of Transportation. In the case of these and other transfers, the previous publications of the agencies will be found in the lists and indexes of the Department of Agriculture, but later ones must be sought elsewhere. At the same time the Farm Credit Administration and the Commodity Credit Corporation were transferred to the Department of Agriculture.

If a publication is a cumulative continuation of earlier ones, the latest publication alone is generally mentioned, unless there is a special reason for listing a previous edition. As a rule the titles explain the scope of the work, but annotations have been added if they appeared desirable. The list below does not, as a rule, include the indexes to specialized types of publications discussed in other chapters, as such indexes are cited in connection with the account of the publications.

ADJUTANT GENERAL OF THE ARMY

Subject index of the general orders of the War Department, Jan. 1, 1809–Dec. 31, 1860, by Jeremiah C. Allen, 1886, 192 pp.

Subject index to the general orders and circulars of the War Department and the headquarters of the Army, Adjutant General's Office, Jan. 1, 1861–Dec. 31, 1880, by Jeremiah C. Allen, 1882, 506 pp.

Same, Jan. 1, 1860–Dec. 31, 1880, 1913, 266 pp.

Same, Jan. 1, 1881–Dec. 31, 1911, 1912, 650 pp.

AGRICULTURAL CHEMISTRY

Index of publications of the Bureau of Chemistry and Soils, originally the "Bureau of Chemistry" and the "Bureau of Soils," 75 years, 1862–1937. List of titles and authors, prepared by H. P. Holman, V. A. Pease, K. Smith, M. T. Reid, A. Crebassa, 1939, 546 pp. Includes both official and nonofficial publications. Author index. Only one volume issued.

AGRICULTURE DEPARTMENT

General Lists

List of publications of the United States Department of Agriculture from 1841 to June 30, 1895, inclusive, by Adelaide R. Hasse, 1896, 76 pp. (Department of Agriculture, Library [Bulletin] 9.)

List, by titles, of publications of the United States Department of Agriculture from 1840 to June 1901, by R. B. Handy and Minna A. Cannon, 1902, 216 pp. (Department of Agriculture, Division of Publications, Bulletin 6.)

List of publications of the United States Department of Agriculture from January 1901 to December 1925, inclusive, by Mabel G. Hunt, 1927, 182 pp. (Department of Agriculture, Miscellaneous Publication 9.)

Same, from January 1926 to December 1930, inclusive, by Mabel G. Hunt, 1932, 46 pp. (Department of Agriculture, Miscellaneous Publication 153.)

Same, from January 1931 to December 1935, inclusive, by Mabel G. Hunt, 1935, 64 pp. (Department of Agriculture, Miscellaneous Publication 252.)

Same, from January 1936 to December 1940, inclusive, by Mabel Hunt Doyle, 1941, 68 pp. (Department of Agriculture, Miscellaneous Publication 443.)

Same, from January 1941 to December 1945, inclusive, by Bertha

Louise Zoeller and Mabel Hunt Doyle, 1946, 56 pp. (Department of Agriculture, Miscellaneous Publication 617.)

List of available publications of the United States Department of Agriculture, compiled by Eleanor W. Clay, revised January 1966, 115 pp. (Department of Agriculture, Office of Information, List No. 11.) This title is revised frequently.

General Indexes

Index to authors, with titles of their publications, appearing in the documents of the United States Department of Agriculture, 1841–97, by George F. Thompson, 1893, 303 pp. (Department of Agriculture, Division of Publications, Bulletin 4.)

[Subject] Index to the annual report of the United States Department of Agriculture for the years 1837–93, inclusive, 1896, 252 pp. (Department of Agriculture, Division of Publications, Bulletin 1.)

Synoptical index of the reports of the statistician [of the Department of Agriculture], 1863–94, by George F. Thompson, 1897, 258 pp. (Department of Agriculture, Division of Publications, Bulletin 2.)

List of publications of the Department of Agriculture, 1862–1902, with analytical index, 1904, 623 pp. (Office of Superintendent of Documents, Bibliography of United States Public Documents, Department List 1.) Arrangement is by Documents Office classification numbers, and index entries refer to them.

Index to publications of the United States Department of Agriculture, 1901–25, by Mary A. Bradley and Mabel G. Hunt, 1932, 2,689 pp. Author and subject index to printed publications of the department except periodicals issued by bureaus. It is a very detailed index, referring to page numbers in publications; titles of bulletins are not always given.

Same, 1926–30, by Mary A. Bradley, 1935, 694 pp.

Same, 1931–35, by Mary A. Bradley, 1937, 518 pp.

Same, 1936–40, ed. by Mary A. Bradley, 1943, 763 pp.

Numerical list of current publications of the United States Department of Agriculture, compiled by comparison with the originals, by Fred L. Zimmerman and Phyllis R. Read, 1941, 929 pp. This list is useful for identifying publications when the number is known but the series is unknown.

Special Lists and Indexes

Agricultural Adjustment Administration

List of publications and other printed material of the Agricultural Adjustment Administration, May 12, 1933–June 1, 1934, 1934, 25 pp.

Consumer services of government agencies, by Iris C. Walker, 1937,

56 pp. (Consumers' Counsel Series, Publication 1, revised.) A selected list of government publications of interest to consumers, with accounts of the work of the several agencies.

Cooperative bookshelf 1937, 13 pp. (Consumers' Counsel Series, Publication 3.) An annotated bibliography of government publications on consumers' cooperation.

Agricultural Economics

Agricultural economic and statistical publications, June 1952, 83 pp.

Monthly checklist of reports issued by the Economic Research Service and the Statistical Reporting Service, April 1961–.

Periodic reports of agricultural economics. Economic Research Service, Statistical Reporting Service, January 1967, 14 pp.

Publications of the Horticultural Crops Branch, Agricultural Marketing Service, October 1963, 24 pp.

Publications of the Transportation and Facilities Research Division, Agricultural Marketing Service, September 1963, 14 pp.

Checklist of reports and charts issued by the Agricultural Marketing Service, December 1953–March 1964.

Publications dealing with farm management, 1903–June 30, 1940. (Bulletins, processed reports, and articles carried in official publications, prepared by federal farm management workers alone or in cooperation with state and other agencies and published in Washington or the states.) Compiled by M. A. Crosby, M. R. Cooper, and Della E. Merrick, December 1940, 132 pp.

Agricultural Research Service

Publications of the horticultural crops research branch, revised April 1966, 25 pp.

List of processed publications of the Bureau of Agricultural and Industrial Chemistry, May 1953, 25 pp.

Animal Industry

Index [author and subject] to literature relating to animal industry in the publications of the Department of Agriculture, 1837–98, by George Fayette Thompson, 1900, 676 pp. (Department of Agriculture, Division of Publications, Bulletin 5.)

Atomic Energy Commission

See Chapter 17.

Cotton

Cotton and cottonseed, a list [and index] of publications of the United States Department of Agriculture, including early reports of the United

States Patent Office, by Rachel P. Lane and Emil L. Day, 1934, 149 pp. (Department of Agriculture, Miscellaneous Publication 203.)

Department Bulletins

Index to department Bulletins 1–1500, by Mabel G. Hunt, 1936, 384 pp.

Entomology

General index to the seven volumes of *Insect Life*, 1885–95, 1897, 145 pp.

Index to [Entomology] Bulletins Nos. 1–30, new series, 1896–1901, by Nathan Banks, 1902, 64 pp. (Entomology Bulletin 36, new series.)

Checklist of publications on entomology issued by Department of Agriculture through 1927, with subject index, by Mabel Colcord, Ina L. Hawes, and Angelina J. Carabelli, January 1930, 261 pp. (Department of Agriculture, Library, Bibliographical Contributions 20; processed.)

List of entomological technique publications, 1935–51, Bureau of Entomology and Plant Quarantine, Division of Insect Pest Survey and Information. Six numbers were issued; then the series was replaced by the Agriculture Research Service series.

Experiment Stations Office

General index to *Experiment Station Record,* Vols. 1–12, 1899–1901, 671 pp.

Same, Vols. 13–25, 1901–11, by M. D. Moore and William Henry, 1913, 1,159 pp.

Same, Vols. 26–40, 1912–19, by Martha C. Gundlach, 1926, 640 pp.

Same, Vols. 41–50, 1919–24, by Martha C. Gundlach, 1931, 709 pp.

Same, Vols. 51–60, 1924–29, by Martha C. Gundlach, 1932, 677 pp.

Same, Vols. 61–70, 1929–34, by Martha C. Gundlach, 1937, 752 pp.

Same, Vols. 71–80, 1934–39, prepared by Indexing Section, Office of Information, 1959, 832 pp.

List of Bulletins of the agricultural experiment stations from their establishment to the end of 1920,[25] 1924, 186 pp. (Department of Agriculture, Bulletin 1199.)

Same, 1921 and 1922, by Catherine E. Pennington, 1924, 24 pp. (Department of Agriculture, Bulletin 1199, Supplement 1.)

Same [with index], 1923 and 1924, by Catherine E. Pennington, 1926, 54 pp. (Department of Agriculture, Bulletin 1199, Supplement 2.)

Same [with index], 1925 and 1926, by Catherine E. Pennington, 1927,

[25] The papers published by the agricultural experiment stations are not government publications, but the work is carried on to a large extent under government subsidy and supervision.

62 pp. (Department of Agriculture, Bulletin 1199, Supplement 3.)

Same [with index], 1927 and 1928, by Catherine E. Pennington, 1930, 78 pp. (Department of Agriculture, Miscellaneous Publication 65.)

Same [with index], 1929 and 1930, by Catherine E. Pennington, 1932, 88 pp. (Department of Agriculture, Miscellaneous Publication 128.)

Same [with index], 1931 and 1932, by Catherine E. Pennington, 1934, 77 pp. (Department of Agriculture, Miscellaneous Publication 181.)

Same [with index], 1933 and 1934, by Catherine E. Pennington, 1936, 81 pp. (Department of Agriculture, Miscellaneous Publication 232.)

Same [with index], 1935 and 1936, by Catherine E. Pennington, 1938, 94 pp. (Department of Agriculture, Miscellaneous Publication 294.)

Same [with index], 1937 and 1938, by Catherine E. Pennington, 1940, 91 pp. (Department of Agriculture, Miscellaneous Publication 362.)

Same [with index], 1939 and 1940, by Catherine E. Pennington, 1941, 86 pp. (Department of Agriculture, Miscellaneous Publication 459.)

Same [with index], 1941 and 1942, by Helen V. Barnes, 1944, 70 pp. (Department of Agriculture, Bibliographical Bulletin 4.)

State Agricultural Experiment Station publications are listed monthly as a section in the Bibliography of Agriculture, and reprints of the section are issued.

Farmer Cooperative Service

List of publications, July 1967, 71 pp.

Farmers' Bulletins

Index to Farmers' Bulletins Nos. 1–1000, by Charles H. Greathouse, 1920, 811 pp.

Index to Farmers' Bulletins Nos. 1001–1500, by Mabel G. Hunt, 1929, 371 pp. Reprinted 1942, 374 pp. The reprint contains a list of Farmers' Bulletins from 1001 to 1500 that have been superseded, together with the publications superseding them up to January 1942.

Index to Farmers' Bulletins Nos. 1501–1750, by Mabel Hunt Doyle, 1941, 135 pp.

Foreign Agricultural Service

Published information on agriculture in foreign countries, January 1937–December 1953, 1954, 65 pp.

Forest Service

The Forest Products Laboratory publishes a semiannual list of publications and lists of available publications on different subjects. The forest experiment stations publish lists of their publications at varying intervals.

Plant Industry

Contents of and index to Bulletins of Bureau of Plant Industry, Nos. 1–100, by J. E. Rockwell, 1907, 102 pp. (Bureau of Plant Industry, Bulletin 101.)

Index to papers relating to plant industry subjects in yearbooks of Department of Agriculture, by J. E. Rockwell, 1908, 55 pp. (Bureau of Plant Industry, Circular 17.)

Checklist of publications issued by the Bureau of Plant Industry . . . 1901–20, and by the divisions and offices which combined to form this bureau, 1862–1901, 1921, 127 pp. (Department of Agriculture, Library, Bibliographical Contributions 3; processed.)

Plant Pathology

A checklist of the publications of the Department of Agriculture . . . on plant pathology, 1837–1918, 1919, 38 pp. (Department of Agriculture, Library, Bibliographical Contributions 1; processed.)

Author and subject index to publications on plant pathology issued by Department of Agriculture to Jan. 1, 1925, by Jessie M. Allen, 1925, 158 pp. (Department of Agriculture, Library, Bibliographical Contributions 8; processed.)

Checklist of publications of the state agricultural experiment stations on the subject of plant pathology, 1876–1920, 1922, 179 pp. (Department of Agriculture, Library, Bibliographical Contributions 2.)

Soils

List of publications on soils issued by United States Department of Agriculture, 1844–1926, by Emma B. Hawks and Charlotte Trolinger, 1927, 63 pp. (Department of Agriculture, Library, Bibliographical Contributions 14.)

List of the publications on soils issued by the state agricultural experiment stations of the United States through 1926, by C. L. Feldkamp and C. E. Pennington, 1927, 81 pp. (USDA Library Bibliographical Contributions 15.)

Index of the publications of the Bureau of Chemistry and Soils, 1862–1937, Vol. 1 (list of titles and authors), prepared by H. P. Holman, V. A. Pease, K. Smith, M. T. Redi, and A. Crebassa, 1939, 546 pp.

List of published soil surveys, Soil Conservation Service, January 1967, 26 pp.

Statistics

Statistical data compiled and published by the Bureau of Crop Estimates, 1863–1920, 1921, 64 pp. (Department of Agriculture, Circular 150.)

Technical Bulletins

Index to Technical Bulletins Nos. 1–500, by Mabel G. Hunt, 1937, 249 pp.

Same, Nos. 501–750, 1941, 169 pp.

Weather Bureau

Checklist of Library of Congress printed catalog cards for Weather Bureau publications, 1917, 39 pp.

Yearbooks

Index to the yearbooks of the United States Department of Agriculture, 1894–1900, by Charles H. Greathouse, 1902, 196 pp. (Department of Agriculture, Division of Publications, Bulletin 7.)

Same, 1901–05, by Charles H. Greathouse, 1908, 166 pp. (Department of Agriculture, Division of Publications, Bulletin 9.)

Same, 1906–10, by Charles H. Greathouse, 1913, 146 pp. (Department of Agriculture, Division of Publications, Bulletin 10.)

Same, 1911–15, by Charles H. Greathouse, 1922, 178 pp. (Department of Agriculture, Division of Publications, general publication.) The department stated that this would be the last index to the yearbooks.

AIR FORCE DEPARTMENT

Air Force scientific research bibliography, by G. Vernon Hooker *et al.*, Bibliography Section, Science and Technology Division, Library of Congress, supported by the Air Force Office of Scientific Research, Office of Aerospace Research. Vol. 1, 1950–56; Vol. 2, 1957–58; Vol. 3, 1959; Vol. 4, 1960.

Materials research abstracts, a review of the Air Force materials research and development, edited by Charles D. Thibault, Science and Technology Division, Library of Congress, published for Directorate of Materials and Processes, Aeronautical Systems Division, Wright-Patterson Air Force Base, Ohio, 1962, 534 pp.

Quarterly index of technical documentary reports, Air Force Office of Scientific Research, Air Research and Development Command, October-December 1956–61.

Office of Aerospace Index of Research Results, January-March, April-June, July-September 1962.

OAR cumulative index of research results, Office of Aerospace Research, 1959–62, 786 pp.; 1963, 238 pp.; 1964, 275 pp.; 1965–66, 557 pp.

ARMED FORCES INFORMATION AGENCY

Armed forces information and education catalog of current information materials, 1966, 37 pp.

AMERICAN HISTORICAL ASSOCIATION

General index to papers and annual reports[26] of the American Historical Association, 1884–1914, 1918, 793 pp. (Vol. 2 of *Annual Report of the American Historical Association* for the year 1914; also issued as H. Doc. 818, 64 Cong. 1 sess.)

ARMY DEPARTMENT

Military publications: Index of administrative publications (army regulations, special regulations, Department of the Army pamphlets, commercial traffic bulletins, general orders, bulletins, circulars, and army procurement circulars), January 1955, 309 pp. (Pamphlet 310–1.) Supplemented by changes.

Index of training publications: Field manuals, Reserve Officers' Training Corps manuals, training circulars, army training programs, programs of instruction, army subject schedules, army training tests, graphic training aids, War Department and Department of the Army posters, and firing tables and charts, October 1954, 83 pp. (Pamphlet 310–3.)

Military publications: Index of technical manuals, technical regulations, technical bulletins, supply bulletins, lubrication orders, and modification work orders, May 1955, 565 pp. (Pamphlet 310–4). Supplemented by changes.

Publications of the Office, Chief of Military History, 1959, 19 pp.

Same, 1964, 24 pp.

Same, 1966, 22 pp.

Same, 1967, 23 pp.

Same, 1968, 23 pp.

Military publications, index of AMC publications and blank forms, Headquarters, Army Materiel Command, January 1968, 53 pp.

BUSINESS AND DEFENSE SERVICES ADMINISTRATION

Activities and services of the federal government in distribution research, a summary report prepared for the President's Conference on Technical and Distribution Research for the Benefit of Small Business, 1967, 60 pp.

United States Department of Commerce publications for use in marketing and distribution, December 1961, 31 pp.

BDSA publications, industrial economics, marketing, industrial mobilization, April 1964, 10 pp.

BDSA publications, working with business for business, 1966, 12 pp.

BDSA publications, 1967, 32 pp.

---

[26] The *Annual Reports of the American Historical Association* have always been issued as government publications; the *Papers* were not issued as government publications, but some of them have been reprinted in the *Annual Reports*.

Selected publications available from your local United States Department of Commerce Field Office, 1961, 24 pp.

Catalog of United States census publications 1790–1945 [annotated bibliography], prepared by Henry J. Dubester, 1950, 320 pp.

Census publications, catalog and subject guide, 1945–51.

Catalog of United States census publications, 1951–. This is issued on a current basis each quarter and cumulated to the annual volume. A monthly supplement is also issued.

Topical index of population census reports, 1900–30, by Olive M. Riddleberger, 1934, 76 pp. (Processed.)

Key to published and tabulated data for small areas, United States censuses of population and housing 1950, 1951, 50 pp. (A preliminary edition was issued for the 1940 census.)

Directory of federal statistics for local areas, a guide to sources, 1966, 156 pp. This is a comprehensive finding guide to sources of published statistics for governmental and socio-economic units below the state level, including one-time programs.

Guide to industrial statistics, 1964, 60 pp. This is a guide to the sources of manufacturing and mining statistics published by the Bureau of the Census and other governmental organizations.

Census tract manual, 1966, 83 pp. (Appendixes B and C also issued.)

Guide to foreign trade statistics, 1967, 89 pp.

Data access descriptions, mathching studies series 1, March 1967–. Intended as means of access to unpublished data of the Bureau of the Census for persons with data requirements not found in published reports.

Availability of published and unpublished data, United States census of the population, 1960. Revised 1964, 36 pp.

Availability of published and unpublished data, United States census of housing, 1960. Revised 1966, 13 pp.

Children's Bureau publications, an index to publications by number, title, author, and subject, 1912–67, 1967, 65 pp.

Publications index, 1967, 33 pp. Revised frequently.

Publications catalog, United States Commission on Civil Rights, 1966, 27 pp.

List and catalogue of the publications issued by the United States

Coast and Geodetic Survey, 1816–1902, by E. L. Burchard, 1902, 239 pp. Reprint with supplement 1903–08, by R. N. Brown, 1908, 237 + 44 pp.
Publications of the Coast and Geodetic Survey, 5th ed., 1955, 42 pp.

COAST GUARD

Directives, publications, and reports index, CG-236, cumulative edition, 1960, 181 pp.

COMMERCE DEPARTMENT

United States Department of Commerce publications, 1952, 795 pp. Publications issued since October 1950 not included.

Same, 1951–52 supplement, 1954, 191 pp. Publications issued from Oct. 1, 1950, to Dec. 31, 1952. Beginning with 1953, supplements have been issued annually.

Business service checklist (weekly), a guide to Department of Commerce publications plus key business indicators.

CONGRESS

See Chapter 6, Congressional Publications.

EDUCATION OFFICE

Index to the reports of the Commissioner of Education, 1867–1907, 1909, 103 pp. (Bureau of Education, Bulletin, 1909, No. 7.)

List of publications of the United States Bureau of Education, 1867–1910, 1910, 55 pp. (Bureau of Education, Bulletin, 1910, No. 3.)

List of publications of the Office of Education, 1910–36, including those of the former Federal Board for Vocational Education for 1917–33, with author and subject indexes, 158 pp. (Office of Education, Bulletin, 1937, No. 22.) This list includes the Bulletins from the first issue in 1906.

Publications of the Office of Education, 1937–59, compiled by Beryl Parke and Zelma E. McIlvain, 1960, 157 pp.

Publications of the Office of Education, 1959, 1959, 49 pp. (Office of Education, Bulletin, 1959, No. 25; OE-11000.) Contains an annotated list of publications issued by Office of Education through April 1959.

Publications of the Office of Education 1961, compiled by Beryl Parke, 1962, 52 pp.

Publications of the Office of Education 1962, compiled by Beryl Parke, 1963, 66 pp.

Publications of the Office of Education 1963, compiled by Martha Walpole, 1964, 76 pp.

Publications of the Office of Education 1966, compiled by Bobbie Doud, 1967, 60 pp.

Publications of the Office of Education 1967, compiled by Bobbie Doud, 1968, 86 pp.

Research in education, Educational Research Information Center, No. 1, January 1967–. Reports cited in this monthly publication are available in printed form or microfiche from ERIC Document Reproduction Service, Bell & Howell Co., Cleveland.

Office of Education research reports, résumés, 1956–65, Educational Research Information Center, 1967, 326 pp.

Same, indexes, 1967, 310 pp.

EMPLOYMENT SECURITY BUREAU

Bureau of Employment Security publications, 1966, 34 pp.

ENGINEER DEPARTMENT

Index to the reports of the Chief of Engineers, United States Army (including the reports of the Isthmian Canal Commissions, 1899–1914), 1866–1912, by John McClure, 1915, 2 vols. (H. Doc. 740, 63 Cong. 2 sess.)

Index to the reports of the Chief of Engineers, United States Army, 1913–17, by Claude Lindsey. Supplemental to index, 1866–1912 . . . including the reports of the Governor of the Panama Canal 1915–17; professional papers of the Corps of Engineers, United States Army; professional memoirs, Corps of Engineers, United States Army and Engineer Department at Large; and congressional documents relating to works of river and harbor improvement, 1905–17, 1921, 445 + xxxv pp. (H. Doc. 724, 66 Cong. 2 sess.)

[Index to] Preliminary examinations, surveys, projects and appropriations for rivers and harbors [from the establishment of the government to Mar. 4, 1915], 1916, 594 pp. (H. Doc. 1491, 63 Cong. 3 sess.)

The annual bulletin of the Beach Erosion Board, Office, Chief of Engineers, Washington, D.C., Vol. 12, July 1958, 115 pp. This issue includes annotated listings of contents of all previous issues of the bulletin and other technical publications of the Beach Erosion Board. Vol. 16, issued July 1962, 114 pp., includes listing of contents of all issues of the Bulletin after Vol. 12 and technical memoranda from No. 106.

List of publications of the Army Engineer Waterways Experiment Station, including hydraulic reports of other Corps of Engineers Laboratories and reports of hydraulic model investigations sponsored by other Corps of Engineers Offices, Waterways Experiment Station, Vicksburg, Miss., January 1965, 125 pp. Supplement No. 1 issued January 1967.

List of publications of the Ohio River Division Laboratories, Army Engineer Division, Ohio River, Corps of Engineers, Ohio River Division Laboratories, Cincinnati, Ohio, July 1962, 25 pp.

List of publications, Army Snow, Ice, and Permafrost Establishment, July 1960, 17 pp.

List of publications of the Arctic Construction and Frost Effects Laboratory, prepared by Arctic Construction and Frost Effects Laboratory, New England Division, Waltham, Mass., January 1961, 20 pp. Miscellaneous paper No. 14.

Military publications, index of engineer regulations and manuals, October 1961, loose-leaf.

Publications available for purchase, Army Engineer Waterways Experiment Station and other Corps of Engineers agencies, January 1967, 56 pp.

ETHNOLOGY BUREAU

General index to [annual] reports of Bureau of American Ethnology, Vols. 1–48, 1879–1931, by Biren Bonnerjea.[27] (In 48th Annual Report of the Bureau, 1930–31, pp. 25–1220.)

List of publications of the Bureau of American Ethnology, with index to authors and titles, revised to Dec. 31, 1961, 1962, 130 pp.

EXPLORATIONS

Reports of explorations printed in documents of United States government, by Adelaide R. Hasse, 1899, 90 pp. (Office of Superintendent of Documents.)

FEDERAL AVIATION ADMINISTRATION

FAA publications, April 1967, 25 pp.

FEDERAL RESERVE SYSTEM BOARD OF GOVERNORS

Index-digest Federal Reserve Bulletin, Vols. I–VI, 1914–20, inclusive, by Charles S. Hamlin, 1921, 249 pp. (Federal Reserve Board.) Similar index-digests were issued for 1921 and 1922. The bulletin for each year also has an index.

FEDERAL TRADE COMMISSION

List of publications, 1958, 11 pp.

FISH AND WILDLIFE SERVICE

An analytical subject bibliography of the publications of the Bureau of Fisheries, 1871–1920, by Rose M. E. MacDonald, 1921, 306 pp. (App. V of Annual Report of the United States Commissioner of Fisheries, fiscal year 1920; also published separately as Bureau of Fisheries Document 899.)

Publications of the United States Bureau of Fisheries, 1871–1940, compiled by Barbara B. Aller, 1958, 202 pp. (Fish and Wildlife Service, Special Scientific Report—Fisheries No. 284.)

Fishery publication index, 1920–54; publications of the Bureau of Fisheries and fishery publications of the Fish and Wildlife Service, by series, authors, and subjects, 1955, 254 pp. (Fish and Wildlife Service, Circular 36.)

Index of fishery technological publications of the Fish and Wildlife Service and the former Bureau of Fisheries, 1918–55, compiled by M. E. Stansby and Rosemary Schairer, 1961, 237 pp. (Circular 96.)

---

[27] The Bureau of American Ethnology also issues a series of bulletins.

Index of publications by the Branch of Technology, Bureau of Commercial Fisheries, 1955–59, by F. Bruce Sanford and Helen E. Plastino, April 1964, 28 pp. (Fishery Leaflet 558.)

List of individual series published by the Fish and Wildlife Service have been issued in its Fishery Leaflet series. Out of print titles are also listed.

List of fishery bulletins of the Fish and Wildlife Service, December 1966, 15 pp. (Fishery Leaflet 597.)

List of circulars of the Fish and Wildlife Service, December 1966, 13 pp. (Fishery Leaflet 596.)

List of fishery leaflets of the Fish and Wildlife Service, December 1966, 29 pp. (Fishery Leaflet 595.)

List of special scientific reports and "special scientific report–fisheries" of the Fish and Wildlife Service, November 1967, 50 pp. (Fishery Leaflet 605.)

Publications of the Bureau of Sport Fisheries and Wildlife, 1954–. Formerly titled Monthly List.

GENERAL ACCOUNTING OFFICE

List of GAO publications, January 1968, Vol. 1, No. 2. This pamphlet is issued every 6 months.

GEOGRAPHIC NAMES BOARD

Catalog of publications and indexes to decisions, February 1953, 20 pp.

GEOLOGICAL SURVEY[28]

Catalogue and index of the publications of the Hayden, King, Powell, and Wheeler surveys, by L. F. Schmeckebier, 1904, 208 pp. (Geological Survey, Bulletin 222.)

Catalogue and index of the publications of the United States Geological Survey, 1880–1901, by Philip C. Warman, 1901, 858 pp. (Geological Survey, Bulletin 177.)

Same, 1901–03, by Philip C. Warman, 1903, 234 pp. (Geological Survey, Bulletin 215.)

Index to the hydrographic progress reports of the United States Geological Survey, 1879–1904, by John C. Hoyt and B. D. Wood, 1905, 253 pp. (Geological Survey, Water-Supply Paper 119.)

Bibliographic review and index of papers relating to underground waters published by the United States Geological Survey, 1879–1904, by Myron L. Fuller, 1905, 128 pp. (Geological Survey, Water-Supply Paper 120.)

Bibliography and index of publications relating to ground water pre-

[28] All the publications cited under this heading, except the last one, were also issued as House documents.

pared by the Geological Survey and cooperating agencies, by G. A. Waring and O. E. Meinzer, 1947, 412 pp. (Geological Survey Water-Supply Paper 992. This supersedes Paper 120 but is somewhat more narrow in scope.)

Bibliography of publications relating to ground water prepared by the Geological Survey and cooperating agencies 1946–55, by Robert C. Vorhis, 1957, 203 pp. (Geological Survey Water-Supply Paper 1492.)

Inventory of unpublished hydrologic data, by W. T. Holland and C. S. Jarvis, 1938, 77 pp. (Geological Survey Water-Supply Paper 837.)

Index to river surveys made by the Geological Survey and other agencies, revised to July 1, 1947, by B. E. Jones and R. O. Helland, 1948, 145 pp. (Geological Survey Water-Supply Paper 995.)

Publications of the Geological Survey 1879–1961, 1964, 475 pp. This catalog is supplemented by a monthly publication, New Publications of the Geological Survey, which is cumulated annually and contains indexes comparable to those in the catalog.

Reports of the Geological Survey released only in the open files have been listed annually in the Circular series since 1951 as follows: 1951, Circular 227; 1952, 263; 1953, 337; 1954, 364; 1955, 379; 1956, 401; 1957, 403; 1958, 412; 1959, 428; 1960, 448; 1961, 463; 1962, 473; 1963, 488; 1964, 498; 1965, 518; 1966, 528. These reports may be consulted at the indicated depositories and may be copied. The annual lists have a subject index and are supplemented by frequently released lists.

Announcement of water-resources reports released for public inspection. This is a listing issued almost every month of open-file reports.

See also Chapter 3, Bibliographies, "Geology" and "Water Resources."

INTERIOR DEPARTMENT

A list of all books, reports, documents, and pamphlets printed or published from 1789 to 1881, 1882, 76 pp. (S. Ex. Doc. 182, 47 Cong. 1 sess.)

INTERNATIONAL COMMERCE BUREAU

Semiannual checklist, Bureau of International Commerce international business publications, July 1967, 39 pp.

INTERNATIONAL LAW TOPICS

General index to international law situations, topics, discussions, documents, and decisions, Vols. 1–30, 1901–30, 1933, 332 pp. (Naval War College.) An earlier index covered Vols. 1–20. The Naval War College at Newport has for some years published an annual volume containing the lectures on international law delivered to student officers.

General index to international law situations, and documents, Vols. 31–40, 1931–40, 1942, 79 pp.

INTEROCEANIC COMMUNICATION

Bibliography of United States public documents relating to interoceanic communication across Nicaragua, Isthmus of Panama, Isthmus of Tehuantepec, 1899, 29 pp. (Office of Superintendent of Documents.) This was reprinted with additions as an appendix to S. Doc. 59, 56 Cong. 1 sess., entitled *List of Books and Articles in Periodicals Relating to Interoceanic Canal and Railway Routes,* by H. A. Morrison.

JUSTICE DEPARTMENT

A list embracing all the publications of that department [1789–1881], 1882, 12 pp. (S. Ex. Doc. 109, 47 Cong. 1 sess.)

LABOR DEPARTMENT

Publications of the United States Department of Labor, subject listing 1948–57, August 1957 [1958], 37 pp.
Same, 1958, June 1963, 24 pp.
Same, 1961, June 1966, 71 pp.
New publications, Department of Labor, Office of Information, Publications, and Reports. (Issued monthly.)

LABOR STANDARDS BUREAU

Selected publications of the Bureau of Labor Standards, 1966, 25 pp.

LABOR STATISTICS BUREAU

Subject index of the publications of the United States Bureau of Labor Statistics up to May 1, 1915, 1915, 233 pp. (Bureau of Labor Statistics, Bulletin 174; issued also as H. Doc. 1707, 63 Cong. 2 sess.)
Subject index of bulletins published by the Bureau of Labor Statistics, 1915–59, 1960, 102 pp. (Bulletin 1281, issued also as H. Doc. 423, 86 Cong.)
Subject index to the *Monthly Labor Review* [of the United States Bureau of Labor Statistics], Vols. 1–11, July 1915–December 1920, by Karoline Klager and Elsie M. Pursglove, 1923, 176 pp. (Bureau of Labor Statistics, Bulletin 695; issued also as H. Doc. 305, 77 Cong. 1 sess.)
Subject index to the *Monthly Labor Review,* Vols. 12–51, January 1921–December 1940, 1942, 421 pp. (Bureau of Labor Statistics, Bulletin 696; issued also as H. Doc. 306, 77 Cong. 1 sess.)
Subject index of the *Monthly Labor Review,* Vols. 52–71, January 1941–December 1950, 1953, 219 pp. (Bureau of Labor Statistics, Bulletin 1080; issued also as H. Doc. 448, 82 Cong. 2 sess.)
Subject index to the *Monthly Labor Review,* Vols. 72–83, January 1951–December 1960, 1962, 58 pp. (Bulletin 1335; issued also as H. Doc. 428, 87 Cong.)

Publications of the Bureau of Labor Statistics (monthly), June 1947–.

Checklist of regular Bureau of Labor Statistics series for states and areas 1955, January 1956, 129 pp.

A directory of BLS studies in industrial relations, July 1953–April 1958, 1958, 9 pp.

A directory of BLS studies in industrial relations, 1954–65, 1965, 21 pp.

A directory of community wage surveys, 1948–June 1966, 1966, 37 pp.

A directory of industry wage studies and union scale studies, 1955–July 1966, 1966, 27 pp.

A directory of wage chronologies, 1948–October 1964, 1964, 14 pp.

Programs and publications of the Office of Foreign Labor and Trade, February 1967, 13 pp.

LIBRARY OF CONGRESS

List of publications of the Library of Congress, 1800–1901. (In report of the Librarian of Congress, fiscal year ending June 30, 1901, 1901, pp. 362–367.)

Publications issued by the Library since 1897, May 1935, 61 pp.

Publications, 1936–46, 1947, 70 pp. From lists in annual reports.

Library of Congress publications in print, March 1966, 1966, 32 pp.

MINES BUREAU

List of publications issued by the Bureau of Mines, July 1, 1910–Jan. 1, 1960, with subject and author index, prepared by Hazel J. Stratton, 1960, 828 pp.

List of journal articles by Bureau of Mines authors, July 1, 1910–Jan. 1, 1960, with subject index, compiled by Mae W. Hardison and Opal V. Weaver, 1960, 295 pp.

List of Bureau of Mines publications and articles Jan. 1, 1960–Dec. 31, 1964, with subject and author index, prepared by Rita D. Sylvester, 1965, 297 pp.

Same, Jan. 1–Dec. 31, 1965, 1966, 89 pp.

Same, Jan. 1–Dec. 31, 1966, 1967, 94 pp.

These are supplemented by a monthly list, *New Publications–Bureau of Mines.*

MISSISSIPPI RIVER COMMISSION

Index to reports of Mississippi River Commission 1879–95, 1896, 100 pp.

Publication list, 1945 [March 1945], 2 + [1] leaves.

NATIONAL ADVISORY COMMITTEE FOR AERONAUTICS

Index of NACA technical publications, 1915–49, 1950, 605 pp.

Same, 1949–May 1951, 1952, 201 pp.

Same, June 1951–May 1953, 1954, 230 pp.

Same, June 1953–May 1954, 1954, 212 pp.

Same, June 1954–May 1955, 1955, 205 pp.

Same, June 1955–June 1956, 1956, 222 pp.

Same, July 1956–June 1957, 1957, 265 pp.

Same, July 1957–September 1958 (final supplement), 1959, 338 pp.

List of NACA reports reprinted as wartime reports, June 1948. This is useful for identifying wartime reports cited by various advance report numbers.

Research abstracts No. 1, June 1951–No. 130, September 1958.

NATIONAL AERONAUTICS AND SPACE ADMINISTRATION

Publications announcements No. 1–70, Nov. 14, 1958–Apr. 26, 1962. Abstracts publications available. British aeronautical publications included are available on loan only. Beginning with No. 7 of June 30, 1959, entitled "Technical publications announcements."

Index of NASA technical publications, October 1958–June 1959, 1959, 166 pp.

Index of NASA technical publications, July 1959–June 1960, 1960, 242 pp.

Index of NASA technical publications with abstracts, July 1960–December 1961, 1962, 427 pp. (NASA SP-9.)

List of selected references on NASA programs, prepared for the National Aeronautics and Space Administration by the Science and Technology Division of the Library of Congress, 1962, 236 pp. (NASA SP-3.)

A selected listing of NASA scientific and technical reports for 1963, 1964, 235 pp. (NASA SP-7005.)

Same, 1964, 1965, 1,130 pp. (NASA SP-7018.)

Same, 1965, 1966, 1,400 pp. (NASA SP-7024.)

Same, 1966, 1967, 2,070 pp. (NASA SP-7028.)

Technical publications announcements, Vol. 2, 1962, 1963, 1,215 pp. Covers period April-December.

Scientific and technical aerospace reports, STAR, Vol. 1, 1963–. See Chapter 17, Technical and Other Department Publications.

NATIONAL ARCHIVES

Federal population censuses, 1790–1890, a price list of microfilm copies of the schedules, 1966, 154 pp.

Federal records of World War II. Vol. I, civilian agencies, 1950, 1,073 pp. Vol. II, military agencies, 1951, 1,061 pp.

Guide to federal archives relating to the civil war, by Kenneth W. Munden and Henry Putney Beers, 1962, 721 pp.

List of National Archives microfilm publications, 1966, 107 pp.

Publications of the National Archives and Records Service, an annual list.

NATIONAL MUSEUM

A list and index of the publications of the United States National Museum (1875–1946), 1947, 306 pp. (National Museum, Bulletin 193.)

Same, Supplement 1, January 1947–June 1958, 1958, 16 pp.

Publications of the National Museum, July 1959–June 1960, 1961, 2 pp.

NATIONAL RESOURCES COMMITTEE

Subject index of reports by the National Planning Board, National Resources Board, National Resources Committee. A National Resources Committee publication issued by the National Resources Planning Board, 1940, 76 pp.

NATIONAL SCIENCE FOUNDATION

Publications of the National Science Foundation, March 1963, 8 pp.

NAVAL MEDICAL RESEARCH LABORATORY

Cumulative bibliography of research reports and publications, 1942 through 1950, May 1951, 53 pp.

List of MRL reports published during 1954, 1955, 3 pp.

NAVAL OBSERVATORY

List of publications issued by the United States Naval Observatory, 1845–1908, by William D. Horigan, 1911, pp. D1–D36. (App. III to *Publications of the United States Naval Observatory*, 2d series, Vol. VI; also issued separately.)

NAVAL OCEANOGRAPHIC OFFICE

Catalog of Oceanographic Office technical reports and special publications, February 1967, 30 pp. (H. O. Pub. 1-TR.)

NAVAL PERSONNEL BUREAU

List of training manuals and correspondence courses, revised semi-annually, April 1967, 48 pp. (NAVPERS 10061-Z.)

Training publications for advancement in rating, March 1966, 95 pp. (NAVPERS 10052-N.)

NAVAL RECORDS

Official records of the Union and Confederate Navies in the War of the Rebellion . . . by Dudley W. Knox, 1927, general index, 457 pp. (Navy Department; issued also as H. Doc. 113, 69 Cong. 1 sess.)

NAVAL RESEARCH LABORATORY

Bibliography of unclassified NRL formal reports numbers 1,000 to 5,700, July 1962, 145 pp. (NRL Report 5,700B.)

Same, Nos. 5,700 to 6,300, January 1966, 131 pp. (NRL Report 6,000B.)

NAVY

List of United States public documents and reports relating to construction of new navy; also references to debates in Congress on the subject, 1880–1901, 1902, 18 pp. (Office of Superintendent of Documents.)

NAVY DEPARTMENT

List of all books, reports, documents and pamphlets issued, printed, or published by the Navy Department [1789 to 1881], 15 pp. (S. Ex. Doc. 37, 47 Cong. 1 sess.)

ORDNANCE DEPARTMENT, WAR DEPARTMENT

Index to reports of Chief of Ordnance, 1864–1912, 1913, 193 pp. (Office of Chief of Ordnance.)

Index to reports of tests of metals and other materials made with the United States testing machine at Watertown Arsenal, and to reports of United States Board for Tests of Metals from 1881 to 1912, both inclusive, 1913, 240 pp.

PATENTS

Index of patents (annual), 1926–.

Index of trademarks (annual), 1927–.

Prior to 1927 all the indexes were in one volume and the title of the volume was *Annual Report of the Commissioner of Patents,* although the index was also issued separately at times. This report, which was made to Congress, was for the calendar year and was discontinued with the issue for 1926 under authority of the act of May 13, 1926 (44 Stat. 552).

Subject-matter index of patents for inventions . . . 1790–1873, 1874, 3 vols.

Women inventors to whom patents have been granted by the United States government, 1790–July 1, 1888; App. 1, July 1, 1888–Oct. 1, 1892; App. 2, Oct. 1, 1892–Mar. 1, 1895.

Index of patents relating to electricity granted . . . prior to July 1, 1881, with an appendix embracing patents granted from July 1, 1881, to June 30, 1882.

Index of patents relating to electricity granted from July 1, 1882, to June 30, 1883.

The same, annually, from 1883–84 to 1896–97.

Official gazette of the United States Patent Office, Vol. 1, 1872–. Contains the patents, trademarks, and designs issued each week and the decisions of the Commissioner of Patents and of the United States courts in patent cases. Before the annual index appears, the official gazette provides a "list of patentees" and "classification of patents," a subject index, with patent numbers arranged by class and subclass. To identify class and subclass, the Manual of Classification should be consulted together with its index. A cumulated "classification of patents" is published in an annual index of patents, 1955–. Through 1953 the index of patents had a section "list of inventions." No subject approach is provided for the year 1954 in printed indexes but is included in the microfilm lists which provide lists of patents by class numbers to October 1959.

Patent abstract series, government-owned patents available for license by the public on a royalty-free, non-exclusive basis. The initial series comprised 7 volumes covering patents to December 1953: Vol. 1, Instrumentation (PB-111 464); Vol. 2, Chemical products and processes (PB-111 465); Vol. 3, Food products and processes (PB-111 466); Vol. 4, Metal processes and apparatus, machinery, and transportation equipment (PB-111 467); Vol. 5, Electrical and electronic apparatus (PB-111 468); Vol. 6, Ordnance (PB-111 469); Vol. 7, Ceramic, paper, rubber, textile, wood, and other products and processes (PB-111 470). Supplement No. 1, January 1954–June 1955. Supplement No. 2, July 1955–June 1958. Supplement No. 3, July 1958–December 1960. Supplement No. 4, January 1961–December 1961. Supplement No. 5, January 1962–December 1962. Supplement No. 6, January 1963–December 1963. An index has been issued covering the period through December 1961.

PUBLIC HEALTH SERVICE

Publications of the Public Health Service, 1927, 129 pp. Complete to January 1927. (Misc. Pub. No. 12.)

List of publications issued by the Public Health Service, annual or semiannual, 1913–. Reprints are included.

Public Health Service numbered publications, a catalog, 1950–62, 1964, 190 pp. (PHS Biblio. Series No. 55.) Supplement No. 1, 1963–64, 1965, 114 pp.

Reference list of publications, water supply and pollution control, by Robert A. Taft Sanitary Engineering Center, Department of Health, Education, and Welfare, Public Health Service, Division of Water Supply and Pollution Control, Cincinnati, Ohio, 1965, 54 pp.

PUBLIC WORKS ADMINISTRATION

Bibliography of PWA publications and official documents pertaining to PWA, September 1938, 20 pp. (Processed.)

RAILROAD ADMINISTRATION

Index to United States Railroad Administration documents, Mar. 1, 1920. (MS. copy in Library of Congress.)

REBELLION RECORDS

War of the Rebellion, compilation of the official records of the Union and Confederate Armies; general index and additions and corrections, by John S. Moodey, indexer, 1901, 1,242 pp. ("index," pp. 1–1087; "additions and corrections," pp. 1089–1242.) (War Department; also issued as H. Doc. 558, 56 Cong. 2 sess.) A six-page pamphlet of additions and corrections to index was issued in 1902.

RECLAMATION BUREAU

Index, 1st to 20th reports of the Reclamation Service. (In 20th Annual Report of Reclamation Service for 1920–21, pp. 583–642.)

RESEARCH REPORTS

See Chapter 17, Technical and Other Department Publications.

SIGNAL OFFICE, WAR DEPARTMENT

Report of O. L. Fassig, bibliographer and librarian [on publications of the United States Signal Service from 1861 to July 1, 1891]. (In Annual Report of the Secretary of War for the year 1891, Vol. IV, pp. 387–409.)

SMITHSONIAN INSTITUTION

Catalogue of publications of the Smithsonian Institution [1846–86],[29] by William J. Rhees. (In Annual Report for 1886, pp. 485–867.)

List of publications of the Smithsonian Institution, 1846–1903, by William J. Rhees, 1903, 99 pp. (Smithsonian Publication 1376; also published in Smithsonian Miscellaneous Collections, Vol. 44.)

List of Smithsonian publications available for distribution June 30, 1958, 1958, 54 pp.

Author-subject index to articles in the Smithsonian annual reports, 1849–1961, compiled by Ruth M. Stemple and the Editorial and Publications Division of the Smithsonian Institution, 1963, 200 pp.

SPECIFICATIONS AND STANDARDS

Index of federal specifications and standards, General Services Administration, Federal Supply Service. Issued annually with monthly supplements. (See page 448.)

Guide to specifications and standards of the federal government, 1965, 35 pp.

[29] This is a more satisfactory work than the later one, which also covers this period.

Department of Defense index of specifications and standards. Pt. 1, alphabetical; Pt. 2, numerical. Issued annually with several cumulative supplements.

Department of Defense federal supply classification listing of DOD standardization documents. Issued annually with several cumulative supplements.

National directory of commodity specifications, classified and alphabetical lists and brief descriptions of specifications of national recognition, prepared by Paul A. Cooley and Ann E. Rapuzzi, 1945, 1,311 pp. (National Bureau of Standards, Miscellaneous Publication No. 178.) A 322-page supplement prepared by Paul A. Cooley was published in 1947. These listings are not confined to government publications.

STANDARDS BUREAU

Publications of the Bureau of Standards 1901–25 [list and index], 1925, 271 pp. (Bureau of Standards, Circular 24.)

Supplementary list [with index] of the publications of the Bureau of Standards, July 1, 1925, to Dec. 31, 1931, 1932, 214 pp.

Same, Jan. 1, 1932–Dec. 31, 1941, with subject and author indexes 1901–41, 1943, 386 pp.

Publications of the National Bureau of Standards 1901 to June 30, 1947, 1948, 375 pp. (Circular 460.) This does not include the annotations that were given in the earlier lists.

Supplementary list of publications of the National Bureau of Standards July 1, 1947–June 30, 1957, 1958, 373 pp.

Publications of the National Bureau of Standards, July 1, 1957–June 30, 1960, by Betty L. Arnold, including titles of papers published in outside journals, 1950–59, 1961, 391 pp. (Misc. Pub. 240.)

Same, July 1960–June 1966, including outside journals, 1960–65, 1967, 740 pp.

Supplementary list of publications of the National Bureau of Standards, July 1, 1960–Feb. 26, 1965, 1965, 50 pp.

STATE DEPARTMENT

Publications of the Department of State, Oct. 1, 1929–Jan. 1, 1953, 1954, 207 pp. Complete list of the numbered publications.

Same, Jan. 1, 1953–Dec. 31, 1957, 1958, 230 pp.

Same, Jan. 1, 1958–Dec. 31, 1959, 1960, 73 pp.

General index to the published volumes of the diplomatic correspondence and foreign relations of the United States, 1861–99,[30] 1902, 945 pp.

Same, 1900–18, 1941, 507 pp.

[30] *Index to United States Documents Relating to Foreign Affairs, 1828–61*, by Adelaide R. Hasse, 3 vols. (1914–21), has been published by the Carnegie Institution of Washington (Publication No. 185).

TARIFF COMMISSION

Publications of the Tariff Commission, 1939, 132 pp.
Same, 1940–52, supplement, 1953, 30 pp.
Same, 1951–60, 1961, 16 pp.

TREASURY DEPARTMENT

Synopsis of executive documents, letters, reports, etc., upon banking coinage, currency, finance, etc., submitted to Congress by Secretaries of Treasury from the 1st Congress to 1st session of 53d Congress, inclusive, 1893, 73 pp.

Tabular material in the annual reports of the Secretary of the Treasury from 1914 to 1927. (Pages 10–18 of *Periodical Publications of the Treasury Department,* revised to Feb. 1, 1928, and summary of tabular material in the annual reports of the Secretary of the Treasury from 1914 to 1927.)

VETERANS ADMINISTRATION

Index to Veterans Administration publications, July 1, 1967, 1967, 236 pp. Revised frequently.

WAR DEPARTMENT

Publications . . . of the respective bureaus of the War Department from Mar. 4, 1789, to Mar. 4, 1881, 1882, 19 pp. (S. Ex. Doc. 47, 47 Cong. 1 sess.)

WORKS PROGRESS ADMINISTRATION (LATER WORK PROJECTS ADMINISTRATION)

Index of research projects, Vol. 1 [1938], 291 pp.
Same, Vol. 2 [1939], 208 pp.
Same, Vol. 3 [1939], 243 pp.
Subject index of research bulletins and monographs issued by Federal Emergency Relief Administration and Works Progress Administration, Division of Social Research, September 1937, 110 pp. (Processed.)

Catalog of research bulletins issued by Research Section, Division of Research, Statistics, and Finance, Federal Emergency Relief Administration and Division of Social Research, Works Progress Administration, October 1938, 20 pp. (Processed.)

Division of Research, Statistics, and Records, Catalog of publications, October 1937, 16 pp. (Processed.)

Bibliography of research projects reports, Feb. 2, 1940–Apr. 30, 1943, 1940–43, 7 vols. (WPA technical series, research and records bibliography Nos. 1, 2, 3, 4, 5, 6, 7, 8.)

Index of Bureau of Yards and Docks publications, January 1966, 29 pp. The Bureau was abolished and its functions transferred to the Naval Facilities Engineering Command, effective May 1, 1966.

Lists of Series

A complete list of all series of government publications, giving both title and number, has never been published. For departmental publications the *Checklist* gives complete lists of annual and unnumbered reports issued up to 1910; for numbered series it gives the series titles and numbers but not titles and dates for the individual publications in the series. For both classes it gives the congressional document number if the publication was issued as a document of Congress.[31]

In the *Checklist* the series are listed under the publishing office, which must be known in order to locate them. If a series was issued at different times by several offices, the *Checklist* contains the necessary cross references.

Similar lists for important series are given in the *Tables and Index* (see pages 32–34) for the period ending with 1892, and in the *Senate Catalogue* (1924 edition) for years prior to 1921. In these books the series are listed under their titles regardless of the name of the publishing bureau. The lists in the *Tables and Index* give the serial number and the document or report number; those in the *Senate Catalogue* do not indicate the serial number, but give the complete citation by congress, session, and document number. For reports and years not covered by these lists, recourse must be had to *Poore's Catalogue*, the *Ames Index*, and the several volumes of the biennial *Document Catalog*.

The lists described above are particularly valuable for locating the annual reports and other series issued in the early years

---

[31] The citation to the document number is given in brackets after the title or series number. Thus Geological Survey Bulletin 180 is listed as follows: 180 [4365-462]. The first number within the bracket is the serial number in the congressional series; the second number is the document number. Reference to the tables of congressional documents shows that No. 462 in serial number 4365 is a House document for the 1st session of the 57th Congress.

of the government. For many years most of these publications were issued or are available only as congressional documents. For years prior to 1859 most of them are listed twice under each year, because the same report was printed as a House document and as a Senate document. The two prints are generally identical in pagination and other features.

A list of congressional documents and reports for each session is given at the end of the several document indexes beginning with the 2d session of the 54th Congress and ending with the 2d session of the 72d Congress, the last one published. It is continued in *Numerical Lists* (see page 22).

A numerical list, with cross references to the subject entry in which the title is given, has been published in each issue of the biennial *Document Catalog* beginning with the issue for the 65th Congress under the main entry "Congressional Documents Lists."

If the document or report number is known and search is being made for the title, it is easier to use the several issues of the *Document Index* and the *Numerical Lists* if they are available. Thus for House Document 23 of the 1st session of the 71st Congress the numerical list of the *Document Index* gives the title directly, but the numerical list in the biennial *Document Catalog* gives a cross reference to "Tariff," and it is necessary to search through the four pages in which material on that subject is cataloged.

Lists of the series available for distribution to depository libraries is contained in the 1950 revision of the *Classified List of United States Government Publications Available for Selection by Depository Libraries*. This list is in the form of 3 × 5 cards so that it can be kept up to date as new publications appear. It is also supplied to depository libraries as a printed list, *List of Classes of United States Government Publications Available for Selection by Depository Libraries*, revised August 1, 1967, 27 pp.

The *Library of Congress Cumulative Catalog of Printed Cards* (see page 80) is also useful for identifying some government titles, especially by personal authors.

CHAPTER THREE

BIBLIOGRAPHIES

MOST OF THE CATALOGS described in the preceding chapter may be regarded as bibliographies so far as government publications are concerned, but the government has also published numerous bibliographies which include publications within specified fields. The Library of Congress has been particularly active in this respect, and the other departments and agencies have issued an appreciable number dealing with subjects coming within their scope. Many of these are separate publications, which may be found under the subject matter in the biennial *Document Catalog* and under both the entry "Bibliography" and the subject matter in the index to the *Monthly Catalog*.

Much more numerous are the bibliographies appended to publications on particular topics. Those printed prior to July 1930 are listed under the entry "Bibliography" in the annual index to the *Monthly Catalog*. In the index for 1930–31, however, only bibliographies which are complete publications in themselves are listed. The more comprehensive listing was resumed with the index to the catalog for 1931–32 and continued through 1947. For the years 1955 through 1967, over 200 individual bibliographies are listed for each year. The subject matter of these bibliographies runs from "accident prevention" to "youth" in the 1967 index.

The compilation of a bibliography of all bibliographies in government publications would be a project worth undertaking. Entries up to 1895 have been prepared by Miss Adelaide R. Hasse and are in the possession of the Superintendent of Documents. They comprise about 4,000 items, but of course the entries for the period since 1895 would be much more extensive.

Some of the outstanding bibliographies and lists which have been published in a continuous series over a period of years are discussed below. Non-series bibliographies are also included.

Aeronautics. Aeronautics is included in a series of bibliographies by Paul Brockett covering the subject from the earliest times and bearing the title *Bibliography of Aeronautics*. The first issue, which covered the literature to 1909, was published by the Smithsonian Institution as Publication 1920, Miscellaneous Collections, Volume 55 (940 pages). Later volumes, the last being in 1932, were published by the National Advisory Committee for Aeronautics. The earlier volumes published by the National Advisory Committee covered the years 1909–16, 1917–19, and 1920–21, respectively, but 1922–32 issues were for single years. The *Air University Periodical Index* is described on page 87.

The Commander-in-Chief, Pacific Air Forces, issues annotated lists for base libraries entitled *PACAF Basic Bibliographies*. There are 25 titles from Accident Prevention to Transportation.

The Federal Aviation Agency published a *Bibliographic List* series.

NASA's complete bibliography is STAR, *Scientific and Technical Aerospace Reports*. (See Chapter 17.) NASA also has many subject bibliographies issued in its SP-7000 series. Some are continuing bibliographies.

SP-7002 High energy propellants, a continuing bibliography, a selection of annotated references to unclassified reports and journal articles introduced into the NASA information system during the period 1962–.
SP-7003 Lunar surface studies, . . . 1962–.
SP-7004 Communication satellites, . . . 1962–.
SP-7006 Bibliographies on aerospace science, . . . 1962–.
SP-7009 Lasers and masers, . . . 1962–.
SP-7011 Aerospace medicine and biology, . . . 1964–.
SP-7017 Planetary atmospheres, . . . 1962–.
SP-7020 Lubrication, corrosion and wear, . . . 1962–.

Other bibliographies are the following:

SP-7010 Extraterrestrial life, a bibliography. Pt. I, Report literature, 1952–64; Pt. II, Published literature, a selection of annotated references to journal articles and books, 1900–64. December 1965.

SP-7021 Ballistocardiography, September 1965.

SP-7022 Space communications; theory and applications, 1958–63, 4 vols.

Africa. The Army Library has issued *Africa, Problems and Prospects,* a bibliographic survey, April 1967, 226 pp. The preface states that analysts selected more than 99 unclassified items from several thousand documents, books, and periodical articles in order to shed light on the problems facing Africa as well as to present the emerging economic, political, and sociological picture of the continent's prospects for the future.

In 1964, the Library of Congress issued *African Music,* a briefly annotated bibliography compiled by Darius L. Thieme, 55 pp. In 1962, the African Section issued *List of American Doctoral Dissertations on Africa,* 69 pp.

Bibliographies of foreign publications in Africa are described on pp. 83–84.

Agriculture and related subjects. The Department of Agriculture has published many valuable bibliographies on agriculture or the sciences related thereto, and on economic conditions in that field. Many of these covered specific topics and were not issued periodically, such as those of the department library in the series Bibliographical Contributions and those formerly issued by the Bureau of Agricultural Economics library in the series Agricultural Economics Bibliography, most of which are processed. They are listed in the biennial *Document Catalog* and in the *Monthly Catalog* after 1936.

Each year the department publishes bibliographies on various subjects, such as the *Bibliography of Forest Disease Research in the Department of Agriculture,* compiled by Agnes Ellis Moore, Department of Agriculture, Miscellaneous Publication 25, 1957 (186 pages), which covers research from 1899 to January 1954. *Abstracts of Recent Published Material on Soil and Water Conservation,* published since 1941, is issued several times a year by the Agricultural Research Service. *Summaries of Studies in Agricultural Education* was first issued in 1935 by the Office of Education. Supplement 16 contains material through the 1960–61 academic year.

Pesticides Documentation Bulletin is a computer-produced permuted title index in three parts—keyword, bibliography, and author. This is an index to the literature on pest control, broadly defined. *Contract Farming and Vertical Integration, 1953–62,* a 77-page list of selected references was issued in 1963. An annotated bibliography of 77 pages, *Agriculture in the European Economic Community, 1958–66,* was published in 1968.

The Department of Agriculture also issued, from 1943 until 1954, a Bibliographical Bulletin Series on a number of subjects. Each Bulletin contains a bibliography of selected references on a particular subject, such as Land Ownership, Rural Electrification, Voluntary Health Insurance, etc. Twenty-five Bulletins were issued.

A bibliographical series entitled, *Library List,* was started in 1942. Many of these numbers are frequently revised, and No. 25 is *Available Bibliographies and Lists.*

The *Bibliography of Agriculture,* Vol. 1, 1942–, is a monthly index to the literature of agriculture and the related sciences received in the library of the Department of Agriculture. For scientific and technical publications it is as complete as possible, but only selected popular publications are indexed. Publications from any country are indexed if they are in one of the languages of western Europe or in Russian, or if they have summaries, abstracts, or titles in one of those languages.

The main library of the Department of Agriculture and the libraries of the bureaus formerly issued periodically the following processed bibliographies, whose contents are indicated by their titles.

Agricultural Economics Literature. Published monthly (except July and August) from January 1927 to June 1942 by the Bureau of Agricultural Economics.

Agricultural Library Notes. Published monthly from January 1926 to June 1942 by the department library. Among other material contained the following: principal library accessions; bibliographies and lists; publications by United States Department of Agriculture workers appearing outside the department; list of state extension publications; and selected list of processed publications.

Commodity Exchange Administration Literature. Published monthly from January 1938 to February 1939 by the library of the Commodity Exchange Administration of the department.

Cotton Literature. Published monthly from January 1931 to June 1942. Prepared in the library of the department with the cooperation of the Bureau of Agricultural Economics, Bureau of Plant Industry, and Bureau of Entomology and Plant Quarantine. Covered all aspects of cotton and cotton products, including production, preparation, marketing, utilization in manufacture, seed and seed products, and legislation.

Current Literature in Agricultural Engineering. Published monthly by the Bureau of Agricultural Engineering.[1] First issued under the above title in August 1931; it was discontinued in March 1942. Before 1931 the contents were included in *Highways and Rural Engineering, Current Literature* (June 23, 1926–April 13, 1927) and *Highways and Agricultural Engineering, Current Literature* (April 20, 1927–June 24, 1931).

Entomology, Current Literature. Published bimonthly from January 1932 to June 1942. Selected references compiled by the staff of the Bureau of Entomology and Plant Quarantine library from publications received in the department library.

Plant Science Literature. Published biweekly from 1934 to 1942. Compiled by the library staff of the Bureau of Plant Industry from publications received in the department library. First issued in January 1919 under the title *Botany, Current Literature;* title and frequency of publication varied.

Soil Conservation Literature. Published bimonthly from January 1937 to June 1942 by the library of the Soil Conservation Service.

The Department also issues a *Bi-Monthly List of Publications and Motion Pictures.* In 1949 there began to be issued *Abstracts of Recent Published Material on Soil and Water Conservation.* In some years only one number has appeared with a range to as many as 5 in 1965. No. 42 was issued in September 1967. An index covering the period December 1954 through August 1961 (Nos. 9–21) was issued in February 1963.

The first 10 volumes of the *Dictionary Catalog of the National Agricultural Library, 1862–1965,* were issued in February

[1] Combined in 1939 with the Bureau of Chemistry and Soils to form the Bureau of Agricultural Chemistry and Engineering. In 1942 most of the research functions were consolidated in the Agricultural Research Administration (now Agricultural Research Service).

1968. The complete work will cover approximately 68 volumes, will include approximately 1,500,000 author, title, and subject cards, arranged in a single alphabet, for all books and journals added to the National Agricultural Library from 1862 through 1965. The *Dictionary Catalog* is kept up to date by the *National Agricultural Library Catalog* which has been published monthly since January 1966.

Air pollution.   The Public Health Service has issued two bibliographies on air pollution: *Air Pollution Publications, Selected Bibliography, 1936–56*, 1966, 144 pp., and *Air Pollution Publications, Selected Bibliography, 1955–64*, 1964, 174 pp. The latter lists publications by Public Health Service personnel and other persons and organizations receiving federal air pollution funds and was compiled by Anna Grossman-Cooper.

The Department of Commerce has published *Air Pollution and Purification*, 1963, 24 pp., and Supplement No. 1, 1965, 14 pp. These list reports and translations in the Clearinghouse for Scientific and Technical Information collection.

American history.   A valuable bibliography which has been issued annually for some years as a government publication, but which is not prepared under government direction, is the series entitled *Writings on American History*. These volumes have been prepared under the auspices of the American Historical Association and the leading historical societies in more limited fields. The volumes that have appeared as government publications form part of the *Annual Report of the American Historical Association*, which is made to the Secretary of the Smithsonian Institution and by him transmitted to Congress and printed under the provisions of the act of January 4, 1889 (25 Stat. 640), incorporating the association.

The volumes in this series published by the government are those for the years 1909–11 and 1918 and thereafter. The issues for 1909–11 formed part of the annual report of the association and were also issued separately; those for 1918–29 were issued in separate volumes as supplements to the annual report; those for 1930 and 1931 were published as Volume 2 of the annual report for those years; the one for 1932 was published as Part III of the annual report for 1931; the volumes for 1933 and 1934 constituted the entire report of the association for those years. All the annual reports of the association are also issued as House documents. Issues in the series which have not been published by the government are as follows:

Writings on American history, 1902, by Ernest C. Richardson and Anson E. Morse, published by Princeton, N.J., Bookstore and now sold by Princeton University Library

Same, 1903, by Andrew C. McLaughlin, William A. Slade, and Ernest D. Lewis, published by the Carnegie Institution of Washington, Publication No. 38

1904 and 1905, not issued

Same, 1906–08, by Grace G. Griffin, published by the Macmillan Company, but now sold by the American Historical Association, Washington, D.C.

Same, 1912–17, by Grace G. Griffin, published by the Yale University Press

Including the latest volume, that for 1958, the series consists of 46 volumes, covering 48 years. Volumes for the years 1904–05 and 1941–47 have not been prepared.

In 1951 the National Historical Publications Commission assumed responsibility for the preparation of the *Writings* and for seeing the volumes through the press. It was also agreed that they would continue to be published as parts of the *Annual Reports of the American Historical Association.*

A similar index, which covers an earlier period, although somewhat narrower in scope, and which overlaps slightly the early volumes of the series described above, is *Bibliography of American Historical Societies (The United States and the Dominion of Canada)* by Appleton P. C. Griffin, Volume II of the *Annual Report of the American Historical Association for 1905,* (1,374 pages), published also as House Document 923, Part 2, 59th Congress, 1st session. This work is broader than its title indicates, as it includes such publications as the Columbia University Studies in History, Economics, and Public Law. The arrangement is alphabetical by states, the studies just cited being under New York. The book has three indexes: (1) subject and author; (2) biographical sketches; and (3) societies.

Arctic regions.   An *Arctic Bibliography*, started in 1953, was prepared for and in cooperation with the Department of Defense under the direction of the Arctic Institute of North America. The latest is Volume 12 issued in 1965. Volume 13 is being printed in Canada under the direction of McGill University.

Another publication covering the arctic regions is *Polar Bibliography*, produced by the Technical Information Division of the Library of Congress. This bibliography was published in two volumes, Volume 1 in 1956 and Volume 2 in 1957. (AFM 200–132.)

A continuing series, *Antarctic Bibliography*, Volume 1, 1965–, containing current abstracts and indexes of Antarctic literature, is prepared at the Library of Congress and sponsored by the Office of Antarctic Programs, National Science Foundation.

The *Bibliography on Snow, Ice, and Permafrost With Abstracts* (CRREL Report 12), Volume 1 published in 1951, is a continuing project of the Cold Regions Bibliography Section, Science and Technology Division, Library of Congress, prepared for the Cold Regions Research and Engineering Laboratory of the Army Materiel Command. CRREL was formerly known as USA SIPRE. Beginning with Volume 20, 1966, the title changed to *Bibliography on Snow, Ice, and Frozen Ground With Abstracts*. In addition to the annual volumes, there have been several cumulative indexes.

Commerce.   The basic volume, *United States Department of Commerce Publications*, covering publications of the Department of Commerce from 1790 to October 1950, has been kept up to date with annual supplements.

The *Catalog of United States Census Publications* is issued on a current basis each quarter and cumulated to the annual volume. A monthly supplement is also issued. The record of the Bureau of the Census publications since the first census in 1790 through the year 1945 is available in the *Catalog of United*

States Census Publications, 1790–1945. Publications issued after 1945 are shown in the annual issues of *Census Publications, Catalog and Subject Guide* through 1951. Publications since 1951 are listed in the *Catalog of United States Census Publications.*

Marketing Information Guide, a monthly publication of the Business and Defense Services Administration, contains annotations of selected current publications and reports with basic information and statistics on marketing and distribution. This publication began in 1954 with the title, *Distribution Data Guide.*

Housing and Planning References, Number 1, 1965–, a bimonthly publication of the Department of Housing and Urban Development Library, is a selected list of publications and an index of articles on housing and planning, newly acquired or noted in the libraries of the Department.

Urban Transportation Research and Planning Current Literature, issued by the Bureau of Public Roads, Volume 7, 1951–, appeared earlier with the title, *Planning, Current Literature.*

The Bureau of the Census issues quarterly *Foreign Statistical Publications Accession List,* January 1956–, which appeared earlier with the title, *Publications on Foreign Countries.*

The Small Business Administration has a series *Small Business Bibliography* which was started as *Small Business Bulletin* in 1958. Most numbers have been revised.

Education. Between 1907 and 1932 the Office of Education[2] issued a series of general bibliographies, many of which were annotated. The general title of the earlier issues was *Bibliography of Education* and that of the later ones *Record of Current Educational Publications.* Most were issued as bulletins, but some were published as library circulars. Prior to 1912 each publication covered a year or more, but in 1913 and thereafter there were monthly or quarterly issues. For some years an index was issued separately, but for other years it was

[2] Bureau of Education prior to October 3, 1929. From 1899 to 1907 the series of bibliographies described in this paragraph had been prepared by J. I. Wyer, Isabel E. Lord, and others and published in the *Educational Review* under the title "Bibliography of Education."

included in the last number for the year. The scope of the bibliographies was materially changed with the one covering the period July–December 1930.[3] The series ended with the issue for January–March 1932.[4]

The bibliographies issued regularly by the Office of Education have been largely confined to those relating to research and investigations in the field of education. These have generally been issued annually as printed bulletins and processed circulars as follows:

Bibliography of research studies in education [in colleges and universities], 1926–27, prepared in Library Division, 162 pp. (Bulletin, 1928. No. 22)[5]

Same, 1927–28, Edith A. Wright, compiler, 225 pp. (Bulletin, 1929, No. 36)

Same, 1928–29, by Edith A. Wright, 308 pp. (Bulletin, 1930, No. 23)

Same, 1929–30, by Edith A. Wright, 475 pp. (Bulletin, 1931, No. 13)

Same, 1930–31, by Edith A. Wright and Ruth A. Gray, 459 pp. (Bulletin, 1932, No. 16)

Same, 1931–32, by Ruth A. Gray, 282 pp. (Bulletin, 1933, No. 6)

Same, 1932–33, by Ruth A. Gray, 349 pp. (Bulletin, 1934, No. 7)

Same, 1933–34, by Ruth A. Gray, 328 pp. (Bulletin, 1935, No. 5)

Same, 1934–35, by Ruth A. Gray, 287 pp. (Bulletin, 1936, No. 5)

Same, 1935–36, by Ruth A. Gray, 338 pp. (Bulletin, 1937, No. 6)

Same, 1936–37, by Ruth A. Gray, 373 pp. (Bulletin, 1938, No. 5)

Same, 1937–38, by Ruth A. Gray, 400 pp. (Bulletin, 1939, No. 5)

Same, 1938–39, by Ruth A. Gray, 411 pp. (Bulletin, 1940, No. 5)

Same, 1939–40, by Ruth A. Gray, 404 pp. (Bulletin, 1941, No. 5)

List of educational research studies of state departments of education and state education associations, No. 1, January 1931, by Edith A. Wright, 40 pp. (Circular 31)

Same, 1930–31, by Edith A. Wright, 43 pp. (Circular 44)

Same, 1931–32, by Edith A. Wright, 44 pp. (Circular 63)

Research and investigations reported by state departments of education and state education associations, 1932–33, by Ruth A. Gray, 24 pp. (Circular 127)

[3] For statement regarding change of plan, see Bureau of Education Bulletin, 1931, No. 3, p. v.

[4] This bibliography has been continued on a somewhat similar plan by *The Elementary School Journal* and *The School Review*.

[5] Also previously issued as unnumbered processed publications entitled *Bibliography of Current Research Studies in Education, March 1928*, and *Bibliography of Current Research Studies in Education, Supplementary List No. 1, May 1928*.

Same, 1933–34, not published

Same, 1934–35, by Ruth A. Gray, 21 pp. (Circular 141)

Same, 1935–36, by Ruth A. Gray, 21 pp. (Circular 160)

List of educational research studies in city school systems, No. 1, August 1930, by Edith A. Wright, 85 pp. (Circular 18)

Same, No. 2, October 1931, by Edith A. Wright, 71 pp. (Circular 42)

Same, 1931–32, by Ruth A. Gray, 63 pp. (Circular 72)

Research and investigations reported by city school systems, 1932–33, by Ruth A. Gray, 37 pp. (Circular 128)

Same, 1933–34, not published

Same, 1934–35, by Ruth A. Gray, 33 pp. (Circular 143)

Same, 1935–36, by Ruth A. Gray, 24 pp. (Circular 161)

For the bibliographies of research studies, the periods indicated by the title are not complete calendar years but portions of two years.

From 1931 to 1945 the Office of Education published a numbered series with the series title "Bibliography No. —." These have the general subject title *Good References* and a subordinate subject title indicating the subject covered. They are small leaflets giving selected annotated references to significant studies and do not pretend to list all the literature on any topic considered. They are not published periodically.

The Office of Education also issues many bibliographies on special phases of educational activities. Examples follow:

OE-80046, Vocational education, annotated bibliography of selected references, 1917–66 (below college), by Alice Songe, 1967, 39 pp.

OE-14004, Bibliography of publications in comparative and international education, prepared for 1958 and issued again for 1959.

OE-14023, Publications of the Office of Education on international education, 1963.

OE-34041, Research in instructional television and film, by J. C. Reid and D. W. MacLennan, 1967, 216 pp.

Fish and wildlife. A quarterly publication of the Fish and Wildlife Service of the Department of the Interior is *Wildlife Review*, which abstracts publications on wildlife management. This publication, started in 1935 by the Biological Survey of the Department of Agriculture, was transferred to the Fish and Wildlife Service in May 1940.

Another publication of the Fish and Wildlife Service is the

monthly catalog *Commercial Fisheries Abstracts.* In addition to the regular abstracts, a bibliography of references of secondary importance (without abstracts) is included.

Wildlife Abstracts, 1935–51, is an annotated bibliography of the publications abstracted in the *Wildlife Review,* Nos. 1–66, compiled by Neil Hotchkiss, 1954 (435 pages). Nos. 67–83, 1952–55, were compiled by Lucille F. Strickel, 1957 (321 pages). Nos. 84–100, 1956–60, were compiled by Nicholas J. Chura, 1964 (335 pages).

The Bureau of Fisheries issues two quarterlies: *Wildlife Review Abstracting Service for Wildlife Management,* issued for the information of cooperators, and *Sport Fishery Abstracts,* Volume 1, 1955–.

Federal Research on Fisheries and Limnology in the Great Lakes Through 1964, an annotated bibliography, by Ralph Hile, was issued in 1966 (53 pages).

Forestry. Publications on forestry, lumber, and allied subjects were listed in the processed publication entitled *Forestry, Current Literature,* issued bimonthly by the Forest Service. The list did not always appear as a government publication, being printed for several periods in private journals. The titles and method of publication have been as follows:

February 1904–November 1905. *New Books Received;* typewritten to March 1905; processed April–November 1905
December 1905. *New Books;* processed
January 1906–March 1907. *Current Literature;* processed
April and May 1907. *Accessions to the Library;* printed in *Field Program* of Forest Service
June–November 1907. *New Forest Literature;* printed in *Field Program* of Forest Service, June–October; processed in November
December 1907–April 1910. *Current Literature;* processed
May and June 1910. *Monthly List;* printed in *American Forestry*
July 1910–December 1927. *Current Literature;* printed in *American Forestry* July 1910–July 1919; processed August 1919–February 1922; printed in *Journal of Forestry* March 1922–March 1927; processed after March 1927
January 1928–April 1940. *Forestry, Current Literature;* processed; discontinued with issue for September–October 1932; resumed in January 1934

with issues for November 1932–June 1933 and July–December 1933; new series begun with Vol. 1, No. 1 for January–February 1934.

This series was discontinued with Volume 7, No. 2, in 1940 and was succeeded by the *Bibliography of Agriculture* (see page 68).

Other publications pertaining to forestry are *A Selected Bibliography of North American Forestry* by E. N. Munns (2 vols.), Department of Agriculture, Miscellaneous Publication 364, 1940 (1,142 pages); *Tree Physiology Bibliography* by Theodore T. Kozlowski, Forest Service, Department of Agriculture, 1958 (316 pages); and *Economics of Forestry*, a bibliography for the United States and Canada, 1940–47, compiled by Frances J. Flick and Elizabeth P. Brown, June 1950 (126 pages). Two supplements have been issued—Supplement 1, June 1955 (136 pages) and Supplement 2, February 1959 (45 pages). *Economics of Forestry*, a bibliography for the United States and Canada, 1960–62, was compiled by Fay Rumsey, October 1965 (45 pages) (Misc. Pub. 1003). *Forest Recreation Research*, a bibliography of Forest Service outdoor recreation research publications, 1942–66, was issued in January 1967 (16 pages). *Bibliography of Publications by Intermountain Forest and Range Experiment Station on Genetics and Breeding of Forest Trees, 1921–64*, was compiled by Vendla K. Roberts, 1966 (8 pages).

Geology. Geology has been covered by the following publications of the United States Geological Survey:

Geologic literature on North America 1785–1918, by John M. Nickles, Pt. 1, bibliography, 1,167 pp. (Bulletin 746); Pt. II, index, 658 pp. (Bulletin 747)
Bibliography of North American geology 1919–28, by John M. Nickles, 1,005 pp. (Bulletin 823)

These publications superseded a long series of earlier bulletins covering shorter periods by N. H. Darton, F. B. Weeks, and John M. Nickles. They have been continued by the following publications:

Bibliography of North American geology, 1929–39, Pt. I, bibliography, Pt. II, index, 1,546 pages (Bulletin 937)
Same, 1940–49, Pt. I, bibliography, Pt. II, index, 2,205 pages (Bulletin 1049)
Same, 1950–59, 4 vols. (Bulletin 1195)
Same, 1960, 777 pp. (Bulletin 1196)
Same, 1961, 663 pp. (Bulletin 1197)
Same, 1962, 834 pp. (Bulletin 1232)
Same, 1964, 944 pp. (Bulletin 1234)

Since 1885 the Geological Survey has published several bibliographies concerning investigations of the natural water of the United States which occurs both above and below the land surface. The *Bibliography and Index of Publications Relating to Ground Water,* Geological Survey Water-Supply Paper 992, is a compilation of all previous works and brings these surveys up to January 1946. A *Bibliography of Publications Relating to Ground Water, 1946–55,* compiled by R. C. Vorhis, was issued in 1957 (203 pages).

Geophysical Abstracts is a quarterly publication of the Geological Survey which includes abstracts of technical papers and books on the physics of the solid earth, the application of physical methods and techniques to geologic problems, and geophysical exploration. It was first published in 1936.

Abstracts of North American Geology is a monthly publication started in 1966 which contains abstracts of technical papers and books and also citations of maps on the geology of North America, including Greenland, the West Indies, the State of Hawaii, Guam and other island possessions.

The *Bibliography of Hydrology of the United States, 1963,* compiled by J. R. Randolph and R. G. Deike, was issued in 1966, 166 pp. An *Annotated Bibliography on Hydrology and Sedimentation, United States and Canada, 1955–58,* compiled by H. C. Riggs, was published in 1962 (236 pages). *Bibliography of Reports Resulting From the U.S. Geological Survey Participation in the United States Technical Assistance Program, 1940–65,* 1965 (51 pages), was compiled by Jo Ann Heath. *Bibliography and Discussion of Flood-routing Methods and Unsteady Flow in Channels,* 1964 (235 pages), was compiled by V. M. Yevdjevich. *Terrestrial Impact Structures—A Bibliography*, 1966 (91 pages), was compiled by J. H. Freeberg.

Geriatrics. The seventh volume, containing a bibliography, of *Studies of the Aged and Aging* was published in November 1956 as a Senate committee print. It was compiled by the staff of the Committee on Labor and Public Welfare. The publications are grouped under several major headings, such as Health, Income, and Employment. An annotated bibliography, *Selected References on Aging*, was compiled for the Special Staff on Aging by the library of the Department of Health, Education, and Welfare, 1959, 110 pages. The title, *Selected References on Aging*, has subsequently been used for several numbered series published by the Department of Health, Education, and Welfare and by its agencies, Welfare Administration and Aging Administration.

Library of Congress. The Library of Congress compiles numerous valuable bibliographies and also issues a number of periodical publications of a bibliographical nature.

Types and Availability of Bibliographies. The special bibliographies of the Library of Congress have been issued in three forms—printed, processed, and typewritten.

Both the printed and the processed bibliographies are listed in the Library of Congress, *Publications in Print*. This document indicates how and where copies may be obtained—both those for sale by the Superintendent of Documents, U. S. Government Printing Office and those available from other sources. These bibliographies are announced, as they are issued, in the weekly *Information Bulletin* of the Library of Congress, and in the *Annual Report of the Librarian of Congress*. They are also listed in the *Monthly Catalog*.

The typewritten lists are available on interlibrary loan through the Loan Division of the Library of Congress, and photostat copies may be obtained from the Photoduplication Service of the Library of Congress.

Union Catalog. *The National Union Catalog, a Cumulative*

Author List, is designed as a current and cumulative continuation of *A Catalog of Books Represented by Library of Congress Printed Cards* and its supplements. It represents the works cataloged by the Library of Congress and by the libraries contributing to its cooperative cataloging program during the period of its coverage. In addition, it includes entries for publications issued in 1956 and thereafter reported by North American libraries and not represented by Library of Congress printed cards. It constitutes a reference and research tool for a large part of the world's production of significant books as acquired and cataloged by the Library of Congress and a number of other North American libraries. It indicates in every case at least one library where the publication is held and, for imprints since 1956, additional locations, and serves thereby, at least for these imprints, as a national union catalog. The Library of Congress catalogs were first reproduced in book form with *A Catalog of Books Represented by Library of Congress Printed Cards,* which was issued under the auspices of the Association of Research Libraries and published in 1942–46 by Edwards Brothers, Inc., Ann Arbor, Michigan. In 1947 the Library began publishing the *Cumulative Catalog of Library of Congress Printed Cards.* With the annual cumulation for 1949, the title was changed to *The Library of Congress Author Catalog.* In 1953 a cumulation in 24 volumes covering the years 1948–52 was released under the title *The Library of Congress Author Catalog 1948–1952.* With the issue of January 1953 the title was changed to *Library of Congress Catalog—Books: Authors,* and in January 1956 the title was changed to *The National Union Catalog, a Cumulative Author List.* It is printed in nine monthly issues, three quarterly cumulations, and annual and quinquennial cumulations. In 1963, the 54-volume *Library of Congress National Union Catalog, Author List 1958–62* was issued by Rowman and Littlefields, New York. Volumes 51–52 cover music and phonorecords, and volumes 53–54, motion pictures and filmstrips. In 1961, J. W. Edwards, publisher, Ann Arbor, Michigan, issued the 30-volume *The Library of Congress Catalogs: The National Union Catalog 1952–55*

Imprints, Author List. This is an author list compiled by the Library of Congress under the auspices of the American Library Association consisting of Library of Congress printed cards and titles reported by other American libraries.

THE LIBRARY OF CONGRESS CATALOG—BOOKS: SUBJECTS. A publication by this title was undertaken, beginning January 1950, as a complement to the *Library of Congress Catalog—Books: Authors.* It is an alphabetical arrangement by subject or form heading. It is designed to serve as a continuing and cumulative subject bibliography of recent works currently received and cataloged by the Library of Congress and other American libraries participating in its cooperative cataloging program, so far as these works are represented by Library of Congress printed cards. It constitutes a reference and research tool by providing a basic subject control over a large portion of the world's current output of significant books. For all the works listed, a location in at least one library in the United States is given. The period 1950–54 was covered by 20 volumes issued by J. W. Edwards, publisher, Ann Arbor, Michigan; 1954–59, by 22 volumes published by Pageant Books, Inc., Paterson, New Jersey; and 1960–64, by 25 volumes issued by J. W. Edwards.

NEW SERIAL TITLES. This is a union list of serials commencing publication after December 13, 1949, and is prepared under the sponsorship of the Joint Committee on the Union List of Serials. This bibliography has been published monthly since 1951, and lists serials received by the Library of Congress and a number of cooperating libraries. Beginning in 1968, it is issued weekly with quarterly cumulations. The R. R. Bowker Co. has issued volumes covering the periods 1950–60 and 1961–65 and 1966.

COPYRIGHT ENTRIES. A publication of the Library of Congress which is valuable for keeping track of new publications, although it does not pretend to be a bibliography, is the *Catalog of Copyright Entries.* This is an administrative publication in which is listed all copyrighted material. As practically all important works are copyrighted, the entries include the greater part of all new productions. As the law does not require the copyright entry to be made immediately after publication, there is some lag between the dates of publication and listing, depending on the promptness with which the owner of the copyright complies with the statutory requirements.

The Catalog of Copyright Entries is issued in 13 parts. The parts, which are issued semiannually and may be subscribed for separately from the Superintendent of Documents, Government Printing Office, are as follows:

> Pt. 1, Books and pamphlets
> Pt. 2, Periodicals
> Pts. 3–4, Drama and works prepared for oral delivery
> Pt. 5, Music
> Pt. 6, Maps and atlases
> Pts. 7–11A, Works of art, reproductions of works of art, etc.
> Pt. 11B, Commercial prints and labels
> Pts. 12–13, Motion pictures and film strips

Entries on motion pictures have also been issued cumulatively in four volumes covering the period 1894–1912, 1912–39, 1940–49, and 1950–59.

FOREIGN PUBLICATIONS. The Library of Congress publishes bibliographic compilations of publications printed in foreign countries. The *East European Accessions Index* was a monthly record of monographic publications issued after 1944 and periodical publications issued after 1950 which were received by the Library of Congress and, as indicated, by other American libraries. Imprints of the following countries, as well as publications issued elsewhere in the languages of these countries, were included: Albania, Bulgaria, Czechoslovakia, Estonia, Hungary, Latvia, Lithuania, Poland, Rumania, and Yugoslavia. Publication was discontinued with the November–December 1961 issue.

The *Monthly Index of Russian Accessions* is a record of the publications in the Russian language and other languages spoken in the U.S.S.R. issued in and outside the Soviet Union that are currently received by the Library of Congress and a group of cooperating libraries. This index consists of three parts: Part A lists monographic literature, but no accessions published earlier than 1945 are included; Part B lists Russian periodicals subsequent to 1946 with their tables of contents translated into English; Part C is a subject guide to both the monographs and periodical articles listed in Parts A and B.

The *Bibliography of Translations from Russian Scientific and Technical Literature* lists translations deposited with or loaned to the Scientific Translations Center by government agencies, scientific societies, industrial laboratories, universities, and similar organizations. It was published monthly from October 1953 to December 1956.

Southern Asia: Publications in Western Languages, A Quarterly Accessions List was a record of publications, pertaining to southern Asia accessioned by the Library of Congress. The list included all monographs received in the library bearing an imprint of 1945 or later and selected articles in periodicals published since January 1953. Only publications in the western languages are included. In 1956 the title was changed to *Southern Asia Accession List,* and in 1960 the list was discontinued.

A reading guide entitled *Introduction to Africa* was published by the University Press of Washington in 1952. In 1954 this was followed by *Research and Information on Africa: Continuing Sources* released by the Reference Department of the Library of Congress. Because of the transformation taking place in Africa and its importance in world affairs today, material relating to this continent was brought up to date in *Africa South of the Sahara* and in *North and Northeast Africa,* both compiled by Helen F. Conover and published in 1957. *Africa South of the Sahara* was revised in 1963. *Official Publications of French West Africa, 1946–58,* compiled by Helen F. Conover, was issued in 1960. *Official Publications of British East Africa* was published in four parts: Part 1, *East Africa High Commission and Other Regional Documents,* compiled by Helen F. Conover, 1960. Parts 2, 3, and 4 were compiled by Audrey A. Walker: *Tanganyika,* 1962; *Kenya and Zanzibar,* 1962; and *Uganda,* 1963. *Serials for African Studies* was compiled by Helen F. Conover in 1961; and *Official Publications of*

French Equatorial Africa, French Cameroons, and Togo, 1946–58, was compiled by Julian W. Witherell in 1964.

The 231-page *Postwar Foreign Newspapers, Union List,* was issued in 1953, and accession lists were also published for India, Pakistan, Middle East, Israel, and Indonesia.

INTERNATIONAL LISTS. On November 25, 1946, a Conference on International Cultural, Educational, and Scientific Exchanges, held at Princeton University, recommended that UNESCO and other suitable agencies stimulate in each country throughout the world the issuance of comprehensive current national bibliographies. The Library of Congress later agreed to prepare such an international list. As a result, *Current National Bibliographies* was published in 1955.

MOTION PICTURES AND FILMSTRIPS. A publication by this title, printed quarterly with an annual cumulation beginning with the April–June 1954 issue, is designed to reproduce the catalog cards for motion pictures and filmstrips currently printed by the Library of Congress. It constitutes a reference and research tool for a large part of these audiovisual materials. Cumulations for 1953–57 and 1958–62 have been issued as volumes of The National Union Catalog. *Music and Phonorecords,* printed semiannually with annual cumulations since the January–June 1954 issue, does the same in its field. Cumulations for 1953–57 and 1958–62 have been issued as volumes of The National Union Catalog.

AIR POLLUTION. The first volume of *The Air Pollution Bibliography* was compiled in 1957 by the Technical Information Division of the Library of Congress for the Public Health Service. This consists of annotated references to open literature, both foreign and domestic, published from 1952 through 1957. A second volume, covering material published between 1952 and 1958, was issued in 1959. The United States Bureau of Mines publication, *Air Pollution, A Bibliography* (Bulletin 537, 448 pages), containing references published prior to early 1952, served as a starting point for the bibliography.

STATE PUBLICATIONS. Another publication of the Library of Congress is the *Monthly Checklist of State Publications*, with annual index. This was first issued in 1910. Only the publications that have been received by the Library of Congress from state offices are listed. It is sold by the Superintendent of Documents.

OTHER LISTS. Other publications of general interest are *The Presidents of the United States 1739–1962*, a selected list of references compiled by Donald H. Mugridge in 1963; *John Fitzgerald Kennedy 1917–63*, a chronological list of references published in 1964; and *Children's Literature Guide to Reference Sources*, compiled by Virginia Haviland in 1966. An annual list of children's books was started in 1964. An unusual publication, *Popular Names of U.S. Government Reports*, compiled by Donald F. Wisdom and William P. Kilroy, published in 1966, contains a selection of significant reports published during the past 75 years which have become identified with personal names such as the chairman of a committee, the head of a research team, or a specialist who performed the work.

Medicine. The *Current List of Medical Literature* was published monthly by the National Library of Medicine, formerly the Armed Forces Medical Library, and lists articles of medical interest contained in current journals received. It also contains author and subject indexes. Approximately 10,000 items are listed in each issue. This publication was discontinued in December 1959. Starting in January 1960, the National Library of Medicine began publishing the *Index Medicus*, a more expansive journal. The first five annual cumulation volumes were published by the American Medical Association. Beginning with Volume 6–, 1965, publication was assumed by the National Library of Medicine. The *Bibliography of Medical Reviews* is included in *Index Medicus* and annual cumulations are published separately. Beginning in 1968, the *Bibliography* is also published separately. A *Bibliography of Medical Translations* has been started, with Volume 1 covering 1959–64 and Volumes 2 and 3 covering 1965–66. Other listings are *Bibliography of the History of Medicine*, Volume 1, 1965–, and

Monthly Bibliography of Medical Reviews, Volume 1, No. 1, January 1968.

The *National Library of Medicine Current Catalog* is a biweekly listing started in 1966 and is cumulated quarterly and annually. It supersedes the *Army Medical Library Catalog,* 1950–64, and the *National Library of Medicine Catalog,* 1960– 65.

The *Index-Catalogue of the Library of the Surgeon General's Office, United States Army,* published by the Armed Forces Medical Library,[6] does not pretend to be a bibliography, but it serves that purpose by reason of the comprehensive character of the library. It was published in four "series," each running through the complete alphabet, with entries by author and subject. The first series contains 16 volumes, the second series 21, the third series 10, and the fourth series 11. Since a volume comprising only a part of the alphabet is issued about once a year, each series as a whole does not include all of the accessions between two fixed years, but each alphabetic subdivision in a series lists the accessions since the similar alphabetic subdivision in the previous series. Thus Volume 1 of the first series, which appeared in 1880, includes all material in the library from *A* to *Berlinski* at the time the volume was prepared; Volume 1 of the second series, published in 1896, includes all the material from *A* to *Azzurri* received between 1880 and 1896; Volume 1 of the third series, published in 1918, lists all entries from *A* to *Army* received between 1896 and 1918; Volume 1 of the fourth series, published in 1936, lists all entries from *A* to *Azzi-leal* received from 1919 to 1936.

The catalog includes books, pamphlets, and articles in journals. Books are listed under both author and subject, but journal articles are entered only under the subject and not under the author. Volumes 6–10 of the third series cover the material in journals only to January 1, 1926.

When interested in a particular author, or in a work on some particular subject, the user of the catalog should consult the

[6] This library was often officially referred to as the Army Medical Library, but that term did not find a place on the title page of the index.

proper volume in all four series; however, if he knows definitely the year of publication of the work desired, he may, obviously, ignore the volumes antedating that year.

The entries included in the 58 volumes are as follows:

Author titles 494,566
Subject titles:
    Books and pamphlets 418,309
    Journal articles 2,556,036
Portraits 9,187

Aerospace Medicine and Biology is a continuing bibliography started by the National Aeronautics and Space Administration in 1964. The Medicine and Surgery Bureau, Department of the Navy, has issued Volume 1 of *Bibliographical Sourcebook of Compressed Air, Diving, and Submarine Medicine.*

Military establishment. The *Air University Library Index to Military Periodicals* is a subject index to significant articles, news items, and editorials appearing in 58 English language military and aeronautical periodicals not indexed in readily available commercial indexing services. The *Index* originated with 23 titles as a quarterly publication in 1949 and has continued on a quarterly basis with annual and triennial cumulations. From 1949 to 1962 it was published as *Air University Periodical Index.*

Other bibliographies issued by the Department of Defense are *Military Manpower Policy*, a survey issued in 1965; *U.S. Security, Arms Control, and Disarmament*, 1960–61 and 1961–65. *Bibliographies and Lists of Publications* of the Research and Development Board include a *Conservation Bibliography,* 1959; *MENEX, Maintenance Engineering Exchange Bulletin,* December 1960; and *Subject Index, Bibliography, and Code Description of Technical Conference on Plastics,* June 1962. Department of the Army Pamphlet 130-2 is entitled *Civilian in Peace, Soldier in War, Bibliographic Survey of Army and Air National Guard,* January 1967. A selected and annotated bibliography issued by the Navy in 1965 is *United States Naval History, Naval Biography, Naval Strategy and Tactics.* The

Marine Corps has a numbered series entitled *Marine Corps Historical Bibliographies.* The Air Force Academy has a numbered special bibliography series which includes *U.S. Air Force Academy* (No. 2), 1957; *About the U.S. Air Force Academy* (No. 9), 1959; *Air Force Libraries* (No. 13), 1961; *International Organizations and Military Security Systems* (No. 25), 1962; *Astronautics 1960–66* (No. 34), 1966. The Military History Office has issued *Publications of the Office of the Chief of Military History,* 1967.

Mines and mining. The Geological Survey published *A Selected Bibliography on Quicksilver, 1811–1953,* Bulletin 1019–A, 1954 (62 pages), which includes publications relating to the geology, mining, and metallurgy of quicksilver. It lists publications of the United States Geological Survey, the United States Bureau of Mines, state organizations, and scientific and professional journals, as well as foreign and miscellaneous publications. Thirteen other bibliographies have been published in this group covering various mineral resources such as trace elements, barite, iron ore, magnesium, thorium and rare earth deposits, titanium deposits, silica, high calcium limestone deposits, salt, nickel, asbestos, selenium, andalusite, kyanite, sillimanite, topaz, and pyrophyllite.

Bulletin 1105 is a *Selected Annotated Bibliography of Gypsum and Anhydrite in the United States and Puerto Rico,* 1960, by C. F. Withington and M. C. Jaster. Bulletin 1107A is *Bibliography of U.S. Geological Survey Reports on Uranium and Thorium,* 1942 through May 1958, compiled by P. E. Soister and D. R. Conklin. Bulletin 86 is *Bibliography of Geological Survey Publications Relating to Coal,* 1882–1949, by Louise R. Berryhill. A supplement has been issued covering the period 1950–51.

One of the publications in the Bulletin Series of the Bureau of Mines is the *Bibliography of the Fischer-Tropsch Syntheses and Related Processes,* Bulletin No. 544. This is printed in two parts, Part I, 1954 (532 pages), being a review and compilation of the literature on the production of synthetic liquid fuels and chemicals by the hydrogenation of carbon monoxide and Part II, 1955 (pages 533–965), containing the patents for these processes.

Bibliography of Pressure Hydrogenation, Bulletin No. 485, is another publication of the Bureau of Mines, in three parts. Part I, 1950 (306 pages), contains a review and compilation of the literature on pressure hydrogenation of liquid and solid carbonaceous materials; Part II, 1951 (pages 307–592), contains the patents on these subjects; and Part III, 1952 (pages 593–646), is a subject index and numerical patent index.

Publications concerning Bureau of Mines investigations of coal and its products since the bureau was established in 1910 to 1960 are listed in *Bibliography of Bureau of Mines Investigations of Coal and Its Products,* 1962, compiled by the staff of the Division of Bituminous Coal. A list of 150 technical and scientific publications that document the nation's progress in fuel technology is found in *Bureau of Mines Publications on Coal Preparation 1910–60* compiled by Albert W. Deurbrouck. Mary S. Esfandiary is the compiler of *Coal Research Organizations: Their Activities and Publications,* 1960.

Bibliography of Zirconium by Eleanor Abshire (Information Circular 7771), 1957 (281 pages), is the most comprehensive bibliography compiled on zirconium. It is the result of a cooperative project of the Bureau of Ships, Department of the Navy, and the Bureau of Mines to accumulate literature on zirconium and hafnium. A supplement was issued in 1958 (Information Circular 7830) and also in 1967 (Information Circular 8048).

The Bureau of Mines issued a *Bibliography of Investment and Operating Costs for Chemical and Petroleum Plants* in 1949, which was supplemented in 1955 and 1956. Supplements have been issued each year through 1965. Other bibliographies include *Rare-Earth Compounds as High-Temperature Refractories,* 1962; *Bibliography of Hafnium,* compiled by Eleanor Abshire and Sarah Notestine, 1960; *Bibliography on Metallurgy of High Purity Tungsten, January 1911 through February 1959,* by Earl T. Hayes and Ruth A. Pritchard; *Bibliography of*

Thermal Methods of Oil Recovery, by W. T. Wertman, N. A. Caspero, and T. E. Steiner, 1960; *Bureau of Mines Articles on Thermodynamics of Petroleum Constituents and Related Compounds, January 1, 1944–December 31, 1960,* by J. P. McCulloch; *Publications Dealing With the Health and Safety in the Mineral and Allied Industries 1910–46,* by Sarah J. Davenport (Technical Paper 705); *Bureau of Mines Health and Safety Publications, January 1947–June 1955,* by H. B. Humphrey and Hazel J. Stratton, 1956 (Bulletin 558), supplemented through June 30, 1961, by Information Circular 812.

National Bureau of Standards. The National Bureau of Standards is engaged in fundamental and applied research in physics, chemistry, mathematics, and engineering. Projects are conducted in seventeen fields: electricity and electronics, optics and metrology, heat, atomic and radiation physics, chemistry, mechanics, organic and fibrous materials, metallurgy, mineral products, building technology, applied mathematics, data-processing systems, cryogenic engineering, radio propagation, radio standards, weights and measures, and basic instrumentation. The NBS Circular Series (now discontinued) contained bibliographies related to these fields, such as *Nitrogen 15, High Polymers, and Electron Microscopy.* Bibliographies are now issued as Monographs, Miscellaneous Publications, and Technical Notes.

An annotative bibliographical survey containing almost 140,000 items is the *Bibliography of Solid Adsorbents 1943–1953,* by Victor R. Deitz, 1956 (1,528 pages), also released in the Circular Series as No. 566.

Some recent NBS bibliographies are *Flame Spectroscopy, Analytical Applications 1800–1966,* compiled by R. Mavrodineau, 1967; *Bibliography of Liesegang Rings 1855–1965,* by Kurt H. Stern, 1967; *Bibliography and Index on Vacuum and Low Pressure Measurements,* by W. G. Brombacher, 1961; *Computer Literature Bibliography 1946–63* by W. W. Youden, 1965; *Bibliography on Ionospheric Propagation of Radio Waves 1923–60,* by W. Nupen, 1960; *Bibliography on Direction Finding and Related Ionospheric Propagation Topics 1955–61,* by

O. D. Remmier, 1962; *A Bibliography on Ion-Molecule Reactions, January 1960 to March 1966,* by F. N. Harllee, H. M. Rosenstock, and J. T. Herron, 1966; *Bibliography of Temperature Measurement January 1953 to June 1960,* by C. Halpern and R. J. Moffat, 1961, supplemented to December 1965 by L. C. Olsen and Carl Halpern, 1967.

Nuclear science. *Nuclear Science Abstracts* is a semi-monthly abstract journal published by the Technical Information Service, United States Atomic Energy Commission. It was started in 1948 and has gained recognition as the only abstract journal devoted exclusively to announcing, abstracting, and indexing unclassified literature on nuclear science.

The expanding coverage and scope of *Nuclear Science Abstracts* is influenced by such factors as the increasing worldwide importance of atomic energy and its applications for peaceful uses; the increasing amount of literature on detailed aspects of the subject from an ever-growing number of sources in the United States and abroad; the discovery of new elements and their relationship to nuclear energy; and the significance of unclassified information on the thermonuclear program.

There are subject, author, and report number indexes in each issue of *Nuclear Science Abstracts,* which are cumulated quarterly, semiannually, and annually.

Nuclear Science Abstracts was preceded by *Abstracts of Declassified Documents,* Volumes 1–2, 1947–48, and *Guide to Published Research on Atomic Energy,* Volume 1, 1946, to Volume 3, 1948, the former indexing Atomic Energy Commission reports and the latter information from other sources.

The Technical Information Service of the Atomic Energy Commission also publishes separate bibliographies. These compilations have ranged from simple short title lists to long, exhaustive, annotated bibliographies that are indexed and categorized. Currently all TIS-originated formal bibliographies are assigned a TID-3000 to TID-3499 number. The informal, less exhaustive bibliographies or literature searches are numbered from TID-3500 to TID-3999. Individual Atomic Energy Commission laboratory-issued bibliographies appear as laboratory reports and bear the originator code number. Bibliographies are listed in *Bibliographies of Interest to the Atomic Energy Program,* compiled by James M. Jacobs, Naomi K. Smelcer, and Hugh E. Voress, March 1962. There have been three supplements issued, the latest of which is dated May 1965. These are further supplemented by *Bibliographies of Atomic Energy Literature* issued every two or three months bearing numbers in the TID 3700's. There are also lists under the word "Bibliographies" in the *Nuclear Science Abstracts* subject indexes.

The New York Operations Office, Atomic Energy Commission, published as NYO-4753 *Annotated Bibliography on Fallout Resulting from Nuclear Explosions,* by Allen G. Horad, Merril Eisenbud, and John H. Harley, September 1956 (48 pages). Three supplements have been issued.

Outdoor recreation. The Bureau of Outdoor Recreation of the Department of the Interior has issued an *Index of Selected Outdoor Recreation Literature,* Volume 1, 1967, and *Guide to Outdoor Recreation Areas and Facilities,* 1966. Other bibliographies are *Outdoor Recreation Literature, Survey and Report to Outdoor Recreation Resources Review,* by the Librarian of Congress, and *Outdoor Recreation, Current Periodicals,* selected by Elaine P. Rosenthal, 1964.

Public health. From 1921 to 1967, the Public Health Service released a monthly publication entitled *Public Health Engineering Abstracts.* The abstracts are according to subject matter and the person abstracting each article is indicated.

The Public Health Service also issues a Public Health Bibliography Series. Each number of the series is devoted to a specific subject. Examples are cancer, cardiovascular disease, occupational health, urban fringe sanitation, water pollution control, mental health, and chronic illness.

The Public Health Service has also issued a *Bibliography of Industrial Hygiene* which contains a selected list of materials published from 1900 to 1943.

An annual publication of the National Library of Medicine

is the *Bibliography of Medical Reviews.* Volume 2 of this series was published in May 1957, Volume 3 in 1958, Volume 4 in 1959, and Volume 5 in 1960. The first *Bibliography* was published in 1955 by the Armed Forces Medical Library without a volume number.

The Public Health Service issues abstract series on special subjects in medicine and public health. Examples are *Artificial Kidney Bibliography,* Volume 1, 1967–; *Cancer Chemotherapy Abstracts,* Volume 1, 1960–; *Diabetes Literature Index,* Volume 1, 1966–; *Epilepsy Abstracts,* Volume 1, 1967–; *Gastroenterology, Abstracts and Citations,* Volume 1, 1966–; *Mental Health Digest,* 1967–; *Mental Retardation Abstracts,* Volume 1, 1964–; *Psychopharmacology Abstracts,* Volume 1, 1961–; *Reading Guide to Cancer Virology Literature,* Volume 1, 1964–.

Roads. Publications received in the library of the Bureau of Public Roads are listed in the weekly processed publication entitled *Highways, Current Literature,* which has had this title since July 1931. This was first issued in November 1921 under the title *Contents of New Periodicals in Public Roads Library.* Later titles were as follows: *Highways and Rural Engineering, Current Literature* (June 23, 1926–April 15, 1927) and *Highways and Agricultural Engineering, Current Literature* (April 20, 1927–June 24, 1931). The library of the Bureau of Public Roads issued *A Bibliography of Highway Planning Reports,* 1950 (48 pages). *Highway Research and Development Studies Using Federal-Aid Research and Planning Funds* has been issued from 1964 to 1967. *Bibliography on Right-of-Way Acquisition,* compiled by Dawn E. Willis, was issued in January 1964, with a supplement in July 1966.

Security. Although not a continuing bibliography, *United States National Security,* Special Bibliography No. 7, compiled by the Army Library, the Adjutant General's Office, Department of the Army, is an introductory presentation and will be supplemented in the future. This publication consists of approximately 1,000 unclassified titles of magazine articles, reports, books, and other materials dealing with security. Special Bibliography No. 7 has been supplemented by *U.S. National*

Security and the Communist Challenge—The Spectrum of East-West Conflict, August 1961 (Department of the Army Pamphlet 20–60). The materials for the most part cover the years 1958–60 and almost all are available in the Army Library.

The Legislative Reference Service of the Library of Congress has compiled *Organizing for National Security Bibliography,* 1959, for the Subcommittee on National Policy Machinery and also *Organizing for National Security, Selected Materials,* 1960. For the Subcommittee on National Security Staffing and Operations, it has compiled *Administration of National Security, Bibliography,* 1963.

Tariff. An outstanding bibliography which consists of a single volume and is not issued as a recurrent series is *The Tariff—A Bibliography—A Select List of References,* 1934 (980 pages), published by the United States Tariff Commission. This includes government publications as well as books and articles published elsewhere. It is arranged topically with voluminous subject and author indexes.

A particularly noteworthy feature consists of citations to the debates in Congress from 1909 to 1933. These are found in all major classifications under the subentry "Congressional Record"; they are also indexed by author and subject.

A similar publication, also issued by the Tariff Commission, is *Reciprocal Trade: A Current Bibliography,* 3d edition, 1937 (272 + 129 pages, processed). This edition consists of two parts: the first part covers the period from March 1933 to December 1936; the second part covers the early part of 1937. Each part has a separate index. At the end of the first part is a list of material printed in the *Congressional Record.* In the second part the material in the *Congressional Record* is not listed in detail, but the index contains specific citations to the several speeches, etc. The indexes to this volume serve also as indexes to the hearings before the House Committee on Ways and Means and the Senate Committee on Finance on the reciprocal trade agreements bill, as the hearings are not indexed. A 232-page supplement was issued in 1940 covering the period 1937–39.

Tennessee Valley Authority. The Technical Library of the TVA at Knoxville has produced an *Indexed Bibliography* of the Tennessee Valley Authority. This list and index of periodical articles, compiled by Harry C. Bauer (since 1943 by Bernard L. Foy) was published July 1, 1936, and covers the period January 1933–June 1936. It is continued by semiannual, annual, or cumulative supplements.

Water resources. The Water Resources Scientific Information Center of the Department of the Interior started publication of a new series entitled *Selected Water Resources Abstracts* with Volume 1, No. 1, bearing the date of January 1968. The recognition of water as a natural resource which is threatened by pollution has given rise to increasing public interest and a number of government agencies have published bibliographies on various aspects. Some are *Selected References on Saline Ground-Water Resources of the United States,* compiled by J. H. Feth and issued as Geological Survey Circular 499, 1965; *Water for Peace,* a representative list of research and development reports available from the Clearinghouse of the Department of Commerce, printed in May 1967 and reprinted with amendments in August; *Water Pollution Control, Sewage Treatment, Water Treatment, Selected Bibliographical References,* compiled by William M. Ingram and Kenneth M. Mackenthun, 1963 (Public Health Bibliography Series 8); *Water Supply and Pollution Control,* Section 3 of *Reference List of Publications of the Robert A. Taft Sanitary Engineering Center,* 1963 (PHS Technical Report W63-1); *Annotated Bibliography of Water-Use Data,* by Lois E. Randall, 1961 (Geological Survey Circular 455); *Bibliography on Socio-Economic Aspects of Water Resources,* by H. R. Hamilton *et al.,* Office of Water Resources Research, 1966. The Office of Water Resources Research has issued a *Water Resources Research Catalog,* which lists research projects in progress, both government and non-government. Volume 1 was issued in two parts in 1965, and Volume 2 in 1967. The latest volume is that for 1968, which comprises 1,503 pages.

CHAPTER FOUR

CLASSIFICATION

GOVERNMENT PUBLICATIONS may be divided into three fairly well-defined groups corresponding roughly to the three coordinate branches of the government; namely, (1) congressional or legislative, (2) judicial, and (3) executive. Congressional publications are those relating to the work or proceedings of Congress, those printed by order of or for the use of either or both houses or their committees, and certain executive publications which are duplicated as documents of the House or the Senate. The subclassification and the characteristics of congressional publications are described in detail in Chapter 6. The duplication of executive publications in the congressional series is discussed on pages 109–16. Judicial publications consist of court decisions published by the United States. The judicial publications as a whole do not constitute a unified series, the reports of each court forming an independent series. The court decisions published regularly and the special compilations are described in Chapter 10.

Executive Publications

Executive publications or departmental series are those published by the several executive departments and independent establishments. However, some reports originating in the executive branch are published as House or Senate documents. This group includes papers submitted to Congress on the initiative of the heads of executive agencies, and reports specifically requested by either house. Executive reports printed as documents are discussed in Chapter 14.

Numbered series were used for publications of Congress in the early years of the 19th century, but it was a long time before the executive branch of the government made use of them to any extent. The reasons for this are obvious. Congress in its early days found itself confronted with a growing mass of printed matter and adopted the expedient of numbering in order to facilitate reference and ways of finding the material.

During approximately the first three quarters of the 19th century the publications of the executive departments were confined mainly to annual reports (generally printed as congressional documents), a few annual statistical reports, sporadic issues of regulations, and occasional reports on a variety of subjects. The annual reports and statistical publications were easily referred to by their dates, and the regulations were not numerous enough to warrant serial numbering. The exploring expeditions were all temporary organizations which, as a rule, issued a general report subdivided into volumes.

It was the development of the research and informational activities of the government which made necessary the use of numbered series in order to keep track of the increasing quantity of publications. There has thus resulted a mass of bulletins and other numbered issues.

Like other aspects of government publishing there is little uniformity in the use of series. In the Departments of the Interior, Labor, and Commerce the products of each bureau appear in its own series. Since July 1913 the general practice in the Department of Agriculture has been to have more important bureau publications appear in a series common to the entire department, although the various services within the department issue many well-defined series of their own, as do the regional forest experiment stations. The numbered series of the Department of State have always been department series. Moreover, practically all Department of State publications bear an over-all control number in addition to a series number. Thus, for example, Department and Foreign Service

Series 65 is also Publication 6484. The major exception to this rule in the State Department is the Treaties and Other International Acts Series. The practice of over-all control numbers for major publications is now also used by the Public Health Service, the Internal Revenue Service, and the Post Office Department. Control numbers are common in bureaus of the Navy Department, such as NAVPERS numbers of the Bureau of Naval Personnel and NAVSHIPS numbers in the Naval Ships Systems Command.

As a general rule, all government publications issued in a series have both a number and a separate title, the usual form being as follows: "Farmers' Bulletin 2142, *Library Service for Rural People.*" Periodicals usually contain only the general title and the serial number, as "*Foreign Commerce Weekly,* Vol. 62, No. 2." Many periodicals contain only the month or date instead of the number, as "*Naval Aviation News,* July 1959." A few are issued with continuing numbers as in a series. One unhappy example of numbering is practiced by the Fish and Wildlife Service, which issues a series called Current Fishery Statistics (designated C.F.S. numbers). Within this series regular monthly reports on various types of statistics are issued; in one group appear numbers 1471, 1496, 1513, all with a common title, representing the reports for September, October, and November 1956. Furthermore, not all of the same month's issues for all titles run in consecutive order, so that it is impossible to bind them in any usable fashion. The *Monthly Catolog* lists these series-within-series in the annual appendix beginning with 1962, but this listing does not identify the C.F.S. numbers. They are listed by number in the Fish and Wildlife Service's *Monthly List of New Publications.*

A recent practice in numbering common-title frequent releases, also used for some series, is to key all of one year's issues by prefixing the last two digits of the date. Thus the tenth issue of 1959 would be numbered 59–10. A similar practice but keyed to the number of a congress was begun by the Federal Register Division of the National Archives and Records Service in publishing the laws of the 85th Congress, so that they are now referred to as Public Law 85–1, 85–2, 85–3 or Private Law 85–1, 85–2, 85–3, and so forth.

Use of subseries within series is practiced on a large scale by the Department of the Army and the Department of the Air Force on a subject basis in such series as Regulations, Manuals, and Pamphlets. A double combined number is used as 30–6, 30–10, 145–6, etc. All those in the 30– group pertain to one subject, the 35– group another subject, etc. However, the same first number will not necessarily be the same subject in another series. On some series there is further subdivision by the use of a third number, such as 110–50–3. One publication may also bear two or more numbers, as DOD pamphlet 5–6, *Our Flag* (1958), which is also numbered DA pamphlet 355–116, NAVPERS 92591, AFP 34–10–7, and NAVMC 5901.

At times the main title of the series is followed by the title of the particular publication, without serial number, as "United States Army in World War II: *Pictorial Record: War Against Japan.*" This method of classification is used extensively in series issued by commercial publishing houses, and has been adopted for several unnumbered series of government publications.

A series that appears only once a year is generally distinguished by the year, thus: "*Statistical Abstract of the United States, 1967.*"

The publications of some agencies are definitely limited by law. In such cases new series may not be started, although old ones may be discontinued by the simple expedient of not publishing any more issues. This restriction promotes stability in series designation, as the process of obtaining legislation is slow and tedious. Other series are established and discontinued in the discretion of the publishing offices. This practice permits adjustments to meet new conditions, but unfortunately the changes are not always well considered. Confusion results. For example, there may be only a few issues in a series before it is abandoned, or one part of a report may appear in one series and the second part in another series.

Probably the Department of Agriculture has the most confusing array of series, both by reason of the frequent changes and the great number of publications issued. The principal printed series of the Department, except periodicals, recently being issued are listed below. A list of the many series and periodic reports issued by the various services and bureaus of the Department of Agriculture would be too long for inclusion in this work. The notations regarding the scope of each series are quoted mainly from the *List of Available Publications of the United States Department of Agriculture,* issued January 1966, compiled by Eleanor W. Clay (List No. 11) or other information supplied by the Department of Agriculture.

AGRICULTURAL ECONOMIC REPORTS

Semipopular or semitechnical reports on production, marketing, and use of agricultural products for professional and technical workers.

AGRICULTURAL STATISTICS

This publication is issued once a year. It contains detailed analytical statistics on agriculture.

AGRICULTURE HANDBOOKS

This series includes useful information designed for use as ready references, such as manuals, guidebooks, specifications, glossaries, and lists of plants or animals.

AGRICULTURE INFORMATION BULLETINS

This series includes subject matter of general interest in both rural and urban areas.

CONSERVATION RESEARCH REPORTS

Reports of conservation research, including reports on less complete research projects than are reported in the Technical Bulletin Series.

FARMERS' BULLETINS

Information on practical methods of applying the results of scientific research to farming and homemaking is given in simple language in this series.

FOREIGN AGRICULTURAL ECONOMIC REPORTS

Semipopular or semitechnical reports with emphasis on keeping the nation's agricultural interest informed of current developments abroad in the supply, demand, and consumption of agricultural products.

FOREST RESOURCE REPORTS

This series for forestry corresponds somewhat to the Soil Survey reports for land and soil.

HOME AND GARDEN BULLETINS

This series presents popular publications on home economics subjects for use by city as well as farm residents.

HOME ECONOMICS RESEARCH REPORTS

Reports of home economics research, including technical reports and semitechnical presentations of research data that will serve professional workers in home economics and related fields.

LEAFLETS

Leaflets carry popular material of the same general character as the Farmers' Bulletin series except that they are simpler and briefer.

MARKETING BULLETINS

Popular presentations of information on agricultural marketing for the general public.

MARKETING RESEARCH REPORTS

In this series the results of marketing research are presented in semi-technical or popular style.

MISCELLANEOUS PUBLICATIONS

This series includes both technical and nontechnical publications that do not conform to the size or type of material specified for the other series.

PRODUCTION RESEARCH REPORTS

Reports of production research, including reports on less complete research projects than are reported in the Technical Bulletin series.

PROGRAM AIDS

This series presents guides in meeting the various farm programs, as well as the aims and progress being made.

SOIL SURVEYS

The Soil Surveys contain: (1) A soil map, in color, showing the extent and distribution of the different soils in the area; (2) descriptions of each of the soils shown on the soil map, giving its texture, color, structure, friability, depth, quality of drainage, degree of stoniness, slope, presence of hardpans or other impermeable layers, reactions, and other characteristics affecting plant growth; (3) estimates of the productivity of each soil in terms of crop yields, and suggestions for its use and management; (4) a technical discussion of the mode of origin of the soils of the area, and of their characteristics in relation to the major soil groups of the nation; (5) a general description of the climate, agriculture, markets, transportation facilities, industries, population, and other items of interest concerning the area.

STATISTICAL BULLETINS

These bulletins consist mainly of tables giving statistics on one or more closely related agricultural commodities. They contain, so far as possible, statistics of foreign and domestic production and marketing, including movement from the farm, receipts at principal markets, reshipments, farm and market prices, and exports and imports. They are of particular interest to persons actually engaged in marketing or any business affected by agricultural production and marketing.

TECHNICAL BULLETINS

Technical Bulletins contain results of research work carried on by the Department of Agriculture and its cooperators. They are written in technical language and are intended chiefly for distribution to scientists and specialists in the fields studied. Usually a comparatively small edition is printed, which limits the number of copies that are available for free distribution.

UTILIZATION RESEARCH REPORTS

Reports of utilization research, including reports on less complete research projects than are reported in the Technical Bulletin series.

YEARBOOKS

Prior to 1936 the *Yearbook* was made up of detailed agricultural statistics and brief summaries of new developments in agriculture. Since 1936 the detailed analytical statistics section has been issued annually as *Agricultural Statistics*, and the section devoted to articles on agricultural problems, new developments in agriculture, and research findings has been printed separately and is known as the *Agriculture Yearbook*. Yearbooks which have been released and the dates of issuance are:

        1936 Yearbook of agriculture
        1937 Yearbook of agriculture
        1938 Soils and men
        1939 Food and life

1940 Farmers in a changing world
1941 Climate and man
1942 Keeping livestock healthy
1943–47 Science in farming
1948 Grass
1949 Trees
1950–51 Crops in peace and war
1952 Insects
1953 Plant diseases
1954 Marketing
1955 Water
1956 Animal diseases
1957 Soil
1958 Land
1959 Food
1960 Power to produce
1961 Seeds
1962 After a hundred years
1963 A place to live
1964 Farmer's world
1965 Consumers all
1966 Protecting our food
1967 Outdoors U.S.A.

The fact that a topic forms the subject of a publication in a particular series should not lead the reader to think that all publications on that topic will be found in series. Thus milk is the subject of several Farmers' Bulletins, but it is also discussed in Circulars, Leaflets, Miscellaneous Publications, and other publications of the Department of Agriculture, as well as in the publications of the Children's Bureau, the Public Health Service, and the Office of Education.

The peculiarities and defects of series are too extensive to be listed in detail, but mention will be made of characteristic or unusual examples. In many cases the series designation and numbering were adopted after the issuance of publications that would have belonged to the series if it had been in existence earlier. In such cases the actual series numbering begins with a number other than 1, and the earlier publications are arbitrarily assigned to the series. Thus the first number appearing on the Bulletins of the Bureau of American Ethnology was 25,

Nos. 1–24, being assigned to publications which had appeared without serial designation and number. Complete lists of series numbered in this manner prior to 1909 may be found in the *Checklist*.

At times the series title and number are inadvertently omitted from a paper in the middle of a series. Thus there is no issue which carries the number "11" in the *Professional Papers of the Engineer Department of the Army*, but an unnumbered report has been assigned to this number. (See *Checklist*, p. 1272.)

Some departments and agencies have found it convenient to have certain numbers in a series processed on their own office duplicating equipment, while others are printed through the facilities of the Government Printing Office. This device creates distribution problems in some instances, as only certain issues will be available to the public by purchase while the others must be obtained from the issuing organization.

Occasionally the title of a series is changed, but the numbering is continuous regardless of title. Thus one series issued by the Navy Department has appeared under the following titles:

> Navy Scientific Papers, Nos. 1–12
> Navy Professional Papers, No. 13
> Naval Professional Papers, Nos. 14–22
> Professional Papers, No. 23

Most of the faults in the numbering of series may be ascribed to carelessness, but there are at least three remarkable instances of deliberate disregard of the simple principles that should be applied to numbers.

The Bureau of Aeronautics (an early predecessor of the Federal Aviation Agency) adopted the practice of assigning the same number to two publications, as is shown by the following examples in the series Aeronautics Bulletins:

> 14. Requirements for approved type certificates (1928)
> 14. Relative lift distribution in any biplane (1929)
> 20. Directory of licensed pilots (1928)
> 20. Suggested city or county aeronautics ordinance and uniform field rules for airports (1929)

One would naturally suppose that the duplication of numbers shown above was due to error, but inquiry developed the fact that it was made designedly. The reason given was that the bulletin listed first under each number was no longer available, and the publishing office did not want any "dead" numbers on its lists.

If the reader found a citation to Information Circular 6005 of the Bureau of Mines, he would be justified in reaching the conclusion that the series was a voluminous one. If he consulted the list of publications of the Bureau of Mines, however, he would find that the Information Circulars began with No. 6000. It is easy to understand why insurance policies and other papers used in different areas should be given certain blocks of numbers in order to facilitate identification, but it is hard to conceive of any such practice in the case of a publication.

The Bureau of Foreign and Domestic Commerce had a Market Research Series, which used decimal numbering in part. Separate bulletins bore the numbers 1, 2, 3, 4, 5.1, 5.2, 5.3, 5.4, 5.5, and 6. The publications numbered 5.1 to 5.5 were not separates from No. 5 as there was no No. 5. It is true that each of these had the general title *Consumer Use of Goods and Services, by Income Classes,* the decimal numbering being applied to the reports on separate cities. Obviously, without a checklist the librarian could not determine where the decimal numbering ended.

The Office of Education has added confusion to an already complicated system of numbering by having three Bulletin series. The first, which continued until 1966, was begun in 1906. In this series the numbering has the following form "Bulletin, 1938, No. 1." The numbers begin with 1 for each year, and therefore the year is an essential part of the series number. In 1933, when the Federal Board for Vocational Education was transferred to the Office of Education, the Vocational Education Bulletins of the Board were continued as Vocational Education Bulletins of the Office of Education, the first issue of the new series being 172. Some of the earlier Bulletins of the Federal Board have been reprinted under the original number as Vocational Education Bulletins of the Office of Education. In 1937 a new series of Bulletins was started having the series title and number in the following form: "Bulletin, 1937, Misc. No. 1." After 1939 the word "Bulletin" and the date were dropped, so that now the designation is simply "Misc." and the number. This series is referred to as "Miscellaneous" and issues are usually printed for public distribution. Less than thirty have been issued to date. In the same vein of series designation the Office of Education also published another "Misc." numbered series. These are referred to as "Miscellany" and, though more numerous, are more limited in application and are usually reproduced within the issuing office. Toward the end of 1959, the Office of Education started an OE series with a group of numbers assigned to a particular subject. For example, adult education was assigned OE 13,000–13,999; library service, OE 15,000–15,999; guidance, testing, counseling, OE 25,000–25,999; manpower development and training, OE 87,000–87,999. There are approximately 40 subject groups. Older established numbers were continued until 1967, with both numbers printed on the publications.

The Soil Surveys of the Soil Conservation Service also began with No. 1 in each year, followed by "Series (year)." The year used for the series does not mean year of publication, but is apparently the year in which the field work was done. In 1966 the numbering system was discontinued, and the classification system arranges the reports by the name of the county.

Several series of numbered Census Bulletins have been issued, and care must be taken not to confuse them. Separate series of numbered bulletins were issued by the Tenth Census (1880), the Eleventh Census (1890), and the Twelfth Census (1900). There is also a general numbered Bulletin Series which was started soon after the organization of the permanent Census Bureau. This series is still being published. Many preliminary reports of the Census have been headed "Bulletin" without series numbering.

Reports of the various decennial, quinquennial, and other

periodic censuses present a special problem. Usually there are preliminary reports issued for each state, industry, type of business, mineral group, or other category, depending on the census. These are generally followed by final figures in printed pamphlet form. When all final figures are completed, bound volumes are made up with special introductory pages and in some cases special appendixes.

The Census Bureau attempts to outline in advance what types and series of reports will be issued, but it is not always able to give firm information concerning this. To some extent this is due to fund limitations since, if funds permit, special reports on certain aspects of the censuses will be issued later. The essential reports for which the censuses are designed are issued first.

Various designations are used by the Census Bureau, generally a combination of letters and numbers. This is particularly true of the preliminary reports. In some cases of final pamphlet reports, however, they are designated simply volume and chapter numbers, or volume, part, and chapter numbers. Some volumes, in addition, are issued only in pamphlet form by parts or chapters, no bound volumes being issued for public distribution.

Fortunately for those seeking information about census reports, the Census Bureau issues a quarterly catalog, which is cumulative through the year and presents an excellent record of what census publications have been issued. Monthly supplements are also issued.

One of the recent trends in government publishing—an unhappy one in certain aspects—is the use of loose-leaf manuals, particularly in the field of regulatory material. An initial manual is usually issued, accurate to a certain date. Thereafter revised pages are issued for insertion in the manual, each group being accompanied by a "Transmittal Sheet," generally numbered, and referred to as TS 1, TS 2, etc. For a complete manual, the original and all of the sets of revised pages must be obtained and assembled.

An example is the *Federal Personnel Manual* issued by the

Civil Service Commission. In this case no basic manual was issued—only transmittal sheets with attached pages or revised pages of the manual. When, after a number of years of publication, it reached the stage where many of the transmittal sheets could no longer be supplied, the Commission reprinted all pages corrected to 1956. The latest corrected printing is 1963.

Another complicated example of the loose-leaf manual is the *Postal Manual*, issued by the Post Office Department, the last revision of which is dated 1954. It is issued in eight chapters; the first two are public information; the remaining six are administrative. Chapters 1 and 2 are therefore sold separately, punched for a three-ring binder. However, since they are also used by the Post Office Department administratively, they (and the other six chapters) are issued in addition, punched for a seven-ring binder. The entire manual is kept up to date by a series of revised pages known as "Issues." Each issue is numbered but does not necessarily pertain to all chapters.

The intensification of research activities of the government which began during World War II has led to the publication of a great mass of material known in general as "research reports." These are the results of scientific studies conducted not only within the government but by colleges, universities, commercial laboratories, and manufacturing corporations under contract with the various agencies of the government, particularly the components of the Department of Defense and the Atomic Energy Commission.

The reports of each contractor with the Atomic Energy Commission form a series in themselves, each laboratory or research agency using a letter symbol keyed to its name or location, with a number for each report it issues. Formats are highly similar as to size and make-up of the reports owing to uniform specifications contained in the contracts. Some of the symbols are ANL for Argonne National Laboratory; IDO for the Atomic Energy Division of Phillips Petroleum Company, Idaho Falls, Idaho; ISC for Iowa State College; and ORNL for Oak Ridge National Laboratory. The AEC has also published some in its own series, although the work was done under contract, some of these, for example, being designated as AECU numbers and others as TID numbers, the former referring to "Atomic Energy Commission Unclassified," the latter to "Technical Information Division" (now Technical Information Service).

Those published by components of the Department of Defense are varied. The Air Force has, for example, AFCRC–TN (Air Force Cambridge Research Center) numbers and AFPTRC–TN (Air Force Personnel and Training Research Center) numbers. These usually have in addition a DOD document number, a project number, and a task number; or perhaps a contract number, and a progress report number or a memorandum number in addition.

Research report series of some agencies, however, are quite regular and uncomplicated, such as the Technical Memorandums, Technical Notes, and printed Reports of the National Aeronautics and Space Administration (until July 1958, National Advisory Committee for Aeronautics), which run each in straight numerical sequence. The sequence of many research report series appears to be broken, as classified reports are numbered in series with reports not classified.

Duplication of Publications

The issuance of the same publication in two or more contemporaneous series is a source of great confusion. Prior to 1860 there were often three contemporaneous editions of some annual bureau reports. The bureau report appeared as an independent publication, while the combined report of the department containing the bureau report was issued in two editions as a House document and as a Senate document. For instance, the *Annual Report of the Commissioner of Indian Affairs for the Fiscal Year 1856* was printed in the following forms:

Separate report of the Commissioner of Indian Affairs, pp. 1–282
As a part (pp. 554–832) of the Annual Report of the Department of the

Interior printed as Pt. 2 of S. Ex. Doc. 5, 34 Cong. 3 sess.
As a part (pp. 554–832) of the Annual Report of the Department of the
Interior printed as Pt. 1 of H. Ex. Doc. 1, 34 Cong. 3 sess.

For some years prior to 1860 most of the important publications originating in the executive branch of the government were printed either as a House or a Senate document, and in the case of annual reports generally as both. In this period there were few prints of executive publications with distinctive departmental title pages, although it is difficult to determine the exact extent to which departmental titles pages were used. There was no agency charged with the contemporaneous cataloging or collecting of government publications, as the collection now in the Public Documents Library was not assembled until after 1895. As regards annual reports, the *Checklist* contains many notes stating that "the Public Documents Library has no edition without congressional document number prior to ——." This statement means exactly what it says and does not mean that there *was* no print without the congressional document number. Since the *Checklist* was prepared, additional volumes without the document number have come to light.

The establishment of the Government Printing Office in 1860 seems to mark the abandonment of the printing of the same publication as both a Senate and a House document, although the first specific legislation preventing duplication was contained in Section 53 of the Printing Act of 1895 (28 Stat. 608).

About this time there developed the practice whereby each executive department printed an edition of the combined annual report as a department publication. From the late seventies down to 1920 there was generally issued for most departments an annual report which was duplicated in the congressional series. Bureau annual reports were also issued as separate publications and as a part of the combined department report. Thus the *Annual Report of the Commissioner of the General Land Office for the Fiscal Year 1905* was published in the following forms:

Separate report of the Commissioner of the General Land Office, pp. 1–218

As a part (pp. 289–504) of Vol. 1 of the Annual Report of the Department of the Interior

As a part (pp. 289–504) of the Annual Report of the Department of the Interior printed as [Pt. 1] H. Doc. 5, 59 Cong. 1 sess.

It is immaterial which edition is used, but in the case of bureau reports which are issued separately and which also form part of the department report the citation should clearly indicate the report used, as the pagination is not the same in the two volumes. Thus, in the case of the annual report mentioned in the preceding paragraph, the separate report may be cited as "Annual Report of the Commissioner of the General Land Office for the Fiscal Year 1905." The same report in the department compilation may be cited as "Annual Report of the Commissioner of the General Land Office in Volume 1 of the Annual Report of the Department of the Interior for the Fiscal Year 1905," as "Report of the Department of the Interior for the Fiscal Year 1905, Vol. 1," or as "House Document 5 [Part 1], 59th Congress, 1st session."

The most confusing example of duplication is the *Annual Report of the Chief of Engineers of the Army,* the first volume of which was formerly available in five editions, three of which were departmental and two of which were congressional. The editions of the report for the fiscal year 1906, which was typical of the practice for some years, were as follows:

BUREAU EDITIONS

[1] Annual report of the Chief of Engineers, United States Army [without appendixes], pp. 1–832, i–lxi

[2] Annual report of the Chief of Engineers, United States Army [with appendixes], Pts. 1 and 2, pp. 1–1432, i–lxii; 1433–2609, i–lxii [Roman pagination is index, which is same in both volumes]

DEPARTMENT EDITION

[3] Annual reports of the War Department, Vol. V. Report of the Chief of Engineers [without appendixes], pp. 1–832, i–lxi

[4] Annual reports of the War Department, Vol. V. Report of the Chief of Engineers [without appendixes], 59 Cong. 2 sess., *House Documents*, Vol. 6, No. 2, Vol. 5, pp. 1–832, i–lxi[1]

[5] Annual report of the Chief of Engineers, United States Army [with appendixes]. Pts. 1 and 2, 59 Cong. 2 sess., *House Documents*, Vols. 41 and 42, No. 22 [Pts. 1 and 2], pp. 1–1432, i–lxii; 1433–2609, i–lxii

The report proper of the Chief of Engineers (pages 1–832) was printed in all five of the editions. It comprised the entire contents of the first, third, and fourth editions listed above. The report proper and the appendixes appear in identical form in the second and fifth editions listed above. The title pages of editions without appendixes do not indicate that an edition with appendixes is available.

Up to 1932 there were still three editions, but by 1934 the editions had been reduced to two—the departmental and the congressional.

With the development of the systematic organization of research work and the publication of the results during the last two decades of the nineteenth century, the laws authorizing publication have often specifically provided that a certain number of copies should be printed for the use of the Senate and the House of Representatives. Such provisions resulted in the issuance of both departmental and congressional editions. It is for this reason that the publications of the Geological Survey and other organizations have been issued as documents of Congress, but the printing of Geological Survey publications as documents has been discontinued. These provisions do not apply to the publications of the Department of Agriculture, the Bureau of Standards, and other important publishing agencies.

Those series or serials currently regularly published in both departmental and congressional document editions are:

Air Force Register
American Ethnology Bureau Bulletins

[1] Note that this is Volume 6 of *House Documents* and also Volume 5 of Document 2. This document was printed in ten volumes, 1 to 10, which are Volumes 2 to 11 of *House Documents*. This example is typical of the complicated system of numbering. For discussion of numbering, see pp. 154–56 and 157–66.

Army Register
Budget of the District of Columbia
Budget of the United States and Appendix
Combined Statement of Receipts and Expenditures
Decisions of the Commissioner of Patents
Economic Report of the President
Merchant Vessels of the United States
Minerals Yearbook
Navy and Marine Corps Register
Statistical Abstract of the United States and Supplements
Weather Modification
Yearbook of Agriculture

Some executive reports are actually transmitted to Congress. If Congress orders a report printed, it may appear both as a document and as an executive publication, or it may be published as a document only. If Congress does not order it printed, it will appear as an executive publication.

Listed below are those agencies whose annual reports are regularly issued at present in both departmental and congressional document editions:

American Historical Association
Arms Control and Disarmament Agency
Atomic Energy Commission
Chief of Engineers, Army
Civil Service Commission
Commissioner of Internal Revenue
Comptroller General of United States
Comptroller of the Currency
Farm Credit Administration
Federal Maritime Commission
Federal Power Commission
Federal Trade Commission
Interstate Commerce Commission
Judicial Conference of the United States (proceedings of
    the annual meeting)
Librarian of Congress
Maritime Administration
National Academy of Sciences
National Aeronautics and Space Administration (semi-
    annual report)
National Science Foundation

Post Office Department
Railroad Retirement Board
Secretary of the Treasury
Securities and Exchange Commission
Smithsonian Institution
State Department (*Report on United States Participation in the United Nations*)
State Department (volumes on *Foreign Relations*)
Tariff Commission
United States Advisory Commission on Information
Veterans Administration

For many of the publications printed as documents the congressional edition is so small that few copies are in circulation in that form. For an appreciable number the document edition reaches a considerable size.

In one instance, that of reports on examination of rivers and harbors prepared by the Army Corps of Engineers, all copies are printed as congressional documents with the exception of those furnished to depository libraries.

The *Monthly Catalog*, the former biennial *Document Catalog*, and the *Checklist* indicate the duplication in editions. The *Monthly Catalog* and the *Document Catalog* have a separate entry for the document edition. The latter gives, in addition to the document number, the volume number and the serial number in the congressional series, the serial number being in black-face type.

In the *Checklist*, which extends to 1909, the serial number and the document number are given in brackets following the main entry. Thus the *Annual Report of the Postmaster General for 1901* is listed as "1901 (4288–4)." This indicates that in addition to the department edition the report is Document 4 of Serial 4288. Reference to the congressional tables in the *Checklist* shows that Serial 4288 contains House documents of the 1st session of the 57th Congress.

The discontinued *Document Index* also indicates what executive publications in regular series were issued as documents, the citations giving both the document and series numbers. Generally each of these indexes is for a session.

It should be noted that the lists in the *Tables and Index* and in the *Document Index* do not necessarily indicate duplication. For publications other than regular series they show that a department publication has been issued as a document, but they do not show whether it has also been printed in a department edition.

The schedule of volumes of congressional documents and reports contained in the *Numerical Lists and Schedule of Volumes,* published by the Superintendent of Documents for each session of Congress, segregates those volumes of House and Senate documents which are published in both editions, with notes to that effect.

The index portion of the *Tables and Index,* which extends to 1892, also gives the serial number and document number of executive publications issued as documents. The congress and session may be ascertained from the numerical tables of serial numbers in the front of the book.

Occasionally a corrected print of a publication is issued without notation regarding edition or duplication other than a star on the front page, the star being a symbol used by the Government Printing Office to indicate a corrected print. Generally the starred corrected print is the only one that finds its way into circulation, as the Government Printing Office endeavors to recall and destroy all copies of the original erroneous print.[2]

In the *Monthly Catalog* and the biennial *Document Catalog* the notation "corrected print" indicates a starred edition. The original print of a starred issue is seldom listed in the *Monthly Catalog,* as the original and the starred prints generally appear

---

[2] Other distinctive marks used by the Government Printing Office at the end of publications are the following: O, in the center of the page immediately following the text, means that publication is complete; X, generally at the bottom of the page, means that additional material is expected to be published. However, these marks are not always conclusive. Thus, in the case of fourteen numbered publications issued in 1937 as committee prints by the Senate Select Committee on Investigation of Executive Agencies of the Government, six, including the last one, carried the all mark, and eight the mark signifying more to come. Each of the fourteen reports was complete in itself but formed part of a series.

during the same month, and the original print is ignored. If, however, the starred print is not issued in the same month as the original, both issues will be noted in separate issues of the catalog, because when the first entry is prepared the compilers do not know that the original edition is to be recalled. The original of a corrected print was not listed in the biennial *Document Catalog*.

CHAPTER FIVE

AVAILABILITY OF PUBLICATIONS

THE GOVERNMENT has generally been liberal in the distribution of its publications, both for personal use and for consultation in libraries. The method of distribution is in part regulated by law and in part determined by the heads of executive departments and agencies. As the distribution to individuals and to libraries is generally on a different basis, each of these groups will be considered separately.

Distribution to Individuals

The distribution to individuals is made by four groups of agencies, as follows: (1) free by members of Congress; (2) free and by sale by the several executive agencies;[1] (3) by sale by the Superintendent of Documents; and (4) by sale by the Clearinghouse for Federal Scientific and Technical Information, Department of Commerce, and by the Photoduplication Service, Publications Board Project, of the Library of Congress. The same publication is often available for distribution by all these agencies and frequently is sold by one and sent free by another. As a rule material which is printed both as a congressional document and as an executive publication may be obtained more readily through the executive agency. An appropriate symbol

---

[1] The executive agencies include the departments as a whole, the bureaus or other subordinate units of the departments, and the independent establishments. See pp. 393–94.

after each entry in the *Monthly Catalog* indicates how the publication may be obtained.

Distribution to individuals by members of Congress. The publications available for distribution by members of Congress are documents, reports, bills, resolutions, the *Congressional Record*, Farmers' Bulletins, and other matter printed for the use of either of the two houses or their committees. While members do not have a specific allotment of hearings, bills, and resolutions, they are generally able to obtain them.

As the edition of a congressional publication is generally limited, the supply available to members is usually small, and it is desirable to make prompt application for copies. Such materials are not usually for sale by the Superintendent of Documents because of the limited demand. On rare occasions when there is likely to be a great demand for a hearing or a lengthy bill in excess of the supply available to the congressional committee, the Superintendent of Documents may offer the document for sale at the request of the committee. There is usually no advantage in applying to a member of Congress for publications printed only in department editions. Such requests are generally forwarded by members to the appropriate executive agency, and the application to a member of Congress generally means additional correspondence and delay.

Distribution to individuals by executive agencies. No universal rule is in effect regarding the distribution by executive agencies. Some make a liberal free distribution, some sell their publications direct, while others make practically no general distribution and refer all applicants to the Superintendent of Documents. The division of the distribution between the executive offices and the Superintendent of Documents is discussed more fully below. In the Department of Agriculture the distribution is almost entirely controlled by a central office for the entire department, while in the other departments which are large publishers—Commerce, Interior, and Labor—the distribution is largely in the hands of the bureaus.

As a rule there is no free distribution of maps, which are

usually sold by the publishing office, although some are sold by the Superintendent of Documents. Information as to where the principal regular series of maps may be obtained is given in Chapter 16. Maps not in regular series are generally sold by the Superintendent of Documents, but there are exceptions.

Practically all processed publications are distributed by the executive agencies. Most of them are distributed free but recently some agencies, particularly the bureaus of the Department of Commerce, have been distributing them directly by sale. The distribution of processed publications is less centralized than that of printed ones; in many cases it is made by divisions or other subordinate units of the bureaus.

Distribution to individuals by Superintendent of Documents. The distribution to individuals by the Superintendent of Documents is entirely by sale. Anyone may order publications by mail by writing to the Superintendent of Documents, and in Washington, D.C., an over-the-counter sales office is maintained at the Government Printing Office at North Capitol and H streets, N.W. The Superintendent also operates three branch sales offices where only a limited number of publications are maintained in stock but where price lists are available and mail orders may be placed. These are located in Washington at 1776 Pennsylvania Avenue, N.W.; in Chicago, Illinois, at the Federal Office Building at 219 South Dearborn Street; in Kansas City, Missouri, at the Federal Building at 601 East 12th Street. The Superintendent confines his sales to publications bearing the imprint of the Government Printing Office,[2] but does not include all such publications. No general statement may be made regarding the type of publications available only through

[2] For many years most processed publications, maps, lithographs, etc., ordered from commercial establishments through the Government Printing Office and all publications printed from type or plates by the Government Printing Office have borne the imprint of that office. Earlier the imprint was not always used, even on some small publications printed from type or plates. Publications printed by executive agencies at their own plant or ordered directly from commercial establishments do not bear the imprint of the Government Printing Office.

purchase from the Superintendent of Documents, but many of the older publications fall in this group. Likewise no general statement may be made regarding publications that are not sold by him; the most that can be done is to point out certain issues that are not sold by him.

No publications of the Organization of American States and the Board of Governors of the Fereral Reserve System are sold by the Superintendent of Documents.

As regards agencies listed below, some publications are sold by the issuing office and some by the Superintendent of Documents.

CENSUS BUREAU. Most publications are sold by the Superintendent of Documents, but the *Catalog of United States Census Publications* lists some which are available from the Bureau. A section of the *Catalog* tells how to obtain access to data files and unpublished materials.

COAST AND GEODETIC SURVEY. Tide and current tables and maps are sold by the survey and its agencies. Other publications are sold by the Superintendent of Documents.

FEDERAL POWER COMMISSION. The maps and some of the publications are sold by the commission. Other publications are sold by the Superintendent of Documents. There appears to be no general rule indicating what is sold by each agency. A list issued by the commission shows where the publications may be obtained.

GEOLOGICAL SURVEY. Maps and charts are sold by mail from the Geological Survey and over the counter at sources listed in *Publications of the United States Geological Survey*. The same sources also sell some books which are also available from the Superintendent.

LIBRARY OF CONGRESS. Most publications are sold by the Superintendent of Documents, but *Library of Congress Publications in Print* lists some which are sold by the Card Division of the Library and some which are distributed by the Office of the Secretary and other divisions of the Library.

NATIONAL BUREAU OF STANDARDS. Publications are primarily available from the Superintendent of Documents. Some are sold by the Clearinghouse for Federal Scientific and Technical Information. The NBS *Supplementary List of Available Publications* suggests the Library of Congress Photoduplication Service as a source for out-of-print titles, and an appendix entitled "Price List of Available Publications" is useful for determining sources.

PATENT OFFICE. Copies of individual patents are sold by the Patent Office, but the other publications are sold by the Superintendent of Documents.

SMITHSONIAN INSTITUTION. The series known as "Smithsonian Miscellaneous Collections" is sold by the Smithsonian Institution, as is the periodical *Smithsonian Journal of History*. Publications not in series are sometimes sold by the Superintendent and sometimes by the Smithsonian. *Publications in Salvage Archaeology* and *Proceedings and Contributions from the National Herbarium* are marked "Distribution made by the issuing office."

Although it is impossible for the Superintendent of Documents to issue a catalog containing the title of every publication carried in stock, the inquirer is usually able to obtain information about current publications through the *Selected List,* the *Monthly Catalog,* and the price lists issued by the Superintendent of Documents. If the desired publication cannot be located through the use of one or another of these aids, information can almost certainly be secured through correspondence, as the office has an excellent reference card catalog which is used as a guide in locating material not in the price lists.

In order to facilitate the sale of publications, the Superintendent of Documents sells coupons in lots of twenty coupons worth five cents each, which may be used in the purchase of publications. This plan makes it unnecessary for the purchaser to obtain a money order or to send small amounts of cash through the mail. Repeated small remittances may also be avoided by making a cash deposit with the Superintendent of Documents and having orders charged as they come in. This is particularly advantageous in the case of publications which are desired promptly and which vary in price. An initial deposit of $25.00 or more is required to open an account. An account number is assigned to each depositor, and a supply of deposit account order blanks is provided.

Outside of Washington, publications are sold for the Superintendent of Documents by the publication distribution centers of the Department of State, by the superintendents of national parks, and by designated agents of several other government agencies. These agencies do not deal in all publications but handle primarily those issued by or relating to their particular services. As a rule they do not fill mail orders. The field offices of the Department of Commerce stock and sell publications of interest to business and also accept mail orders. They offer a reference service to help individuals locate useful publications, and they will place orders with the Superintendent of Documents and the Clearinghouse. Publications may also be ordered through book dealers, as the act of June 30, 1932 (47 Stat. 409), permits the Superintendent of Documents to allow a discount to authorized dealers.

The most satisfactory procedure in ordering current publications is to use the *Monthly Catalog* as a guide and to order from the Superintendent of Documents all items which the notations indicate are sold by him. It should be noted that some priced items are sold by the issuing agencies, but this fact is always shown in the catalog. Some publications sold by the Superintendent of Documents are also distributed free by the departments, but there is so little uniformity of practice by the departments in the method of distribution that the applicant is never sure he can obtain a copy from the issuing office. Since the Superintendent of Documents has a very limited supply of some publications, it is advisable to order promptly.

Distribution to individuals by the Clearinghouse for Federal Scientific and Technical Information of the Department of Commerce. The Clearinghouse is responsible for the collection and distribution of technical reports, usually originating in agencies of the United States government, in the interest of American science and industry. The more important are reprinted for sale to the public by the Clearinghouse. Many of the reports, however, are so specialized that the demand for them does not warrant reprinting. Orders are accepted for copies at a uniform price of $3.00 for paper copies or 65 cents for microfiche copies.

Distribution to Libraries

Probably all libraries in the country receive some government publications through one or more of the following methods of distribution: (1) designated depository libraries which are entitled to receive from the Superintendent of Documents all publications, with certain exceptions; (2) libraries which are not depositories and which receive the publications through executive agencies; (3) Clearinghouse for Federal Scientific and Technical Information, Department of Commerce, and Photo-duplication Service, Publications Board Project, of the Library of Congress (see preceding paragraph); (4) Documents Expediting Project; (5) microcopies (see Chapter 19); and (6) Atomic Energy Commission depositories.

Distribution to depository libraries. Many years ago Congress recognized the desirability of making government publications available to the public. It therefore provided that one library could be designated in each congressional district by the representative and two in each state by the senators to be depositories of one copy of every government publication, with certain exceptions. Later the depository privilege was extended to the libraries of the executive departments existing in 1895, state and territorial libraries, libraries of land-grant colleges, and a few specified institutions. Under the earlier laws an existing depository designated by a senator or a representative could be displaced by another library at the discretion of the senator or representative entitled to make the designation, but the act of June 23, 1913 (38 Stat. 75), definitely placed on a permanent basis the then existing depositories and those designated later. In 1962, the law was changed to provide for two depositories in each congressional district to be designated by the representative and two in each state to be designated by each senator. The number of depositories in the executive departments and agencies was also increased. Under the provisions of the law, there is a potential of approximately 1,350 depositories, of which about 955 have been designated. There are also 36 regional depositories, so designated by the Superintendent of Documents, which agree to accept and keep permanently a complete collection of publications, thus making it possible for other depositories to dispose of some of their documents after five years in accordance with regulations of the

Superintendent and with approval of the regional repository.

Prior to the passage of the Printing Act of 1895, the depository libraries received only the publications included in the congressional series and bearing a congressional series number.[3] The act of 1895, which is still in force, provides that the depository libraries shall receive "all publications of the executive departments, not intended for their especial use, but made for distribution" (28 Stat. 610). This clause has been interpreted as excepting only confidential publications, and so various manuals intended for the internal administrative use of the departments have been included in the depository distributions.

While the publications included in the congressional series as a whole have not changed, those sent to depository libraries have varied from time to time. The first change was made by the Printing Act of 1895, which limited the library distribution of the *Senate Journal* and the *House Journal* to three libraries designated by the Superintendent of Documents in each state and territory (28 Stat. 609).[4] For the 54th Congress (1895–97) and the 1st session of the 55th Congress (1897) serial numbers were not assigned to these journals; thereafter numbers were assigned as before, until the 1st session of the 83d Congress, when they were again discontinued.

The second change was effected by the act of January 20, 1905 (33 Stat. 610), which amended Sections 54 and 55 of the Printing Act of 1895. The effect of this act was to eliminate reports on private bills and simple and concurrent resolutions from the depository sets of the congressional series by providing that a limited number should be printed.[5] The act provided, however, that the excepted reports should be bound for the Senate and the House libraries. Copies have also been bound for the Library of Congress and the Public Documents

[3] These included many departmental series and annual reports. See pp. 151–54 for contents of congressional series.

[4] By the act of June 25, 1938 (52 Stat. 1206), the journals were made available to all depository libraries.

[5] Reports on private bills and simple and concurrent resolutions were again made available to depository libraries by the act of June 25, 1938 (52 Stat. 1206).

Library. Private bills for the purpose of this act were defined as "all bills for the relief of private parties, bills granting pensions, bills removing political disabilities, and bills for the survey of rivers and harbors."

The act of 1905 resulted in the exclusion of many important reports from the accessions of depository libraries, for the reports on simple resolutions often contain the results of detailed and exhaustive investigations by committees. Thus Senate Report 563 of the 67th Congress, 2d session (46 pages), on the membership of the World War Debt Commission is printed with the reports on private bills. This report contains exhaustive and able discussions on the eligibility of members of Congress to serve on commissions having executive duties and reviews precedents covering such cases. Thus its importance is not to be measured by the effect on the individual members concerned. Another general Senate report of the same congress and session bound with the reports on the private bills is No. 794 (37 pages), which contains the results of an inquiry by a Senate committee on the occupation and administration of Haiti.

This division of reports became effective on the date the act was approved, so that the depository set for the 3d session of the 58th Congress includes reports on private bills, etc., made prior to January 20, 1905, but no reports submitted at a later date. The volume designation of the books containing the reports on private bills, etc., was alphabetical from the time this legislation took effect until the end of the 75th Congress. These volumes were not given serial numbers during the 3d session of the 58th Congress (1904–05) and the 59th Congress (1905–07). They were assigned serial numbers in the 60th Congress (1907) and thereafter, but as they were not sent to depositories there resulted gaps in the serial number sets in libraries using the serial number classification. Beginning with the 76th Congress these reports were not segregated, and all reports were bound in numerical order, but beginning with the 84th Congress they were again bound separately.

The next change, a purely formal one, resulted from the operation of the joint resolution of January 15, 1908 (35 Stat. 565). This provided that publications originating in executive departments or establishments should not be given any congressional series of numbers on the copies distributed to depository libraries. It also provided that the volumes should be bound as directed by the Joint Committee on Printing. This resulted in the buckram binding, which was used for the depository volumes of the 60th Congress and thereafter. Hence the congressional document number, the volume number, and the serial number were no longer printed on the title page or stamped on the binding of the executive publications sent to depositories, although they still appeared on the books for the Senate and House libraries, the Library of Congress, and the Public Documents Library. The strictly congressional series, as represented by the copies in these libraries, therefore remained unchanged. Moreover, if several publications were bound in one book for these libraries, the same arrangement was followed for books sent to depository libraries. Beginning in the 2d session of the 88th Congress serial numbers were again printed on copies sent to depositories.

This method of titling and marking gave the librarians the choice of two methods of shelving: (1) they could stamp the volume and serial number on the books and continue the congressional series arrangement, or (2) they could shelve the books according to some other classification. If they continued the serial number arrangement, the congressional series remained a mixture of congressional and executive publications; if they used some other classification, many gaps in the document numbers, volume numbers, and serial numbers of the congressional series occurred. An alternative was to duplicate the executive publications if possible and keep intact both the congressional and other classifications.

The next change, effective with the publications of the 63d Congress (1913), altered still further the form in which department publications were distributed to depository libraries. Under this rule all publications of executive departments included in the congressional series are distributed to depositories in the form issued by the departments; that is, if the department edition is bound in paper, the libraries receive the volumes in paper. Moreover, the serial publications of the departments are not assembled in volumes corresponding to those in the congressional series, as before. For instance, Volume 118 of the *House Documents* of the 63d Congress, 2d session (Serial 6715), contains Bureau of Labor Statistics Bulletins 135, 137, 143, and 146. Under the plan in use prior to the 63d Congress, these would have gone to the depositories in one bound volume corresponding to the congressional series except in title page and back title. Under the new plan the depositories receive each bulletin separately, as issued, in paper covers. However, such publications as are issued in bound editions by the departments are sent to depositories in that form.

All the department publications heretofore included in the congressional series still remain in the limited edition provided for the libraries of the House and the Senate, the National Archives, the Public Documents Library, and the Library of Congress, to which sets volume and serial numbers are assigned as before.

Except in the five libraries in Washington—the Senate, House, National Archives, Public Documents, and Library of Congress—this last change probably marked the end of the set known under the names of the congressional set, the sheep set, and the serial number set. The libraries are able to maintain this set as heretofore, but to do so it is necessary to assemble and bind a number of separate publications and this they are unlikely to do since it would mean trouble and expense. Thus under the old plan the publications included in Serial Nos. 8461 to 8501 would have gone to the depositories in the form of 41 bound volumes; under the present plan they are sent in 8 bound volumes and 75 publications in paper covers.

Up to 1922 each depository library received a copy of all publications available for depositories, regardless of whether it wanted them. Far-seeing librarians had long desired the privilege of selecting the publications desired, and selective distribution had been recommended by the Superintendent of Documents and the committees of Congress as early as 1909. But nothing was done until the passage of the appropriation act for the fiscal year 1923 (42 Stat. 436), which provided that the appropriation for distributing books to depository libraries should not be used to supply them with publications not requested. This was made permanent law by language in the Legislative Branch Appropriation Act, 1957 (70 Stat. 369).

Since the Superintendent of Documents must know the number of copies needed in advance of printing, it is impracticable for libraries to select individual publications. Hence they are selected in advance by classes. There are about 2,184 such classes, but many include only one publication issued once a year, notably the annual reports; others include an entire series, such as the Bulletins of the Bureau of Labor Statistics.[6]

The next change, by order of the Joint Committee on Printing of May 21, 1924, and effective with the publications of the 1st session of the 68th Congress (1923), was also a purely formal one. Under this order the volume number is omitted from the bound copies of publications originating in Congress. This change was made in order to make an earlier distribution. If the volume number were placed on the books, it would be necessary to hold them until the end of the session. Bound volumes containing reports or documents which have been distributed in unbound form at the time of printing include a volume title page, but the volume and serial numbers do not appear on the cover.

The act of June 25, 1938 (52 Stat. 1206), again made available to depository libraries the reports on private bills and simple and concurrent resolutions. It also broadened the distribution by the inclusion of the *Senate Journal* and the *House*

[6] The classification used in ordering publications for depositories and the call number assigned in the Public Documents Library are given in *Classified List of United States Government Publications Available for Selection by Depository Libraries* . . . (revised 1967 in card form).

Journal and all publications, except administrative and confidential ones, ordered by any committee of Congress. The inclusion of committee publications made the hearings available for free distribution to depository libraries for the first time, beginning with hearings dated 1941.

The Depository Library Act of 1962 (PL 87-579) provided for the distribution to depositories by the Superintendent of Documents of non-Government Printing Office publications. No appropriations were made available for this purpose for three years. In 1963, the Superintendent of Documents began this distribution with Census Bureau publications. The August 1967 list of publications available for selection by depositories contained 65 classes of publications from three departments, Commerce, Interior, and Labor. Publications of the State Department will soon be included in the program. This is a program with tremendous problems of administration and coordination. Since the cost of the non-Government Printing Office publications sent to the depositories must be borne by the appropriations of the agencies, there may be a danger that more and more publications will be designated as "administrative," which removes the requirement for depository copies but which also eliminates listing in the *Monthly Catalog*.

At present (1969) publications are being distributed by the Superintendent of Documents to depository libraries in the following manner. (1) Publications originally published by the departments are distributed in the same form as the department edition; and, regardless of whether the same publication is also published as a congressional document, it bears no document number. (2) Documents and reports originating in Congress are distributed in bound volumes with serial numbers on the cover and, except for those bound immediately, in unbound form at the time of printing; each one bears the numbers of the documents or reports included in the volume. (3) Hearings and other committee publications are distributed in the form in which they are printed for the use of the committee.

Depositories do not receive the publications listed below.

Administrative publications intended for use within agencies

Briefs filed in various courts on behalf of the United States (only a small edition printed; no copies available for distribution)

Comptroller General (monthly pamphlet containing decisions)

Congressional committee prints, with some exceptions

Confidential publications

Federal Deposit Insurance Corporation (very little of the printing of the FDIC executed at the Government Printing Office; only a few isolated publications distributed to depositories by the Superintendent of Documents)

Federal Reserve System Board of Governors (same as FDIC)

Maps issued in separate form

National Research Council publications

Patent Office (copies of individual patents)

Private laws, slip copies

Publications not printed at the Government Printing Office (impossible to specify these, as some agencies print publications both at the Government Printing Office and at private establishments)

Senate executive documents and reports

Separate decisions of the Board of Tax Appeals, Interstate Commerce Commission, Federal Trade Commission, and Interior Department; separate opinions of the Attorney General; extracts from periodicals and other publications

Smithsonian Institution (miscellaneous collections)

Special publications, such as those relating to naval historical documents (48 Stat. 414), which may be excepted by the law authorizing their publication

Treasury decisions under the customs, internal revenue, industrial alcohol, narcotic, and other laws (weekly edition)

Distribution to libraries not depositories.   Libraries which are not designated depositories receive publications from the several publishing offices. Some of the executive agencies maintain library mailing lists for all publications, but the practice is not uniform in this respect. If a library is not on a mailing list, the method of distribution is the same as in the case of an individual.

The Superintendent of Documents has no control over any mailing list for libraries that are not depositories and does not supply publications regularly to them. Generally, libraries which are not depositories must purchase current publications from the Superintendent of Documents, if not available from the issuing offices.

Documents Expediting Project

Sponsored by the Joint Committee on Government Publications of the Association of Research Libraries, the American Library Association, the American Association of Law Libraries, and the Special Libraries Association, the Documents Expediting Project was organized in 1946 to facilitate the procurement and distribution of government documents of all types for interested public, university, and special libraries.

The project is concerned primarily with the documents which are not distributed by the Superintendent of Documents or which are difficult to obtain through the usual channels. It distributes publications to libraries according to priority based on the amount of their voluntary subscription. Libraries are also supplied with forms on which to request particular documents.

In addition to distributing publications to its member libraries, the Documents Expediting Project endeavors to have its participants placed on mailing lists to receive government publications distributed by various agencies.

One copy of every publication distributed by "DocEx" to its member libraries is sent to the Public Documents Library, so that it may be available for listing in the *Monthly Catalog of United States Government Publications.*

Atomic Energy Commission Depositories

The 99 United States Atomic Energy Commission depositories receive unclassified United States Atomic Energy Commission reports and some domestic non-AEC reports and foreign atomic energy reports. Until 1965, whenever there was an inadequate supply of printed copies, distribution to depositories was in the form of microcards. Since 1965, almost all reports sent to depositories are in the form of micronegatives. Publications sent to AEC depositories and the form in which they are sent are indicated in *Nuclear Science Abstracts, Cumulative Report Number Index With Public Availability Citations.* Volumes 1 through 15 (revised) covered the period 1947–61. Volumes 16 through 20 covered the period 1962–66.

Collections of Publications

There is probably no complete collection of government publications in existence, but the one in the Public Documents Library is probably the most nearly complete. This library was not started until 1895, however, and some of the earlier publications are missing. For ordinary printed books and pamphlets issued since 1895, the collection is almost complete, but there are some publications that were never received.

The catalog of the Public Documents Library is a single-entry shelf list arranged by publishing offices as in the *Checklist* and the *Monthly Catalog,* the shelf numbers being the same as those given in these publications.[7] It may at times be difficult to find the publications of executive agencies unless the publishing unit is known. However, many citations by subject or author may be obtained from a separate reference index maintained by the Inquiries Section of the Office of the Superintendent of Documents. The reference index, however, does not pretend to be complete, although entries are continually

[7] The publication of shelf numbers was begun in the *Monthly Catalog* for July 1924. There was no published list of shelf numbers assigned between Dec. 31, 1909, the closing date for the *Checklist,* and April 1910, when class numbers began to be included in *Depository Invoices.* However, Cutter numbers for individual documents were not given in the *Invoices.* Some of these were included in the *Price List.* To fill this gap, Mary Elizabeth Poole, Document Librarian, the D. H. Hill Library, North Carolina State University, Raleigh, N.C., has been working for a number of years and has authored *Documents Office Classification through 1966,* published by University Microfilms, Ann Arbor, Mich., 1966. Miss Poole and Ella Frances Smith, Alderman Library, University of Virginia, have authored a two-part publication entitled *Documents Office Classification Numbers for Cuttered Documents 1910–1924,* published by University Microfilms, 1960.

added as inquiries are answered. All publications issued as documents and reports of Congress are arranged according to the serial numbers (see pages 161–66).

The most complete collection of maps produced by the United States government is on file in the National Archives, which publishes inventories and descriptive catalogs for public use. The Library of Congress also has an excellent map collection.

Neither the Public Documents Library nor the Library of Congress has a complete file of processed material. This arises from the fact that these publications are issued by many minor units of the executive agencies and are not made available to the libraries. The Public Documents Library has all issues listed in the *Monthly Catalog* and the biennial *Document Catalog*. It also has some material not so listed, as back issues are often sent to the library after the catalogs are printed. The Library of Congress card catalog shows what is available there. If a processed publication cannot be found in these libraries, the only other source is the issuing office, and sometimes not even there since some agencies do not have complete files of their own processed publications.

The Library of Congress has an extensive collection of government publications, the card catalog giving entries by author, subject, and title. It has a set of congressional documents and reports arranged according to the serial numbers, and the correct volume may be obtained by calling for the serial number. An important feature of the Library of Congress collection is a bound set of bills and resolutions.

As has been explained on preceding pages, designated depository libraries are entitled to receive all publications, with certain exceptions. All designated depositories are required to make the publications available for the free use of the general public. A complete list of the depository libraries is given in the appendix.

CHAPTER SIX

CONGRESSIONAL PUBLICATIONS

CONGRESSIONAL PUBLICATIONS as here described include anything published under the authority of Congress as a whole, of either house, or of any committee of either house.[1] At the present time the congressional series is composed of the *Congressional Record,* the journals of the two houses, the numbered documents and reports, and certain other publications of the Senate and the House of Representatives. Hearings and other publications issued by committees are not congressional publications in the technical sense, but are discussed in this chapter as they relate to the work of Congress.

Debates

The debates of Congress have been reported in four series of publications, the names of which are as follows:

Annals of Congress, 1st Congress to end of 1st session of the 18th Congress, 1789–1824

Register of Debates, 2d session of the 18th Congress to end of 1st session of the 25th Congress, 1824–37

Congressional Globe, 1st session of the 23d Congress to end of the 42d Congress, 1833–73

Congressional Record, 1st session of the 43d Congress and thereafter, 1873 to date

It will be noted that the *Register of Debates* and the *Congressional Globe* overlap for a short period. The *Annals of*

[1] See also William F. Willoughby, "The Legislative Branch and Research," in National Resources Committee, *Research—A National Resource* (1938), pp. 113-64.

Congress,[2] the *Register of Debates,* and the *Congressional Globe*[3] were issued by commercial printers, but as copies were purchased for the use of the government, they have generally been regarded as government publications. During a portion of its existence the *Globe* was published under a contract which covered both the reporting and the printing. The *Record* has been printed at the Government Printing Office during its entire history.

Each series has independent numbering. A complete list of the volume and part numbers to the end of the 79th Congress (1947) is given in "Proceedings of Congress," *Price List 49,* 31st edition, issued by the Superintendent of Documents; a list to the end of the 66th Congress (1921) is given on pages 705–27 of the *Senate Catalogue,* 1924 edition; and a list to the end of the 1st session of the 61st Congress (1909) will be found on pages 1463–75 of the *Checklist.* The list in the *Senate Catalogue,* however, does not give the volume numbers for the *Globe.* All three lists show the limiting dates of the debates and proceedings in each volume and part.

For many of the early years the indexes to the debates are poor, but the student may locate the material in the debates in an indirect way by use of the indexes to the House and the Senate journals.[4] An example will illustrate the method. A law approved July 21, 1840 (6 Stat. 813), is entitled "An act for the relief of Chastelain and Ponvert, and for other purposes." In the index to the debates the only reference to Chastelain and Ponvert is in the index to the House proceedings on the day the bill came back to the House with the Senate amendments. There is no reference to its introduction or passage by the House, nor is there any reference to the proceedings in the Senate. But in the index to the *Senate Journal* we find under "Chastelain and Ponvert" a cross reference to H. R. 27. The table of bills in the index to the *Senate Journal* gives references to the pages therein showing action. The *House Journal* contains no

[2] Hereafter referred to as the *Annals.*
[3] Hereafter referred to as the *Globe.*
[4] See pp. 144–45.

entry for Chastelain and Ponvert, but we have already found
from the *Senate Journal* that the bill is H. R. 27. The *House Journal* also has a table of bills which gives references to the pages
therein showing action. From the journals we obtain the dates
on which action was taken, and it is easy to find the same dates
in the volumes of debates. While this method is time consuming, it is not so wasteful as examining page after page of the
debates, which is the alternative.

Annals of Congress

The *Annals* comprise 42 volumes, covering the first 17 congresses and the 1st session of the 18th (1789–1824). Some volumes are for a single session, some for a portion of a session, a
few for an entire congress, and some for portions of two sessions. The volumes are not numbered on the title pages, but
numbers have been assigned and generally appear on the back
titles. Each volume has separate indexes for Senate and House
proceedings. The indexes cover the entire session, but are repeated in each volume if the session proceedings require more
than one volume.

This series is generally known by the short title *Annals of
Congress*. The full title is *The Debates and Proceedings in the
Congress of the United States; with an Appendix, Containing
Important State Papers and Public Documents and All the
Laws of a Public Nature; with a Copious Index*. The series is
occasionally cited as *History of Congress*, which is the running
head on the pages. Volumes 1 and 2 for the 1st Congress are
duplicated by another compilation with the same title page (as
regards wording, but not typography) and imprint date (1834),
but with the running page head "Gales and Seaton's History of
Debates in Congress."[5] The text in the two sets is apparently
the same, but they are not printed from the same type, and
after the first few pages the text breaks differently at the end of

[5] The statement in the footnote on page 112 of the first edition of this book
regarding the use of the words "Old Series" on the back title is evidently
erroneous. It was based on a statement in the *Checklist* (p. 1463) and a rebound copy in the Public Documents Library. That library has another set of
these two volumes in the original binding, which do not have the words "Old
Series" on the back title.

each page. In the books with the running head "History of Congress," Volume 1 includes the proceedings from March 4, 1789, to February 10, 1790 (pages 1–1169 + lxx),[6] and Volume 2 includes proceedings from February 10, 1790, to March 3, 1791 (pages 1171–2353 + lxx). In the books with the running head "History of Debates," Volume 1 includes the proceedings from March 4, 1789, to February 18, 1790 (pages 1–1322 + xxx), and Volume 2 includes the proceedings from February 18, 1790, to March 3, 1791 (pages 1323–2418 + xxx). Why two sets with different make-up should have been published in the same year is somewhat of a mystery.

The volumes for the 2d and 4th Congresses were evidently printed in more than one edition, as different imprint dates appear on volumes covering the same period and apparently containing the same text.

The *Annals* were not published contemporaneously but were issued in 1834 and thereafter by Gales and Seaton, who compiled the text from newspapers and other sources, the debates from October 1800 being taken from the *National Intelligencer*. The proceedings are not given verbatim but are more in the nature of abstracts. The appendix in the last volume for each congress contains the public laws and some executive reports.

The general indexes to the journals of Congress from 1789 to 1821 listed on page 145 contain citations to the *Annals*. While these volumes may not serve as a complete index to the *Annals*, they will be found convenient.

Register of Debates

The *Register of Debates*[7] comprises 14 numbered volumes, beginning with the 2d session of the 18th Congress and ending with the 1st session of the 25th Congress (1824–37). Each volume covers a session; but as most of the volumes are arbitrarily divided into parts, there are 29 books in the series. The publi-

[6] The pages have two columns, and each column is numbered as if it were a page.
[7] The complete series entitled the *Register of Debates* was published by Gales and Seaton. Another *Register of Debates, Giving Speeches Delivered in Congress during the 1st Session of the 23d Congress from Dec. 2, 1833, to May 31, 1834*, was published in two volumes by Duff Green in 1834.

cation of the *Register of Debates* was contemporaneous with the proceedings, but the series does not pretend to be a verbatim account. Each volume has separate indexes for Senate and House proceedings covering an entire session, but the index is repeated in each book if the volume is divided into parts. The index is at the end of each book, but occasionally other matter, such as the text of laws, follows the index, so that at times it is necessary to search for it. The last volume for each session contains the messages of the President, some department and committee reports, and the laws. Like the *Annals* each page has two columns, each column a page number.

Congressional Globe

The *Globe* comprises 109 books in 46 volumes, beginning with the 1st session of the 23d Congress and ending with the 42d Congress (1833–73), the first five volumes overlapping the *Register of Debates*. The first 14 volumes bear numbers on the title page; some of the succeeding volumes are numbered on the title pages and some are not. The scheme of volume numbering on the title pages after Volume 14 is not consistent with that in the preceding volumes, and therefore the *Checklist* has disregarded the original volume numbers after Volume 14 and supplied a new set of numbers according to the consistent plan of a volume number for each session. As many libraries have numbered the back titles according to the *Checklist* plan, the title page number and the *Checklist* number may not agree. On the other hand, in some sets the back title numbers may be the same as the title page. In order to avoid confusion, citations to the *Globe* should be by congress and session instead of by volume number.

There are separate indexes for the Senate and House proceedings for each session, and in many volumes the index is repeated in each part. In some volumes the index appears only in Part 1. In this series the index is at the front of the book.[8]

---

[8] As the index has a Roman pagination, it is not unlikely that the position of the index and the matter of its repetition vary in sets which were bound at different times.

During its earlier years the text of the *Globe* was, in general, the same as that of its predecessor, the *Register of Debates*, namely, an abstract of the debates. Beginning with the 32d Congress (1851), more of the debates are given in the first person, and gradually the *Globe* approached a more nearly verbatim report.

In addition to the debates, the appendix to each volume of the *Globe* contains the following material: up to the close of the 2d session of the 40th Congress (1833–68), the messages of the President and reports of heads of departments; beginning with the 2d session of the 32d Congress (1853–73), the text of the laws; up to the close of the 36th Congress (1833–61), a detailed statement of appropriations.

The appendix to the *Globe* contains many speeches to which there is no reference on the pages containing the debates. Therefore the appendix should be consulted if all the material on any subject is desired.

Congressional Record

The *Congressional Record* has been published continuously beginning with the 1st session of the 43d Congress in 1873. The *Record* is published in three forms: (1) the daily *Record*, which appears on the morning after the day to which it relates; (2) the paper-bound biweekly *Record*, which is simply an assemblage of the daily issues; and (3) the permanent bound *Record*. In the permanent bound *Record* the proceedings for each session constitute a numbered volume, beginning with 1 for the special session of the 43d Congress, and divided into parts of approximately equal size.

The *Record* is presumably a complete and verbatim account of the words spoken in the two houses, but neither the daily nor the permanent *Record* fills this description. The daily edition falls short of being a complete account of the debate because a member may withhold his remarks for revision. While the major part of the material withheld may be the remarks of one member, there are often questions and remarks by other members during the course of the debate.[9] Remarks withheld are later published in the appendix to the daily edition, but they appear in the bound edition in their proper place in relation to the proceedings, except at the end of a session, when they may be printed in the appendix. The *Record* is not a verbatim account in that the remarks are edited and revised before the copy is sent to the printer. Therefore at times it does not contain statements reported in the papers by reputable and experienced correspondents.[10]

The bound *Record* is not a verbatim account for the reasons given above and for the further reason that the House proceedings contain many speeches which were not delivered on the floor but which are inserted under "leave to print." This leave-to-print privilege is exercised in two forms. Under one, the member obtains permission to address the House for a few minutes and when his time expires he asks leave to extend his remarks in print. Under the second, he is merely recognized by the chair, and obtains leave to print his remarks without speaking a single word on the floor. Under each method the *Record* is burdened with a mass of material which has never been spoken in debate. In the daily *Record* these leave-to-print speeches are printed in the appendix after the regular proceedings. In the bound edition they are printed as part of the proceedings, except at the end of the session, and there is no way of distinguishing between a speech actually delivered and one which is included under leave to print. The bound *Record* is, therefore, a guide to the opinions of members, but it cannot be relied upon as a report of words spoken in debate.

Other material in the *Record* not germane to the proceedings includes speeches and articles delivered elsewhere than on the floor or previously printed in other places. Such material is

---

[9] See *Congressional Record,* daily ed., Feb. 24, 1936, pp. 2775-80, which contains remarks in the Senate, with questions by other members on H. R. 9870. The remarks were made on January 20 (p. 697), and the bill was passed over the President's veto on January 27.

[10] For history of the reporting of debates in the House of Representatives, see *Hinds' Precedents of the House of Representatives,* Vol. 5, pp. 974-88; for rulings on matter included in the *Record,* see the same volume, pp. 978-1008, and *Cannon's Precedents of the House of Representatives,* Vol. 8, pp. 876-903.

ordinarily printed in the appendix to the daily *Record,* but since the beginning of the 2d session of the 83d Congress has not been included in the bound *Record.* This class of material, which is not considered germane to the proceedings, includes reprints of editorials, magazine articles, and at times extracts from books, as well as speeches by officers of the executive branch and persons not connected with the government.

The paper-bound biweekly edition is an assemblage of the copies of the daily edition. As it duplicates the daily edition, it includes all matter ordered expunged. It is printed primarily for the use of members of Congress, and it is doubtful if copies are available except in the Library of Congress and in the Public Documents Library. If the daily or biweekly edition is bound, it may be distinguished from the permanent bound edition by the fact that the proceedings for each day begin on a new page with the caption "Congressional Record," while in the permanent bound *Record* the text runs without break.

Occasionally the daily *Record* contains material that is not in the bound volume because it has been expunged. Thus on June 12, 1933, a member of the Senate offered a motion to print in the *Record* an article by another person.[11] The article, which appeared in the appendix for that day,[12] contained an attack on an officer of the executive branch of the government. On the next day the senator explained to the Senate that he had not read the article, expressed his regret over its appearance, and moved that it be expunged.[13] This motion was adopted without debate, and the bound *Record* does not contain the original motion to print, the article, or the explanation and motion to expunge.

Again, on April 5, 1934, two senators engaged in an acrimonious debate, but the next day both agreed to expunge a portion of the remarks.[14] As a result thirteen pages of debate in the daily *Record* were condensed to five pages in the bound volume. In this case the motion to expunge is given in the bound

[11] *Congressional Record,* daily ed., June 12, 1933, p. 5811.
[12] *Ibid.,* p. 5902.
[13] *Ibid.,* June 13, 1933, p. 5929.
[14] *Ibid.,* Apr. 5, 1934, p. 6263, and Apr. 6, 1934, p. 6339.

volume, and the reader is given an indication of the change in the text.

While the pagination of the daily *Record* runs through an entire session, it is not the same as that in the bound edition, by reason of the insertion, in their proper places in the bound volumes, of leave-to-print and "withheld for revision" speeches. Therefore, in citing the daily *Record*, it should be referred to as such. In citations to the daily *Record* it is desirable to include the date, as the use of the date enables the reader more easily to locate the material in the bound volume.

An index to the *Record* is issued every two weeks. At the end of the session an index to the bound volumes is prepared. The biweekly indexes cannot be used for the bound *Record*, nor can the complete session index be used for the daily *Record*, since, as we have noted, the daily and bound-volume paginations are not the same. However, the session index can be used as a key to material in the appendix of the daily *Record* which was excluded from the bound *Record* as not being germane to the proceedings.

The biweekly indexes are not cumulative, and a bill is indexed under the name of the member and the subject matter only at the time it is introduced. Bills are indexed under their number when introduced and whenever action is taken, but these references are cumulative, so that the latest index giving references to a bill shows the entire history for the session.

Bills are numbered consecutively through a congress, and a bill may reach certain stages in one session and other stages in a later session. Therefore, the index for a session after the first one does not necessarily give citations to all the proceedings, as some action may have been taken at a previous session, and the index for that one must be consulted to complete the history.

The index reference to the report on the bill generally gives the report number in parentheses. For earlier years the report number may generally be obtained by referring to the page of the *Record* where the action is reported.

The first classification in both the biweekly and the bound indexes is by names of members and subject matter. In this classification the subject matter of bills and resolutions is indexed without page reference but with a cross reference to the bill or resolution number. This classification is followed by eight separate indexes, arranged by series numbers, of Senate bills, Senate joint resolutions, Senate concurrent resolutions, Senate resolutions, House bills, House joint resolutions, House concurrent resolutions, and House resolutions.

The index to the *Congressional Record* is strong in citations to action on bills and remarks of members but weak in citations under subject headings. In order to locate the debates on a particular topic, the reader must generally ascertain the number of the bill in the entry under the subject and then turn to the index by bill numbers in order to obtain the references.

If there are several bills on the same subject, the one on which action has been taken is indicated by an asterisk. As a rule speeches are not made on unreported bills.

Unless there is a short special session the index of the bound *Record* has generally formed a separate part, although at times it is combined with the appendix. At first the index volume contained separate indexes for House and Senate proceedings, but beginning with the 2d session of the 48th Congress (1884) there has been one general index for both the House and Senate. The index volume generally was not numbered as a "part" prior to Volume 64 for the 4th session of the 67th Congress.

Citations to speeches on the tariff between 1909 and 1933 are given in *The Tariff—A Bibliography—A Select List of References*, 1934 (980 pages), published by the Tariff Commission. These citations are found in the major classifications under the subentry "Congressional Record." The volume also has detailed author and subject indexes. Similar material from 1933 to 1937 on reciprocal trade relations is given in *Reciprocal Trade: A Current Bibliography*, 3d edition, 1937 (282 + 129 pages), published by the Tariff Commission.

Daily Digest

A *Daily Digest* was added to the daily issues of the *Congressional Record* beginning with the 80th Congress. The *Digest* contains the highlights of the day's sessions; actions taken by each chamber, including page references to the proceedings; a résumé of committee actions; and lists of committee meetings for the following day. It also lists bills signed by the President.

Proceedings

While the proceedings, except those of closed executive sessions of the Senate, are included in the publications giving the debates, they are also published in more convenient form in the journals, which include all motions, all action taken, and the votes on roll calls or divisions. The journals do not include any speeches or explanatory matter. The journals are the only publications required by the Constitution, which provides that each "house shall keep a journal of its proceedings, and from time to time publish the same, excepting such parts as may in their judgment require secrecy" (Article 1, Section 5, Clause 3).

Legislative Journals

No edition of the journals is available until the end of the session, when the entire proceedings are included in one volume for each house. The journals of the first 13 congresses (1789–1815) were reprinted by separate orders of the House and Senate, and the reprints are the only copies generally available. For the first 13 congresses the reprint of the *House Journal* is in nine volumes and that of the *Senate Journal* in five volumes. For later years there is, as a rule, a separate volume of the journal of each house for each session, although the journals for the 3d and 4th sessions of the 67th Congress are included in one volume each for the Senate and the House. At the end of the *House Journal* for each session is a compilation of all rulings made on points of order.

The journals are included in the congressional set from the 15th to the 82d Congress, but prior to the passage of the act of June 25, 1938 (52 Stat. 1206), the library distribution was limited to three libraries in each state.

Each volume of both journals is indexed separately, by both subject matter and bill number. If information is desired regarding the action taken by either house, the journals will be found more convenient than the voluminous *Congressional Record*. The journals, however, do not contain any account of motions or proceedings in the Committee of the Whole, the record being confined to a report of the action taken by the Committee.

General indexes to the journals of the first 16 congresses are given in the following volumes:

General index of the journals of Congress, from the 1st to the 10th Congress, inclusive [1789–1809], by Albert Ordway, 1880, 151 pp. (H. Rept. 1776, 46 Cong. 2 sess.)

Same, from the 11th to the 16th Congress, inclusive [1809–21], by Albert Ordway, 1883, 118 pp. (H. Rept. 1559, 47 Cong. 1 sess.)

General personal index of the journals of Congress, from the 1st to the 8th Congress, inclusive [1789–1805], 1885, 134 pp. (H. Rept. 2692, 48 Cong. 2 sess.)

Same, from the 9th to the 16th Congress, inclusive [1805–21], 1887, 191 pp. (H. Rept. 3474, 49 Cong. 1 sess.)

The two volumes of general indexes to the journals contain also citations to the *Annals*, the *Statutes at Large*, *American State Papers*, the *Senate Documents*, the *House Documents*, and annual reports of executive officers. While the period covered by these indexes antedates the publication of the *Statutes at Large*, the indexes were not compiled until after the publication of that series.

Executive Journal of the Senate

The *Senate Journal* does not include proceedings in executive session. These are printed separately as the *Executive Journal* some years after the event by special order of the Senate. They have volume numbers, and the volumes cover unequal periods of time. There have been only seven printings of the *Executive Journal* authorized, as follows:

Order of Apr. 4, 1828. Journals of the 1st to the 19th Congress, 1789–1829, Vols. 1–3, printed by Duff Green. 700 copies.

Order of June 28, 1886. Journals of the 20th to the 40th Congress, 1829–69, Vols. 4–16 (Vols. 14 and 15 each in two parts). Only 18 of 125 copies printed were available for general distribution.

Order of Jan. 21, 1901. Journals of the 41st to the 51st Congress, 1869–91, Vols. 17–27. 150 copies printed.

Order relating to the 52d to the 58th Congress. Journals of the 52d to the 58th Congress, 1891–1905, Vols. 28–34 (Vols. 29 and 31 each in two parts). 250 copies printed.

Order of Feb. 28, 1931. Journals from the 59th Congress to end of the 71st Congress, 1905–31, Vols. 35–39. 500 copies printed.

Order of July 6, 1939. Provided for 500 copies of all journals beginning with the 72d Congress, 1st session, and continuing for each session thereafter.

Order of Feb. 9, 1950. Provided for disposing of volumes from Dec. 1, 1901, through Dec. 31, 1948. Also cut future printings to 50 copies of each volume.

Like the other journals, the *Executive Journal* does not contain any speeches, as it is confined to motions and actions. It is chiefly useful in determining the action taken on nominations, treaties, and other matters considered in executive session. Many of the executive sessions of the Senate are open sessions, and the proceedings and debates appear in the *Congressional Record*.

Issues of the *Executive Journal* form a separate series and do not constitute a part of any other series of congressional papers.

Extracts from the *Executive Journal* in cases of impeachment are given in *Extracts from the Journal of the Senate in All Cases of Impeachment, 1798–1904*, issued as Senate Document 876, 62d Congress, 2d session (594 pages). Those relative to treaties rejected by the Senate are given on pages 83–280 of Senate Document 26, 66th Congress, 1st session, which has the main title *Ratification of Treaties; Methods and Procedure in Foreign Countries relative to the Ratification of Treaties*.

Journals of the Continental Congress

The *Journals of the Continental Congress* were published contemporaneously and in several series of reprints. The contemporaneous prints were in 13 volumes, some of which were issued in several editions. The several volumes, the period indicated on the title page, and the name of the printer are as follows:

Vol. 1. Sept. 5, 1774–Jan. 1, 1776, Aitken
Vol. 2. 1776, Aitken
Vol. 2. Jan. 1, 1776–Jan. 1, 1777, Dunlap
Vol. 3. Jan. 1, 1777–Jan. 1, 1778, Dunlap
Vol. 3. Jan. 1, 1777–Jan. 1, 1778, Patterson
Vol. 4. Jan 1, 1778–Jan. 1, 1779, Claypoole
Vol. 5. Jan. 1, 1779–Jan. 1, 1780, Claypoole
[Vol. 6]. Jan. 1, 1780–Jan. 1, 1781, Claypoole
Vol. 6. 1780, Dunlap
Vol. 7. 1781, Claypoole
Vol. 7. 1781, Patterson
Vol. 8. From first Monday in November 1782 to first Monday in November 1783, Claypoole
Vol. 9. Nov. 3, 1783–June 3, 1784, Dunlap
[Vol. 10]. From first Monday in November 1784 [to Nov. 4, 1785], Dunlap
[Vol. 11]. Nov. 3, 1785–Nov. 3, 1786, Dunlap [this volume reads Vol. 12 on title page]
Vol. 12. Nov. 6, 1786–Nov. 5, 1787 [Dunlap]
Vol. 13. Nov. 5, 1787–Nov. 3, 1788, Dunlap

The reprints have been as follows: a 13-volume edition printed by Folwell in 1800 and 1801; a 4-volume edition printed by Way and Gideon in 1823; and the Library of Congress reprint in 34 volumes, begun in 1904 and completed in 1937.

The earlier editions of originals and reprints are not complete, as certain portions, known as the *Secret Journals,* were withheld from publication. These portions were published in four volumes by Wait in 1821. In the Library of Congress edition they appear in their proper chronological place without differentiation from the other proceedings.

As the volumes in the several editions cover different periods, the edition should be included in the citation. It is desirable to cite the date also in order that the action cited may be located easily in other editions.

Journals of the Congress of the Confederate States

The *Journals of the Congress of the Confederate States* have been printed in seven volumes as Senate Document 234, 58th Congress, 2d session.

Compilations of Debates and Proceedings

Occasionally the debates and proceedings over a period of years are assembled in a special compilation. The proceedings in the Senate from 1789 to 1911 relating to the election of the president pro tempore are given in *President of the Senate Pro Tempore*, 1911, issued as Senate Document 104, 62d Congress, 1st session (255 pages).

Agriculture Department

A guide to the debates up to 1911 on laws relating to the Department of Agriculture is afforded by *Index to Legislative History of Acts of Congress Involving the United States Department of Agriculture*, by Otis A. Gates, 1912 (53 pages). This compilation covers legislation from the act of July 26, 1866, to the act of March 4, 1911. The several steps of each bill are cited to the *Congressional Record*, with notations regarding the House and Senate reports.

Copyright

Lists of bills, reports, and documents, and chronological abstracts of proceedings relating to copyright are given in *Copyright in Congress, 1789–1904 . . .* , by Thorvald Solberg, 1905 (468 pages), published by the Library of Congress as Copyright Office Bulletin 8. The volume covers the period to January 27, 1905, although the title page reads April 28, 1904. A separate four-page addendum brings the record to the end of the 58th Congress on March 3, 1905.

Tariff

The speeches on the tariff bills from 1839 to 1857 and much

other material are given in *Tariff Proceedings and Documents, 1839–57*, 1911, issued as Senate Document 72, 62d Congress, 1st session (three volumes). The documents include messages of the President, reports of the Secretary of the Treasury, reprints of bills, memorials, statistics, tables of duties, and other matter.

The yea and nay votes in the Senate on several tariff bills have been assembled and published as follows:

Votes on reciprocity and tariff bills . . . during 1st session of 62d Congress, 1912, 57 pp. (S. Doc. 275, 62 Cong. 2 sess.)

Underwood-Simmons tariff bill [of 1913], yea and nay votes in Senate on all amendments . . . 1914, 155 pp. (S. Doc. 556, 63 Cong. 2 sess.)

Fordney-McCumber tariff bill of 1922, yea and nay votes in Senate on bill and all amendments . . . compiled by C. A. Loeffler, 1922, 418 pp. (S. Doc. 264, 67 Cong. 2 sess.)

Smoot-Hawley tariff bill of 1930, yea and nay votes in Senate . . . on bill and all amendments . . . compiled by C. A. Loeffler, 1930, 369 pp. (S. Doc. 177, 71 Cong. 2 sess.)

The debates, special reports, and other publications on reciprocity with Canada from 1848 to 1911 have been assembled in Senate Document 80, 62d Congress, 1st session (five volumes), entitled *Reciprocity with Canada, Compilation of 1911*. The compilation has no index and the volumes have inadequate tables of contents.

Trusts

Congressional activity on trusts from 1887 to 1913 is reflected in three volumes entitled *Bills and Debates in Congress relating to Trusts*. Volume 1 (pages 1–1113), issued as Senate Document 147, 57th Congress, 2d session, compiled by J. A. Finch, includes the bills and debates from the 50th Congress (1887) to the 1st session of the 57th Congress (1902). Volumes 2 and 3, compiled by J. J. Speight, were issued by the Judiciary Committee of the House of Representatives as committee publications. Volume 2 (pages 1115–2403) extends from the 2d session of the 57th Congress (1902) to the 61st Congress (1911).

Volume 3 (pages 2405–3408) extends from the 62d Congress (1911) to the 1st session of the 63d Congress (1913).

Documents and Reports

The House and Senate documents and the House and Senate reports comprise most of the collection variously known as the "congressional set," the "sheep set," the "serial number set," or the "congressional series." The *Congressional Record* and the *Senate* and *House Journals* are not a part of the congressional series.

For some time the reports have included only the reports of congressional committees. These reports deal with proposed legislation and contain findings on matters under investigation.[15] At times reports on investigations include testimony taken, but as a rule the congressional committee before which the testimony is heard orders it to be published separately as "hearings." (See pages 166–67 and 180–83.)

The documents include all other papers ordered printed by either house of Congress. These papers include many reports of executive departments and establishments. Some of these reports are submitted in accordance with permanent law, some result from resolutions calling on executive officers for information, and some are published in the series because a specified number is available for distribution by members of Congress.[16]

[15] A report as a rule does not indicate the membership of the committee since the chairman makes the report for the committee. In some cases the majority report does not indicate any dissenting report (see S. Rept. 1236, Pt. 2, 75 Cong. 1 sess., issued as a separate pamphlet and containing individual views of Senator Byrd). The committee memberships are given in the *Congressional Record* and the journals when the committees are appointed; they also appear in the *Congressional Directory* as of date of compilation. The membership changes from time to time, and for any times other than those given above, it is necessary to compile the changes from the *Congressional Record* or the journals. The lists of members of committees have been printed from time to time at the end of the daily edition of the *Congressional Record*, but these lists are used to fill out a signature and consequently do not appear at regular intervals.

[16] The duplication of publications is discussed on pp. 109–16.

The documents cover a wide variety of topics, an appreciable number being treatises on many subjects printed upon motion of members of Congress. For instance, the issues for the 70th Congress include such diverse matters as a report of the National Conference on Outdoor Recreation (S. Doc. 158), a committee report of the American Bar Association on judicial salaries (S. Doc. 188), a report on the sinking of the steamship *Vestris* (S. Doc. 177), prayers offered before the Senate (S. Doc. 266), and a monograph on proposed amendments to the Constitution (H. Doc. 551).[17]

The publications printed regularly not dealing with government activities have included the following:

American Instructors of the Deaf, proceedings of meetings, 22d (1920) and thereafter

American Legion, proceedings of national convention, 1924 and thereafter

Boy Scouts of America, annual report, 1918 and thereafter

Disabled American Veterans, proceedings of annual convention, 1930 and thereafter

Girl Scouts of America, annual report, 1950 and thereafter

Grand Army of the Republic, journal of annual encampment, 1914 through 1949 with a final journal covering 1866–1956

Military Order of the Purple Heart; reports were printed from 1941 through 1944

National Society of Daughters of the American Revolution, report, 1897 and thereafter

United Spanish War Veterans, proceedings of national encampment, 1924 and thereafter

Veterans of Foreign Wars of the United States, proceedings of national convention, 1925 and thereafter

Veterans of World War I of the United States, Inc., 1963 and thereafter

General Classification of Documents and Reports

The classification of congressional publications began with the 1st session of the 15th Congress. For the 15th Congress (1817–19), the classified publications are generally known as *House Documents* and *Senate Documents*. These names do not appear on the publications. The publications are merely desig-

[17] See the indexes described on pp. 6–27 for subject matter covered by the series.

nated by series numbers, one series of numbers for House publications and one series for Senate publications. During this congress the reports of congressional committees were published as documents, there being no publications entitled *Reports*.

For the 16th to the 29th Congress (1819–47), the classified publications were known as *House Documents, Senate Documents,* and *House Reports,* such reports of Senate committees as were published being issued as *Senate Documents.* The documents series included reports of the executive departments transmitted to Congress and miscellaneous publications originating in Congress other than committee reports.

A joint resolution approved August 3, 1846 (9 Stat. 113), prescribing the methods of procuring printing for Congress, apparently determined the classification for almost half a century. At that time government printing was done by contract, and the resolution provided that the printing of the respective houses should be classified as follows:

1. Bills and resolutions
2. Reports of committees
3. Journals
4. Executive documents [or reports made to Congress by the executive branch]
5. Every other description of printing [publications other than committee reports originating in Congress]

The application of this legislation evidently resulted in the six following series:

House Reports Senate Reports	Reports of committees
House Executive Documents Senate Executive Documents	Reports made to Congress by the executive branch
House Miscellaneous Documents Senate Miscellaneous Documents	All other publications except reports ordered by Congress or either house

This classification continued long after contract printing was abandoned, its period covering the 30th to the 53d Congress (1847–95), extending from December 6, 1847, to March 2, 1895.

The act of January 12, 1895 (28 Stat. 621), which was a revision of all the laws relating to public printing, provided for four series of documents and reports: *House Documents, Senate Documents, House Reports,* and *Senate Reports.* This law and classification are in effect at present.

The equivalents of the present series are as follows:

House Documents	House Documents, 15th to 29th Congress (1817–47) House Executive Documents and House Miscellaneous Documents, 30th to 53d Congress (1847–95) House Documents, 54th Congress (1895) and thereafter
Senate Documents	Senate Documents, 15th to 29th Congress (1817–47) Senate Executive Documents and Senate Miscellaneous Documents, 30th to 53d Congress (1847–95) Senate Documents, 54th Congress (1895) and thereafter
House Reports	House Documents, 15th Congress (1817–19) House Reports, 16th Congress (1819) and thereafter
Senate Reports	Senate Documents, 15th to 29th Congress (1817–47) Senate Reports, 30th Congress (1847) and thereafter

Although the classification of congressional publications began with the 1st session of the 15th Congress, only gradually did the complete series designation appear on the separate pamphlets. Many volumes have no title pages, and the back titles often are too indefinite to be of value. The safest guide to proper citation of the series is to follow the classification as given on pages 5 and following of the *Checklist.*

Three series of numbers have been used in connection with the documents and the reports series: (1) the number given the individual publication; (2) the numbers given to volumes of each series for each session; and (3) the serial number. Documents and reports should always be cited by the number of the individual publication and not by volume number or serial number.

Numbering of Individual Documents and Reports

The individual documents and reports have had numbers beginning with the 15th Congress (1817), but the method of numbering has not been uniform. At times the numbers have run consecutively through all sessions of a congress, while at other times they have begun with 1 at each session. The practice has been as follows:

Senate and House documents: 15th to 59th Congress (1817–1907), new series of numbers for each session; 60th Congress (1907) and thereafter, consecutive numbers throughout the congress

Senate reports: 30th Congress (1847) and thereafter,[18] consecutive numbers throughout the congress

House reports: 16th to 46th Congress (1819–81),[19] new series of numbers for each session; 47th Congress (1881) and thereafter, consecutive numbers throughout the congress

For periods during which the numbers begin with 1 for each session, the congress and session form essential parts of the series number and should be included in a citation. If the numbers run consecutively through a congress, the publication can be identified without the session number but, as the session number appears on the publication, its inclusion in a citation is desirable for several reasons. The printing of the session number on the publication makes it a part of the series designation, which is therefore not complete unless it is given. The use of the session number also frequently facilitates locating the document or report. Moreover, since it is not easy to remember the congresses during which the session number is significant, the inclusion of the session number facilitates the making of citations and reduces the possibility of error.

It should be noted that one document number may be used for several books, each book being given a second number as

[18] Senate reports began with the 30th Congress (1847). Previously the committee reports were in the document series.

[19] House reports began with the 16th Congress (1819). Previously the committee reports were in the document series.

a "part." At times the several books are parts of one publication, as in the case of the *Report of the Coal Commission of 1922*, which was issued as Senate Document 195 of the 68th Congress, 2d session, the separate books being designated as Parts 1 to 5. At other times unrelated publications have been given the same document number, being divided into parts and again subdivided into volumes and parts. House Executive Document 1 of the 1st session of the 51st Congress, for instance, was published in 21 subdivisions, as follows:

Pt. 1. President's Message and Foreign Relations
Pt. 2. Report of the Secretary of War, Vol. 1
Pt. 2 [*Con.*]. Report of the Secretary of War, Vol. 2, Report of the Chief of Engineers, Pt. 1
Pt. 2 [*Con.*]. Report of the Secretary of War, Vol. 2 [*Con.*]. Report of the Chief of Engineers, Pt. 2
Pt. 2. [*Con.*]. Report of the Secretary of War, Vol. 2 [*Con.*]. Report of the Chief of Engineers, Pt. 3
Pt. 2 [*Con.*]. Report of the Secretary of War, Vol. 2 [*Con.*]. Report of the Chief of Engineers, Pt. 4
Pt. 2 [*Con.*]. Report of the Secretary of War, Vol. 3. Report of the Chief of Ordnance
Pt. 2 [*Con.*]. Report of the Secretary of War, Vol. 4. Report of the Chief Signal Officer
Pt. 3. Report of the Secretary of the Navy, Vol. 1
Pt. 3 [*Con.*]. Report of the Secretary of the Navy, Vol. 2
Pt. 4. Report of the Postmaster General
Pt. 5. Report of the Secretary of the Interior, Vol. 1. Secretary and Public Lands
Pt. 5 [*Con.*]. Report of the Secretary of the Interior, Vol. 2. Indian Affairs
Pt. 5 [*Con.*]. Report of the Secretary of the Interior, Vol. 3. Miscellaneous
Pt. 5 [*Con.*]. Report of the Secretary of the Interior, Vol. 4. Report of the Director of the Geological Survey, Pt. 1
Pt. 5 [*Con.*]. Report of the Secretary of the Interior, Vol. 4 [*Con.*] Report of the Director of the Geological Survey, Pt. 2
Pt. 5 [*Con.*]. Report of the Secretary of the Interior, Vol. 5. Report of the Commissioner of Education, Pt. 1
Pt. 5 [*Con.*]. Report of the Secretary of the Interior, Vol. 5 [*Con.*]. Report of the Commissioner of Education, Pt. 2
Pt. 6. Report of the Commissioners of the District of Columbia
Pt. 7. Report of the Secretary of Agriculture
Pt. 8. Report of the Civil Service Commission

Later the reports for each department were given separate document numbers but the subdivision into volumes and parts was continued.

Indexing of Documents and Reports

Prior to the 54th Congress each volume of documents and reports contained an index for the session to the particular series contained in the volume, but there was no general index covering all the series. From the 54th to the 72d Congress the documents and reports are listed and indexed by sessions in the annual *Document Index*. For the 73d Congress and thereafter they are listed but not indexed in the *Numerical Lists*. These publications do not include committee documents or Senate executive documents and reports. There are no other separate indexes exclusively for documents and reports, but information regarding them may be obtained from the general and periodic catalogs and indexes discussed in Chapter 2. The listing and indexing of reports are also discussed on page 179.

If a complete citation is not available, the individual documents and reports may be identified in the manner described below.

If the number (the congress and session being an essential part of the number) is known, the title may be ascertained as follows:

15th to 54th Congress, 2d session (1817–97). There are no complete numerical lists prior to the 2d session of the 54th Congress, but the titles of the more important or voluminous publications issued from the 15th to the 60th Congress (1817–1909) may be obtained from the "Congressional Tables" on pages 5–169 of the *Checklist*. Pages 16–109 of *Tables and Index* contain similar information for the 15th to the 52d Congress (1817–93), but there are few notations on reports and not many on documents. *Poore's Catalogue* may be used as a last resort for publications issued prior to 1881. The items in Poore are arranged chronologically regardless of numerical sequence or series, and it may take some time to find the item desired. It should be noted that, if several annual reports are printed in one publication, a separate entry is made for each one, and that the titles given in Poore are often descriptive rather than literal. In some cases the citation "Senate Document" or "House Document" is used without indication as to whether the publication is a miscellaneous document or an executive document. In other cases the citation is "Executive Document," without indication as to whether it is a House or a Senate document.

54th Congress, 2d session, to 72d Congress (1897–1933). Numerical lists at end of each annual *Document Index.*

65th Congress (1917) to 76th Congress (1940). Consult the entry "Congressional Documents Lists" in each biennial *Document Catalog.* There are two of these lists. In the first the publications are arranged by document and report numbers with cross references to the subject entries. In the second the listing is by volume and serial numbers. The second list is of no assistance in finding the title unless each volume contains only one document or report.

73d Congress (1933) and thereafter. *Numerical Lists,* which is issued annually by the Superintendent of Documents and which supersedes the annual *Document Index.* Prior to the publication of the *Numerical Lists,* there is no convenient method of obtaining the titles of documents and reports if the series number only is known. All issues are listed in the *Monthly Catalog.*

If the title is known, the number may be ascertained from the subject entries in the sources given below:

Prior to the 47th Congress (1881). *Poore's Catalogue,* but, as noted above, the citations there are not always complete.

15th to 52d Congress (1817–93). *Tables and Index,* but the index in this publication does not have entries for all documents and reports.

47th to 53d Congress (1881–94). *Ames Index.*

54th Congress (1895) and thereafter. Annual *Document Index* up to the end of the 72d Congress and the biennial *Document Catalog* up to the end of the 76th Congress. All documents and reports are listed in the *Monthly Catalog* serially and in the monthly and annual indexes of the *Monthly Catalog* by subject.

Volume Numbers

The documents and reports were assembled in volumes beginning with the 1st session of the 15th Congress (1817), and this practice has continued to the present day. Title pages were not always used, but the present practice is to provide title pages and tables of contents where needed for all volumes containing several documents or reports, and title pages are always provided for all volumes of the official set maintained by the United States Government.[20]

As a rule the volumes in each series are numbered consecutively, beginning with Volume 1 for each session, although in some of the earlier publications the volume number appears neither on the title page nor on the back title. Occasional publications ordered printed by Congress or by either house which were not assigned to any series do not bear the volume number. From the 3d session of the 58th Congress (1904) to the 3d session of the 75th Congress (1938) the volumes containing reports on private bills and simple and concurrent resolutions were designated alphabetically, starting with Volume A for each series in every session. Beginning with the 1st session of the 76th Congress (1939) the volumes containing these reports were again designated numerically. For classification purposes the term "private bills" was defined by law to mean "all bills for the relief of private parties, bills granting pensions, bills removing political disabilities, and bills for the survey of rivers and harbors."

Of more importance than the reports on private bills are those on resolutions. Frequently a simple resolution directs a committee to make an investigation on a matter of public interest. Under the law in force since 1904 all such reports were assembled in the volumes containing reports on private bills, and must be sought there.

As the reports were thus arbitrarily divided, they did not appear in numerical sequence in the several books. The documents likewise do not appear in numerical sequence, since from the beginning an endeavor has been made to keep the books of a fairly uniform thickness. Thus in the *House Documents* for the 2d session of the 15th Congress (1818), Nos. 31–

[20] A list by sessions, from the 15th to the 60th Congress, but not by volumes, showing wording of title pages or absence of title pages, is given on pp. 175-84 of the *Checklist*. It should be noted that many volumes have title pages reading "Index to" the several classes of documents and reports. This does not mean that the volumes contain only the indexes. The title pages for indexes which are in the front of the volumes are the only ones in the books and constitute misleading title pages for the volumes.

46 and 48 appear in Volume 2, while No. 47 comprises Volume 3. The volume number does not always indicate a single book, as at times the same number was assigned to several books and at times to all the books that were parts of one document number. Thus the 21 subdivisions of House Executive Document 1 (51st Congress, 1st session) listed on page 155, were bound in 20 books, which were numbered Volumes 1–18, but Volume 18 also contained Part 8 of Document 1 and Documents 4 and 7; Volumes 14 and 15 were in two parts.

The final volumes of the Eleventh Census made 30 books, all of which were published as parts of Volume 50 of *House Miscellaneous Documents* for the 1st session of the 52d Congress. All the volumes are also parts of Document 340, but the parts assigned to subdivisions of the volume number do not correspond to the parts assigned to the document number. In fact, the 30 books make Parts 1–19 of the volume number, and Parts 1–29 of the document number. Eleven parts (2, 3, 5, 8–13, 16, and 19) of the document number are missing, as they were never published. The subdivisions of Volume 50 and the corresponding subdivisions of Document 340 are as follows:

Pt. 1. Mineral Industries. (Doc. 340, Pt. 1)
Pt. 2. Wealth, Debt, and Taxation. Pt. 1, Public Debt. (Doc. 340, Pt. 4)
Pt. 2 [*Con.*]. Wealth, Debt, and Taxation. Pt. 2, Valuation and Taxation. (Doc. 340, Pt. 4 [*Con.*])
Pt. 3. Compendium. Pt. 1, Population. (Doc. 340, Pt. 6)
Pt. 4. Compendium. Pt. 2, Vital and Social Statistics, etc. (Doc. 340, Pt. 6 [*Con.*])
Pt. 4 [*Con.*]. Compendium. Pt. 3, Population, etc. (Doc. 340, Pt. 6 [*Con.*])
Pt. 5. Insurance Business. Pt. 1, Fire, Marine, and Inland Insurance. (Doc. 340, Pt. 14)
Pt. 5. [*Con.*]. Insurance Business. Pt. 2, Life Insurance. (Doc. 340, Pt. 14 [*Con.*])
Pt. 6. Indians. (Doc. 340, Pt. 15)
Pt. 7. Churches. (Doc. 340, Pt. 17)
Pt. 8. Population. Pt. 1. (Doc. 340, Pt. 18)
Pt. 8 [*Con.*]. Population. Pt. 2 [and report on education]. (Doc. 340, Pt. 18 [*Con.*])
Pt. 9. Alaska. (Doc. 340, Pt. 7)
Pt. 10. Agriculture, Irrigation, and Fisheries. (Doc. 340, Pt. 20)

Pt. 11. Transportation Business. Pt. 1, By Land. (Doc. 340, Pt. 21)

Pt. 11 [*Con.*]. Transportation Business. Pt. 2, By Water. (Doc. 340, Pt. 21 [*Con.*])

Pt. 12. Manufacturing Industries. Pt. 1, Totals for States and Industries. (Doc. 340, Pt. 22)

Pt. 12 [*Con.*]. Manufacturing Industries. Pt. 2, Statistics of Cities. (Doc. 340, Pt. 22 [*Con.*])

Pt. 12 [*Con.*]. Manufacturing Industries. Pt. 3, Selected Industries. (Doc. 340, Pt. 22 [*Con.*])

Pt. 13. Real Estate Mortgages. (Doc. 340, Pt. 23)

Pt. 14. Crime, Pauperism, and Benevolence. Pt. 1, Analysis. (Doc. 340, Pt. 24)

Pt. 14 [*Con.*]. Crime, Pauperism, and Benevolence. Pt. 2, General Tables. (Doc. 340, Pt. 24 [*Con.*])

Pt. 15. Farms and Homes. (Doc. 340, Pt. 25)

Pt. 16. Insane, Feeble-minded, Deaf and Dumb, and Blind. (Doc. 340, Pt. 26)

Pt. 17. Occupations. (Doc. 340, Pt. 27)

Pt. 18. Vital and Social Statistics. Pt. 1, Analysis and Rate Tables. (Doc. 340, Pt. 28)

Pt. 18 [*Con.*]. Vital and Social Statistics. Pt. 2, Vital Statistics, Cities of 100,000 Population and Upward. (Doc. 340, Pt. 28 [*Con.*])

Pt. 18 [*Con.*]. Vital and Social Statistics. Pt. 3, Statistics of Deaths. (Doc. 340, Pt. 28 [*Con.*])

Pt. 18 [*Con.*]. Vital and Social Statistics. Pt. 4, Statistics of Deaths [*Con.*]. (Doc. 340, Pt. 28 [*Con.*])

Pt. 19. Statistical Atlas. (Doc. 340, Pt. 29)

This subdivision into parts probably arises from the fact that a publication is authorized or ordered but not completed during a certain session and when the schedule of volumes is prepared definite information is not always available regarding the number of books.

If several publications are bound in one volume, there is no volume pagination. Therefore, citation to the volume number is not generally advisable, a preferable citation being to the separate document or report, which must be known in order to locate the publication in the volume. Moreover, for many years, the volume number has been omitted from the back titles of books distributed to depository libraries and placed only on the sets bound for the Library of Congress, the Public Documents Library, the libraries of the Senate and the House of Representatives, and the National Archives. Beginning with the 60th Congress, the volume number was omitted from books distributed to depository libraries for documents that were also printed as department publications. Beginning with the 68th Congress (1923) it was omitted from back titles of all books containing documents and reports.[21]

If the citation is to the volume number and the volume contains only one document or report, the title may be obtained from the following sources:[22]

15th to 67th Congress (1817–1923). Pages 979–1210 of the 1924 edition of the *Senate Catalogue;* also earlier editions for shorter periods
15th to 60th Congress (1817–1909). Pages 5–169 of the *Checklist*
15th to 52d Congress (1817–93). Pages 16–109 of the *Tables and Index*
47th to 52d Congress (1881–93). Pages 274–93 of Volume 1 of the *Ames Index*
53d to 76th Congress (1893–1941). Entries "Congressional Documents" or "Congressional Documents Lists" in biennial *Document Catalog.* Beginning with the *Catalog* for the 65th Congress (1917) there are two lists under this entry, the second being arranged by volume numbers and giving the title if the volume contains only one publication
54th to 72d Congress (1895–1933). Schedules at end of annual *Document Index*
73d Congress (1933) and thereafter. Schedules at end of annual issues of *Numerical Lists*

The sources cited above also indicate the numbers of the individual documents and reports contained in each volume and the serial numbers assigned to the several volumes.

Serial Numbers

The serial number is a number applied to each book in the congressional series of publications, the numbers running consecutively beginning with the 15th Congress (1817). It has not been possible to apply it to the first 14 congresses (1789–1817),

[21] For detailed information regarding changes in the numbering of books distributed to depository libraries, see pp. 124–29.
[22] In many cases these lists give the subject matter of the volume rather than the title.

as the publications were not assembled in book form. A special series of numbers, 01 to 038, has been applied to the volumes known as *American State Papers*, which contain reprints of the publications of the first 14 congresses, as well as those of some later congresses. The only other congressional publications not given serial numbers are the reports on private bills for the 3d session of the 58th Congress (1904–05) and the two sessions of the 59th Congress (1905–07). After the passage of the joint resolution of January 20, 1905 (33 Stat. 610), the volumes containing these reports were no longer available to depository libraries and consequently they were not assigned serial numbers. Beginning with the 60th Congress (1907) these volumes were again given serial numbers, but their distribution to depository libraries was not resumed until the 76th Congress (1939), pursuant to the act of June 25, 1938 (52 Stat. 1206).

The serial number applies to the documents and the reports, but it has never been applied to the *Congressional Record* or its predecessors. Prior to the 83d Congress, serial numbers were given to the *House* and *Senate Journals*, although they did not belong with the documents and reports, being more closely akin to the *Congressional Record*. The serial number should not be confused with the separate series numbers of the documents and the reports, which include the number of the congress and session as a part of the designation (see page 154). It is a continuing number regardless of congress or series and is a complete designation of itself.

The sets of congressional publications in the Library of Congress, the National Archives, and the Public Documents Library are arranged according to the serial numbers, and the numbers are stamped on the books, but the serial number may not appear on many of the volumes available in libraries outside of Washington. The plan was developed by John G. Ames in the last decade of the 19th century. Necessarily the serial number did not appear on the original binding of volumes issued earlier; but in libraries where the serial classification is used the numbers have been added. Many of the publications that are listed in the document catalogs and document indexes as forming part of the congressional series have been sent to the depository libraries without serial numbers or in volumes that did not correspond to the serial number classification.[23]

The serial number is not suitable for citation, as the volumes represented by many numbers contain several publications with separate pagination. Furthermore, the complete serial number sets are available in only a limited number of libraries. The serial numbers, however, afford a convenient and quick method of locating publications in libraries in which the books are arranged according to this plan—notably in the Library of Congress, the National Archives, and the Public Documents Library.

While each serial number generally represents a single book, there are cases in which the same number is applied to several books, the differentiation being by a letter, a superior number, or a volume number. In the case of earlier issues, this probably resulted from the fact that a publication was overlooked when the list was originally prepared; in the case of later ones it results from the fact that the work was not completed when the numbers were originally assigned, and more than one book was needed for a particular work.

The serial numbers follow the sequence of the volume numbers for each series in each session, but the sequence of series has not always been the same. The arrangement at various times has been as follows:

> 15th Congress (1817–19)
> > Senate Journal
> > Senate Documents
> > House Journal
> > House Documents
>
> 16th to 29th Congress (1819–47)
> > Senate Journal
> > Senate Documents
> > House Journal
> > House Documents
> > House Reports
>
> 30th to 53d Congress (1847–95)
> > Senate Journal
> > Senate Executive Documents

[23] For information regarding changes in the numbering of congressional publications sent to depository libraries, see pp. 124–29.

Senate Miscellaneous Documents
Senate Reports
House Journal
House Executive Documents
House Miscellaneous Documents
House Reports
54th Congress to 57th Congress, 1st session (1895–1902)
Senate Journal
Senate Documents
Senate Reports
House Journal
House Documents
House Reports
57th Congress, 2d session, to 82d Congress (1902–52)
Senate Journal
House Journal
Senate Reports
House Reports
Senate Documents
House Documents
83d Congress and thereafter (1953–)
Senate Reports
House Reports
Senate Documents
House Documents

As the serial number applies to the same material as the volume number, the documents and reports do not appear in numerical sequence. Serial numbers have been assigned to the *Senate* and *House Journals,* but this practice was discontinued with the 83d Congress, 1st session. Serial numbers have been assigned to a few other early volumes which do not carry document or volume numbers. An example of this is the index to House documents and reports for the 22d to the 25th Congress, which carries Serial Number 350.

If the serial number is given as a citation and the volume contains only one document or report, the title may be found by consulting the sources given below.[24]

15th to 67th Congress (1817–1923): Pages 979–1210 of the 1924 edition of the *Senate Catalogue;* also earlier editions for shorter periods

---

[24] In many cases these lists give the subject matter of the volume rather than the title.

15th to 60th Congress (1817–1909): Pages 5–169 of the *Checklist*

15th to 52d Congress (1817–93): Pages 16–109 of the *Tables and Index*

47th to 52d Congress (1881–93): Pages 274–93 of Volume 1 of the *Ames Index*

54th to 75th Congress (1895–1938): Under "Congressional Documents List" in biennial *Document Catalog*. The serial number appears in brackets at the end of the entry; beginning with the *Document Catalog* for the 65th Congress (1917) there are two lists under this entry, the second being arranged by volume and serial numbers and giving the title if the volume contains only one publication

55th to 72d Congress (1897–1933): Schedule at end of each annual *Document Index*. Prior to the volume for the 1st session of the 56th Congress, the serial number appears in brackets at the end of each entry

73d Congress (1933) and thereafter: Schedule at end of annual *Numerical Lists*

The foregoing references show the numbers of the individual documents and reports contained in each book in the serial number set and also the equivalent volume numbers. They may be used to ascertain the serial set number if the individual document or report number or the volume number is known.

As the assemblage of the documents and the reports in books is determined largely by the format and number of pages, the numbers of individual documents and reports are not always continuous in the book. All of the lists cited above are arranged by the serial numbers with notations showing the documents and the reports included. It is therefore necessary to examine a complete list in order to locate the volume desired. Thus the *Checklist* includes the following information on the *House Miscellaneous Documents* for the 1st session of the 47th Congress:

Serial Number	Documents in Book
2035	1–7, 9, 10, 12, 13
2036	8, 53
2037	11
2038	14, 2 pts.; 15, 2 pts.
2039	16–18, 21

Likewise, the list shows that Serial Number 2069 contains House Reports 1277–1617, but the annotation in another column states that Reports 1325 and 1465 were not printed, and that Report 1559 is in Serial Number 2071.

The subject entries in the *Document Catalog* beginning with the 56th Congress (1899) and in the *Document Index* beginning with the 1st session of the 68th Congress (1923) contain references to the serial number.

Senate Executive Documents and Reports

The Senate has a series generally known as *Senate Executive Documents,* with an alphabetical instead of a numerical designation, and another series known as *Senate Executive Reports,* which is numbered. Individual documents are headed "— Congress — Session. Confidential. Executive —." They contain treaties submitted to the Senate with the correspondence from the President and the Secretary of State. Individual Senate executive reports are headed "In Executive Session, Senate of the United States — Congress — Session. Senate Report No. —." They contain the reports of the Committee on Foreign Relations. Both are confidential publications and are not available until released by order of the Senate. Being confidential, neither is listed in the *Monthly Catalog* unless made public when printed. The executive documents and the executive reports do not form part of the regular series of Senate documents and reports and they are not distributed to depository libraries.

Hearings

Hearings contain the transcript of testimony given before committees. Technically speaking they are not publications of Congress, as they are not ordered by either house. They are the most important publications originating in Congress, however, and the most elusive, owing to inadequate methods of distribution.

The testimony given before committees is not always printed, although the publication of transcripts of hearings has increased during recent years. Occasionally hearings are printed as documents or as parts of reports. The printing is ordered by the committee, and usually the entire stock is delivered to it except for the copies which are sent to depository libraries and those occasional hearings which are placed on sale by the Superintendent of Documents at the request of the committee. Copies may generally be obtained from the committee as long as the supply lasts, but it is not always possible to secure older issues, as a new committee clerk may consign the accumulated stock to the waste basket.

The hearings do not constitute a real series, although the word "Hearings" generally appears on the title page. Some committees have given a serial designation to their publications for their own convenience, too often to the mystification of the user, but there is no uniformity in designation. Some are designated numerically, some alphabetically; some series run through a session, some through a congress, and some continuously.[25] Some committees now number their hearings by Congresses, with a number for the Congress followed by consecutive numbers for each hearing.

Other Committee Publications

Among the vagaries of committee printing is a series of numbered documents published by some of the committees. These are headed "House of Representatives, Committee on ——, Document No. —." Care must be taken not to confuse them with the regular series of *House Documents*.

At times the committees issue numbered publications, which, in addition to the name of the committee and the title, contain the series designation "— Congress, — Session, Senate Committee Print No. —." These form an independent series. Some committee prints are issued without series designations or numbering. Committee prints frequently contain material prepared just for the use of the committee. Copies are not sent to depositories and are not sold by the Superintendent of Documents

[25] Information on indexes to and lists of hearings is given on pp. 180–83.

unless the committee issuing the publications makes a specific request. Some committee prints are preliminary publications which are later printed, often with revisions, as *House Documents, House Reports, Senate Documents,* or *Senate Reports.* Others are released to the press and to the public and are never printed as *Documents* or *Reports.* In rare instances committee prints have been disapproved by the committee and all copies ordered destroyed. Word of these leaks out and librarians spend much time vainly attempting to obtain copies. In exceptional cases a committee may send a copy of a committee print to the Superintendent of Documents to be listed in the *Monthly Catalog,* and in other cases a committee may arrange for a committee print to be placed on sale. Certain libraries in cooperation with the Library of Congress and the American Library Association have established a Documents Expediting Project in Washington to obtain for the subscribing libraries committee prints and other government publications not available through regular channels. The Documents Expediting Project furnishes copies of committee prints to the Superintendent of Documents, and these are listed in the *Monthly Catalog* after permission is secured from the issuing committee.

Committee publications issued prior to 1910 are listed under the names of the respective committees on pages 1532–1652 of the *Checklist.* Later issues are listed in the biennial *Document Catalog* under the names of the committees and the subject matter; current issues are listed in the *Monthly Catalog* under the names of the committees.

Bills and Resolutions

Bills and resolutions have been printed for many years, and current ones may generally be obtained from senators and representatives. It is usually impossible to secure bills introduced in previous congresses. Files of bills and resolutions of previous sessions are available for consultation in the Library of Congress, the Office of the Clerk of the House of Representatives, the Office of the Secretary of the Senate, and the National Archives and Records Service. The copies in the Library of Congress are bound, but the files are not complete for earlier years.

Bills and resolutions are numbered in series beginning with each congress. A bill or resolution introduced at one session of a congress may be acted on during any subsequent session of the same congress, but all bills and resolutions die at the end of a congress.[26] The several series and the abbreviations appearing on them are as follows:

Senate:
Bills (S.)
Resolutions (S. Res.)
Joint resolutions (S. J. Res.)
Concurrent resolutions (S. Con. Res.)
House of Representatives:
Bills (H. R.)
Resolutions (H. Res.)
Joint resolutions (H. J. Res.)
Concurrent resolutions (H. Con. Res.)

A bill is the usual form in which legislation is formally proposed. After passage and approval or passage over veto all bills become laws. The legal effect of joint resolutions is the same as that of bills. With the exception of those proposing amendments to the Constitution, they are signed by the President, and become laws after enactment.[27] They "are used for what may be called the incidental, unusual, or inferior purposes of legislating."[28]

A resolution, generally known as a simple resolution, may affect only the business, procedure, or organization of the house to which it relates, including its committees and em-

[26] The numbering of bills apparently started during the 15th Congress. It seems that beginning with that congress House bills were numbered continuously through a congress, and remained alive beyond the first session. Until the 30th Congress, Senate bills were numbered beginning with 1 for each session and appear to have died at the end of the session.

[27] However, several joint resolutions proposing amendments have been signed by the President.

[28] See footnote 6, p. 209.

ployees. A concurrent resolution is used for matters in which the two houses are interested, but which do not have the force of law. It is used for such matters as joint sessions, the appointment of joint committees, adjournment for more than three days, etc.

There are probably more bills introduced in the Congress of the United States than in any other legislative body in the world. Only a small percentage become laws, and most of them never receive serious consideration.

A bill or resolution is introduced by a member and ordinarily is immediately referred to a committee. By constitutional requirement all bills for raising revenue originate in the House of Representatives and by long-established custom the general appropriation bills originate in the same body, but there is no constitutional provision requiring this practice and at times bills making specific appropriations originate in the Senate.

The various printings and the distinctive headings of a House bill are described below. The procedure is the same in the case of a Senate bill, except that "Senate" is substituted for "House of Representatives" at corresponding stages. Joint and concurrent resolutions are printed in a similar form.

When introduced a bill is given a number which it retains through all its stages. The first print, made when the bill is introduced, bears the following headings:

86th Congress
2d Session

H. R. 15269

IN THE HOUSE OF REPRESENTATIVES
February 11, 1960

Mr. . . . introduced the following bill; which was referred to the Committee on Interstate and Foreign Commerce and ordered to be printed

A BILL

To extend [etc., title of bill]

Few bills proceed beyond the stage described above, and many are not given consideration by the committees. Often hearings are held, and the transcript of the hearing may be printed (see page 166). Notice of hearings of House committees open to the public is generally printed in the *Congressional Record* a day in advance.

When the committee has concluded its consideration of a bill, a report is made and the bill is generally printed a second time, although this print may be omitted if the committee does not recommend changes. In this print the changes made by the committee are indicated by printing new matter in italics and by canceling the portions to be omitted. The bill is then ready for consideration by the House. The headings in this print are as follows:

House Calendar[29] No. 531

86th Congress
2d Session

H. R. 15269
[Report No. 2003]

IN THE HOUSE OF REPRESENTATIVES
February 11, 1960

Mr. . . . introduced the following bill; which was referred to the Committee on Interstate and Foreign Commerce and ordered to be printed

April 8, 1960

Reported with an amendment,[30] referred to the House Calendar,[31] and ordered to be printed

A BILL

To extend [etc., title of bill]

After the bill passes the House it goes to the Senate, where it is again printed. It should be noted that the bill as passed by

---

[29] Or "Private Calendar" or "Union Calendar."

[30] If there are no amendments the words "reported with an amendment" are omitted.

[31] Or "committed to the Committee of the Whole House" or "committed to the Committee of the Whole House on the State of the Union."

one house is not printed by that house, but is printed when received by the other house. After the bill has passed one house the heading is changed from "A Bill" to "An Act." The writer has never been able to ascertain why this change is made at this stage. The headings are then as follows:

86th Congress
2d Session

H. R. 15269

IN THE SENATE OF THE UNITED STATES

April 14 (calendar day, April 18), 1960

Read twice and referred to the Committee on Commerce

AN ACT

To extend [etc., title of bill]

When the Senate committee reports the bill it is again printed, and if amended the new language is indicated by italics and the deletions by a canceling line. The headings are as follows:

Calendar No. 1558

86th Congress
2d Session

H. R. 15269

[Report No. 1533]

IN THE SENATE OF THE UNITED STATES
April 14 (calendar day, April 18), 1960

Read twice and referred to the Committee on Commerce
April 29,1960

Reported by Mr. . . ., without amendment[32]

AN ACT

To extend [etc., title of bill]

This is generally the last print available for distribution. In the case of appropriation and other bills on which the two houses are in disagreement, another print is often made when

[32] Or "with amendments."

the bill is returned to the House. This print gives the text of the bill as it passed the House and shows the amendments made by the Senate. The portions stricken out by the Senate are indicated by a canceling line, and the new wording is printed in italics, each amendment being numbered. This print is headed as follows:

86th Congress
2d Session

H. R. 15269

IN THE HOUSE OF REPRESENTATIVES
March 21, 1960

Ordered to be printed with the amendments of the Senate numbered

AN ACT

To extend [etc., title of bill]

The bill then goes to a conference committee consisting of members appointed by the two houses. The report of the conference committee is printed in the *Congressional Record* and is generally printed separately by one or both houses. If printed by the House it appears in the report series; if printed by the Senate, in the document series. If either house rejects a conference report in part, there may be a second report on the items still in disagreement.

The final print, which is not for public distribution, is in the form in which the bill has been agreed to by the two houses. This is the enrolled print which goes to the President for his signature and, after being signed or becoming law without being signed, is filed in the National Archives. An exact copy of this print, even to typographical errors in enrollment, is printed, generally from the same type, in the slip laws and the *Statutes at Large*.

If a bill is vetoed and returned to Congress, the text of the bill is generally printed in the document containing the veto message, and occasionally in the *Congressional Record* and the journals of the two houses. If the adjournment of Congress prevents the return of the bill and it fails by reason of a pocket veto, no print of the bill in the form in which it was presented to the President is available. In such a case the final form must be built up from the latest print and amendments as shown by the *Congressional Record* or the journals.

A general appropriation bill is printed somewhat differently in the initial stage. Ordinarily the House Committee on Appropriations holds hearings in advance of the introduction of the bill, and the form in which it is to be reported is determined before it is introduced. It is then introduced by a member of the committee, generally the chairman of the subcommittee in charge of the bill. There is no print of it as introduced, because it is immediately reported and printed with the following notation:

Mr. . . . from the Committee on Appropriations, reported the following bill; which was committed to the Committee on the Whole House on the State of the Union and ordered to be printed.

This print corresponds to the second print of other bills; the subsequent prints are in the forms noted above.

Legislative History

The steps in the enactment of legislation begin with the introduction of a bill (or joint resolution) in either house and its reference to a committee. During the consideration of the bill the committee may hold hearings, which may or may not be printed. The committee then makes a report; the bill goes on the calendar, is discussed on the floor, and is passed or rejected.

It then goes to the other house, where the same steps are taken. If the bill is amended in the other house, it goes back to the house in which it originates and the amendments may be debated on the floor. If they are accepted, the bill goes to the President for his signature; if they are not agreed to, the bill goes to a conference committee consisting of members from each house.[33] After the conferees report, either house may

[33] See Ada C. McCown, *The Congressional Conference Committee*, Columbia University Press, 1927 (275 pp.).

again debate the bill and there may be several conference reports before it is finally passed or rejected.

If the President signs the bill while Congress is in session, he notifies the house in which it originates and it is then printed as a slip law. If he vetoes the bill while Congress is in session, he returns it with his objections to the house in which it originated. Each house then votes on passing the bill over the veto. If Congress is in session and the President does not sign the bill within ten days, the bill becomes law without his signature. If Congress has adjourned and the President does not sign the bill within the ten-day period, the bill fails to become law. This is known as a pocket veto.[34]

There are two variations in the procedure outlined above. If a special rule limiting debate or restricting amendments in the House of Representatives is proposed, the House Committee on Rules may hold hearings and bring in a special report. The Committee on Rules also has jurisdiction over proposals to create committees to make investigations. Therefore the

[34] The power of the President to sign after adjournment has been established. In 1886 President Cleveland made the following notation on a resolution after adjournment: "This resolution reached me five minutes after the adjournment of the two houses of Congress, and is the only enactment of the session which came to me too late for official action" (H. Doc. 493, 70 Cong. 2 sess., p. 28). The power to sign after adjournment was finally settled in 1932 in the case of *Edwards* v. *United States* (286 U. S. 482).

In 1936 Congress adjourned sine die on June 20, but Public Law 849 (49 Stat. 2041) was not approved until July 13, after an interval of twenty-three days. The language of the Constitution regarding the period allowed the President was "ten days (Sundays excepted) after it [the bill or resolution] shall have been presented to him." In this case the bill was not received by the President until July 11, and he had ten days from that date in which to sign. (For account of the circumstances see *American Political Science Review*, Vol. 33, pp. 52-54.)

For validity of pocket vetoes see *The Pocket Veto Case* (279 U.S. 655) decided in 1929. In *Wright* v. *United States* (302 U.S. 583), decided in 1938, the Supreme Court held that a recess of one house was not an adjournment in the sense used in the Constitution.

On January 25, 1939, Representative Sumners introduced a bill (H. R. 3233, 76 Cong.) to repeal all bills and joint resolutions which prior to the beginning of the 76th Congress had been presented to the President less than 10 days prior to an adjournment (other than a final adjournment at the end of a congress). For summary of the Wright case and explanation of reasons for this bill, see H. Rept. 16, 76 Cong. 1 sess.

For text and lists of veto messages and pocket vetoes, see pp. 337–39.

hearings before the Committee on Rules often go to the merits of the proposed measure. A second variation is the holding of joint sessions by committees of the two houses.

The history of legislation may be obtained from seven main sources: (1) the *Congressional Record*, (2) the *House Journal*, (3) the *Senate Journal*, (4) the *House Calendar*, (5) *Senate Reports*, (6) *House Reports*, and (7) *Hearings*. Occasionally the *Senate Documents* and *House Documents* include publications dealing with pending legislation.

The *Congressional Record* and the journals of the two houses contain the same information as regards action, the difference being that the *Record* gives the debates, while the journals show only the proceedings. If information is desired on the action taken, the journals will be found more convenient; but as they are not printed until the close of the session, the *Record* must be used for contemporaneous information.

In tracing the history of legislation it should be borne in mind that the entry for the bill enacted may not indicate the entire legislative consideration. A bill may be considered in part as a House bill in the House of Representatives or its committee, and in part as a Senate bill in the Senate and its committee, and at some stage in the proceeding one bill may be substituted for the other. Therefore the entire consideration may be found only by looking up the debates, reports, and hearings on the several bills. The specific substitution of bills has been indicated in the index to the *Congressional Record* and also in the daily and final editions of the *House Calendar*, but hearings may be held on one bill and a new bill reported without notation in the index.

In the biennial *Document Catalog* an entry for a report on a bill that has become law contains a cross reference to the slip-law entry and gives a citation to the page in the *Statutes at Large*. There is no cross reference from reports on a bill for which another bill may have been substituted at some stage of the proceedings. Thus Public Law 867, 68th Congress, regulating the sale of oleomargarine, was under consideration as S. 5745 and H. R. 16836, and the House bill was substituted for the Senate bill. Public Law No. 867 is listed in the *Document Catalog* (page 1867) under the subhead "Congress" as the enacted form of H. R. 16836. Under the subhead "Agriculture Committee, House" is listed House Report 2532 on H. R. 16836. There is no entry for the report on H. R. 16836 under the subhead "Agriculture and Forestry Committee, Senate," as the Senate committee did not report that bill. There is, however, under this subhead an entry (without cross reference) for Senate Report 1450 on S. 5745, for which H. R. 16836 was substituted. The catalog also contains an entry for a Senate Committee hearing on S. 5745, without cross reference. Therefore, all references to bills, reports, and hearings on the subject under consideration should be utilized if the complete history is desired.

Some indexes and catalogs list committees and government offices under the first significant word (Appropriations Committee) while others list them under the first word (Committee on Appropriations).

Numerous references to the history of tariff legislation are given in *The Tariff—A Bibliography—A Select List of References*, 1934 (980 pages), published by the Tariff Commission. The items cited in the index under the entry "Tariff Act of—" will be found particularly useful.

Bills

In both the *Congressional Record* and the journals of the two houses the bills introduced in and reported to the House are listed by title and bill number at the end of each day's proceedings, public and private bills being segregated. Those introduced in and reported to the Senate are listed in the body of the proceedings.

The indexes to the *Record* and the journals furnish alternative guides to legislative action. In each case the detailed entries are under the bill number, the subject indexes giving merely cross references to the bill numbers. The indexes have generally indicated the report and slip-law numbers.

The biweekly indexes to the daily *Record* contain references only if the bill has been acted upon during the period covered by the index. As the daily edition of the *Record* has a different pagination from the bound edition, the index for one cannot be used for the other. As the life of a bill extends to the end of a congress, references may be found in all sessions until it is enacted.

Beginning with the 2d session of the 74th Congress (1936) the Legislative Reference Service of the Library of Congress has prepared a *Digest of Public General Bills*. At first this was published weekly; later it was issued at irregular intervals. At present there are four or five cumulative issues per session, the final one appearing after the close of the session, and supplements are issued to the earlier cumulations at approximately two-week intervals. It contains a digest of the provisions of every bill which the compiler considers general and public in character. It does not include a complete history, but gives only the introduction, the committee reference, and the last action. The arrangement is by bill numbers, with a subject index. It is the only guide to the scope of bills giving information beyond the title.

The *House Calendar* is limited to information on bills which have been reported to either house, or on which later action has been taken. For each bill reported this publication gives a cumulative history, showing the dates on which action was taken and the slip-law number if the bill became law. The arrangement is by bill numbers, but a subject index is issued once a week. The *Calendar* is issued on every day the House is in session.

The final edition is published sometime after the close of a congress under the title *Calendar of the United States House of Representatives and History of Legislation*. This volume includes also a list of all bills which failed to become law. This list is the only place where all these bills are segregated; there is no other official publication of lists of bills which failed to become law by reason of the fact that the President did not approve them after the adjournment of Congress (pocket veto).

Bills vetoed and returned to Congress are listed in the index to the *Congressional Record.*

For some years the Senate has published at the end of each congress a *History of Bills and Resolutions Introduced in the Senate. . . .* Within its more limited scope it contains the same information as the final edition of the *House Calendar.* The primary arrangement is by the names of the senators who introduced the bills, the secondary classification being by bill numbers. There is no index.

If a bill has become law, the bill number may be obtained from the slip law, the *Statutes at Large,* the daily and the final edition of the *House Calendar,* or the *Monthly Catalog.* In the slip law it appears immediately below the act number; in the *Statutes at Large,* in the margin immediately below the date of the act; in the final edition of the *House Calendar,* in a separate list giving slip-law numbers and bill numbers; in the *Monthly Catalog,* in the entry for the slip law; and in the biennial *Document Catalog,* in the entries for the slip law and for the reports.

Reports

Reports on bills and resolutions may be located by means of the *Monthly Catalog,* the annual *Document Index,*[35] the biennial *Document Catalog,*[36] the *House Calendar,* and the indexes to the *Congressional Record* and to the journals of the two houses. In the *House Calendar* and the indexes to the *Record* and the journals the references are found in the numerical lists of bills.

In the *Monthly Catalog* reports were listed by subject until September 1947 when a change was made to a serial listing under House of Representatives and Senate, each entry including the report number, the full title of the report, with the bill number and explanatory matter, the date submitted, and the number of pages. The index is by subjects.

[35] This publication was discontinued with the issue for the 2d session of the 72d Congress.

[36] This publication was discontinued with the 76th Congress.

In the discontinued annual *Document Index* the reports were listed by subject, and the entry gave only the title, the bill number, and the report number. All the reports are listed in the successor to the *Document Index*—the *Numerical Lists*. This list, however, is arranged entirely by report numbers; it gives the title, but not the bill number. As there is no index, the report on a particular subject is not readily located.

In the biennial *Document Catalog* the detailed information regarding reports is given under the subject, the entry including the bill number, the title of the report, the name of the member presenting the report, the date, the number of pages, and the report number. There is also a numerical list of reports under the heading "Congressional Documents Lists," with cross references to the entries under the subject. Under the name of each committee are cross references to the subject entries under which the committee reports are listed.

Compilations of committee reports and indexes are described on pages 31–32 and 188–92.

Hearings

As published the hearings are listed in the *Monthly Catalog*. An illustration of the difficulty in determining what subjects are considered by the several committees is offered by the hearings on control of radio. In the Senate these have been before the Committee on Interstate Commerce. In the House, although there is a Committee on Interstate and Foreign Commerce, hearings on radio legislation were held for some years by the Committee on Merchant Marine and Fisheries. This assignment in the House grew out of the fact that originally legislation relating to radio was largely limited to its use on merchant ships. Later the name of the committee was changed to Merchant Marine, Radio, and Fisheries. In the early part of 1935 the name of the committee was again changed to Merchant Marine and Fisheries, and bills relating to radio were placed in the jurisdiction of the Committee on Interstate and Foreign Commerce.

Likewise the House Committee on Agriculture has printed

hearings on a bill extending to the District of Columbia the provisions of the act making grants to the several states and territories for the so-called land-grant colleges. While this bill was of primary interest to the District of Columbia and was concerned with problems within the field of education, it was not referred to the Committee on the District of Columbia, to the Committee on Education and Labor, or to the Committee on Public Lands, but to the Committee on Agriculture, which has always reported on land-grant college legislation.

The 1959 *Rules and Manual of the United State Senate* enumerates the subjects considered by the standing committees of the Senate. The *House Manual* contains annotations showing some of the topics considered by each committee. The index to the *Monthly Catalog* gives references under the committees and the subject matter.

The 1924 edition of the *Senate Catalogue* affords a convenient guide to most hearings issued up to March 3, 1923. The *Senate Catalogue* is no longer printed, but the list of hearings has been published separately several times, both before and after 1924. One is the *Index of Congressional Committee Hearings . . . Prior to March 4, 1935 in the United States Senate Library*, 1935 (1,056 pages). The latest edition is the *Cumulative Index of Congressional Committee Hearings 1963–66* (664 pages). The hearings in the House of Representatives Library are listed in volumes entitled *Index to Congressional Committee Hearings Prior to January 1, 1951 in the Library of the United States House of Representatives* (485 pages) and *Supplemental Index to Congressional Committee Hearings, January 3, 1949, to January 3, 1955, 81st, 82d, and 83d Congresses, in the Library of the House of Representatives* (127 pages).

Each of these lists is in three parts, the classification being by subjects, by committees, and by bill numbers. Except for the few hearings which have been printed as documents or reports, the citations in the bill index are not of much value to persons outside Washington, as the references are to the numbers assigned to the books in the Senate and House libraries. However, this section is of value in showing that hearings have been published. If the student has only the bill number, he may ascertain from the *Congressional Record* the title of the bill and the committee to which it was referred, and then find the full title in the subject matter or committee index of the lists.

The Senate and House lists cited above are not identical, as each one lists some hearings not cited in the other. It should be borne in mind that neither pretends to include all hearings, but each is confined to the material in a specified collection. However, it is likely that most of the published hearings are listed, particularly those of recent years.

Hearings prior to the 61st Congress (1909) are listed, with other committee publications, on pages 1532–1652 of the *Checklist*. The primary arrangement is by committees, the secondary classification by subjects. The hearings are not segregated, but are interspersed with other publications. Occasionally hearings are printed as documents, but this practice is exceptional.

For hearings on appropriation bills, see pages 384–87.

The Library of Congress has issued a *Checklist of Hearings before Congressional Committees through the 67th Congress*, by Harold O. Thomen, in nine parts as follows:

Pt. 1. Committee on Agriculture, 1942.
Pt. 2. House Committee on Appropriations, 1949, 50 pp.
Pt. 3. House Committee on Accounts through House Committee on Coinage, Weights and Measures, 1951, 61 pp.
Pt. 4. House Committee on District of Columbia through House Committee on Industrial Arts and Expositions, 1957, 122 pp.
Pt. 5. House Committee on Insular Affairs through House Committee on Merchant Marine and Fisheries, 1957, 130 pp.
Pt. 6. House Committee on Military Affairs through House Committee on Public Expenditures, 1957, 111 pp.
Pt. 7. House Committee on Public Lands through House Committee on Woman Suffrage, 1957, 115 pp.
Pt. 8. Senate Committee on Agriculture and Forestry through Senate Committee on Interstate Commerce, 1958, 171 pp.
Pt. 9. Senate Committee on Irrigation and Reclamation through Senate Committee on Woman Suffrage and Joint Committees, 1958, 166 pp.

An unofficial listing of hearings, memorial addresses, contested elections, and speeches has been compiled by Ella Frances Smith, Alderman Library, University of Virginia. This has been issued as Part 2 of a compilation entitled *Documents Office Classification Numbers for Cuttered Documents 1910–1924*, compiled by Miss Smith and Miss Mary Elizabeth Poole, Document Librarian, the D. H. Hill Library, North Carolina State University, Raleigh, North Carolina, and published by University Microfilms, 1960.

Slip Laws

Slip laws (see page 208), both public and private, are listed contemporaneously in the *Monthly Catalog* under the main heading "Congress." They are listed serially with law number, bill number, title, date, and pages. The index is by subjects.

In the biennial *Document Catalog* slip laws and resolutions are listed under the subject to which they relate. The entry gives the bill or resolution number, the full title, the date of approval (or date it became law if passed over a veto), the slip-law number, and a citation to the *Statutes at Large*. The entries for the slip laws and resolutions are under the subhead "Congress."

Miscellaneous Publications

The publications here classified as miscellaneous deal mostly with the work of Congress. Although some of them contain general information not readily available elsewhere, most of them are issued as documents, the term "miscellaneous" being used in a descriptive sense and not as the title of a series. Only the more important of the publications not mentioned elsewhere in this volume are described in this chapter. Some of the publications of a miscellaneous character are described in other chapters.

Congressional Directory

The *Congressional Directory* is a compendium of information relating to Congress and other branches of the government. While designed primarily for the use of members of Congress, it contains much information of value to the public. Like most other publications of this character its contents vary from time to time, the tendency being to add new features. At present the book includes the following:

INFORMATION CONCERNING MEMBERS OF CONGRESS: Biographies of incumbent senators and representatives, their addresses, party affiliation, terms of service, committee assignments,[37] certain staff members, and election statistics

OTHER INFORMATION REGARDING CONGRESS: Sessions of Congress from 1789, court of impeachment, principal officers of Senate and House, description of the Capitol Building and grounds, maps of congressional districts, as well as rules governing the press galleries, with lists of members of the press entitled to admission

INFORMATION REGARDING OTHER GOVERNMENT BODIES AND OFFICIALS: List of governors of states and territories, biographies of the President, Vice President, and Cabinet members, lists of principal administrative officers of executive departments and agencies, the United States diplomatic and consular offices, the District of Columbia government and officials, and information regarding the judiciary, including biographies of judges

OTHER INFORMATION: Officials of international organizations, and foreign diplomatic and consular representation in the United States

The *Congressional Directory* appears to have been published first in 1809, being printed by private printers until 1847.[38] During the early years one edition was issued for each session of Congress, but for later years several editions were issued during each session. Since the 81st Congress (1949), only one edition has been issued for each session.

Biographical Congressional Directory

A collection of biographies of all members of Congress from 1774 to 1949 is contained in the *Biographical Directory of the American Congress* (2,057 pages), published as House Docu-

[37] For changes in membership of committees, see footnote 15, p. 150.
[38] A list of the issues to the 2d session of the 61st Congress (1909) is given in the *Checklist*, pp. 1616–21.

ment 607, 81st Congress, 2d session. A list of members of each congress by states and of the Cabinet officers under each administration is also given. This volume was compiled by James L. Harrison, staff director of the Joint Committee on Printing, and is a revision of the *Dictionary of the United States Congress and the General Government,* published in 1859 and again revised in 1869, by Charles Lanman; the *Biographical Annals of the Civil Government of the United States,* published in 1876, by Charles Lanman and James Anglim, and the Lanman edition of 1876 as corrected by Joseph M. Morrison in 1887; the *Political Register and Congressional Directory of 1878,* by Ben Perley Poore; the *Biographical Congressional Directory of 1903,* by O. M. Enyart; the *Biographical Congressional Directory,* published in 1911, and the *Biographical Directory of the American Congress, 1774–1927,* by Ansel Wold, published in 1928. A further revision of the *Biographical Directory of the American Congress, 1774–1961,* was published in 1961 as House Document 442, 85th Congress, 2d session. Data in Lanman not generally available elsewhere are complete lists, since 1789, of presidential electors, of diplomatic appointments, and of state and territorial governors.

House Rules

The publication which is generally known as the *House Manual* but which is entitled *Constitution, Jefferson's Manual, and Rules of the House of Representatives* includes the material indicated by its title and the principal rulings made on the several sections. The "Notes" give a brief history under each rule, and the rules relating to committees set forth the history of the committee and its jurisdiction. The *Manual* is generally published every other year as a House document.

The rulings of the presiding officers of the House of Representatives are given in detail in *Hinds' Precedents of the House of Representatives, Including References to Provisions of the Constitution, the Laws, and Decisions of the Senate,* by Asher C. Hinds, published in 1907 and 1908 in eight volumes, both as an unnumbered publication and as House Document 355, 59th Congress, 2d session. This set comprised five volumes of text and three volumes of index.

An edition, with additions by Clarence Cannon, was published in eight volumes in 1936 without document number.[39] The volumes in this edition are numbered consecutively from one to eight. The title pages and back titles of Volumes 1–5 read *Hinds' Precedents of the House of Representatives,* and bear the date 1907, although they were printed in 1936. These volumes were reprinted from the original plates. The title pages and back titles of Volumes 6–8 read *Cannon's Precedents of the House of Representatives;* the title pages bear the date 1935, but the back titles have the date 1936. Thus there are no Volumes 1–5 with the title *Cannon's Precedents.* Volumes 9–11 contain the index-digest of *Cannon's Precedents* and were published in 1941.

The latest edition is *Cannon's Procedure in the House of Representatives,* by Clarence Cannon, House Document 610, 87th Congress, 1963 (542 pages).

Senate Rules

The Senate rules are contained in the *Senate Manual Containing the Standing Rules and Orders . . . the Constitution . . . Declaration of Independence, Articles of Confederation, the Ordinance of 1787, Jefferson's Manual. . . .* This does not contain interpretation of the rules, as does the *House Manual,* but, in addition to the subjects indicated by the title, it includes the following material not readily available elsewhere:

Presidents pro tempore of the Senate since the 1st Congress
Senators from each state since the 1st Congress, with dates of commencement and expiration of term
States admitted since adoption of the Constitution, with area, population, and other information

[39] It was originally announced that the Cannon revised edition would be published as House Document 1020, 66th Congress, 3d session; as the document edition has been abandoned, this number will remain blank in the congressional set.

Data on territorial and insular possessions
Electoral votes by states at each presidential election
Justices of the Supreme Court since 1789, with length of service
Heads of departments under each President, with dates of appointment

The book generally appears every other year, and is published as a Senate document.

The rulings in the Senate are given in *Precedents, Decisions on Points of Order with Phraseology in the Senate* . . . by Henry H. Gilfry. This book, covering the period from 1789 to 1913, was issued as Senate Document 1123, 62d Congress, 3d session. The latest edition, *Senate Procedure, Precedents and Practices,* by Charles L. Watkins and Floyd M. Riddick, was issued as Senate Document 44, 88th Congress, 2d session. In compiling this edition the authors perused the Senate portions of the *Congressional Record* and the *Senate Journal* for the period from December 3, 1883, to the date of publication for rulings by presiding officers and practices which relate to Senate procedure.

Platforms of Political Parties

The platforms of the political parties have been issued as unnumbered publications under the general title *Platforms of the Two Great Political Parties* with the following subtitles:

1856–1908, three editions, compiled by Alexander McDowell, August 1908, and by South Trimble, July 1911 and March 1912
1856–1916, compiled by South Trimble
1856–1920, compiled by George D. Ellis
1856–1928, compiled by George D. Ellis
1856–1932, compiled by George D. Ellis
1932, compiled by Leroy D. Brandon
1932 and 1936, compiled by Leroy D. Brandon
1932–40, compiled by Leroy D. Brandon
1932–44, August 1944, compiled by William Graf
1932–44, June 1945, compiled by William Graf (includes some revisions)

The following publications have also been issued:

Supplement to platforms of the two great political parties, 1948, compiled by William Graf

Same, 1952, compiled by Earl Rockwood

Platforms of the Democratic Party and the Republican Party, 1956, by Ralph R. Roberts

Same, 1960

Same, 1964

Factual campaign information, compiled by Richard D. Hupman and Senate Library staff, corrected to Mar. 20, 1956

Same, revised, Sept. 12, 1956

Same, February 1960

Same, revised, Aug. 15, 1960; Oct. 1, 1960

Same, March 1962

Same, revised Jan. 22, 1964; July 8, 1964; Oct. 5, 1964; Jan. 31, 1966; June 27, 1966; Sept. 24, 1966; Jan. 15, 1968; May 15, 1968

Manner of selecting delegates to national political conventions and nomination and election of Presidential electors, compiled by Senate Library, corrected to April 1, 1952

Same, compiled by Richard D. Hupman, Senate Library, and Samuel H. Still, Jr., Legislative Reference Service, Library of Congress, January 1966

Nomination and election of President and Vice President of the United States, including manner of selecting delegates to national political conventions, compiled by Richard D. Hupman and Samuel H. Still, Jr., January 1960

Same, compiled by Richard D. Hupman, Eiler C. Ravnholt, and Robert L. Tienken, January 1964

Same, compiled by Richard D. Hupman and Robert L. Tienken, January 1968

Compilations of Congressional Publications

One general compilation of congressional publications and several of limited extent have been published. Only the more important of the limited publications are discussed below.

American State Papers.   The most comprehensive compilation of congressional publications is entitled *American State Papers, Documents, Legislative and Executive, of the Congress of the United States . . .* but is generally known as *American State Papers* from the back title. This was published by Gales and Seaton between 1832 and 1861. It is divided into ten classes, which have subtitles and dates indicated below:

Class 1. Foreign Relations, 6 vols., 1st Congress to 20th Congress, 1st session; June 11, 1789 to May 24, 1828

Class 2. Indian Affairs, 2 vols., 1st Congress to 19th Congress; May 25, 1789 to Mar. 1, 1827

Class 3. Finance, 5 vols., 1st Congress to 20th Congress, 1st session; Apr. 11, 1789 to May 16, 1828

Class 4. Commerce and Navigation, 2 vols., 1st Congress to 17th Congress; Apr. 13, 1789 to Feb. 25, 1823

Class 5. Military Affairs, 7 vols., 1st Congress to 25th Congress, 2d session; Aug. 10, 1789 to Mar. 1, 1838

Class 6. Naval Affairs, 4 vols., 3d Congress to 24th Congress, 1st session; Jan. 20, 1794 to June 15, 1836

Class 7. Post Office Department, 1 vol., 1st Congress, 2d session, to 22d Congress; Jan. 22, 1790 to Feb. 1, 1833

Class 8. Public Lands, 8 vols.,[40] 1st Congress to 24th Congress; July 31, 1789 to Feb. 28, 1837

Class 9. Claims, 1 vol., 1st Congress, 2d session, to 17th Congress; Feb. 5, 1790 to Mar. 3, 1823

Class 10. Miscellaneous, 2 vols., 1st Congress to 17th Congress; Apr. 18, 1789 to Mar. 3, 1823

The compilation does not include all documents and reports, but comprises those considered the most important. Each paper is numbered, beginning with 1 for each class, but these numbers bear no relation to the regular document and report numbers and should not be confused with them. Many of the papers in this compilation are indexed in Ordway's *General Indexes to the Journals of Congress* listed on page 145, but it is likely that those indexes cannot be depended upon for references to all the papers.

McKee's committee reports. At various times some of the committees have published compilations of their reports or other papers dealing with the subjects under their jurisdiction. The most extensive compilation of this character is that of T. H. McKee, which embraces the reports made by all com-

[40] Another series in five volumes relating to public lands was published by Duff Green under the title *American State Papers, Documents, Legislative and Executive, of the Congress of the United States in Relation to Public Lands*, selected and edited by Walter Lowrie. This series extends from the 1st Congress to the 1st session of the 23d Congress, or to June 15, 1834. The first three volumes of the Duff Green series are apparently the same as those in the Gales and Seaton series. Volumes 4 and 5 of the Duff Green series do not contain some documents given in the Gales and Seaton series.

mittees from 1815 to the end of the 49th Congress in 1887. The reports of each standing committee form a separate series, those of the special and select committees of the House being assembled in one series of 89 volumes and the similar committees of the Senate in another series of 46 volumes. In all there were 515 volumes in 94 series.

Although each series has a printed title page and an index, this compilation cannot be regarded as a publication, as it was not a reprint of the reports but merely an assemblage of the separate prints. There are indexes to each of the 94 series, the indexes being also issued separately.[41]

It is doubtful whether a complete set of these volumes is available in any one place, and probably none may be obtained outside Washington. The Public Documents Library has a partial set and some of the committees may have the volumes relating to their own work. The indexes are doubtless available in other libraries.

For the House Committee on Banking and Currency the McKee compilation was continued in *Reports of the Committee on Banking and Currency, U. S. House of Representatives, 50th to 52d Congress,* compiled by Ruter W. Springer, 1893.

Contested election cases. Contested election cases in the Senate from 1789 to 1913 are reported in *Compilation of Senate Election Cases from 1789–1913,* by Charles A. Webb and Herbert R. Pierce, published as Senate Document 1036, 62d Congress, 3d session (1,233 pages). This volume contains the reprints of the proceedings and reports of committees and references to the debates. It also treats cases dealing with the expulsion of senators. Earlier editions are as follows:

1789–1903, by George M. Buck. S. Doc. 11, 58 Cong. spec. sess.
1789–1893, by George P. Furber. S. Misc. Doc. 67, 52 Cong. 2 sess.
1789–1885, by George S. Taft. S. Misc. Doc. 47, 49 Cong. 1 sess.

Senate contested election cases up to 1865 are also contained in the first two publications listed on page 191.

Senate contested election cases up to 1865 are also contained in the first two publications listed on page 191.

[41] The indexes are described on p. 32.

House contested election cases are described in the series of publications (most of which were published as *House Documents*) enumerated below.

Cases of contested elections in Congress from the year 1789 to 1834, inclusive, by M. St. Clair Clarke and David A. Hall. Gales and Seaton, 1834, 1,025 pp. Contains the committee reports and the debates.

Cases of contested elections in Congress from 1834 to 1865, inclusive, compiled by D. W. Bartlett, 1865, 660 pp. Contains reports and abstracts of debates. H. Misc. Doc. 57, 38 Cong. 2 sess.

Digest of election cases. Cases of contested elections in the House of Representatives from 1865 to 1871, inclusive, compiled by D. W. Bartlett, 1870, 955 pp. Contains committee reports. H. Misc. Doc. 152, 41 Cong. 2 sess.

Digest of election cases. Cases of contested elections in the House of Representatives, 42d, 43d, and 44th Congresses, from 1871 to 1876, inclusive, compiled by J. M. Smith, 1876, 699 pp. Contains committee reports. H. Misc. Doc. 52, 46 Cong. 2 sess.

Digest of election cases. Cases of contested elections in the House of Representatives, 45th and 46th Congresses, from 1876 to 1880, inclusive, compiled by J. H. Ellsworth, 1883, 522 pp. H. Misc. Doc. 57, 47 Cong. 1 sess.

Digest of election cases. Cases of contested elections in the House of Representatives, 47th Congress, from 1880 to 1882, inclusive, compiled by J. H. Ellsworth, 1883, 692 pp. Contains committee reports. H. Misc. Doc. 35, 47 Cong. 2 sess.

Digest of contested election cases arising in the 48th, 49th, and 50th Congresses, compiled by William H. Mobley, 1889, 785 pp. Contains committee reports. H. Misc. Doc. 63, 50 Cong. 2 sess.

Digest of contested election cases in the 51st Congress, compiled by Chester H. Rowell, 1891, 834 pp. Contains committee reports and a digest of points established. H. Misc. Doc. 137, 51 Cong. 2 sess.

Digest of contested election cases in the 53d Congress, compiled by Alfred J. Stofer, 1895, 203 pp. Contains reports and digest. H. Misc. Doc. 77, 53 Cong. 3 sess.

A complete review of all cases up to 1901 is contained in *A Historical and Legal Digest of All the Contested Election Cases in the House of Representatives of the United States from the 1st to the 56th Congress, 1789–1901*, by Chester H. Rowell, 1901 (864 pages). This volume was published as House Document 510, 56th Congress, 2d session. It contains not only a digest of each case, but a subject digest of the points raised with references to the cases. This review of cases has been continued under the same title for the 57th through the 64th Congress (1901–17) by Merrill Moores. It was published as House Document 2052, 64th Congress, 2d session (1917) in 133 pages.

Contested election cases are discussed also in *Hinds' Precedents of the House of Representatives*, Volume 2, pages 1–748, and in *Cannon's Precedents of the House of Representatives*, Volume 6, pages 220–373.

Reports of Senate Committee on Foreign Relations.   The reports of the Senate Committee on Foreign Relations up to 1901 were reprinted and published as Senate Document 231, 56th Congress, 2d session, in eight volumes. This compilation resulted from a search of all available material and presumably includes some reports which did not appear previously in the regular Senate reports. The eight volumes were divided as follows:

Vols. 1 and 2. Claims of citizens of the United States against foreign governments

Vol. 3. Claims of citizens of United States against foreign governments; claims of citizens of United States against United States; claims of citizens of foreign countries against United States; claims against United States of diplomatic and consular officers of the United States for reimbursement and extra pay

Vol. 4. Mediterranean commerce, etc.; nominations; authorizations to accept decorations from foreign governments; international expositions; international conferences; maritime canals; Pacific cables; trade and commerce with foreign nations; tariff restrictions

Vol. 5. Foreign tariffs; boundary and fishery disputes

Vol. 6. Diplomatic relations with foreign nations; Hawaiian Islands

Vol. 7. Diplomatic relations with foreign nations; affairs in Cuba

Vol. 8. Treaties and legislation respecting them

There is an index in each volume and a general index in Volume 8.

Papers relating to expenditures.   A volume published in 1939 by the Brookings Institution, entitled *Control of Federal*

Expenditures: A Documentary History, 1775–1894, by Fred W. Powell, contains reprints of the significant materials, official and unofficial, underlying the financial history of the United States on the disbursement side, from the beginning to 1894, when the Cockrell-Dockery Act introduced fundamental changes in the system.

Included in the scope of the volume are: proceedings, resolutions, orders, and ordinances of the Continental Congress as shown by its *Journals;* pertinent and informative remarks, speeches, and debates in Congress, as reported in its proceedings *(Annals, Register, Globe, Record);* congressional committee reports; and reports of administrative officers. Supplementing them are excerpts from unofficial papers of men whose experience as participants in legislation or administration gave value to their words.

CHAPTER SEVEN

FEDERAL AND STATE CONSTITUTIONS

As a rule government publications on federal and state constitutions contain only the adopted text or preliminary proposals. While the interpretations of the federal Constitution are contained in the decisions of the Supreme Court, they have not usually been assembled by the government, most of the general books on constitutional law having been issued by commercial publishers. Much material dealing with the federal Constitution is contained in the committee reports and debates on proposed legislation, but the discussion below is confined to works dealing with the federal Constitution as a whole, the publications dealing with amendments, and the state constitutions.

The Federal Constitution as a Whole

The Constitution has been published in pamphlet form by the Department of State and the Department of Justice and appears in all the complete compilations of federal statutes issued by the government. It may be found in Volume 1 of the *Statutes at Large,* in the *Revised Statutes,* and in the *United States Code.* It is also printed regularly in the *Senate Manual* and the *House Manual,* described on pages 185–86, and in the *United States Government Organization Manual.*

Congress on June 17, 1947 (61 Stat. 133), authorized the printing of a new annotated edition of the Constitution. This compilation, prepared by the Legislative Reference Service of the Library of Congress under the supervision of Edward S. Corwin, was published under the title *The Constitution of the United States of America* (1,361 pages), Senate Document 170, 82d Congress, 2d session. The annotations include cases decided by the Supreme Court to June 30, 1952.[1] Public Law 86–754, enacted September 18, 1960, authorized a new edition to "bring the volume up to date, maintaining the present text intact to the degree possible." An edition was published in 1964 as *The Constitution of the United States of America, Analysis and Interpretation, Annotation of Cases Decided by the Supreme Court of the United States to June 22, 1964,* prepared by the Legislative Reference Service of the Library of Congress, Edwin S. Corwin, editor of the 1952 edition, Norman J. Small, editor, and Lester S. Jayson, supervising editor of the 1964 edition, Senate Document 39, 88th Congress, 1st session.

Under each clause are listed citations to leading cases, an abstract of the ruling of the court, and in some cases a brief quotation from the decision. At the end are lists of cases cited and of acts of Congress held unconstitutional, with citations to the cases.

An earlier list of acts declared unconstitutional, prepared by the Legislative Reference Service of the Library of Congress, is given in the *Congressional Record,* 74th Congress, 2d session (Volume 80, Part 9, pages 9251–54).

In 1936 the Library of Congress published *Provisions of Federal Law Held Unconstitutional by the Supreme Court of the United States* (148 pages), prepared by W. C. Gilbert. The cases are analyzed on pages 1–86, the analysis being confined to the point of unconstitutionality; notes and miscellaneous

---

[1] Three earlier editions of this work, compiled by George Gordon Payne and Wilfred C. Gilbert, were published. S. Doc. 96, 67 Cong. 2 sess. (780 pp.), entitled *Constitution of the United States of America as Amended to January 1, 1923 (Annotated),* contains notes on decisions to the end of the October term 1922. S. Doc. 154, 68 Cong. 1 sess. (876 pp.), entitled *Constitution of the United States of America as Amended to December 1, 1924 (Annotated),* contains notes on decisions of the October term 1923; this volume was issued also in an edition without document number. S. Doc. 232, 74 Cong. 2 sess. (1,246 pp.), entitled *The Constitution of the United States of America (Annotated),* contains notes on decisions rendered by the Supreme Court to January 1, 1938.

data of interest relating to the court are given on pages 87–148.

In addition to the writings of the founders, two publications deal with the origin of the Constitution. In 1894 the Department of State began the publication of the *Documentary History of the Constitution of the United States,* which was completed in five volumes, Volumes 1 and 2 appearing in 1894, Volume 3 in 1900, and Volumes 4 and 5 in 1905. Volumes 1–3 were also issued as House Document 529, 56th Congress, 2d session. Volumes 4–5 were issued only in the department edition. Volumes 1–3 also appeared originally as appendixes to Bulletins 1, 3, 4, 7, and 9, and Volumes 4–5 as Bulletin 11, Parts 1 and 2, of the Bureau of Rolls and Library of the Department of State.

The lack of headings and explanatory notes makes the work somewhat baffling to one not familiar with the form of the papers. The papers reproduced are the following:

VOLUME I

Report of the Annapolis Convention of 1786 relative to a Federal Convention

Proceedings of the Continental Congress of Feb. 21, 1787, convening the Federal Convention

Credentials of delegates to the Federal Convention

Proceedings of the Federal Convention

Letter from Charles Pinckney to John Quincy Adams, with draft of Constitution

Plan presented by William Paterson

Plan presented by Alexander Hamilton[2]

Resolutions of the Federal Convention preparatory to the formation of the Constitution, recommended Sept. 17, 1787

Report of the Grand Committee July 5, 1787

Plan of the Constitution as reported Aug. 6, 1787

Plan of the Constitution brought in Sept. 13, 1787, with final changes indicated

VOLUME II

Letter of the President of the Federal Convention to the President of Congress, transmitting the Constitution

The Constitution

[2] This volume gives only one text of the Hamilton plan; five variants are given in *Documents Illustrative of the Formation of the Union of the American States,* described below.

Resolution of the Federal Convention submitting the Constitution to
Congress
Resolution of Congress submitting the Constitution to the several states
Circular letter of the Secretary of Congress transmitting copy of the Constitution to the several governors
Resolution of ratification by the several states
Proceedings of Congress relating to the Constitution between July 2 and
Sept. 13, 1788
Resolutions of Congress and of the several states relating to amendments

VOLUME III

Debates in the Federal Convention of 1787 as reported by James Madison
Plan submitted by Hamilton to Madison
Speech of Charles Pinckney June 25, 1787
Additional notes to Madison's debates

VOLUME IV

Letters and papers relating to the Constitution to July 31, 1788

VOLUME V

Letters and papers relating to the Constitution from Aug. 1, 1788, to the
death of Madison
Bibliography

In 1927 the Library of Congress published a new compilation by Charles C. Tansill of basic documents relating to the Constitution, entitled *Documents Illustrative of the Formation of the Union of the American States,* issued also as House Document 398, 69th Congress, 1st session. One edition has the back title *United States, Formation of the Union, Documents.* The material in this volume is as follows:

Declaration and resolves of the First Continental Congress Oct. 14, 1774
Resolves adopted in Charlotte Town, Mecklenburg County, N.C., May
31, 1775
Declaration of the causes and necessity of taking up arms July 6, 1775
Resolution of secrecy adopted by the Continental Congress Nov. 9, 1775
Preamble and resolution of the Virginia Convention May 15, 1776,
instructing the Virginia delegates in the Continental Congress to "propose to that respectable body to declare the United Colonies free and
independent states"
Resolution introduced in the Continental Congress by Richard Henry Lee
(Virginia) proposing a Declaration of Independence June 7, 1776
Declaration of Independence July 4, 1776
Articles of Confederation Mar. 1, 1781

Resolution of the General Assembly of Virginia Jan. 21, 1786, proposing a joint meeting of commissioners from the states to consider and recommend a federal plan for regulating commerce

Proceedings of commissioners to remedy defects of the federal government, Annapolis, Md., 1786

Report of proceedings in Congress, Wednesday, Feb. 21, 1787

Ordinance of 1787, July 13, 1787

Credentials of the members of the Federal Convention

List of delegates appointed by the states represented in the Federal Convention

Notes of Major William Pierce (Georgia) in the Federal Convention of 1787: (a) loose sketches and notes taken in the convention May 1787; (b) characters in the convention of the states held at Philadelphia May 1787

Debates in the Federal Convention of 1787 as reported by James Madison

Secret proceedings and debates of the convention assembled at Philadelphia in the year 1787 for the purpose of forming the Constitution of the United States of America (from the notes taken by the late Robert Yates, Esq., Chief Justice of New York, Albany, 1821)

Notes of Rufus King in the Federal Convention of 1787

Notes of William Paterson in the Federal Convention of 1787

Notes of Alexander Hamilton in the Federal Convention of 1787

Papers of Dr. James McHenry on the Federal Convention of 1787

Variant texts of the Virginia plan presented by Edmund Randolph to the Federal Convention May 29, 1787

The plan of Charles Pinckney (South Carolina) presented to the Federal Convention May 29, 1787

Variant texts of the plan presented by William Paterson (New Jersey) to the Federal Convention June 15, 1787

Variant texts of the plan presented by Alexander Hamilton to the Federal Convention June 18, 1787

The Constitution of the United States

Letter of the President of the Federal Convention Sept. 17, 1787, to the President of Congress transmitting the Constitution

Resolution of the Federal Convention submitting the Constitution to Congress Sept. 17, 1787

Resolution of Congress Sept. 28, 1787, submitting the Constitution to the several states

Circular letter of the Secretary of Congress Sept. 28, 1787, transmitting copy of the Constitution to the several governors

Ratification of the Constitution by the several states, arranged in the order of their ratification

Resolution of Congress July 2, 1788, submitting ratifications of the Constitution to a committee

Amendments to the Federal Constitution

In addition to the papers on the amendments that have been adopted, reference is made below to the publications relating to proposed amendments. The distinction between amendments proposed *in* Congress and those proposed *by* Congress must be borne in mind. An amendment may be proposed in Congress by any member. It then goes through the usual legislative stages and, after it has been voted by the necessary two-thirds vote of each house, it becomes an amendment proposed by Congress. It is then ready for submission to the legislatures or conventions in the several states, ratification by three-fourths of the states being necessary for its adoption. Several thousand amendments have been proposed in Congress but no action has been taken on most of them.

Amendments to the Constitution proposed by Congress to the states are in the form of joint resolutions and are therefore printed in the *Statutes at Large.* They do not need the approval of the President, but several have been so approved.

In 1950, the function of transmitting these resolutions containing constitutional amendments to the states was transferred from the State Department to the General Services Administration. When the legislatures of three-fourths of the states have ratified a proposed amendment, the Administrator of General Services issues a proclamation declaring the proposal officially part of the United States Constitution. The certification of amendment is published in the *Federal Register,*[3] and in that

[3] Information as to the progress of ratification by the states of proposed amendments was also given in *Press Releases* of the State Department from 1929 to 1939 and in the *Department of State Bulletin* from 1939 to 1950. Prior to 1929 there was no contemporaneous printed official source of such information.

portion of the *Statutes at Large* containing private laws, concurrent resolutions, proclamations, etc.[4] The certificates announcing the adoption of the Thirteenth and Fifteenth Amendments between 1865 and 1879 were included with presidential
proclamations. All later certificates have been under a separate
caption.

Senate Document 163 of the 87th Congress, entitled *Proposed
Amendments to the Constitution,* contains amendments proposed from the 69th Congress, 2d session, through the 87th
Congress, 2d session. Proposed amendments are reported annually by the Senate Committee on the Judiciary. Senate Report 1017, 88th Congress, and Senate Report 458, 89th Congress, cover the 1st and 2d sessions of the 88th Congress. Senate
Report 1335 of the 89th Congress and Senate Report 191 of the
90th Congress cover the 1st and 2d sessions of the 89th Congress.

The dates of ratification of the first 24 amendments by the
several states are given on pages 57–74 of the edition of the
Constitution published as Senate Document 39, 88th Congress,
1st session. *Ratification of the Constitution and Amendments
by the States,* Senate Document 240, 71st Congress, 3d session
(17 pages), also gives the votes in each house of the legislature
on the ratification or rejection of each amendment. The date of
ratification of amendments 11 through 25 is also included in the
1967–68 edition of the *United States Government Organization
Manual.* The following amendments have been proposed by
Congress but have not been ratified by three-fourths of the
states:

1789. Number of members of House of Representatives (1 Stat. 97). For
action on this proposed amendment, see Ames, pp. 54, 320 (complete
citation on p. 201).

[4] In the case of the Twenty-first Amendment, which repealed the Eighteenth
Amendment, the Secretary of State issued a certificate that the amendment
had been adopted (48 Stat. 1749), and the President issued a proclamation to
the same effect (48 Stat. 1720). The proclamation by the President was made
necessary by Sec. 217(a) of the act of June 16, 1933 (48 Stat. 208), which
provided for certain reductions in taxation within specified periods after repeal.
The proclamation by the President in this case was therefore made necessary
by reason of the modification of the tax laws and not by the necessity for
establishing the validity of the amendment.

1789. No law changing compensation of senators and representatives to take effect until an election of representatives had intervened (1 Stat. 97). For action on this proposed amendment, see Ames, pp. 34, 317.

1810. Any citizen receiving a title, office, or emolument from any foreign power without the consent of Congress to cease to be a citizen and to be incapable of holding any office (2 Stat. 613). For action on this proposed amendment, see Ames, pp. 186–89, 329.

1861. No amendment to be made which will authorize Congress to abolish or interfere with the domestic institutions, including slavery, of any state (12 Stat. 251). For action on this proposed amendment, see Ames, pp. 194–97, 363.

1924. Congress to have power to regulate child labor (42 Stat. 670).

For a discussion of the time in which action must be taken by the states, see *Dillon* v. *Gloss* (255 U.S. 368).

In 1938 the Department of Justice published *The Sixteenth Amendment: A Compilation of Extracts from Messages of the Governors and Other Material Contained in Legislative Journals* (78 pages). This amendment was the one authorizing the federal income tax.[5]

A topical discussion of the amendments proposed in and by Congress prior to 1889 is given by Herman V. Ames in "Proposed Amendments to the Constitution of the United States during the First Century of Its History," *Annual Report of the American Historical Association, 1896, Part 2* (442 pages), published also as House Document 353, Part 2, 54th Congress, 2d session. It contains both a detailed discussion and a list of all proposed amendments.[6]

A discussion of the amendments to the Constitution proposed in Congress, particularly those since 1889, is given in *Proposed Amendments to the Constitution*, by Michael A. Musmanno, published as House Document 551, 70th Congress, 2d session, 1929 (253 pages). This work was not prepared under government

[5] For papers on the repeal of the Prohibition Amendment, see Everett S. Brown, *Ratification of the Twenty-first Amendment to the Constitution of the United States, State Convention Records and Laws,* University of Michigan Press, 1938 (718 pp.).

[6] This work received a prize offered by the Executive Council of the American Historical Association for the best monograph based upon original investigation in history, submitted to the Council in 1896. It was published by the government by reason of its inclusion in the *Annual Report of the American Historical Association,* which is issued regularly as a document of Congress.

auspices but was printed under a resolution of the House of Representatives.

An enumeration of the 1,316 amendments to the Constitution proposed in Congress between December 4, 1889, and July 2, 1926, is given in *Proposed Amendments to the Constitution of the United States,* by Charles C. Tansill, published as Senate Document 93, 69th Congress, 1st session, 1926 (148 pages). By 1957 there were 1,543 additional proposals listed in *Proposed Amendments to the Constitution of the United States Introduced in Congress* from the 69th Congress, 2d session, through the 84th Congress, 2d session, December 6, 1926–January 3, 1957, revised by the Senate Library in 1957 (170 pages).

The resolutions of the legislatures of the several states requesting the calling of a convention for the purpose of amending the Constitution are given in the publication entitled *Federal Constitutional Convention,* Senate Document 78, 71st Congress, 2d session, 1930 (32 pages).[7] The House of Representatives Judiciary Committee of the 87th Congress, 1st session, has also issued a committee print on this subject entitled *State Applications Asking Congress To Call a Federal Constitutional Convention,* prepared by Cyril F. Brickfield, 1961 (40 pages).

Legal as well as practical problems presented by a constitutional convention method of amendment and suggested means for disposing of these problems are contained in *Problems Relating to a Federal Constitutional Convention,* by Cyril F. Brickfield, 1957 (112 pages). This is a committee print of the Judiciary Committee of the House of Representatives, 85th Congress, 1st session.

State Constitutions

Acts creating territories and authorizing the formation of state governments are printed with other laws in the *Statutes at Large.* Some of the enabling acts contain definite limitations

[7] The publication does not give the author, but a statement made on the floor of the Senate indicates that the compilation was made by the Secretary of the Senate. (*Congressional Record,* 71 Cong. 2 sess., Vol. 72, Pt. 3, p. 2813.)

on the powers of the state government, although some of these have become inoperative. Some papers relating to the constitutions of the states created after the adoption of the federal Constitution were printed as separate congressional documents and may be located under the names of the states in the Index portion of the *Tables and Index.*

The first compilation that purported to include the constitutions of all states was made by Ben Perley Poore, under a resolution of the Senate, and was published in two volumes in 1877 under the title *The Federal and State Constitutions, Colonial Charters, and Other Organic Laws.* . . . A second edition, which is apparently a reprint of the first one, was issued without document number but has been assigned Serial Nos. 1730 and 1731. The index to this work contains citations to specific subjects on which there are provisions in the several state constitutions.

The acts providing for the creation of territories are assembled in Senate Document 148, 56th Congress, 1st session, entitled *Organic Acts for the Territories of the United States, with Notes Thereon . . . Also Appendixes Comprising Other Matters Relating to the Government of the Territories,* 1900 (283 pages).

The act of June 30, 1906 (34 Stat. 759), made an appropriation for the purchase of the manuscript of a new edition of state constitutions from Francis N. Thorpe. This work was published in 1907 in seven volumes under the title *The Federal and State Constitutions, Colonial Charters, and Other Organic Laws.* . . . It was also issued as House Document 357, 59th Congress, 2d session.[8]

An index-digest to existing state constitutions, including all amendments up to January 1, 1914, by the Legislative Drafting Research Fund of Columbia University, was published by the New York State Constitutional Convention Commission

[8] For reviews of this work and comments upon its defects see *American Historical Review,* Vol. 15, p. 153; *American Political Science Review,* Vol. 4, p. 135.

For specific errors in Thorpe and later amendments up to 1911, see Alfred Z. Reed, *The Territorial Basis of Government under the State Constitutions* (Columbia University Studies in History, Economics, and Public Law, Vol. 40, No. 3), pp. 242–50.

under the title *Index Digest of State Constitutions,* 1915 (1,546 pages). A second edition was issued in September 1959, copyrighted by Columbia University and distributed by Oceana Press (1,132 pages). In 1918 Charles Kettleborough made a compilation entitled *The State Constitutions and the Federal Constitutions and Organic Laws of the Territories and Other Colonial Dependencies of the United States of America,* Indianapolis, B. F. Bowen & Co. (1,645 pages). The texts of the state constitutions as of January 1, 1938, are given in *Constitutions of the States and United States,* published by the New York State Constitutional Convention Committee (1,845 pages).

State constitutional limitations on taxation are given in *Provisions of State Constitutions Relating to Taxation,* 1938 (161 pages), published by the Joint Committee on Internal Revenue Taxation.

The Works Progress Administration (later Work Projects Administration) issued a series of processed publications dealing with state constitutions in their relation to public welfare. The titles, which are identical for those issued except for the name of the state, read *Analysis of Constitutional Provisions Affecting Public Welfare in the State of. . . .* States for which analyses were not issued are California, Kentucky, Louisiana, Mississippi, Oklahoma, Oregon, South Carolina, Tennessee, Texas, Virginia, and West Virginia. Citations to the constitutional provisions relating to general relief, old age assistance, blind assistance, aid to dependent children, veterans' relief, and organization of public assistance are given in *State Public Welfare Legislation,* by Robert C. Lowe, 1939 (398 pages), published by the Works Progress Administration.

CHAPTER EIGHT

FEDERAL LAWS

THE PUBLISHED LAWS OF THE UNITED STATES fall into three well-defined groups: (1) series embracing all the laws printed in chronological order; (2) codifications of all the permanent and general laws in force; and (3) compilations dealing with laws on particular services or subjects.

All of these groups contain only the laws enacted since the adoption of the Constitution and do not include a collection of the laws, or "ordinances" as they are generally termed, enacted by the Continental Congress during the period of the Confederation. These have never been brought together in any official or private publication.[1] The act of March 3, 1877 (19 Stat. 406), provided for the compilation and publication of these papers under the supervision of the Librarian of Congress. In his report for 1877 the Librarian stated that a comparison of the printed journals with the original manuscript showed so many omissions that he had suspended the work until "Congress should be consulted as to the expediency of printing the jour-

---

[1] The ordinances relating to public lands are contained in *Laws of the United States, Resolutions of Congress under the Confederation, Treaties, Proclamations, Spanish Regulations, and Other Documents Respecting the Public Lands*, compiled by Matthew St. Clair Clarke, clerk of the House of Representatives, Washington, Gales and Seaton, 1828 (1,095 pp.). These ordinances are not arranged chronologically, and some appear on pages after those containing laws enacted subsequent to the adoption of the Constitution. Those relating to the staff departments of the Army are assembled in *Legislative History of the General Staff*, by Raphael P. Thian, 1901 (800 pp.), published also as S. Doc. 229, 56 Cong. 2 sess. Some of the ordinances are given in Volume 1 of the Bioren and Duane edition of the *Laws of the United States* (see p. 214 for more information about this edition). The last are indexed in the *Synoptical Index to the Laws and Treaties*, described on p. 221.

nals in full."[2] The reprinting of the journals was not begun until 1904 and was finished in 1937 (see pages 146–47). The project for printing the ordinances was apparently never revived, although James A. Garfield, then a member of the House of Representatives, referred to the act of 1877 as a provision "for the publication of a document precious to every man who wishes to know the early history of the country."[3]

A compilation of the ordinances is desirable because in most cases there is no place where they appear in final form. In the journals of the Continental Congress they are ordinarily given in full as introduced. Later proceedings may show that portions were amended, but the complete text as amended is seldom given. Consequently the student has to reconstruct the ordinances by taking account of the additions, deletions, and amendments.

Series Embracing All Laws

The series containing all the federal laws enacted since the adoption of the Constitution are of particular importance from the historical approach, as the codifications give only the laws in force, and throw no light on the development of legislation, on appropriations, on repealed or temporary measures, or on acts for the particular benefit of individuals.

In all editions of the laws of the United States there is a definite classification into public and private laws. The line of demarcation is not easily defined, but the present practice of the General Services Administration[4] is as follows:

There are, strictly speaking, no rules which determine automatically the division of laws into private or public acts. There are, however, cer-

[2] S. Misc. Doc. 24, 45 Cong. 2 sess., p. 3.
[3] *Congressional Record*, 41 Cong. 2 sess., Vol. 5, Pt. 3, p. 2139.
[4] The publication of the *Statutes at Large* and of acts and joint resolutions in slip form was transferred from the State Department to the General Services Administration by Reorganization Plan No. 20. (*Federal Register*, Vol. 15, No. 101, May 25, 1950, p. 3178.)

tain considerations of which note is taken and which have been followed generally in order to determine in which classification any legislation should fall. In arriving at the conclusion, an act is always examined and considered as a unit, rather than paragraph by paragraph, in order to determine the intent of Congress when the act was passed. The determination of the intent of Congress is based upon the debate of the legislation as it appears in the *Congressional Record;* the nature of the legislation; its effect and scope; whether it is amendatory of legislation which has been classified previously; and upon personal opinion. In addition, an effort is made to follow precedent in order that certain classes of legislation will appear consistently in the proper part of the *Statutes at Large.*

Legislation classed generally as public may be listed as that in which the interest of the government is paramount, particular, or outweighs the other considerations of the act; that in which by the nature and scope of the act, the interest of the public as a whole is affected. Legislation classed generally as private may be stated to include that which is passed for the particular benefit of an individual or group of individuals, in the enactment of which the government or public has no direct or immediate interest.

In borderline cases the general practice is to classify the law as public.

The closeness of the differentiation is indicated by the fact that an act approved March 4, 1927 (44 Stat. 1845), authorizing the Secretary of the Interior to issue a patent to the County of Del Norte, California, for land to be used as a public wharf, was classed as a private act, while an act of February 12, 1927 (44 Stat. 1090), providing for a grant of land to the County of San Juan, Washington, for park purposes, was classed as a public act.

Acts granting land to counties or municipal corporations will generally be found among the public acts, but occasionally they will be classified as private acts. It therefore may be desirable to search among the private acts. Laws pertaining to natural or legal persons will generally be classified as private acts, although occasionally their character may cause them to be included in the public acts.

A curious instance of a law which contains both public and private provisions is the act of July 21, 1840 (6 Stat. 813), "for the relief of Chastelain and Ponvert, and for other purposes," which is classed as a private act. After making several appropriations for the benefit of individuals, the law makes appropriations for public buildings and enacts substantive law governing the duties and salaries of the Commissioner of Public Buildings. Part has thus the character of a private act and part that of a public act. The explanation of this hybrid law is that it was introduced as a private bill, and the public provisions were added by amendment.

The two successive stages in the publication of the laws are as follows: (1) slip laws, and (2) the *Statutes at Large.* All the laws are prepared for printing by the General Services Administration, which is the custodian of the official copy, but the public distribution (except of private slip laws) is through the Superintendent of Documents.

Slip Laws

In the slip-law edition each act is published separately as soon as enacted, regardless of whether it makes one page or one hundred pages. The slip laws are divided into two series—public acts and private acts, each of which is numbered separately beginning with 1 for each congress.[5] While the slip laws form a distinct series, the title "Slip Law" does not appear on it.

Examples of captions are:

Public Law 85–24, 85th Congress, H.R. 71, April 25, 1957. 71 Stat. 25.
AN ACT To prohibit the payment of pensions to persons confined in penal institutions for periods longer than sixty days
Public Law 85–32, 85th Congress, S.J. Res. 22, May 16, 1957. 71 Stat. 30. JOINT RESOLUTION Requesting the President to designate the third Friday of May of each year as National Defense Transportation Day
Private Law 85–14, 85th Congress, S. 394, May 16, 1957. 71 Stat. 11.
AN ACT To waive the limitation on the time within which a Medal of

[5] Formerly there were four series, but beginning with the 77th Congress, January 1941, through agreement of the State Department (which published the laws at that time), the Committee on Revision of the Laws, and the Joint Committee on Printing, public and private resolutions are no longer treated separately but are numbered in the public or private law series and are designated as such.

Honor may be awarded to Commander Hugh Barr Miller, Junior, United States Navy

Volume and page citations to the *Statutes at Large* volume in which the acts will appear are given in marginal notes, with underscoring extending part way into the text to show page divisions. Marginal notes are also used to indicate subjects covered in the text and to give citations to earlier laws referred to. Marginal notes are similar to marginal information in the *Statutes at Large.* The slip laws have been issued for many years, but as they are superseded by the *Statutes at Large,* they have no practical significance after the volume of the *Statutes at Large* is published.

Legally there is no essential distinction between an act and a public or private resolution, as both have the force of law.[6] All joint resolutions are signed by the President except those proposing amendments to the Constitution. However, several resolutions proposing amendments have been approved. Concurrent resolutions of the two houses are not ordinarily printed separately after adoption. These govern the actions or express the wishes of the legislators, but as they are not signed by the President they have not the force of law. At the time of passage they may be found only in the *Congressional Record.* Later they are in the *Statutes at Large,* the *Senate Journal,* and the *House Journal.*

Simple resolutions, which govern the action of only one house, may be found at time of passage only in the *Congressional Record.* They later appear in the journals of both houses.

Public laws in the slip-law edition may be obtained from the Superintendent of Documents either individually or by subscription. Individual copies of private slip laws are not stocked,

---

[6] "They [joint resolutions] are used for what may be called the incidental, unusual, or inferior purposes of legislating. . . ." (*House Manual,* 73 Cong. 2 sess., H. Doc. 413, Sec. 397.) However, some do not appear to fall within these categories, such as the public resolution of June 5, 1933 (48 Stat. 112), which provided that obligations payable in gold could be paid in any kind of legal currency, and Public Resolution 11, approved Apr. 8, 1935 (49 Stat. 115), appropriating $4,880,000,000 for relief purposes, cited as the "Emergency Relief Appropriation Act of 1935."

but a subscription may be placed for all private slip laws. Single copies of recent private acts may generally be obtained from the Document Rooms of the House of Representatives or the Senate.

Occasionally a voluminous act is not printed in the slip-law form. The slip-law print was omitted in the case of the enactment into law of Title 10 and Title 12 of the United States Code of Laws in 1956, the Canal Zone Code in 1962 (see page 220), and the Tariff Schedule in 1963.

The slip laws are listed contemporaneously in the *Monthly Catalog*, arranged serially under the heading "Congress."

Session Laws

The *Session Laws* are now of historical interest only, as they were discontinued with the issue for the 2d session of the 74th Congress (1936). They are noted here because copies are probably extant, although they were always superseded by the *Statutes at Large*. At the end of each session of Congress the laws were assembled in unbound volumes generally known as the *Session Laws* or *Pamphlet Laws*, which bear the title *Session Laws—Statutes of the United States of America, Passed at the . . . Session of the . . . Congress. . . .*[7] In their later years, the *Session Laws* were generally published in two parts. Part 1 contained the public acts and resolutions, while Part 2 contained the private acts and resolutions, concurrent resolutions, treaties, proclamations, and, since 1930, executive agreements. Occasionally when legislation was slight, as at a special session, the *Session Laws* were published in one volume. This was true of the issue containing the laws of the 1st session of the 73d Congress (1933).

The pagination for the public acts and resolutions as given in the *Session Laws* was the same as that in the *Statutes at Large*, so that for public acts and resolutions the *Session Laws* may be cited as the *Statutes at Large*.

In the *Session Laws* there were separate paginations, con-

[7] Prior to the volume for the 1st session of the 73d Congress (1931–33), the words "Session Laws" did not appear on the title page.

tents, and indexes for the private laws, the concurrent resolutions, the treaties, the proclamations, and the executive agreements. The pagination began with 1 for each of the five groups for the first session of each congress and was continuous throughout the congress. As the pagination for each of these five groups was different in the *Statutes at Large,* the *Session Laws* for these groups cannot be cited as the *Statutes at Large.* Some form such as the following must be used: "Session Laws, —Congress, — session, Treaty Section, p. —."

Statutes at Large

The laws are published in the final and permanent form in the *Statutes at Large.* Beginning with Volume 52 (1938) each volume contains the laws enacted during a calendar year. The earlier volumes cover varying periods, as indicated below.

Prior to the adoption of the Twentieth Amendment to the Constitution, the period of each congress ran for two years from March 4 of each odd-numbered year, but for some time prior to 1934 Congress did not convene until December unless a special session was called, although the date of assembling was not fixed by the Constitution. The effect of the Twentieth Amendment is that the period of a congress begins on January 3 of each odd-numbered year, and Congress meets on that day, "unless they shall by law appoint a different day." This amendment became effective after the end of the 1st session of the 73d Congress. The 2d session of the 73d Congress convened in January 1934, and the 1st session of the 74th Congress in January 1935. Therefore the period of a congress now covers two calendar years beginning with each odd-numbered year.

The *Statutes at Large* were printed from the same type as the *Session Laws,* and the chapter numbering was the same. In the *Statutes at Large* all the papers for each group (public acts and resolutions, private acts and resolutions, concurrent resolutions, proclamations, treaties, and executive agreements) were assembled in a continuous series for the entire period covered by the volume.

The issuance of the volumes in parts began regularly with

Volume 32 for the 57th Congress (1901–03); and in Volumes 32 to 50 the public laws and resolutions constituted Part 1, except in the case of Volume 44 for the 69th Congress (1925–27). The pagination was continuous throughout the parts[8] through Volume 60 (79th Congress, 2d session) except in Volume 44.[9] Volume 51 (75th Congress, 2d session) was in one part, as the session was a short one. Volume 52 (75th Congress, 3d session) was also in one part, as many of the treaties that would ordinarily have gone in this volume were published in Volume 51. In Volume 53 (76th Congress, 1st session) Part 1 contained only one act—Public Law 1, the Internal Revenue Code, approved February 10, 1939. Section 9 of the act provides that it shall be published as a separate part of the *Statutes at Large* "with an appendix and index." Part 2 contained public laws and reorganization plans, while Part 3 covered private laws, concurrent resolutions, treaties, international agreements other than treaties, and proclamations. From Volume 53 (76th Congress, 1st session) to Volume 60 (79th Congress, 2d session) public laws and reorganization plans (if any) appeared in Part 1 and private laws and all other papers in Part 2. Volume 61 (80th Congress, 1st session) was issued in six parts, Parts 5 and 6 containing only the General Agreement on Tariffs and Trade, and being paged separately as "A" pages. Part 1 covered public laws, reorganization plans, and the proposed Twenty-second Amendment to the Constitution; Part 2, private laws, concurrent reso-

---

[8] The title of the volume containing the laws for the 43d Congress reads "Vol. 18, Pt. 3," but the volume is always cited as Volume 18. What are regarded as Parts 1 and 2 bear neither volume number, part number, nor the words "Statutes at Large" on their title pages. What is regarded as Part 1 is the first edition of the *Revised Statutes*. What is regarded as Part 2 has the title *Revised Statutes Relating to the District of Columbia and Post Roads . . . with Public Treaties in Force December 1, 1873.* The three sections of this part have separate title pages, pagination, and indexes. The three parts are occasionally found bound separately. It is likely that the separates were not issued in that form, but that the original volume was torn apart and rebound.

[9] Volume 44 for the 69th Congress (1925–27) is in three parts. Part 1 is the code of the laws of a general and permanent character in force Dec. 7, 1925; Part 2 contains public acts and resolutions; and Part 3 contains private acts and resolutions, concurrent resolutions, treaties, and proclamations. Part 2 of this volume corresponds to Part 1 of the others and may be cited as Volume 44, without part number.

lutions, proclamations, and treaties; and Parts 3 and 4, international agreements other than treaties. Volume 62 (80th Congress, 2d session) consisted of three parts, the third one being a continuation of international agreements other than treaties.

Beginning with Volume 63 (81st Congress, 1st session) the compilation, editing, indexing, and publication of the *United States Statutes at Large* has been in the hands of the General Services Administration, having been transferred to that agency from the State Department by Reorganization Plan No. 20 of 1950.[10] The portion pertaining to treaties and other international agreements, however, remained vested in the State Department, so that for Volume 63 (81st Congress, 1st session) Part 1 was published under the direction of the Administrator of General Services and Parts 2 and 3 under the direction of the Secretary of State, although all three parts were still paged consecutively; and for Volume 64 (81st Congress, 2d session) Parts 1 and 2 were published under the direction of the Administrator of General Services and Part 3 under the direction of the Secretary of State. In this volume each part carried separate pagination, with the letter "A" preceding the numbers of pages in Part 2 and the letter "B" those in Part 3.

After Volume 64 the treaties and international agreements other than treaties were dropped entirely from the *Statutes at Large* and contained in a new series of volumes published by the State Department called *United States Treaties and Other International Agreements*, Volume 1 of which covered the year 1950. Succeeding volumes cover succeeding calendar years, the number of parts to a volume varying according to the number of agreements. Each volume replaces a definite sequence of the unbound Treaties and Other International Acts Series, just as a volume of the *Statutes at Large* replaces the public and private acts in slip-law form of a particular session of Congress.

The present form of issuance of the *Statutes at Large* by the Office of the Federal Register in the General Services Adminis-

<hr>

[10] *Federal Register*, Vol. 15, No. 101, May 25, 1950, p. 3178.

tration gives the public laws and reorganization plans in Part 1 and the private laws, concurrent resolutions, and proclamations in Part 2. A section entitled "Laws Affected in Volume 80" is designed to serve as a guide to prior laws and other Federal instruments which were amended, repealed, or otherwise patently affected by the provisions of public laws enacted during the years 1956–65 and published in Volumes 70 through 79 of the *Statutes at Large.*

Prior to Volume 39 (1915–17) the public and private resolutions were assembled separately and were not given chapter numbers. The concurrent resolutions were first printed in Volume 28 (1893–95) in accordance with the provisions of the act of January 12, 1895 (28 Stat. 615). In Volumes 28 and 29, they appear in the appendix following the index and are not listed in the main table of contents. In Volume 30 and thereafter they appear in a separate section in the main portion of the volume. Executive agreements were first printed in Volume 47 (1931–33).[11]

The *Statutes at Large* have been published by the government beginning with Volume 18 (1873–75), the earlier volumes having been issued by private publishing houses with official authority under the titles *Laws of the United States* and *Statutes at Large.*

The first edition of the *Laws of the United States* was the so-called Folwell edition, published under authority of the act of March 3, 1795 (1 Stat. 443). This set comprised twelve volumes covering the first 13 congresses (1789–1813). Only the first four volumes were printed by Folwell. A list of the editions of the several volumes with the names of the publishers is given on page 963 of the *Checklist.*

The second edition of the *Laws of the United States,* known as the Bioren and Duane edition, resulted from the act of April 18, 1814 (3 Stat. 129). This edition also went back to the beginning of the government but was continued to include the 28th Congress (1789–1845). It embraced ten volumes, only five of which were published by Bioren and Duane. The titles of

[11] For additional data on executive agreements see pp. 363–65.

the several volumes and the names of the publishers are given in the *Checklist*, pages 964–65.

A third edition of the laws, published by Little, Brown and Company, was authorized by the joint resolution of March 3, 1845 (5 Stat. 798).[12] This edition also went back to 1789 and continued to the end of the 42d Congress (1873). The title of this edition is *Statutes at Large*, which is used for all citations. The last volume was 17. The act of June 20, 1874 (18 Stat. 113), provided for the publication of the *Statutes at Large* by the government, and the official edition was made a continuation of the earlier private one. Volume 18 was the first in the set to be printed by the government.[13] No provision has ever been made for reprinting the earlier volumes, which must still be obtained from private sources.

As the first eight volumes of the *Statutes at Large* form a compilation, the contents are arranged in volumes of convenient size, the treaties and private acts being in separate volumes. Volume 9 covers three congresses; Volumes 10–12 cover two congresses each; Volumes 13–49 include the laws of one congress each. Volume 50 covers the 1st session, Volume 51 the 2d session, and Volume 52 the 3d session of the 75th Congress. Volume 53 and later volumes each cover a calendar year.[14]

Volumes 1–5 contain the public laws of the first 28 congresses (1789–1845); Volume 6 the private acts passed by these congresses; Volume 7 the treaties with Indian tribes from 1778 to 1845; and Volume 8 treaties with foreign nations from 1778

[12] The act of 1845 laid down definite provisions for the numbering of the chapters and the running head for the pages. These provisions are still observed, although it is doubtful whether they still constitute a legal requirement.

[13] See footnote 8, p. 212.

[14] The act of June 20, 1936, which effected the change from the biennial volume, provided that the *Statutes at Large* should be issued after each session of Congress. The evident intention was to have an annual volume, but the drafters overlooked the possibility of a special session. During the 2d session of the 75th Congress, which lasted from November 15 to December 21, 1937, only five laws, making as many pages, were enacted. The inclusion of the treaties, however, made a volume of 407 pages. The act of June 16, 1938 (52 Stat. 760), provides for the issuance of the *Statutes at Large* after the end of each regular session. In the event of an extra session the laws and concurrent resolutions of the extra session will form part of the volume for the next regular session. This places the volumes on a calendar year basis.

to 1845. Each volume subsequent to Volume 8 contains the public and private acts and, before Volume 65, the treaties for the years covered by the volume.[15]

Volumes 1–3 have no indexes; Volume 5 has an index to Volumes 1–5, and Volume 8 an index to Volumes 1–8. Each later volume has a separate index. For many years Part 1 (public laws) has contained an index to that volume only; prior to Volume 46, a consolidated index of Parts 1 and 2 was given in Part 2. Subsequent practice has been to have a separate index for each part. The pagination has been continuous through the two volumes constituting the two parts.

If the earlier volumes of the *Statutes at Large* are not available, the laws passed during the periods specified below may be found in the appendixes to the volumes containing the proceedings of Congress, as follows:

1st Congress to 18th Congress, 1st session (1789–1824), in *Annals of Congress*

18th Congress, 2d session, to 25th Congress, 1st session (1824–37), in *Register of Debates*

32d Congress, 2d session, to 42d Congress, 3d session (1852–73), in *Congressional Globe*

Codifications

Under this heading will be discussed all the codifications of the entire body of permanent federal law which have been made and published officially. There are several excellent codifications published commercially which are particularly valuable by reason of the annotations giving the decisions of the courts. There are also official codifications on particular fields, which are discussed under the heading "Limited Compilations of Federal Laws," page 226.

Revised Statutes, 1873

The first and only real codification of the laws of the United States is contained in the *Revised Statutes*, enacted June 22,

---

[15] For comment on treaties omitted, see p. 354; for comment on volumes containing proclamations, see p. 344.

1874, which embraces the permanent law in force on December 1, 1873. This code formed Part 1 of Volume 18 of the *Statutes at Large,* although neither volume number, part number, nor the words "Statutes at Large" appear in the title. It does not include provisions regarding post roads or the District of Columbia, which are included in a separate volume regarded as Part 2 of Volume 18 of the *Statutes at Large.*[16]

A second edition of the *Revised Statutes,* which contains all corrections and which is the one that should be used, was published in 1878 under the title *Second Edition, Revised Statutes of the United States Passed at the 1st Session of the 43d Congress.* This edition, however, does not contain the laws relating to post roads or the District of Columbia included in the separate volume mentioned above. A table at the end gives cross references from the original acts to the appropriate sections of the *Revised Statutes.*

The act enacting the *Revised Statutes* specifically repealed all laws embodied in the codification, and the text of the *Revised Statutes* is the law actually in force on December 1, 1873, and not merely a statement of the law.

Supplement to the Revised Statutes, 1874–1901

Two volumes bearing the title *Supplement to the Revised Statutes* have been published as follows:

Supplement to the Revised Statutes . . . , Vol. 1, 2d ed.; revised and continued, 1874–91, 43d to 51st Congress, inclusive
Supplement to the Revised Statutes . . . , Vol. 2. . . . Legislation of the 52d to the 56th Congress, 1892–1901[17]

In these supplements the general acts of a permanent nature are reprinted in chronological order without any attempt at codification or revision. In reality they form a condensed edition of Volumes 18–31 of the *Statutes at Large* rather than a supplement to the *Revised Statutes.* Volume 1 of the *Supple-*

[16] For full title of this volume and comments, see p. 212, footnote 8.
[17] This had been published separately in parts as follows: [Nos. 1, 2], 52d Congress; Nos. 1–5, 52d and 53d Congress; No. 6, 54th Congress, 1st session; No. 7, 54th Congress, 2d session; No. 8, 55th Congress; No. 9, 56th Congress.

ment is made prima facie evidence of the laws by the act of April 9, 1890 (26 Stat. 50), but there appears to be no similar provision for Volume 2.

Code of Laws of the United States

On June 30, 1926, there was approved a code "intended to embrace the laws of the United States, general and permanent in their character, in force on the 7th day of December, 1925." This was published under the title *The Code of the Laws of the United States . . . of a General and Permanent Character in Force December 7, 1925, and Appendix with Laws to December 6, 1926. . . . Volume 44 — Part I of the United States Statutes at Large.* It includes all general and permanent laws in force at the end of the 68th Congress through Volume 43 of the *Statutes at Large.* This is generally known as the *United States Code.*

Cumulative supplements to the *United States Code* are issued after each session of Congress. The supplements contain all enactments and repeals subsequent to the *Code,* as well as corrections.

The *United States Code* and the cumulative supplements were superseded by a second edition in 1934, a third in 1940, a fourth in 1946, a fifth in 1952, a sixth in 1958, and a seventh in 1964. The last mentioned, officially called *"United States Code, 1964 edition"* contains a consolidation and codification of all the general and permanent laws of the United States in force on January 3, 1965, and was prepared and published under authority of Title 1, *U. S. Code,* Section 202(c), by the Committee on the Judiciary of the House of Representatives.[18]

The *United States Code* described above is the official restatement of the law in force. It is prima-facie evidence and is presumed to be the law, but the presumption is rebuttable if the *Code* is at variance with the law as given in the *Statutes at Large,* inasmuch as many of the general and permanent laws

[18] The code has been published commercially under the title *United States Code, Annotated.*

which are required to be incorporated in the *Code* are redundant, archaic, and obsolete. There has been started a comprehensive project of revising and enacting the *Code,* consisting of 50 titles, into positive law, title by title. In furtherance of this plan bills have been enacted to revise, codify, and enact into positive law the following titles:

Title 1 General Provisions. June 30, 1947
Title 3 The President. June 25, 1948
Title 4 Flag and Seal, Seal of Government, and the States. June 30, 1947
Title 5 Government Organization and Employees. Sept. 6, 1966
Title 6 Official and Penal Bonds. July 30, 1947
Title 9 Arbitration. July 30, 1947
Title 10 Armed Forces. Aug. 10, 1956
Title 13 Census. Aug. 31, 1954
Title 14 Coast Guard. Aug. 4, 1949
Title 17 Copyrights. July 30, 1947
Title 18 Crimes and Criminal Procedure. June 25, 1948
Title 23 Highways. Aug. 27, 1958
Title 28 Judiciary and Judicial Procedure. June 25, 1948
Title 32 National Guard. Aug. 10, 1956
Title 35 Patents. July 19, 1952
Title 37 Pay and Allowances of the Uniformed Services. Sept. 7, 1962
Title 38 Veterans' Benefits. Sept. 2, 1958
Title 39 The Postal Service. Sept. 2, 1960

When this work is completed all the titles of the *Code* will be legal evidence of the general and permanent law and recourse to the numerous volumes of the *Statutes at Large* will be unnecessary.

The actual work of preparing and editing the material for this edition was done by the West Publishing Company of St. Paul, Minnesota, and the Edward Thompson Company of Brooklyn, New York, under the supervision of the Committee on the Judiciary of the House of Representatives. These companies prepared the original *Code,* which Congress enacted in

1926, and have continuously served the committee since that time in the preparation of the authorized new editions and supplements to the *Code*.

Index references are to title and section number and there is a separate index of acts cited by popular name.

Canal Zone

All the laws relating to the Panama Canal Zone were codified and re-enacted by the act of June 19, 1934, and again by the act of October 18, 1962. The complete code, entitled *Canal Zone Code*, is published in three volumes. Volume 1 contains Titles 1–4, Volume 2 contains Titles 5–6, and Volume 3 contains Titles 7–8 and treaties, tables, and the index.

Internal Revenue

Laws relating to internal revenue have been codified in the Internal Revenue Code, approved February 10, 1939, and August 16, 1954, published as Volumes 53 and 68A of the *Statutes at Large*, respectively. They were also published in volumes issued by the Treasury Department entitled *Internal Revenue Code, 1939* (743 pages) and *Internal Revenue Code, 1954* (984 pages). All of these volumes contain an appendix consisting of reference tables. The 1954 volumes give a comparison of the provisions of the 1954 code with those of the 1939 code.

District of Columbia

The code of laws of the District of Columbia was prepared and published pursuant to the act of May 29, 1928 (45 Stat. 1007), as amended by the act of March 2, 1929 (45 Stat. 1541). The 1967 edition was published in three volumes as *District of Columbia Code* (annotated), on January 9, 1967, and contains laws, general and permanent in nature, relating to or in force in the District of Columbia (except such laws as are of application in the District of Columbia by reason of being general and permanent laws of the United States).

General Indexes to Federal Laws

Volume 1 of the *Statutes at Large* contains classified chronological lists of public acts passed by the first 28 congresses (1789–1845), with references to Volumes 1–5 of the *Statutes at Large*. The classification is as follows:

Judiciary
Imports and tonnage:
   Duties on merchandise
   Duties on tonnage
   Drawbacks
   Internal duties
   Register of vessels
Post Office:
   Post Office Department
   Post roads
   Franking privilege
Public lands:
   Survey and sale

Relief and purchasers
Pre-emption
Lands given for colleges, schools, seats of government, seats of justice, etc.
Lands granted for internal improvements
Virginia military land
Donation land
Lands for military services
Lands granted to individuals
Acts for the adjustment of private land claims

Citations to the *Statutes at Large* for laws passed during the first 16 congresses (1789–1821) are given in the general indexes of the journals of Congress listed on page 145. Although the period indexed antedates the publication of the *Statutes at Large*, the indexes were prepared at a later date and the citations are to that series.

A general index to the laws up to March 3, 1851, which is at times useful in the study of the early legislation, is the *Synoptical Index to the Laws and Treaties . . . from March 4, 1789 to March 3, 1851* (747 pages), prepared under the direction of the Secretary of the Senate and published by Little, Brown and Company.[19] The references are to both the Little, Brown and the

---

[19] There are five editions of this work bearing the dates 1852, 1853, 1854, 1856, and 1860, but all cover the same period. In the debate on the publication of this index Senator Benton stated that it was made by Harris Heap (*Congressional Globe*, 31 Cong. 1 sess., Pt. 1, p. 510). No information regarding Harris Heap has been located; he is evidently one of the forgotten men.

Bioren and Duane editions. This is the only general index to the statutes which contains citations to laws relating to specific localities and to temporary statutes and to private acts. As the index contains also citations to the Bioren and Duane edition of the laws, it includes references to such ordinances of the Continental Congress as are included in that series.

This index is particularly valuable for tracing the historical development of legislation, as the subentries are arranged chronologically. It should be noted, however, that related subentries are grouped in chronological order without captions. On first glance many of the subentries do not appear to be arranged in the order of their dates, but detailed scrutiny shows that citations relating to laws on the same phase of a general subject are brought together. Under the main heading "Appropriations" (subentries for specific subjects) are listed all grants made during the period covered; under "Compensation of Public Officers" are citations to all statutes fixing salaries.

In 1906 a four-volume index to the *Statutes at Large* was printed under the title *Consolidated Index to Statutes at Large, March 4, 1789 to March 3, 1903*. This index is merely a consolidation of existing indexes to the *Statutes at Large*. It is undoubtedly a useful work, but only 25 copies were printed. It may be found in the Senate Library and in the Library of Congress.

The next general index to the *Statutes at Large* is the two-volume Scott and Beaman index covering the period from 1789 to 1907. This work covers only the general and permanent law and takes no account of local, personal, and temporary statutes. It is in two volumes—one for the years 1789–1873 and one for the years 1873–1907. The volume of this work covering the earlier period is entitled *Index Analysis of the Federal Statutes (General and Permanent Law) 1789–1873*, by Middleton G. Beaman and A. K. McNamara. It covers the legislation prior to the enactment of the *Revised Statutes*. The volume covering the later period is entitled *Index Analysis of the Federal Statutes . . . Volume I (1873–1907); General and Permanent Law in the Revised Statutes of 1873 and the Statutes at Large 1873–1907 (Vols. 18–34)*, by George W. Scott and Middleton G. Beaman. This index takes the *Revised Statutes* as its point of departure and includes all later permanent and general legislation up to March 3, 1907. It contains no direct citations to the acts which were incorporated in that compilation, in all such cases references being to the *Revised Statutes*. Valuable features of both volumes are the tables of repeals and amendments and lists of popular names of statutes.

The Scott and Beaman index was superseded by a volume published in 1933 entitled *Index to the Federal Statutes 1874–1931, General and Permanent Law Contained in the Revised Statutes of 1874 and Volumes 18–46 of the Statutes at Large, Revision of the Scott and Beaman Index Analysis of the Federal Statutes* (1,432 pages). This index was prepared by Walter H. McClenon and Wilfred C. Gilbert of the Legislative Reference Service, Library of Congress. Every worker in the field of federal law will welcome this valuable tool in locating many provisions of the law buried in acts pertaining to another subject. It does not represent a mere bringing up to date of the Scott and Beaman references; it embodies a complete recasting of the entries. The citations are to the *Revised Statutes* and the *Statutes at Large* by volume, page, section, and date and to the *United States Code* by title and section.[20]

As is indicated by the title, the volume covers only laws which are both general and permanent. It therefore excludes private acts, laws relating to specific territories and possessions, acts authorizing specific public works, and all measures which were of a temporary character at the time of their enactment. As the term "permanent" is used in the sense of "intended to be permanent" the index includes citations to acts creating and abolishing various units and activities. It should be noted, how-

---

[20] For Title 26 of the *United States Code*, Internal Revenue, the citations are to the 1925 edition of the *Code*, as that title was recodified for the 1934 edition of the *Code* after the index was published. The internal revenue laws have been entirely recodified by the acts of Feb. 10, 1939, and Aug. 16, 1954.

ever, that many units are established by administrative action and not by law; and as they are not in the laws they are not indexed. More detailed information regarding such units is given on pages 394–99.

The *Index to the Federal Statutes* includes all laws of a permanent character at the time of passage, with indications as to the provisions repealed, superseded, or no longer in force. In addition to the main index entries, it has voluminous footnotes giving convenient lists of statutes, treaties, and proclamations on particular subjects. The subjects and the pages on which they appear follow:

This index has ample cross references, but the alphabetical
arrangement is contrary to that generally used, as the divisions
between words are disregarded; thus "Postal Service" precedes
"Post Office Department" and "Publicity" appears between
"Public Health Service" and "Public Lands." Unless the user
bears this in mind he is likely to miss the entry desired. The
appendix contains the following useful material:

[21] Earlier lists of this character are in both volumes of the Scott and Beaman
index and were issued in pamphlet form in several editions by the Library
of Congress under the title *Popular Names of Federal Statutes*. The Library
of Congress lists were compiled under the direction of Henry J. Harris and,
later, James B. Childs.

Limited Compilations of Federal Laws

Practically every office which has contact with the public issues a compilation of the laws in force relating to its powers. These are generally issued in pamphlet form at frequent intervals and embody the latest amendments.

There have also been many compilations of a broad character. Only the more important or voluminous issues of this character are cited below. In cases where these have been issued in several editions, only the latest edition is noted.

Compilations of judicial decisions relating to Federal Trade Commission cases and railroads also contain the text of the laws; these are discussed in Chapter 10.

Agriculture Department. The volume entitled *Revised Edition of Laws Applicable to the United States Department of Agriculture,* 1945, 2 volumes, by Robert H. Shields and Nora C. Saur (1,723 pages), contains laws applicable to the department up to and including the 78th Congress, reorganization plans, executive orders reflecting the origin and organization of agencies of the department, and current appropriation provisions. It also contains statutes relating to the Agricultural Adjustment Act and the Soil Conservation and Domestic Allotment Act, as Amended. To facilitate reference, in addition to a subject index, all statutes administered by each bureau or agency are listed together. For legislative history of laws relating to the Department of Agriculture, see page 148.

The *1945–1950 Supplement to Laws Applicable to the United States Department of Agriculture (1945 edition),* by W. Carroll Hunter and Ralph J. De La Vergne (898 pages), embraces statutes of a permanent character, reorganization plans, and executive orders affecting the Department of Agriculture which were not included in the revised edition of 1945 or which have been enacted or issued between January 1, 1945, and December 31, 1950.

The laws and regulations governing the extension work of the Department of Agriculture are given in *Federal Legislation, Regulations, and Rulings Affecting Cooperative Extension Work in Agriculture and Home Economics* (61 pages), issued as Department of Agriculture Miscellaneous Publication No. 285, revised, January 1946 (61 pages).

Laws governing the Agricultural Stabilization and Conservation Service are given in *Compilation of Statutes Relating to Soil Conservation, Acreage Diversion, Marketing Quotas and Allotments, Wheat Certificates, Commodity Credit Crop Insurance, Sugar Payments and Quotas, Marketing Agreement and Orders, School Lunch, Child Nutrition, Food Stamp, and Related Statutes* (429 pages), issued as Agriculture Handbook No. 327, January 7, 1967.

Two publications of the Agricultural Marketing Service are *Compilation of Statutes,* relating to marketing activities, including research, service and regulatory work as of June 30, 1957, Agriculture Handbook No. 130 (210 pages), and *Compilation of Agricultural Marketing Agreement Act of 1937* as of January 1, 1958, Handbook No. 124 (28 pages).

A review of agricultural legislation enacted has been published after each Congress beginning with the 83d. The most recent is entitled *Agricultural Legislation in the 89th Congress* (59 pages), December 15, 1966. A *Digest of Agricultural Legislation Enacted During the 90th Congress, 1st Session,* is published by the Office of Budget and Finance. The Packers and Stockyards Administration has issued *Packers and Stockyards Act, 1921, as Amended; Regulations; Statements of General Policy* (65 pages), August 1967.

Atomic energy. *The Legislative History of the Atomic Energy Act of 1954,* Public Law 703, 83d Congress, 1955 (3,994 pages), is compiled in three volumes. A manual to provide security officers in the atomic energy program with information concerning United States statutes of general interest is entitled *U. S. Statutes of General Interest to Security Officers in the Atomic Energy Program, August 1964* (110 pages) 1965. *Atomic*

Energy Legislation Through the 89th Congress, 2d Session, (342 pages) was published in 1967.

Banking and currency. At frequent intervals the Federal Reserve Act, as amended, is published by the Board of Governors of the Federal Reserve System. All the amendments to the Federal Reserve Act are given in full on pages 305–583 of *Digest of Rulings of the Board of Governors of the Federal Reserve System to October 1, 1937.* By the use of canceled words and italics, each amendment shows the changes from the original or from the last preceding amendment. It is thus possible to ascertain quickly the changes that have been made in any paragraph.

Laws relating to national banks are issued by the Comptroller of the Currency. While the publications listed below do not give the current laws, they will be found of value for historical purposes.

Laws of the United States relating to loans, paper money, banking, and coinage, 1790 to 1895, 1896, 602 pp. (S. Rept. 831, 53 Cong. 3 sess.)

Laws of the United States concerning money, banking, and loans, 1778–1909, by A. T. Huntington and Robert J. Mawhinney, 1910 (Vol. 2 of the Reports of the National Monetary Commission; also S. Doc. 580, 61 Cong. 2 sess.)

Coinage laws of the United States, 1792–1894, 1894, 874 pp. (Finance Committee, United States Senate, S. Rept. 235, 53 Cong. 2 sess.)[22]

Copyright. Copyright laws in force are printed currently by the Copyright Office of the Library of Congress, which in 1906 issued also a compilation of all copyright laws entitled *Copyright Enactments of the United States, 1783–1906,* compiled by Thorvald Solberg, 1906 (174 pages), published as Bulletin No. 3, second edition, revised. In addition to the laws, this volume contains also proclamations from 1891 to 1905; treaties from 1899 to 1906; state laws to protect dramatic and musical works, 1895–1905; and some rulings of the Attorney General

---

[22] Only 77 pages are devoted to the laws. The remainder of the volume contains statistical matter and reprints of congressional proceedings, bills, documents, and reports. Three earlier editions of this work were published in 1893.

and decisions of the Treasury Department. In 1963 a 150-page loose-leaf revision of Bulletin No. 3 was issued. Copyright laws are now printed as Bulletin 14 of the Copyright Office of the Library of Congress, latest issue, 1967, contains 87 pages. For legislative history of laws relating to copyright see page 148.

Federal Reserve System. The Federal Reserve Act, including all amendments and provisions of other statutes affecting the Federal Reserve System, are contained in *The Federal Reserve Act as Amended Through December 31, 1966* (353 pages).

Fisheries. The Fish and Wildlife Service of the Department of the Interior released Regulatory Announcement 60 in 1959 entitled *Laws and Regulations for Protection of the Commercial Fisheries of Alaska* (33 pages). A *Compilation of Federal Laws Relating to the Conservation and Development of Our Nation's Fish and wildlife Resources* (472 pages) was issued in 1965.

Foreign relations. A collection of laws and related material was published in 1967 as a Committee Print of the Senate Foreign Relations Committee of the 90th Congress, 1st Session, entitled *Legislation on Foreign Relations,* with explanatory notes (876 pages). The collection contains the texts of the laws as amended through the 2d session of the 89th Congress, and annotations show pertinent history or cross reference.

Government administration. Included under this caption are the compilations dealing primarily with administrative law as distinguished from the substantive law included under other classifications. However, most of the volumes on substantive activities also contain administrative provisions, so that considerable detail on administration will be found in the volumes described under other headings.

Laws relating to the classified civil service are given in *Civil Service Act and Rules, Statutes, Executive Orders, and Regulations,* issued by the Civil Service Commission at irregular intervals and under slightly varying titles from 1883 to 1943. This publication was superseded May 4, 1945, by the *Federal Personnel Manual,* which consists of 10 basic or initial volumes each of which is kept current by the issuance in loose-leaf form of transmittal sheets.

Persons interested in the history of statutory provisions for the organization of the government will find useful references in the report of the Dockery-Cockrell Commission of 1893, entitled *References to Laws Organizing Executive Departments and Other Government Establishments at the National Capital* (175 pages), published as Senate Report 41, 53d Congress, 1st session.

Considerable legislation has always been embodied in appropriation acts, although this practice is not so widespread as it was some years ago. Legislation enacted in this manner from the 55th to the 63d Congress (1897–1915) is given in the volume entitled *General Legislation Enacted on Appropriation Acts, 55th and Subsequent Congresses, Compiled under the Direction of the Committee on Appropriations, House of Representatives,* 1915 (530 + lii pages).

A codification of the laws of the United States relating to estimates of appropriations,[23] the appropriations, and reports of receipts and expenditures, compiled by the Bureau of the Budget, was published as House Document 129, 67th Congress, 2d session, 1921 (232 pages).

An earlier summary of the laws relating to estimates of appropriations and governing the use of appropriations appears on pages 387–438 of the report made in 1912 by the Commission on Economy and Efficiency, entitled *The Need for a National Budget,* published as House Document 854, 62d Congress, 2d session.

The *Digest of Appropriations* was issued annually by the Treasury Department from 1873 through 1954, when it was discontinued as an economy measure. The *Digest* contained the

[23] An estimate of appropriation is the amount requested by the executive branch of the government. The regular annual estimates were formerly in the volume entitled *Estimates of Appropriations;* they are now in *The Budget of the United States Government.* Supplemental and deficiency estimates are submitted separately from time to time.

text, not a digest, of all new laws making or authorizing appropriations.[24] As the laws authorizing appropriations often include those establishing administrative units, the volumes generally contained the organic acts relating to government agencies. However, many subordinate administrative units are established under the general authority conferred on the heads of major units, and there are no laws relating specifically to them.

The *Digest of Appropriations* usually included all legislation of this character enacted at one session of Congress, but if there had been a special session it may have included the laws of two sessions. As the volume for a particular year was prepared prior to or in the early part of the fiscal year, it did not contain appropriations made or laws enacted at a later session during the same fiscal year. Such laws must be sought in the volume for the following year. Therefore deficiency or supplemental appropriations must be sought in the volume for the year following the one to which the volume primarily relates, and occasionally in the volume for the second following year. The series as a whole contained all appropriations, but it is necessary to use several volumes to obtain all the data for any one year.

The text of appropriation acts is given in the annual volume entitled *Appropriations, Budget Estimates, etc.*, compiled annually beginning with the fiscal year 1889 by the clerks of the House and Senate Committees on Appropriations and published as a Senate document. Prior to the volumes for the 68th Congress (1923–25), this compilation was entitled *Appropriations, New Offices, etc.*; the two issues for the 68th Congress were entitled *Appropriations, Estimates, etc.*

The essential difference between *Appropriations, Budget Estimates, etc.*, and *Digest of Appropriations* is in the arrangement of the appropriations. In *Appropriations, Budget Estimates, etc.*, it is according to the several acts of Congress, while

[24] An authority for an appropriation does not make any money available. It is antecedent to an appropriation, but is not legally obligatory. It is granted in order to meet the requirements of the House rule that no "appropriation shall be reported in any general appropriation bill . . . not previously authorized by law" (*House Manual*, 73 Cong. 2 sess.; H. Doc. 413, Sec. 834). Unless there is authority for an appropriation, any member may make a point of order against the item; if the point of order is sustained, the item is dropped from the bill.

in the *Digest of Appropriations* it is according to administrative units. A particularly interesting feature of *Appropriations, Budget Estimates, etc.*, is a tabular comparison item by item of the budget estimates and the amount appropriated. This table has been included only since the creation of the Bureau of the Budget in 1921.

Prior to the 68th Congress (1923–25), this publication gave the number of new positions created and omitted and the positions for which the compensation was increased or diminished. The information was classified by organization units and classes of positions. This tabulation applied only to positions for which specific appropriations were made—the so-called statutory positions. For some years salaries for many other positions had been paid from lump-sum appropriations, and the tabulation did not give a complete picture of appropriations for government personnel.[25] The passage of the Classification Act of 1923, and the consequent use of lump-sum appropriations for personal services, made the compilation of these statements impossible and they were discontinued.

In 1922 the Bureau of the Budget issued a small volume entitled *Compilation of Principal Federal Statutes Relating to Public Contracts*, 1922 (xv + 134 pages).

The budget for each fiscal year is now contained in two volumes entitled *The Budget of the United States Government* and *The Budget of the United States Government, Appendix*. *The Budget* is divided into four parts. Part I contains summary tables; Part II, the detail of the budget for federal funds, including various types of tables and schedules, explanatory statements of the work to be performed, the money needed, and the text of the language proposed for enactment by Congress on

---

[25] A lump-sum appropriation is one for all the expenses, including personal services, of a unit or of an activity. The number of positions and the salaries to be paid are determined by the administrative officer. A specific appropriation which carried the so-called statutory positions mentioned each position or group of positions separately and fixed the compensation. As a rule, the statutory positions were carried in the Legislative, Executive, and Judicial Appropriation Act, and lump-sum appropriations were carried in the other acts. The general appropriation acts are listed on pp. 385–86.

each item of authorization. Part III contains a summary table on trust and deposit funds, and detailed schedules and explanatory statements on the various trust funds. Part IV contains special analyses of budget data and federal programs. The *Appendix* consists of schedules showing details of the personal services which are reflected in the budget. These schedules are furnished to the Congress in accordance with the provisions of Section 204 of the Budget and Accounting Act, 1921 (31 U.S.C. 581).

A small pamphlet entitled *The Federal Budget in Brief* summarizes the budget recommendations and contains charts and graphs depicting the manner in which the money is allocated. A second pamphlet-like publication, *Special Analyses of the Budget of the United States,* contains a number of special analyses of significant aspects of the federal budget, including those printed in the budget document itself.

House Document Room compilations. For many years the House Document Room has been publishing pamphlet compilations of laws on particular topics or government agencies. Most of these have been compiled by the superintendent of the House Document Room. Recent issues may generally be purchased from the Superintendent of Documents. As they are inexpensive they constitute good working papers for a person dealing with a limited field. They are frequently reprinted and brought up to date. The list below includes only the latest editions. Some of the earlier ones are probably out of print.

Agricultural trade development and assistance act of 1954 and amendments (July 10, 1954–Nov. 11, 1966), 1966, 54 pp.
Anti-trust laws, with amendments (1890–1966), 1966, 140 pp.
Army, postal, and Navy air service laws (Mar. 2, 1913–Aug. 8, 1958), 1960, 240 pp.
Atomic energy act of 1946 and amendments (Aug. 1, 1946–Oct. 13, 1966), 1966, 231 pp.
Bankruptcy laws of the United States (July 1, 1898–Oct. 3, 1964), 1964, 375 pp.
Civil service preference, retirement, and salary classification laws (Jan. 15, 1920–Aug. 21, 1964), 1966, 298 pp.

Civil service salary and classification laws, Vol. 2 (Apr. 7, 1961–Oct. 6, 1964), 1964, 148 pp.

Compilation of laws relating to mediation, conciliation, and arbitration between employers and employees; laws relating to disputes between carriers and employers, employees, and subordinate officials under labor board; eight-hour laws; employers' liability laws; and labor and child labor laws; by Gilman G. Udell, 1967, 1035 pp.

Cotton and grain futures act, commodity exchange and warehouse acts, and other laws relating thereto (Aug. 11, 1916–July 2, 1958), 1958, 215 pp.

Crime, kidnaping, and prison laws (June 21, 1902–Nov. 11, 1966), 1966, 515 pp.

Emergency tariff laws of 1921 and reciprocal trade agreements act of 1934, with all amendments (May 27, 1921–Oct. 11, 1962), 1962, 82 pp.

Farm relief and agricultural adjustment acts (June 15, 1920–Oct. 11, 1962), 1962, 656 pp.

Federal farm loan act, with amendments, and farm mortgage and farm credit acts (July 17, 1916–Nov. 8, 1966), 1966, 361 pp.

Federal Power Commission laws and hydroelectric power development laws (June 10, 1920–Oct. 4, 1966), 1966, 329 pp.

Federal reserve act of 1913, with amendments and laws relating to banking (Dec. 23, 1913–Nov. 5, 1966), 1966, 651 pp.

Home owners' loan acts and housing acts (June 22, 1932–Sept. 25, 1965), 1966, 964 pp.

Hospital survey and construction act, with amendments (Aug. 13, 1946–Aug. 27, 1964), 1965, 82 pp.

Laws authorizing issuance of medals and commemorative coins (June 20, 1874–Oct. 13, 1964), 1964, 277 pp.

Laws relating to agriculture (May 29, 1884–Nov. 5, 1966), 1966, 726 pp.

Laws relating to commercial air service and miscellaneous air laws (May 10, 1916–July 14, 1960), 1960, 320 pp.

Laws relating to espionage, sabotage, etc. (June 15, 1917–July 4, 1966), 1966, 147 pp.

Laws relating to federal aid in construction of roads (Aug. 24, 1912–Nov. 8, 1966), 1966, 380 pp.

Laws relating to federal corrupt practices and political activities, federal corrupt practices act, Hatch political activities act, and miscellaneous related acts and regulations (Feb. 28, 1925–Aug. 9, 1955), 1956, 42 pp.

Laws relating to forestry, game conservation, flood control, and related subjects (Mar. 1, 1911–Nov. 5, 1966), 1966, 607 pp.

Laws relating to interstate commerce and transportation (Aug. 29, 1916–Nov. 10, 1966), 793 pp.

Laws relating to national defense enacted during 77th Congress, 1st and 2d sessions (Jan. 29, 1941–Dec. 29, 1942), 1943, 634 pp.

Laws relating to national defense enacted during 78th Congress (Feb. 19, 1943–Dec. 20, 1944), 1945, 320 pp.

Laws relating to Securities Commission, exchanges, and holding companies (May 27, 1933–Aug. 22, 1964), 1964, 328 pp.

Laws relating to shipping and merchant marine (Sept. 7, 1916–Sept. 22, 1964), 1964, 980 pp.

Laws relating to social security and unemployment compensation (Aug. 14, 1935–Jan. 2, 1968), 1968, 858 pp.

Laws relating to veterans, Vol. 1 (September 1914–November 1941), 1950, 469 pp.; Vol. 2 (December 1941–January 1951), 1951, 554 pp.; supplement to compilation of veterans laws (Apr. 25, 1951–Nov. 7, 1966), 1966, 767 pp.

Laws relating to vocational education and agricultural extension work (May 8, 1914–June 29, 1966), 1966, 618 pp.

Liberty loan acts (Apr. 24, 1917–Sept. 22, 1959), 1959, 65 pp.

Liquor laws (Aug. 8, 1890–Sept. 2, 1958), 1960, 315 pp.

National defense acts with amendments (1916–23), 1924, 147 pp.

Naturalization laws (May 9, 1918–Dec. 23, 1963), 1964, 403 pp.

Neutrality laws (Aug. 31, 1935–Aug. 13, 1953), 1959, 33 pp.

Oil land leasing act of 1920, with amendments and other laws relating to mineral lands (Mar. 2, 1919–Sept. 14, 1960), 1960, 415 pp.

Opium and narcotic laws (Feb. 9, 1909–July 14, 1960), 1964, 149 pp.

Passport control acts (Feb. 5, 1917–Aug. 1, 1956), 1958, 27 pp.

Pension laws (June 25, 1918–Sept. 25, 1965), 1966, 174 pp.

Public building act of 1926, with amendments; condemnation laws, with amendments; public works and construction laws (June 24, 1910–Oct. 13, 1964), 1965, 640 pp.

Radio laws of United States (June 24, 1910–Oct. 23, 1962), 1962, 238 pp.

Railroad retirement and unemployment insurance acts as amended (June 29, 1935 Oct. 30, 1966), 1966, 197 pp.

Seamen's act as amended and other laws relating to seamen (Mar. 4, 1915–Sept. 10, 1962), 1962, 167 pp.

Selective service act as amended (May 18, 1917–Aug. 30, 1965), 1966, 160 pp

Small Business Administration and investment act with amendments (July 30, 1953–Aug. 31, 1964), 1964, 85 pp.

Soldiers' and sailors' civil relief act of 1940, with amendments (Oct. 17, 1940–Mar. 3, 1966), 1966, 39 pp.

Surplus property act of 1944, with amendments (Oct. 3, 1944–July 28, 1964), 1964, 124 pp.

War Finance Corporation laws, with amendments (Apr. 5, 1918–Mar. 1, 1929), 1936, 36 pp.

Government operations.   The Committees on Government Operations of the Senate and the House of Representatives have issued compilations of laws concerning matters falling within their legislative jurisdictions. A partial list follows:

Compilation of statutes enacted by Congress of particular concern to the House Committee on Government Operations, December 1966, 240 pp.

Federal statutes on availability of information, compiled by Elizabeth Edward, Library of Congress, and edited by staff of subcommittee on government information, March 1960, House Committee on Government Operations, 303 pp.

Legislation authorizing appropriations and establishing revolving funds, as of March 1965, compiled by the Bureau of the Budget for the Senate Committee on Government Operations, Sept. 29, 1965, 101 pp.

Statutory authority for medical and other health-related research in the United States government and the basis for international cooperation, prepared for the Senate Committee on Government Operations and its subcommittee on reorganization and international organizations pursuant to S. Res. 347, 85th Congress, and S. Res. 42, 86th Congress, Feb. 25, 1959, 66 pp.

Housing.   All of the laws authorizing or affecting the programs of the Department of Housing and Urban Development are contained in a committee print of the House Committee on Banking and Currency entitled *Basic Laws and Authorities on Housing and Urban Development*, revised through Jan. 15, 1968, 749 pages.

Indian affairs.   The laws, executive orders, proclamations, and treaties relating to Indian affairs in effect up to June 29, 1938, are contained in *Indian Affairs, Laws and Treaties*, by Charles J. Kappler (five volumes).

Volume 1 contains the laws, executive orders, and proclamations up to December 1, 1902, and was issued as Senate Document 319, 58th Congress, 2d session. Volume 2 contains the treaties and was published as Part 2 of the same document.[26]

Volume 3 contains the laws, executive orders, and proclama-

---

[26] An earlier edition of Volumes 1 and 2 was published as S. Doc. 452, 57 Cong. 1 sess.

tions that took effect between December 1, 1902, and December 1, 1913. It was published as Senate Document 719, 62d Congress, 2d session. This volume contains also a reprint of the section relating to Indians from Volume 22 of the *Cyclopedia of Law and Procedure,* published by the American Law Book Company.

Volume 4, published as Senate Document 53, 70th Congress, 1st session, contains the laws, proclamations, and executive orders that took effect between December 1, 1913, and March 4, 1927, and the text of unratified treaties negotiated at various times. It also contains discussions of the power of Congress over Indian tribes and treaties; of federal jurisdiction over Indian lands, allotments, alienation, and inheritance; of Indian citizenship; and of the doctrine of Indian right of occupancy and possession of land. A noteworthy feature of this volume is the reprint of Title 25 of the *United States Code,* with the historical notes and notes of decisions published in *United States Code, Annotated,* a private publication. It also contains a few addenda to Volumes 1 and 3 as well as separate indexes to Volumes 1–4.

Volume 5, containing the laws, executive orders, and proclamations from December 22, 1927,[27] through June 29, 1938 (885 pages), was published in 1941 as Senate Document 194 of the 76th Congress, 3d session.

Most of the treaties up to October 1842 are printed in Volume 7 of the *Statutes at Large,* although a few were omitted and were published in later volumes. Abstracts of all the treaties, with quotations of important provisions, are given in *Indian Education and Civilization,* by Alice C. Fletcher, published as Senate Executive Document 95, 48th Congress, 2d session. There were several earlier collections of treaties.

The executive orders relating to Indian reservations have been printed by the Office of Indian Affairs in two pamphlets: *Executive Orders Relating to Indian Reservations from May 15, 1855, to July 1, 1912,* and *Executive Orders Relating to Indian*

[27] There were no laws, executive orders, or proclamations relating to Indian affairs promulgated between Mar. 4 and Dec. 22, 1927.

Reservations from July 1, 1912, to July 1, 1922. A more limited compilation is the volume entitled *Laws Relating to Five Civilized Tribes of Oklahoma 1890–1914,* published by the House Committee on Indian Affairs in 1915.

A *Handbook of Federal Indian Law,* with reference tables and index (662 pages), was compiled by Felix S. Cohen for the Department of the Interior in 1941. This book, which had its fourth printing in 1945, supplements the historical approach with an analysis of the actual functioning of legal rules and concepts and the actual consequences of statutes and decisions. It also contains an annotated table of statutes and treaties and a table of federal cases. *Federal Indian Law* by Frank B. Horne, assisted by Margaret F. Hurley, 1958 (1,106 pages), is a revision through 1956 of the *Handbook.*

House Resolution 698, 82d Congress, authorized the Committee on Interior and Insular Affairs to conduct an investigation of the Bureau of Indian Affairs. The results of this investigation are contained in House Report 2503, 82d Congress, 2d session, 1953 (1,594 pages, 157 maps, and index).

Interior Department.   From the 1st session of the 59th Congress to the 1st session of the 66th Congress, with the exception of the 2d session of the 65th Congress, an annual volume was issued by the Interior Department entitled *Laws Relating to the Department of the Interior . . . Congress . . . Session.* These volumes consist of reprints from the plates for the slip laws.

Labor.   The Bureau of Labor Standards in its bulletin series publishes an *Annual Digest of State and Federal Labor Legislation.* The Department of Labor has also issued *Growth of Labor Law in the United States,* 1967 (311 pages). Two House committee prints contain compilations of labor laws:

Federal labor laws (not including social security or unemployment compensation) and legislative action affecting labor, 1789–1966 (not including wartime controls), 1967, 161 pp.

Federal legislation to end strikes, documentary history prepared for Subcommittee of Labor, by James R. Wason, Library of Congress, 1967, 1354 pp.

Land-grant colleges and experiment stations. The laws relating to these institutions are given in *Land-Grant Colleges and Universities, 1862–1962,* by Henry S. Brunner, published by the Office of Education, 1962 (78 pages).

The laws relating to the state agricultural experiment stations are given in Department of Agriculture Miscellaneous Publication 515, revised January 1959 (24 pages), entitled *Federal Legislation, Rulings, and Regulations Affecting the State Agricultural Experiment Stations.*

Maritime Commission and War Shipping Administration. The United States Maritime Commission was established by the Merchant Marine Act, approved June 29, 1936; and the War Shipping Administration was created, pursuant to the First War Powers Act of 1941, by Executive Order 9054 of February 7, 1942. All laws governing these agencies are contained in the publication of the House Committee on Merchant Marine and Fisheries, *Laws, Proclamations, and Executive Orders, September 8, 1939, to December 31, 1944, No. 55A* (605 pages).

Merchant marine. The laws governing the merchant marine and registration and measurement of vessels have been published at intervals since 1903. The latest edition of this publication under the title of *Navigation Laws of the United States* was released in 1940 by the Bureau of Marine Inspection and Navigation of the Department of Commerce. Prior to 1932 the publishing office was the Bureau of Navigation. In 1932 it was changed to the Bureau of Navigation and Steamboat Inspection, and in 1936 to the Bureau of Marine Inspection and Navigation; by Executive Order No. 9083, dated February 28, 1942, the functions of this bureau were transferred to the United States Coast Guard of the Treasury Department.

Statutes on inspection of vessels have been issued under the title *Laws Governing Marine Inspection.* The latest pamphlet was issued March 1, 1965, by the United States Coast Guard. Earlier issues by the Steamboat Inspection Service and the Bureau of Navigation and Steamboat Inspection bore the title *Laws Governing Steamboat Inspection.*

A publication entitled *Laws Relating to Shipping and Merchant Marine,* 1964 (980 pages), contains laws enacted from September 7, 1916, through September 22, 1964, and another entitled the *Merchant Marine Act, the Shipping Act, and Related Acts,* 1966 (288 pages), contains laws as amended through the 89th Congress, 1st session.

Military establishment.   The permanent and general laws of the United States now in force which affect the Department of Defense are contained in Titles 10 and 37 of the *United States Code,* which have been enacted into law and which were amended by Public Law 89–718, approved November 2, 1966.

The laws and regulations governing military courts are contained in the *Manual for Courts-Martial United States—1951* (665 pages), which was published under authority of Executive Order 10214 of February 8, 1951. The Army, Navy, and Air Force have issued yearly supplements to this manual for use by the respective services.

Laws relating to military and other reservations under the War Department are given in the volume entitled *United States Military Reservations, National Cemeteries, and Military Parks* (544 pages), published by the Office of the Judge Advocate General in 1916. The work contains the general and special laws relating to the reservations, dates of original purchase and additions, and names of grantors from whom the United States obtained title.

All the laws relating to the several staff departments of the Army prior to 1901 are given consecutively in *Legislative History of the General Staff, 1775–1901,* by Raphael P. Thian, 1901 (800 pages), issued also as Senate Document 229, 56th Congress, 2d session.[28]

National forests.   Statutes relating to national forests are given in *Principal Laws Relating to Establishment and Administration of National Forests and Other Forest Service Activities,*

---

[28] This is not a legislative history, as it does not contain any citations to the proceedings in Congress. It is a compilation of laws arranged chronologically under several categories.

prepared by the Division of Legislative Reporting and Liaison of the Forest Service. This is issued as Agriculture Handbook 20, revised July 1964 (127 pages).

National parks. The acts governing the administration of national parks are contained in the volume entitled *Laws Relating to the National Park Service, the National Parks, and Monuments*, compiled by Hillory A. Tolson, 1933 (318 pages). This compilation was issued before the duties of the National Park Service were extended by Executive Order No. 6166 of June 10, 1933. Supplement 1, covering the period from July 1933 to April 1944, was compiled by Thomas A. Sullivan in 1944 (207 pages). The duties of this agency relating to public buildings were assigned to the newly created Public Buildings Administration in 1939 and to the Public Buildings Service in the General Services Administration in 1949. Supplement 2 was issued in 1963, compiled by Hillory A. Tolson and covering the period May 1944 to June 1963 (585 pages).

Nationality laws. The laws pertaining to immigration and nationality, including changes through June 30, 1952, are contained in *Laws Applicable to Immigration and Nationality*, 1953 (1,557 pages), which was compiled by the Immigration and Naturalization Service of the Department of Justice. This book is divided into three parts as follows: Part I contains the law. The Immigration and Nationality Act of June 27, 1952, which recodified former law, is presented first. Following this, in chronological order, is presented prior immigration law and then prior nationality law. Part II contains treaties, executive orders, and proclamations having to do with immigration and nationality. Part III, the appendix, contains laws that do not specifically relate to either immigration or nationality but are generally applicable.

Supplement I, 1954, of this volume (53 pages) covers all laws enacted and executive orders and presidential proclamations issued, as well as treaties entered into which concerned immigration and nationality from July 1, 1952, through December 31, 1953. Supplement II, 1955 (52 pages), covers the period from January 1, 1954, through December 31, 1954. Supplement III, 1960 (152 pages), covers the period January 1, 1955, through December 31, 1959. Supplement IV, 1963 (189 pages), covers the period January 1, 1960, through December 31, 1962.

Laws and Regulations Affecting the Control of Persons Entering and Leaving the United States, February 1, 1942, was issued by the Department of State as Publication 1709 (43 pages). And the House Judiciary Committee issued a committee print in 1965 entitled *Immigration and Nationality Act With Amendments and Notes on Related Laws and Summaries of Pertinent Judicial Decisions,* which was prepared by Garner J. Cline (260 pages).

Navigable waters. The laws governing the navigable waters of the United States, with the exception of the Great Lakes, are assembled in the publication entitled *Rules and Regulations Relating to the Navigable Waters of the United States with the Exception of Those for the Northern and Northwestern Lakes and Their Connecting and Tributary Waters . . .* issued by the War Department, Corps of Engineers, 1927 (351 pages).

Acts governing the improvement of rivers and harbors are given in the three-volume compilation entitled *Laws of the United States Relating to the Improvement of Rivers and Harbors from August 11, 1790, to March 4, 1913,* prepared in the office of the Chief of Engineers, 1913 (H. Doc. 1491, 62 Cong. 3 sess.). Laws applying to specific localities are given in Volumes 1 and 2, Volume 1 covering the period 1790–1896 and Volume 2 the period 1897–1913. Volume 3 contains general provisions. There were several earlier editions. A later volume containing both general and local laws from June 23, 1913, to March 4, 1925, was issued under the same general title and also as House Document 347, 67th Congress, 2d session.

The construction of bridges over navigable waters is regulated by general laws, and, in addition, many special acts are passed authorizing specific projects. All the laws from 1805 to 1903 have been assembled in the work entitled *Laws of the United States Relating to the Construction of Bridges over*

Navigable Waters of the United States. This work was issued in three volumes, as follows:

[Vol. 1], 2d ed., Mar. 2, 1805–Mar. 3, 1887, 335 pp.[29]
Vol. 2, Mar. 4, 1887–Mar. 3, 1893, 1893, 431 pp.
Vol. 3, Mar. 4, 1893–Mar. 3, 1903, 1903, 463 pp.

Navy. Laws affecting the Navy are contained in the publication entitled *Laws Relating to the Navy* (annotated), 1949, published by the Office of the Judge Advocate General. This publication is in loose-leaf form in two volumes and contains sections on the Constitution of the United States, treaties and other international acts, proclamations of the President, executive orders of the President, *Revised Statutes of the United States, United States Statutes at Large* (public laws), and the *United States Code.* Supplements are issued at intervals to keep the material current.

For many years the Navy Department issued an annual volume entitled *Acts and Resolutions Relating Chiefly to the Navy, Navy Department and Marine Corps, Passed at . . . Session . . . Congress, together with Certain Executive Orders.* The laws were reprints from the plates for the slip laws.

The laws and regulations affecting naval courts are given in detail in the book entitled *Naval Courts and Boards* (582 pages), published by the Navy Department, the last edition appearing in 1945 (588 pages).

The *Navy Yearbook* was issued annually from 1903 to 1921. It contains all the acts passed after 1883 authorizing construction of naval vessels, and a résumé of annual appropriation acts. Each issue is cumulative and contains previous legislation. This volume was always published as a Senate document, the last issue being Senate Document 428, 66th Congress, 3d session. Citations to the document numbers of the earlier volumes are given in the *Senate Catalogue.*

Pacific railroads. The laws relating to Pacific railroads are assembled in an unnumbered publication of the Senate en-

[29] The first edition covered the period Mar. 2, 1805–Mar. 3, 1881.

titled *Acts and Joint Resolutions of Congress and Decisions of Supreme Court of United States Relating to Union Pacific, Central Pacific, and Western Pacific Railroads,* 1897 (255 pages).

Postal laws and regulations.   The first major overhauling of postal publications in the history of the Postal Service resulted in consolidating and reconciling overlapping, conflicting, and duplicating materials from the 1948 edition of the *Postal Laws and Regulations,* the 1952 edition of the *Post Office Manual,* and the July 1953 edition of the *Postal Guide, Part I, Domestic,* and *Part II, International.* The material formerly contained in these publications is now found in the following: *Postal Manual,* 1954 (Chapters 1 and 2); *Postal Laws; The Directory of Post Offices;* and the *Directory of International Mail.* Many procedural simplifications were made, of benefit to users of all classes of mail, and the general readability of the publications was improved.

Chapter 1 of the *Postal Manual* contains regulations and procedures for public use pertaining to domestic mail, and Chapter 2 covers international mail. The material in this book explains the services available, prescribes rates and fees, and sets forth conditions under which postal services are available to the public. Loose-leaf supplements are issued periodically.

Postal Laws is a loose-leaf compilation of all laws affecting the Post Office Department. New and revised pages are issued as needed together with a transmittal sheet. It contains all of Title 39 of the *United States Code* as well as pertinent parts of Titles 2, 3, 5, 6, 7, 15, 16, 17, 18, 22, 26, 28, 31, 38, 40, 41, 45, 48, 49, and 50.

The *Directory of Post Offices* is a part of this series, although it is not a compilation of laws or regulations. It is revised annually. It includes the following: list of regional offices, list of inspection service divisions, the number of post offices by class in each state and territory, the zip code system, zip code prefixes, sectional center facilities, abbreviations of state names, list of post offices in each state and territory, and parcel post information.

The *National Zip Code Directory* was issued in 1967 and contains a national zip code map; two-letter state abbreviations; sectional center facilities; zip code prefixes; alphabetical list of states and cities; numerical list of post offices by zip codes; zip codes for Army posts, camps, and stations and Air Force bases, fields, and installations; and mandatory presorting list for second- and third-class mail.

The *Directory of International Mail* contains detailed information about postage rates, services available, prohibitions, import restrictions, and other conditions governing mail to other countries. The countries are listed alphabetically, with the specific requirements applicable to mail addressed to each of them.

The Post Office Department has also issued a book entitled *United States Domestic Postage Rates, 1789–1956,* which traces the development of postal rates through the many steps that have led to the present-day structure. It contains short histories of and tables of rates and fees for first-, second-, third-, and fourth-class mail rates and special services (registration services, domestic money orders, postal savings, special delivery, special handling, collect-on-delivery, insured mail, and certified mail). Appendix A contains abstracts of laws passed between 1789 and 1955 fixing rates of postage on domestic mail matter. Appendix B presents abstracts of laws enacted between 1789 and 1955 relating to the transmission of matter in the mails under the franking, penalty, and free-mailing privileges.

The several acts of Congress passed up to June 26, 1906, are given in chronological order in *Laws of Congress Governing the Post Office Department and the Postal Service,* 1907 (245 pages), compiled under the supervision of R. P. Goodwin.

A general review of the application of the government monopoly of mail transportation is given in *The Private Express Statutes,* 1937 (18 pages), by Karl A. Crowley, solicitor of the Post Office Department.

Abstracts of the laws fixing rates of postage and according free mail privileges are contained in *Postage Rates 1789–1930* (55 pages), published by the Post Office Department.

Presidential elections. The constitutional provisions and federal and state laws relating to Presidential elections and the rules of the two major political parties governing the nomination of Presidential and Vice Presidential candidates are given in *Nomination and Election of the President and Vice President of the United States,* compiled by Richard D. Hupman, Senate Library, and Robert L. Tienken, Library of Congress, under the direction of the Secretary of the Senate, 1968 (261 pages).

Prisoners. Digests of federal and state laws governing the release of prisoners are given in *The Attorney General's Survey of Release Procedure* (see page 271).

Public debt. The General Counsel for the Department of the Treasury in collaboration with the Commissioner of the Public Debt has published *A Compilation of the Principal Laws of the United States Relating to the Public Debt, to Which is Added the Second Liberty Bond Act (as Amended), in Effect January 1, 1938* (143 pages). This was brought to a later date by *Cumulative Supplement II,* December 31, 1939 (48 pages).

Public Health Service. The laws relating to the Public Health Service are contained in *Compilation of Selected Public Health Service Laws,* issued in 1963 by the House Interstate and Foreign Commerce Committee (158 pages). Included are the Public Health Service act, the federal water pollution control act, and acts relating to air pollution. The Public Health Service has issued *The Clean Air Act,* 1967 (14 pages), and the *Public Health Service Act,* revised November 1961 (19 pages).

Public lands. A general collection of laws relating to the public lands is *Public Land Statutes of the United States* (855 pages), compiled by Daniel M. Greene and published by the General Land Office in 1931. This contains all the "general and permanent statutes of practical importance" in force at the end of the 2d session of the 71st Congress (1930). An earlier compilation by John W. Keener was published by the House Committee on Public Lands of the 67th Congress, 4th session, under the title *Public Land Statutes of the United States,* 1923 (696 pages). The Senate Interior and Insular Affairs Committee published *Public Lands—Background Information on Operation of Present Public Land Laws,* in 1963 (129 pages).

The Public Land Law Review Commission was organized in 1965 to make a comprehensive review of the laws, rules, and regulations promulgated by the various agencies of the government to determine whether and to what extent revisions are necessary. In June of 1968, the Commission published *Digest of Public Land Laws* (1,091 pages), prepared by Shepard's Citations, Inc. The *Digest* assembles in one work a brief summary of each of the statutes currently in effect relating to the administration, management, or disposition of public lands.

The laws of the United States relating to the acquisition of public lands for mining purposes, with annotations giving the decisions of courts, are contained in Bureau of Mines Bulletin 94, in two volumes entitled *United States Mining Statutes, Annotated,* by J. W. Thompson, 1915. *Petroleum Laws of All America,* by J. W. Thompson, was issued by the Bureau in 1921 (645 pages), and *Summary of Mining and Petroleum Laws of the World,* Information Circular 8017, in 1961 (215 pages).

Of considerable historical importance is a compilation in three volumes prepared by the Public Lands Commission of 1879 and published in 1884 without document number and as House Miscellaneous Document 45, 47th Congress, 2d session, in three parts.[30] Part 1 contains the laws of a general and permanent character in force in August 1882. Parts 2 and 3 contain the laws of a local or temporary character and show "the entire legislation of Congress upon which the public land titles in each state and territory have depended." They include also a digest of all Indian treaties affecting the titles to public lands; an abstract of the authority for and the boundaries of the existing military reservations; and a table of judicial and executive decisions affecting the various subjects arising under the public land system.

Federal Reclamation Laws (annotated) is a chronological

[30] An earlier edition appeared in 1880 without document number and as H Ex. Doc. 47, 46 Cong. 3 sess.

compilation of public statutes of the United States enacted through the 79th Congress relating to activities of the Bureau of Reclamation in the development and use of water for irrigation and related purposes, with notes of decisions and opinions of the courts, the Comptroller, the Comptroller General, the Attorney General, the Department of the Interior, and the Bureau of Reclamation: Volume 1, March 2, 1861–August 14, 1946, 1958 (927 pages); Volume 2, April 30, 1947–September 2, 1958 [1959] (620 pages). *Federal Reclamation Laws* (without annotations) is a chronological reprint of public statutes of the United States affecting the Bureau of Reclamation covering the period June 23, 1959, to November 8, 1965, 1966 (204 pages).

Roads.   In 1966 the Bureau of Public Roads issued *Federal Laws, Regulations, and Other Material Relating to Highways* through December 1965 (325 pages).

Social security.   All of the laws affecting social security have been combined in a publication entitled *Compilation of the Social Security Laws,* 1968 (478 pages). This material, compiled by the Department of Health, Education, and Welfare, includes the Social Security Act, as amended, and related enactments through January 2, 1968. It was published as House Document 266, 90th Congress, 2d session.

Taxation (including tariff).   The Internal Revenue Code, approved August 16, 1954, has been published as Volume 68A of the *United States Statutes at Large.* It is also available in a publication entitled *Internal Revenue Code, 1954* (984 pages), issued by the Treasury Department. Both volumes also contain an appendix, which compares the provisions of the Internal Revenue Code of 1954 with the provisions of the Internal Revenue Code of 1939.

An unnumbered publication compiled by the staffs of the Joint Committee on Internal Revenue Taxation and the Treasury Department is entitled *Internal Revenue Code of 1954, Comparison of the Principal Changes Made in the 1939 Code by H. R. 8300 After Action by House, Senate, and Conference, August 13, 1954* (48 pages).

A list of terms used in the 1954 code, with citations to the sections in which they are defined or described, was prepared by the staff of the Joint Committee on Internal Revenue Taxation under the title *Terminology of the Internal Revenue Code of 1954,* 1956 (106 pages). The Committee has also prepared *Internal Revenue Code of 1954 as Amended and In Force on January 3, 1961* (1,148 pages) and *Cross-References Within the Internal Revenue Code of 1954 as of January 1, 1965* (17 pages).

Rates for federal taxes, except duties on imports, under successive acts are given in *Sources and Rates of Federal Taxation, Corrected to January 1, 1939* (53 pages), published by the House Committee on Ways and Means.

A useful compilation to the student of internal revenue laws is Senate Report 1123, 55th Congress, 2d session, which contains in chronological order laws of this type passed from August 5, 1861, to March 3, 1873.

The Ways and Means Committee of the House of Representatives published the text of each internal revenue act and the preceding one under the title *Comparison of Revenue Acts of* . . . . The acts included in these compilations are as follows:

1918 and 1921, 1923, 240 pp.
1921 and 1924, 1924, 242 pp.
1924 and 1926, 1926, 258 pp.
1926 and 1928, 1928, 247 pp.
1934 and 1936, 1936, 290 pp.
1936 and 1938, 1938, 336 pp.

The tariff acts passed from 1789 to 1909 are contained in House Document 671, 61st Congress, 2d session, 1909 (1,040 pages). The title is *Tariff Acts Passed by the Congress of the United States from 1789 to 1909 Including All Acts, Resolutions, and Proclamations Modifying or Changing Those Acts.*

The rates of duty imposed by the several tariff acts from 1883 to 1909 are given in Part 1 of the publication of the Finance Committee of the Senate entitled *Comparison of Customs Tariff Laws, 1789 to 1909, Inclusive, and Intermediate Legislation Thereon, with Statistical Tables of Imports and Other Tariff Data,* 1911 (541 pages). In spite of its title, this publication contains no data prior to 1883. Part 2 is entitled *Tables of Imports from 1894 to 1909 Inclusive, Arranged by Paragraphs of the Tariff Law of 1897,* 1911 (1,021 pages).

The text of the laws relating to specific items under various tariff acts is given in the digests of customs decisions described on page 286. The 1908 volume contains the laws from 1883 to 1897; the 1918 volumes, those from 1883 to 1913; the 1936 volumes, those from 1909 to 1934; and the 1941 supplement, those from 1935 to 1940.

The Tariff Act of 1930, which became effective June 18, 1930, is the latest general tariff revision by the United States Congress. Since 1930, a number of articles in the dutiable and the free lists of the act have been made subject to import taxes in addition to the other duties, if any, specified in the tariff act. These taxes, originally imposed by various revenue acts, are now incorporated in the Internal Revenue Code, but are required by law to be treated for virtually all purposes as ordinary customs duties.

Many of the rates specified in the Tariff Act of 1930 and many of the import-tax rates subsequently imposed have been changed by presidential proclamations and a few by direct congressional amendments. Changes by the former method were made either under Section 336 of the Tariff Act or in pursuance of reciprocal trade agreements entered into under the Trade Agreements Act of June 12, 1934, and thereafter amended at various times. These changes are reflected in the publication of the United States Tariff Commission entitled *United States Import Duties,* 1952, Miscellaneous Series (447 pages). Until January 1968, supplements were used to keep the material current. At that time this publication was replaced by *Tariff Schedule of the United States, Annotated* (459 pages). The basic publication is in loose-leaf form, punched for a three-ring binder. Supplements keep the information current. In 1967, *General*

Agreements on Tariffs and Trade (5 volumes), House Document 184, 90th Congress, 1st session was issued.

Territories and noncontiguous possessions. The laws relating to Alaska in 1913 were published in a volume entitled *Compiled Laws of the Territory of Alaska, 1913* (924 pages), issued as Senate Document 1093, 62d Congress, 3d session.

Laws enacted from the 58th to the 62d Congress (1903–13) and decisions relating to noncontiguous territory, Cuba, Santo Domingo (after 1905), and military affairs are contained in five volumes, one for each Congress, entitled *Acts of Congress, Treaties, Proclamations, and Decisions of the Supreme Court of the United States Relating to Noncontiguous Territory, and Cuba, Santo Domingo*[31] *and to Military Affairs,* issued by the Bureau of Insular Affairs of the War Department.

All of the general and permanent laws in force in the Virgin Islands on September 1, 1957, are contained in the set of publications entitled *Virgin Islands Code* (annotated), prepared by the Secretary of the Interior, 1957. There are five volumes in this set.

Vol.   I. Historical Documents, Organic Acts,
           and Constitution, Titles 1–5, 589 pp.
Vol. II. Titles 5 (*con.*)–13, 753 pp.
Vol. III. Titles 14–20, 650 pp.
Vol. IV. Titles 21–32, 576 pp.
Vol. V. Titles 33–34, Tables and Index, 491 pp.

Veterans. The provisions of federal law pertaining to veterans, enacted from the 63d Congress (1914) through the close of the 81st Congress (1950) are included in the volume entitled *Federal Laws Pertaining to Veterans 1914–1950,* published as House Document 78, 82d Congress, 1st session (1,022 pages). Cumulative supplements were issued in 1952, 1954, and 1956. The last, entitled *Supplement III* (338 pages), with the same main title, was issued as House Document 471, 84th Congress, 2d session. The laws are listed according to subject.

House Committee Print 322, 81st Congress, 2d session, Octo-

---

[31] "Santo Domingo" is not in title for volume for 58th Congress.

ber 6, 1950 (83 pages), entitled *Laws Relating to Veterans and Their Dependents,* is a chronological compilation of laws enacted between September 16, 1940, and September 30, 1950. House Committee Print 290, 84th Congress, 2d session, with the same title, dated September 6, 1956 (112 pages), lists the laws enacted between June 27, 1950, and August 10, 1956. A committee print of the House Subcommittee on Veterans Affairs entitled *Legislation Affecting Veterans Enacted by 88th Congress, 1963–64,* 1965 (64 pages), lists the laws enacted during that period.

Abstracts of the laws granting benefits to veterans are contained in *Veterans' Benefits* (56 pages), published in 1938 as House Document 701, 75th Congress, 3d session. A chronological summary of laws relating to veterans is given in *Veterans' Laws . . . Chronological Résumé of Veterans' Laws, January 1, 1939, No. 1* (116 pages), published by the House Committee on Pensions. It includes also abstracts of executive orders issued under authority of the act of March 20, 1933 (48 Stat. 8).

War legislation. The war legislation enacted prior to December 1917, as well as presidential proclamations, executive orders, and analogous legislation since 1775 by the United States, the several states, and the Confederate states, is collected in the volume published by the Department of Justice entitled *Emergency Legislation Passed Prior to December 1917 Dealing with the Control and Taking of Private Property for the Public Use, Benefit or Welfare . . . ,* by J. Reuben Clark, Jr., 1919 (1,150 pages). There were two editions of this publication—one of 1,150 pages with title as indicated above and a second of 110 + 1,150 pages with one title page reading "Emergency Legislation . . . Summary Memorandum," and a second title page as noted above. The two editions are identical with the exception of the 110 additional pages in the second edition. In the 87th Congress, 2d session, the House Judiciary Committee issued a committee print entitled *Provisions of Federal Law in Effect in Time of National Emergency,* prepared by Margaret Fennell, American Law Division, Library of Congress.

The laws and regulations governing World War II are contained in several publications. The legislative history, amendments, appropriations, cognates, and prior instruments of security are contained in a five-volume monograph entitled *The Selective Service Act,* published by the Selective Service System, 1954. These volumes contain the following material:

Vols. 1 and 2. Text, Chaps. I–XXIV, 797 pp.

Vol. 3. Apps. A–B, 438 pp. This volume contains background instruments of security from 1181 A.D. through Aug. 31, 1918, and legislative foreground documents from June 4, 1920, through Aug. 5, 1940.

Vol. 4. Apps. B–D, 307 pp. This is a continuation of Vol. 3 and covers the legislative foreground documents through Jan. 2, 1941, and the Selective Service Act from Sept. 16, 1940, through amendments to 1954.

Vol. 5. Apps. E–F, 301 pp. This volume contains the appropriations for and cognates of the Selective Service Act, a bibliography, and subject and name indexes.

The Office of the Judge Advocate General of the Army prepared a publication for the use of the Committee on Military Affairs, United States Senate, 79th Congress, January 1945 (275 pages). This publication contains *The National Defense Act,* approved June 3, 1916, and the *Pay Readjustment Act,* approved June 16, 1942, both with amendments to January 1, 1945, and army-navy pay tables.

The principal statutes conferring war powers, with particular reference to the circumstances of their termination, are contained in *Report to the President by the Attorney General Concerning the Limitation, Suspension, or Termination of Emergency, National Defense and War Legislation,* Department of Justice, 1945 (97 pages).

Bulletin No. 5, *Acts of Congress Applicable in Time of Emergency as of April 12, 1941,* Legislative Reference Service, Library of Congress, 1941 (58 pages), contains a brief analysis of those provisions of federal law which are specifically applicable in time of emergency, including war.

The Federal Bureau of Investigation, Department of Justice, compiled the *Statutes, Proclamations and Executive Orders*

Pertaining to National Defense Matters, 1941 (108 pages). This publication contains statutes defining criminal offenses, statutes relating to nationality and naturalization, aliens, manner of enforcement, proclamations, and executive orders.

A compilation of statutes, executive orders, regulations, and other documents relating to the construction, financing, operation, and maintenance of community facilities under the Lanham Act, as amended, are contained in *War Public Works,* Office of General Counsel, Federal Works Agency, 1943 (171 pages).

Laws relating to the control of prices are contained in *Price Control Laws and Executive Orders,* as amended, Office of Price Administration, 1946 (65 pages).

A selective list of statutes, proclamations, and executive orders pertaining specifically to World War II is contained in *Tabulation of War Emergency Legislation Relating to the Navy,* Revision 3, 1948, Office of the Judge Advocate General (21 pages).

Laws, executive orders, etc., pertaining to safeguarding military information are included in *Military Security,* Army Regulation No. 380–10, Department of the Army, 1951 (39 pages).

The National Security Act of 1947 as amended to August 1953, Committee Print 3, 83d Congress, 1st session, 1953 (38 pages), includes the National Security Act amendments of 1949, 1952, and 1953, as well as Reorganization Plan No. 6 of 1953.

To inform the general public of their responsibilities under federal laws relating to sabotage, espionage, etc., the Department of Defense issued a small brochure entitled *Federal Laws Covering Espionage, Sabotage, and Subversive Activities,* 1953 (12 pages).

A reference manual on all phases of the problem of protecting our internal security is found in the *Internal Security Manual, Revised,* Senate Document 40, 84th Congress, 1st session, 1955 (409 pages). This manual contains the provisions of federal statutes, executive orders, and congressional resolutions relating to the internal security of the United States through

June 30, 1955, and is a revision of Senate Document 47, 83d Congress, 1st session.

Water resources. A guide to laws and other official documents relating to water resources is contained in *A Compilation of the More Important Congressional Acts, Treaties, Presidential Messages, Judicial Decisions, and Official Reports and Documents Having to Do with the Control, Conservation, and Utilization of Water Resources,* by Francis W. Laurent, 1938 (117 + lvi pages, processed), issued by the Tennessee Valley Authority.

This volume contains only abstracts of the laws and summaries of the decisions, with citations to the sources. The material is arranged chronologically under five heads: (1) navigation; (2) flood control; (3) irrigation; (4) water power; and (5) multiple-purpose planning. Two appendixes are of special interest. Appendix J is a chronological list of reports and documents on the Tennessee River system, subdivided as follows: (1) reports and documents, 1824–1933; (2) legislation, 1828–1937; (3) presidential messages, 1902–33; (4) federal court decisions, 1934–38; (5) reports and studies of the Tennessee Valley Authority; and (6) miscellaneous articles. Appendix O is a chronological list of acts making provision for the improvement of rivers and harbors, 1824–1937.

CHAPTER NINE

STATE LAWS

THE PRINTING OF STATE SESSION LAWS or complete codes is obviously not one of the duties of the federal government, and such volumes must be sought among the publications of the states and private publishers. However, several federal research agencies have at times regularly published compilations of the state laws on subjects within their particular fields. Those interested in state legislation should apply to the federal agency dealing with the subject on which information is desired. Isolated compilations which give state laws within a limited field are also available, but they are not kept current by subsequent issues.

Important and typical compilations of state laws published by the federal government are discussed below.

General Indexes and Digests to State Laws

While the federal government has not published state laws in their entirety, it did provide until 1949 a valuable guide to state legislation through general indexes to state session laws entitled *State Law Index—An Index and Digest to the Legislation of the States of the United States* . . . published by the Library of Congress. Discontinuance of this series with the twelfth volume covering 1947–48 was the result of restrictive language regarding the Legislative Reference Service in appropriation laws for the Library beginning with the fiscal year 1952.

Volume 1 covers the years 1925 and 1926. Since state legislatures as a rule do not meet oftener than once in two years, the biennial period is used for the compilation. In addition to the states, the index covers Alaska, Hawaii, and Puerto Rico.

The *State Law Index* is confined to general and permanent laws and therefore excludes private acts; local and special acts dealing with specific localities, classes, or institutions (with occasional exceptions); temporary acts; acts pertaining to specific courts; appropriation acts; and acts dealing with administrative personnel and organization.

By reason of the special interest in legislation arising out of the depression, Volumes 4 to 6 (for the years 1931–36) index the temporary and local laws enacted to meet emergency conditions. These are included under the general heading "Rehabilitation," divided to include the following subheadings: "Banking, Investments, etc.," "Economies," "Relief," "Revenue," and "Schools."

The user of the index should note that under each main heading the subentries are grouped by states, all the subentries for one state being given before another state is taken up. Therefore, subentries relating to the same subject but in different states are not in juxtaposition, but may be separated by other entries. Thus in the index for 1931–32 under the main entry "Legislature," the subentry "Apportionment in Alabama" is followed by four entries under other key words pertaining to Alabama, Arizona, and Arkansas; then follows the entry for apportionment in California.

Under each state the arrangement is chronological. Thus in the index for 1931–32 under the entry "Local Government Finance" for Alabama, the first entry is "Reports of County Officers" (March 9, 1931), and the tenth and last entry is "Bond Issues, Temporary Borrowing, etc." (November 8, 1932).

In Volumes 1–5 the laws relating to personnel and administrative organization are abstracted in text form in appended digests. In the volume covering 1931 and 1932 these digests give the provisions of 476 acts not cited in the index. These volumes also include textual digests of important statutory changes in each state. There are independent indexes for the two sections containing the digests. Volume 6 for 1935–36 and the volumes that follow contain no digests and consist of one continuous index. Volume 5 for 1933–34 contains citations to court decisions interpreting important statutory changes made during the period of the volume.

Collateral information on state legislation is contained in two series begun by the Library of Congress in 1938. One of these series is called "State Law Digest Reports" and contains the following issues:

Current ideas in 1938 state legislatures, a review of reported bills introduced between January 1 and March 31 in legislatures meeting in 1938, compiled by Margaret W. Stewart, 1938, 26 pp. (Report No. 1)

Recent state laws on transportation and public utilities, a digest of important statutory changes and new laws enacted in 1935–38, compiled by Jennie Wellend and Lottie M. Manross, 1940, 83 pp. (Report No. 2)

Crime control, state laws, 1935–38, inclusive, compiled by Elizabeth A. Banks, 1940, 76 pp. (Report No. 3)

Digest of outstanding state legislation on agriculture, 1935–39, compiled by May H. Pendleton, 1940, 113 pp. (Report No. 4)

Current ideas in 1939 state legislatures, a review of bills introduced and laws enacted during the year, compiled by Margaret W. Stewart, 1941, 86 pp. (Report No. 5)

Current ideas in state legislatures, 1940–41, a review of laws enacted during the biennium, compiled by Margaret W. Stewart, 1942, 146 pp. (Report No. 6)

The same, 1942–43, compiled by Margaret W. Stewart, 1945, 85 pp. (Report No. 7); a 93-page mimeographed supplement, giving citations to the laws, and an index were also issued.

The same, 1944–45, compiled by the staff of the State Law Section, Legislative Reference Service, 1947, 98 pp. (Report No. 8)

The other series is called "Special Reports" and contains the following three issues:

Sources of information on legislation of 1937–38, a bibliographical list of published material reporting legislative bills and enactments of 1937 and 1938, compiled by Jacob Lyons, 1938, 38 pp. (Special Report No. 1)

United States Supreme Court cases declaring state laws unconstitutional, 1912–38, compiled by Margaret W. Stewart and Agnes M. Brown, 1938, 20 pp. (Special Report No. 2)

Sources of information on legislation, 1939, a bibliographical list of published material received in the Library of Congress prior to Jan. 1,
1940, compiled by Jacob Lyons, 1940, 36 pp. (Special Report No. 3)

The Legislative Reference Service in the Library of Congress published a series of mimeographed works known as "Public Affairs Bulletins." Among these were several treating of
special types of state laws as follows:

State labor relations acts, an analysis and comparison, by Agnes M.
Brown and Mollie Margolin, April 1947, 70 pp. (Public Affairs Bulletin
No. 52)

State aviation laws, a summary of the laws of the 48 states, by Samuel
Hutchins Still, May 1947, 235 pp. (Public Affairs Bulletin No. 53)

State rent control laws, an analysis of the statutory provisions, by Carrie
E. Hunter, February 1948, 77 pp. (Public Affairs Bulletin No. 62)

Antidiscrimination legislation in the American states, by W. Brooke
Graves, November 1948, 92 pp. (Public Affairs Bulletin No. 65)

Fair employment practice legislation in the United States, federal-state-
municipal, by W. Brooke Graves, April 1951, 239 pp. (Public Affairs
Bulletin No. 93)

Compilations in Specific Fields

Aging. The Department of Health, Education, and Welfare
has issued *Highlights of Legislation on Aging Enacted by the
States,* January–March 1968 (3 pages).

Air pollution. The latest issue of *Digest of State Air Pollution Laws,* was published by the Department of Health, Education, and Welfare in 1967 (556 pages).

Airports. *Survey of State Airport Zone Legislation,* by
John M. Hunter, June 1939 (13 pages) (Technical Development
Report No. 21), originally printed as Report No. 6, was pub-
lished by the Civil Aeronautics Authority.

Banking. The state banking laws in force in 1910 are given
in the report entitled *Digest of State Banking Laws,* by Samuel
A. Welldon, 1910, published as Volume 3 of the *Reports of the
National Monetary Commission,* and also as Senate Document
353, 61st Congress, 2d session.

Bedding and upholstery. Laws regulating the manufacture and sale of bedding and upholstery were compiled by the Division of Consumers' Counsel of the Agricultural Adjustment Administration with the assistance of the Work Projects Administration and published by the Department of Agriculture in 1940 as Consumers' Counsel Series, Publication No. 9. This 160-page pamphlet, entitled *Survey of State Laws and Judicial Decisions on Bedding and Upholstery*, gives the principal provisions of the laws of 36 states and the District of Columbia, as well as a comparison chart of the features.

Consumers' cooperatives. Laws relating to consumers' cooperatives are given in *Consumers' Co-operative Statutes and Decisions to January 1, 1937* (219 pages), published by the Consumers' Project of the Department of Labor. The volume contains only a few decisions. A tabular comparison of the principal provisions was published by the same agency in a single sheet with the title *Comparison of Provisions in State Consumers' Co-operative Statutes, as of January 1, 1937.*

Debt pooling. The Labor Standards Bureau of the Department of Labor has issued *Summary of State Laws Prohibiting the Business of Debt Pooling*, July 1967 (13 pages).

Education. The text or general reviews of state laws relating to education were published by the Office of Education (formerly the Bureau of Education) from 1903–40, with the exception of 1925 and 1926. This material was published either as a separate issue in the Bulletin Series or as a chapter entitled "Review of Educational Legislation" in the *Biennial Survey of Education.*

From time to time between 1933 and 1935 the Office of Education issued processed circulars giving abstracts of legislative proposals and enactments. These were included in the series of numbered circulars, and had the title *Legislative Action in . . . Affecting Education* or *Educational Measures before . . . State Legislatures.* The Office of Education has also issued compilations dealing with special features of educational administration, among which the following have been carried in the Bulletin Series:

Education for freedom as provided by state laws, by Ward W. Keesecker, 1948, 38 pp. (Bulletin, 1948, No. 11); excerpts from state laws requiring instruction on United States constitution, history, ideals, etc.

School census, compulsory education, child labor; state laws and regulations, by Maris M. Proffitt and David Segel, 1945, 200 pp. (Bulletin, 1945, No. 1)

State boards of education and chief state school officers, their status and legal powers, by Ward W. Keesecker, 1950, 114 pp. (Bulletin, 1950, No. 12)

State legislation for education of exceptional children, by Elise H. Martens, with the collaboration of others, 1949, 61 pp. (Bulletin, 1949, No. 2)

State law on compulsory attendance, by August W. Steinhilber and Carl J. Sokolowski, 1966, 103 pp. (Circular 793, OE-23044)

State laws relating to transportation and textbooks for parochial school students and constitutional protection of religious freedoms, by August W. Steinhilber and Carl J. Sokolowski, 1966, 45 pp. (OE-20087)

State legislation relating to higher education, Jan. 1, 1964 to Dec. 31, 1964, by S. V. Martorana and Jeanne D. Brandt, 1966, 150 pp. (No circular number, OE-50008-64)

State provisions for financing public school capital outlay programs, a cooperative study by the Office of Education and the University of California under the sponsorship of the National Council of Chief State School Officers, 1951, 170 pp. (Bulletin, 1951, No. 6)

State provisions for school lunch programs, laws and personnel, by Myrtis Keels Jeffers, 1952, 40 pp. (Bulletin, 1952, No. 4)

State school laws and regulations for health, safety, driver, outdoor, and physical education (with list of citations to state laws), compiled by Zollie Maynard and Salvatore Rinaldi, 1964 (Miscellaneous Publication 41, OE-28006)

Survey of state legislation relating to higher education, July 1, 1958, to Dec. 31, 1959, by Ernest V. Hollis, William G. Land, and S. V. Martorana, 1960, 200 pp. (Circular 618, OE-50008)

Same, Jan. 1, 1960, to Dec. 31, 1960, 1961, 92 pp. Circular 647, OE-50008-60)

Same, Jan. 1, 1961, to Dec. 31, 1961, by S. V. Martorana and Ernest V. Hollis, 1962, 273 pp. (Circular 684, OE-50008-61)

Same, Jan. 1, 1962, to Dec. 31, 1962, 1963, 135 pp. (Circular 716, OE-50008-62)

Same, Jan. 1, 1963, to Dec. 31, 1963, by Ernest V. Hollis, S. V. Martorana, and Jeanne D. Brandt, 1964, 274 pp. (Circular 748, OE-50008-63)

Another publication of the Office of Education is *Certification of School Librarians*, a compilation of state requirements, by Mary Helen Mahar, 1958 (73 pages) (Bulletin, 1958, No. 12).

Election laws.   The United States Senate has issued several editions of *Election Law Guidebook*, a summary of federal and state laws regulating the nomination and election of United States Senators, the latest being revised to January 1, 1968 (180 pages), and published as Senate Document 76, 90th Congress, 2d session.

Fire control.   The Forest Service in the Department of Agriculture has published *Analysis of State Fire Control Laws*, July 1966 (1 page).

Hard of hearing and deaf.   "A Digest of State Laws Affecting the Acoustically Handicapped, with Supplementary Notes on Administrative Acts, Orders, and Policies" is contained in *The Hard of Hearing and the Deaf*, 1943 (122 pages), prepared by the Legislative Reference Service, Library of Congress, and published as House Document 154, 78th Congress, 1st session. This is a revision of an original 1941 document.

Health.   From 1911 to 1928 the state laws and regulations relating to public health were published by the Public Health Service. After 1928 the publication of the detailed laws was discontinued and the compilation was limited to indexes issued under the title *Citations to Public Health Laws and Regulations*. Beginning with 1910 the Public Health Service published municipal ordinances on public health. These compilations have appeared in the two series known as "Reprints from Public Health Reports" and "Supplements to Public Health Reports."

A later work relating to public health is *State Laws Governing Local Health Departments*, Public Health Service Publication No. 299, 1953 (68 pages). This presents in tabular form data obtained from a study of the provisions of each state's laws, regulations, and practices applicable to the establishment and operation of local health departments.

Other issues of the Public Health Service in the field of health are as follows:

Digest of state air pollution laws, 1967, 556 pp. Public Health Service (Publication No. 711). Earlier editions were issued in 1959, 1960, 1962, 1963, and 1966, with supplements in 1961 and 1964.

Digest of state enabling legislation for mosquito abatement, through 1955, by B. F. Keefe and L. D. Beadle, Communicable Disease Center, Atlanta, Ga., 1956, 83 pp.

Occupational health and safety legislation, a compilation of state laws and regulations, by Victoria M. Trasko, 1954, 315 pp. (Public Health Service Publication No. 357)

Premarital health examination legislation, analysis and compilation of state laws, in part by J. K. Shafer, 1954, 114 pp. (Public Health Service Publication No. 383)

Prenatal health examination legislation, analysis and compilation of state laws, in part by Laura M. Halse and Dominic V. Liberti, 1954, 55 pp (Public Health Service Publication No. 369)

State legislation and regulations involving ionizing radiation, 1965, by Patrick A. Thibeau, 1967, 47 pp. (Public Health Service Publication No. 1574)

Summary of state legislation relating to public health, 1962, prepared upon recommendation of Association of State and Territorial Health Officers, 1963, 64 pp. (Public Health Service Publication No. 1089)

Digest of state air pollution laws, 1967, 556 pp.

Housing and redevelopment. The National Housing Agency, predecessor of the Housing and Home Finance Agency and the Department of Housing and Urban Development, issued on April 1, 1947, an 88-page mimeographed *Comparative Digest of the Principal Provisions of State Urban Redevelopment Legislation.* This covered the general nature of the laws, citations, short titles, and the principal provisions. An earlier edition was issued on October 31, 1945.

A publication of the Department of Agriculture, *Rural Zoning in the United States,* January 1952, by Erling D. Solberg, Agriculture Information Bulletin No. 59 (85 pages), includes a legal bibliography of state enabling legislation empowering counties, towns, or townships, or other local governmental units, to enact rural-zoning regulations.

An earlier survey of enabling legislation was made by the National Resources Planning Board and issued in mimeograph form as its Circular XII (revised), dated December 15, 1941, with the title *State Legislation on Planning, Zoning, and Platting*. This gives citations to the laws as well as an abstract of the coverage of each act.

Another work on planning was issued by the Housing and Home Finance Agency, entitled *Planning Laws; Housing, Urban Planning Assistance, Community Facilities, Urban Renewal; a Comparative Digest of State Statutes for Community, County, Region, and State Planning Through December 1957*. This 77-page pamphlet is the second edition of one of a series. One other work in the series published so far is *Comparative Digest of Municipal and County Zoning Enabling Statutes*, for reference in community planning, housing, slum clearance, and urban redevelopment programs, as of October 31, 1952 (70 pages). Both publications give citations and principal provisions and include a comparative chart. *State Enabling Legislation, Urban Redevelopment, and Urban Renewal*, is a list of citations to statutes, constitutional provisions, and court decisions, 1962 (21 pages). *Fair Housing Laws* gives summaries and texts of state and municipal laws in this field, 1964 (369 pages). The Intergroup Relations Service and the General Counsel's Office have prepared *State Statutes and Local Ordinances and Resolutions Prohibiting Discrimination in Housing and Urban Renewal Operations*, 1962 (115 pages).

Income taxes.   The provisions of state laws are given in *Digest of State Laws Relating to Net Income Taxes, 1938*, by Robert H. Holley, 1938 (133 pages, plus 5 pages of revisions and errata; also corrected reprint of 132 pages), published by the Bureau of the Census. The volume includes abstracts of laws levying income taxes on individuals and corporations in effect January 1, 1938. A 1939 supplement of 37 pages in processed form was also issued.

Inheritance, estate, and gift taxes. Abstracts of state laws in force on January 1, 1938, are given in *Digest of State Laws Relating to Inheritance and Estate Taxes, 1938,* by Robert H. Holley (147 pages), originally issued by the Bureau of the Census in 1938, but reprinted in 1939 with corrections. The original edition also gives a digest of the federal estate tax, but the data are incomplete, as no reference is made to the additional taxes imposed by the Revenue Act of 1932, as amended by the Revenue Act of 1935 (49 Stat. 1021). In the second edition the credit allowed on the federal tax on account of estate tax payment to states is given in place of the federal rates. A 1939 supplement of 32 pages in processed form was also issued.

An earlier, but more comprehensive, report is *Federal and State Death Taxes,* 1933 (256 pages), published by the Joint Committee on Internal Revenue Taxation. Only abstracts of the laws are given, but the volume includes information on the history, development, principles, and difficulties of these taxes. An appendix gives statistics.

The Veterans Administration has published *Digest of Inheritance Laws, States and Territories of the United States,* 1966 (118 pages).

Internal security. A committee print of the Senate Judiciary Committee prepared by Raymond J. Celada of the Library of Congress, *Internal Security and Subversion,* covers the principal state laws and cases, 1965 (703 pages).

Irrigation districts. Abstracts of laws on irrigation districts are given in *Summary of Irrigation District Statutes of Western States,* by Wells A. Hutchins, 1931 (127 pages), published by the Department of Agriculture as Miscellaneous Publication 103.

Labor. One of the long-continued series of compilations of state laws was that of the Bureau of Labor Statistics relating to labor. This series extends back to 1903, but the complete compilations were discontinued with the volume for 1932. Summaries of legislation for later years have been published in the

Monthly Labor Review. A summary of the laws for 1937 was published as Bulletin No. 654.

Abstracts of state laws relating to labor have been published by the Bureau (formerly Division) of Labor Standards of the Department of Labor. The *Digest of Principal State Labor Legislation Enacted in 1935, as Reported to September 15* was issued in a revised edition in 1935 (61 pages). The *Digest of State and Federal Labor Legislation, Enacted September 15, 1935–September 15, 1936* (33 pages), was issued as Bulletin No. 9. This publication has been issued in the Bulletin Series from 1936 to date, covering periods from nine months to two years. In 1944 the title was changed to *Annual Digest of State and Federal Labor Legislation.*

A continuing report on labor legislation was issued in mimeographed form by the Bureau of Labor Standards from January 14, 1939, to August 31, 1951. It was called *Legislative Report* from 1939 to 1947, *Legislative Report, A Current Summary of Legislative Action* in 1948, and *Legislative Report, A Current Summary on Labor Legislation* from 1949 to 1951. In January 1967 *State Labor Relations Acts,* prepared by David A. Swankin, was issued (39 pages).

The Bureau of Labor Standards issues a *Fact Sheet Series,* which is revised periodically. The titles are as follows:

1. Brief outline of labor law in the United States.
2. Status of agricultural workers under state and federal labor laws.
3-A. Brief summary of state child labor laws.
3-B. Questions and answers on child labor laws.
3-C. Brief summary of state compulsory school attendance laws.
4-A. Brief summary of state minimum wage laws.
4-B. Brief summary of state wage payment and wage collection laws.
4-C. Brief summary of state prevailing wage laws.
5. Brief summary of state laws regulating private employment agencies.
6-A. Brief summary of state fair employment practice acts.
6-B. Brief summary of state laws prohibiting discrimination in employment because of age.
6-C. Age discrimination prohibited under state laws—a table.
7-A. Brief summary of state labor relations acts.
7-B. Brief summary of state mediation laws.
7-C. Brief summary of state union regulatory provisions.

8. Brief summary of state laws regulating industrial homework.

9-A. Brief summary of state occupational safety and health legislation.

9-B. Brief summary of state laws and regulations for the control of radiation hazards.

10. Brief summary of state workmen's compensation laws.

Special compilations have been published on particular phases of labor legislation as given in the paragraphs that follow.

ANTI-INJUNCTION. Laura H. Dale has prepared *State Anti-injunction Laws, Brief Discussion of Major Provisions,* 1963 (9 pages).

EMPLOYMENT AGENCIES. *Private Employment Agencies; Laws Relating to Their Regulation,* as of September 1, 1943, prepared by Marian L. Mel, with the assistance of Charles F. Sharkey and Hester M. Hood (514 pages), was issued as Bulletin No. 57 of the Bureau of Labor Standards.

FARM LABOR. *Major Provisions of State and Federal Farm Labor Contractor Laws,* prepared by Deborah T. Bond, was published in 1965 (21 pages).

HOURS OF WORK. The Bureau of Labor Standards issued a set of processed loose-leaf charts in 1938 entitled *Chart Showing State and Federal Hours Limitations* (48 pages). This compilation was supplemented in 1940 by a 53-page supplement on hours of service of bus and truck operators; in addition numerous revised pages were issued. The latest printed compilation issued was *State and Federal Hours Limitations, A Summary,* December 15, 1950, prepared under the general direction of Marian L. Mel (143 pages), Bulletin No. 116, revised.

MEDIATION LAWS AND AGENCIES. The Bureau of Labor Standards has published the following:

State authorities engaged in mediation and conciliation activities, September 1947, prepared by Flora Y. Hatcher, 32 pp., processed (Bulletin No. 91)

A guide to state mediation laws and agencies, Sept. 1, 1954, prepared by Robert G. Rodden, 57 pp. (Bulletin No. 176); a revision, prepared by Norene M. Diamond, released in 1959 (63 pages)

RIGHT-TO-WORK LAWS.   Since the passage of the Taft-Hartley Act more than a third of the states have passed laws or amended their constitutions to make null and void, or unlawful, contracts requiring membership in a labor union as a condition of employment. The Bureau of Labor Standards gathered information on these and published in September 1959 an eight-leaved pamphlet entitled *State Right-to-Work Laws* (Bulletin No. 204).

SAFETY CODES.   The Bureau of Labor Standards in September 1950 made an analysis of the state safety codes for woodworking machinery under the title *Requirements of State Safety Codes for Woodworking Machinery Compared with A.S.A. Safety Code 01.1,* 43 leaves (mimeographed).

TIME OFF FOR VOTING.   A pamphlet entitled *Time Off for Voting under State Laws,* consisting mainly of a tabular chart of comparative provisions of state laws, was issued first in 1950 with 11 pages, and revised in 1952, 1954, 1956, 1958, 1960, 1962, and 1964. The last revision consisted of 21 pages and was issued as Bulletin No. 138 of the Bureau of Labor Standards.

WAGES.   *Wage Payment and Wage Collection Laws, State Legislation and Administration, 1959,* prepared by Lloyd W. Larson (43 pages), was issued as Bureau of Labor Standards Bulletin 203, June 1959. The Women's Bureau has issued *State Minimum-wage Law and Order Provisions Affecting Working Conditions,* July 1, 1942–January 1, 1961 (147 pages), Women's Bureau Bulletin 280; *State Minimum-wage Laws and Orders,* July 1, 1942–January 1, 1963, Part 2: *Analysis of Rates and Coverage,* 1963 (107 pages), Women's Bureau Bulletin 267; *Analysis of Coverage and Rates of State Minimum Wage Laws and Orders,* August 1, 1965 (130 pages), Women's Bureau Bulletin 291; *Fringe Benefit Provisions From State Minimum-wage Laws and Orders,* September 1, 1966 (112 pages), Women's Bureau Bulletin 293.

WOMEN AND CHILDREN.   For compilations of state laws regarding women and children, see pages 274–76.

WORKMEN'S COMPENSATION LAWS.   A publication summarizing the main provisions of the state workmen's compensation laws, with comparative tables for the principal features of the laws, has been published by the Bureau of Labor Standards in various editions, the latest being *State Workmen's Compensation Laws,* as of September 1964, prepared by Norene M. Diamond, Bulletin No. 161, revised (83 pages).

State Workmen's Compensation Laws: A Comparison of Major Provisions with Recommended Standards, issued as Bureau of Labor Standards Bulletin 212 in 1959, was revised in 1961, 1964, and 1967 (37 pages).

A 3- or 4-page article on state workmen's compensation legislation enacted during the year usually appears in the *Monthly Labor Review* and reprints are available. However, these articles do not appear each year as most state legislatures meet only every two years. The same is true of state labor legislation, but this seems to appear more frequently. Articles on special phases of state legislation also appear from time to time.

In addition to the material issued by the Bureau of Labor Standards, the Bureau of Employment Security has made several analyses of state laws relating to unemployment insurance. These publications report state by state what types of workers are covered under the state laws; how the program is financed; what benefits are payable and under what circumstances; and how the states have organized to do the job. The latest issue is *Comparison of State Unemployment Insurance Laws,* as of January 1, 1964 (156 pages). Revised annually is a publication entitled *Significant Provisions of State Unemployment Insurance Laws. Unemployment Insurance, State Laws and Experience* was last revised in February 1965 (32 pages).

During 1941, 1942, 1945, and 1947 the Bureau of Employment Security issued in mimeographed form a periodic *Legislative Report* on bills relating to the employment security program introduced or enacted during the legislative sessions. For the years 1943, 1945, and 1946, an *Annual Legislative Report* was also issued giving a synopsis of major amendments to state unemployment compensation laws. Synopses for 1941 and 1942 were included in the Legislative Report Series.

Legislative jurisdiction. "State constitutional provisions and statutes of general effect relating to the acquisition of legislative jurisdiction by the United States" over federally owned real property within the states can be found as Appendix B, Part A, of *Jurisdiction over Federal Areas Within the States,* report of the Interdepartmental Committee for the Study of Jurisdiction over Federal Areas Within the States, Part 1, the facts and committee recommendations, April 1956 (250 pages).

Marketing laws survey. This survey, made by the Work Projects Administration in the Federal Works Agency (Works Progress Administration prior to July 1, 1939), had as its primary purpose "the compilation, review, and analysis of the text of all the state laws directly affecting the marketing of goods from the point of production to the point of consumption." Two preliminary works were produced: *Comparative Charts of State Statutes Illustrating Barriers to Trade Between States,* May 1939 (88 pages), and *Digest of State Laws Relating to Problem of Interstate Trade Barriers for States Whose Legislatures Convene in 1940,* 1940 (22 leaves). In addition, the volumes listed below were issued:

Vol. 1. State antitrust laws, 1940, 880 pp.; also supplement presenting Code revisions, new legislation, court decisions, 1940, 1941, and 1942, 1942, 79 pp.
Vol. 2. State price control legislation, 1940, 558 pp.; also two supplements presenting Code revisions, new legislation, court decisions, 1940, 1941, and 1942, 1942, 197 pp. and 185 pp.
Vol. 3. State milk and dairy legislation, 1941, 595 pp.
Vol. 4. State liquor legislation, 1941, 910 pp.
Vol. 5. Interstate trade barriers; outlines of studies, 1942, 244 pp.

Mentally retarded. *State Laws and Regulations Affecting Mentally Retarded* is a checklist prepared by the Subcommittee on State Laws in Mental Retardation of the Advisory Committee to the Special Assistant to the President for Mental Retardation, 1964 (27 pages).

Mines and mining. In 1918 and 1920 the Bureau of Mines published annotated compilations of the mining statutes of California (Bulletin 161), Illinois (Bulletin 169), and Pennsylvania (Bulletin 185). This bureau has also issued compilations dealing with special features of mining laws in all the states.

Narcotics. The text of existing state laws on narcotics and digests of previous legislation are given in *State Laws Relating to the Control of Narcotic Drugs and the Treatment of Drug Addiction*, 1931 (330 pages), issued by the Public Health Service as Public Health Reports, Supplement No. 91.

Parks. Abstracts of the laws of all states on state parks are given in *Digest of Laws Relating to State Parks*, 1936, compiled by Roy A. Vetter (3 volumes, processed), issued by the National Park Service.

Poultry and eggs. The Department of Agriculture has issued two pamphlets in this field in recent years, one, *State Egg Laws and Regulations*, a summary, December 1956, Agriculture Handbook No. 112 (44 pages); and the other, *Digest of Laws and Regulations Affecting the Sale of Hatching Eggs, Chicks and Poults*, revised January 1956 (ARS 53–12) in chart form (6 pages).

Prisoners. Federal and state laws governing the release of prisoners are digested in Volume 1 of *The Attorney General's Survey of Release Procedure*, 1939 (1,228 pages). This volume bears the subtitle *Digest of Federal and State Laws on Release Procedure*. There are included statutes, court decisions, and administrative rules on suspension of sentence, probation, parole, executive clemency, good-time deductions, and procedure at expiration of sentence. Volumes 2, 3, 4, and 5 contain discussions of probation, parole, pardon, and prisons.

Public welfare. Beginning in 1936 the Works Progress Administration issued separate processed publications on the public welfare laws of each state. The titles, which are identical except for the name of the state, read *Digest of Public Welfare Provisions under the Laws of the State of.* . . . The subjects included are general poor relief, aid to dependent children, care of dependent and neglected children, assistance to the blind and aged, veterans' relief, and administrative organization. Digests have been issued for all states except Illinois, Massachusetts, New Jersey, New York, Ohio, Pennsylvania, and Rhode Island.

The Works Progress Administration also issued the following:

Digest of blind assistance laws of the several states and territories as of Sept. 1, 1936, by Robert C. Lowe, 19 lvs. (processed)

Digest of old age assistance laws of the several states and territories as of Sept. 1, 1936, by Robert C. Lowe, 23 lvs. (processed)

Digest of state and territorial laws granting aid to dependent children in their own home, as of Sept. 1, 1936, by Robert C. Lowe, 20 lvs. (processed)

Digest of poor-relief laws of the several states and territories, as of May 1, 1936, by Robert C. Lowe, 24 lvs. (processed)

Recent laws [Sept. 1936–Dec. 31, 1937] enacted by state legislatures relating to works progress and social welfare, 256 lvs. (processed)

Information for all states on the topics listed above is contained in *State Public Welfare Legislation* by Robert C. Lowe, 1939 (398 pages), issued by the Works Progress Administration as Research Monograph XX. This contains a general discussion of legislative and constitutional provisions as of January 1, 1939, followed by a tabular abstract of provisions relating to general relief, old age assistance, blind assistance, aid to dependent children in their own home, dependent and neglected children (institutions and agencies), veterans' relief, and state and local boards. Citations to constitutional and statutory provisions for each of the foregoing categories are in a separate table. There are also charts showing the welfare organization in each state and textual summaries of statutory provisions governing organization.

The Department of Health, Education, and Welfare issues a tabular analysis of state laws relating to public assistance with the title *Characteristics of State Public Assistance Plans under the Social Security Act*. It covers old age assistance, aid to the blind, aid to dependent children, and aid to permanently and totally disabled. The latest revision brought such material up to 1965 and was issued as Public Assistance Report No. 53.

Taxation.   Local provisions for taxation are given in the following reports issued by the Bureau of the Census:

Taxation and revenue systems of state and local governments, 1912; in *Wealth, Debt, and Taxation*, 1913, Vol. 1, pp. 447–715; also published separately

Digest of state laws relating to taxation and revenue, 1922, 1924, 544 pp.

In 1932 the Bureau of the Census again planned a digest of state laws relating to taxation and revenue, but the publication of the assembled volume was apparently abandoned. Separate pamphlets were issued containing digests for the following states: Arizona, Indiana, Kansas, Maine, Nevada, New Hampshire, Ohio, Oklahoma, Rhode Island, South Dakota, Virginia, and Washington.

Union reporting requirements. The Bureau of Labor Standards issued a processed publication, *Union Reporting Requirements in State Laws,* which was a summary of requirements for reporting organizational data or financial statements to state officials or to the membership, in July 1958. In September 1958 the Bureau issued a reprint (10 pages) of the July publication.

Veterans. Résumés of the provisions of state laws granting rights, benefits, and privileges to veterans, their dependents, and their organizations are contained in *State Veterans Laws, Digests of State Laws,* revised to July 1, 1967 (277 pages). This was published by the House Committee on Veterans' Affairs as House Committee Print No. 265, 86th Congress, 2d session. This gives in tabular form, for each state, the type of law, a brief résumé of its provisions, and citations to the laws.

The Retraining and Reemployment Administration of the Department of Labor, which functioned from 1944 to 1947, issued *Comparative Charts of State Statutes Creating Veterans Departments or Similar Agencies* in January 1947 "as an aid to those interested in making a comparative study of the various types of State agencies charged with veterans affairs." Citations to the laws are given, with brief information on their provisions.

Water. Summaries of the water-law doctrines of the 17 western states, with citations to the statutes and court decisions, are found in Appendix B to *Water Resources Law,* Volume 3 of the Report of the President's Water Resources Policy Commission, published in 1950. An earlier work, which contains an appendix giving abstracts of state statutory provisions relating to important principles governing the appropriation of water, determination of rights, and administration of rights is entitled *Selected Problems in the Law of Water Rights in the West,* by Wells A. Hutchins, Department of Agriculture Miscellaneous Publication No. 418, 1942 (513 pages).

Water pollution statutes are treated in tabular form in Appendix 1 to *Water Pollution in the United States, Third Report of the Special Advisory Committee on Water Pollution,* prepared by William J. Ponorow, House Document 155, 76th Congress, 1st session, 1939 (165 pages). It bears the title "Summary of State Laws and Regulations Affecting Pollution of Waters, Revised as of November 1938."

Another Department of Agriculture publication is *State Water-rights Laws and Related Subjects,* a bibliography compiled by Jack R. Turney and Harold H. Ellis, 1962 (199 pages). The Soil Conservation Service has published *Status of State Legislation Relating to Watershed Protection and Flood Prevention Act as Amended,* by Frank Hedges and L. M. Adams, 1961 (14 pages).

Weights and measures. Both federal and state laws relating to weights and measures in force in 1925 are given in the publication of the Bureau of Standards entitled *Federal and State Laws Relating to Weights and Measures,* by William Pany (Miscellaneous Publication No. 20, 3d edition, 1926, 976 pages). A 4th edition, issued in 1951, includes laws through the 1949 enactments (Circular 501, 1,182 pages).

Women and children. Some compilations and digests of state laws relating to women and children have been made by the Women's Bureau and the Children's Bureau, but neither has issued continuous publications giving all the laws. The most comprehensive work was Publication No. 10 of the Children's Bureau, entitled *Child-Labor Legislation in the United States,* by Helen L. Sumner and Ella A. Merritt. This book of 1,131 pages contains the text of all the laws relating to child labor in the several states in force October 1, 1915.

A state-by-state summary of laws affecting the employment of minors under eighteen years of age entitled *State Child-Labor Standards*, September 1965, prepared by Ora Mitchell, was issued as a Bureau of Labor Standards Bulletin. A 2-page leaflet entitled *State Laws Governing the Age of Majority* was issued January 1, 1964. Two other publications concerning minors are *State Laws Governing Emancipation of Minors Permitted by Court Order*, January 1, 1964 (3 pages), and *State Laws Governing Rights of Minor, 14 Years of Age or Over, To Nominate Own Guardian*, 1964 (5 pages).

Beginning in 1938 the Women's Bureau of the Department of Labor has issued *The Legal Status of Women in the United States of America*. Initially intended to be a full report, it has so far been issued only in separate parts—one for each state, one for the District of Columbia, and one for the territories and island possessions as a group. These are continually being brought up to date. Summary reports covering all the states have also been issued. The dates of these summaries correspond roughly with the dates of revisions of the separate parts for each state. The series is designated as Women's Bureau Bulletin No. 157, with part numbers such as 157–1 for Alabama, 157–2 for Arizona, etc. Each part is a 10- to 38-page pamphlet. The summary bulletins have been issued as plain Bulletin No. 157, with editions as follows:

Jan. 1, 1938, prepared by Sara L. Buchanan, with the assistance of Mary L. Sullivan, 89 pp., with supplement, 1943, 16 pp., and cumulative supplement, 1938–43, 31 pp.
Jan. 1, 1948, rev. ed., prepared by Sara L. Buchanan, 105 pp.
United States summary, as of Jan. 1, 1953, prepared by Laura H. Dale, with the assistance of Laura H. Harris, 103 pp.

Several over-all analyses of state laws relating to the employment of women have also been published by the Women's Bureau in its Bulletin Series. Much of this material is in chart form and gives pertinent features on a state-by-state basis rather than digests of specific laws. *Highlights of 1966 State Legislation of Special Interest to Women* (3 pages) and *Civil and Political Status* (3 pages) were issued in 1967. *Laws on Sex Discrimination in Employment* (4 pages), covering federal civil rights, Title 7, and state fair employment practices laws, was issued in 1965. *Weightlifting Provisions for Women by State* (3 pages) was issued in March 1966. *Inventory of State Equal Pay Legislation* (4 pages) was published in 1965.

Many bulletins on special phases of state laws relating to employment of women have also been published by the Women's Bureau, and annual changes have been issued in less permanent form. The principal groups are given below.

HOURS OF WORK. *Hours of Work; Summary of State Hour Laws for Women and Minimum Wage Rates,* by Mary Elizabeth Pidgeon, Bulletin No. 137, 1936 (54 pages), and *State Hour Laws for Women,* as of October 1, 1953, Bulletin No. 250 (114 pages), have been issued by the Women's Bureau.

LABOR LEGISLATION. *Chronological Development of Labor Legislation for Women in the United States,* revised December 1931 by Florence P. Smith, Bulletin No. 66–II (176 pages), is a state-by-state digest of laws by date with citations. It was originally published as part of whole Bulletin No. 66 in 1929.

LIGHTING. *State Requirements for Industrial Lighting* is a handbook for the protection of women workers, showing lighting standards and practices, by Marie Correll, Bulletin No. 94, 1932 (65 pages).

MINIMUM-WAGE LAWS. The Women's Bureau has published a continuing series of bulletins giving analyses of state laws as follows:

State minimum-wage laws and orders, 1939, by Florence P. Smith, 34 pp. (Bulletin No. 167)

Same, 1942, by Florence P. Smith, 52 pp. (Bulletin No. 191)

Same, July 1, 1942–Mar. 1, 1953, by Mary L. Sullivan and Alice M. Rand, 84 pp. (Bulletin No. 247)

Same, July 1, 1942–July 1, 1958, by Regina M. Neitzey; Pt. I, Historical development and statutory provisions, 31 pp. and 10 folders; Pt. II, Analysis of rates and coverage, 142 pp. (Bulletin 267, 1959). Pt. II was issued in a loose-leaf form to facilitate periodic revision; a supplement to the analysis for Puerto Rico was issued separately.

State minimum-wage law and order provisions affecting working conditions, July 1, 1942–Apr. 1, 1959, by Regina M. Neitzey, 141 pp. (Bulletin 269)

Same, July 1, 1942–Jan. 1, 1961, by Regina M. Neitzey, 147 pp. (Bulletin 280)

Analysis of coverage and wage rates of state minimum wage laws and orders, Aug. 11, 1965, by Regina M. Neitzey and Mary C. Manning, 130 pp. (Bulletin 291)

CHAPTER TEN

COURT DECISIONS

ALMOST ALL THE COURT DECISIONS published by the government are those of the federal courts, although decisions of state courts are included in some of the special compilations. However, the reports do not include decisions of all federal courts. Those of the circuit courts of appeals and the district courts have never been published regularly by the government, this work being entirely in the hands of commercial publishers. Many of the decisions of these courts are given in the compilations dealing with particular branches of federal law.

The District Court of the United States for the District of Columbia[1] is the court of first instance in which many suits are brought against government officers in their official capacity. Its decisions are not regularly published by the government. Appeals from this court lie to the United States Court of Appeals of the District, which also has direct appellate jurisdiction over many rulings of administrative officers. Its decisions are not published by the government, but prior to April 1, 1929, when the court had jurisdiction over appeals from the decisions of the Commissioner of Patents, its decisions in patent cases were published weekly in the *Official Gazette of the United States Patent Office,* and in the annual volume entitled *Decisions of the Commissioner of Patents.*

The published decisions will be discussed in two groups: those published regularly, which comprise all the decisions of the courts, and those included in compilations of special topics.

---

[1] Formerly Supreme Court of the District of Columbia; name changed by act of June 25, 1936 (49 Stat. 1921).

All court decisions are sold by the Superintendent of Documents and not by the courts or by the agencies compiling them. Some court decisions dealing with special topics are published in connection with administrative rulings and decisions, as enumerated in Chapter 11.

Decisions Published Regularly

The decisions of the following courts are or have been published regularly by the government: Supreme Court of the United States, Court of Claims, Court of Customs and Patent Appeals, Customs Court, Commerce Court, Tax Court, and the United States Court of Military Appeals.

Supreme Court of the United States. The publication of the decisions of the Supreme Court of the United States has run the gamut from entirely commercial publishing, through commercial publishing with official sanction, to complete government publishing. Whether the several editions should be regarded as government issues depends entirely on the definition of a government publication.

The original editions of the volumes issued by the first two reporters, Dallas and Cranch, should apparently be regarded as commercial publications, as there is no record that there was any official distribution by the government.[2]

The first legislative provision for the decisions of the Supreme Court was the act of March 3, 1817 (3 Stat. 376), which provided for the appointment of a reporter who was to print the reports and deliver "without any expense to the United States" a specified number of copies to the government. Various later acts made changes in the number of copies to be de-

[2] "The minutes of the clerk's office of the Supreme Court contain no entry of the appointment of Mr. Dallas as reporter, and he appears to have acted as such only with the acquiescence of the court. On the retirement of Mr. Dallas, this work was taken up by Judge Cranch, who, as stated by Mr. [Hampton L.] Carson in his *History of the Supreme Court*, was the first regularly appointed reporter, although no such entry appears in the minutes of the court." Alexander B. Hagner, "William Cranch," in *Great American Lawyers*, edited by William Draper Lewis, Vol. 3 (1907–09), p. 93.

livered free of charge and in other details, but there was no essential departure until 1922. During this period the copies delivered to the government were solely for distribution to its own officers; the sale to the public was in the hands of the reporter or his authorized publisher. This arrangement was recognized by law, and several acts placed a maximum price on the copies sold.

By the act of July 1, 1922 (42 Stat. 816), the entire plan of publication was revised. This act provided that the printing should be done at the Government Printing Office and the sale to the public made by the Superintendent of Documents; the reporter was divested of all interest in the reports, and his salary was adjusted to meet the new conditions. The first volume issued under the new plan was Volume 257. At present each volume is first issued in four parts as a preliminary print in paper covers, the final bound volume being printed later.

The first 90 volumes of the reports are generally known by the names of the reporters. In 1875 the designation *United States Reports* was adopted beginning with Volume 91, and numbers 1–90 were assigned to the preceding issues, the original names and numbering and the equivalents being as follows:

Dallas 1–4 (1790–1800) .... United States Reports 1–4
Cranch 1–9 (1801–15) .... United States Reports 5–13
Wheaton 1–12 (1816–27) .... United States Reports 14–25
Peters 1–16 (1828–42)[3] .... United States Reports 26–41
Howard 1–24 (1843–60) .... United States Reports 42–65
Black 1–2 (1861–62) .... United States Reports 66–67
Wallace 1–23 (1863–74) .... United States Reports 68–90

Volumes 91–107 (1875–82) have the designation of "1 to 17 *Otto*" as well as "*United States Reports* 91–107" on both the title page and the back title. The volumes after 107 have the designation "*United States Reports*" only; they carry the name of the reporter on the title page, but not on the back title, and they are not cited by the name of the reporter.

The reprints of the early volumes generally bear both the

[3] There is also a 17 *Peters* which duplicates 1 *Howard;* 17 *Peters* is not regarded as part of the official set.

United States Reports numbers and the original numbers with the names of the reporters. They also indicate the pagination of the original edition.

While 1 *Dallas* has been numbered as Volume 1 of the *United States Reports,* it contains no decisions of the Supreme Court, its contents being decisions of the Supreme Court of Pennsylvania (1754–89), of the Court of Common Pleas of Philadelphia County (1785–89), of the Court of Oyer and Terminer at Philadelphia (1785–88), and of the Court of Errors and Appeals of Pennsylvania (1786–88). The decisions of the Supreme Court begin in Volume 2, which contains also the decisions of the Federal Court of Appeals (1781–87) established by the Continental Congress in January 1780 to hear appeals in prize cases.[4] All the volumes of Dallas contain decisions of the appellate courts of Pennsylvania; Volume 4 includes decisions of the United States Circuit Court for Pennsylvania (1799–1806) and of the Court of Errors and Appeals of Delaware for the September term 1788.

The appendix to Volume 131 of the *United States Reports,* prepared by J. C. Bancroft Davis, the reporter, contains an account of the federal courts before the Constitution (pages xix–lxiii); reports of cases omitted from the preceding volumes (pages lxiv–cclxxx), some given in detail and some merely listed; a list of cases in which federal and state statutes were held invalid up to the end of the October term, 1888 (pages ccxxxv–cclxiii); and comments on the completeness of opinions and changes (pages xv–xviii). As the volumes were published in several editions, there is variation in the matter contained in the appendixes.

Occasionally collateral matter of interest appears in the reports, some of which is referred to in the preceding paragraph. After the death of one of the justices the reports generally contain the remarks made at the memorial proceedings. Almost every volume of Wheaton has an appendix containing notes on diverse subjects, the most voluminous being a discussion of prize courts in Volumes 1, 2, 5, and 6.

[4] Additional cases are listed in 131 U. S. xxxv–xliv.

In one sense none of the reports prior to Volume 257 were government publications, as the government did not place its imprint on them or distribute them to the public. They were issued by commercial publishers and sold through trade channels. It is true that beginning with 1 *Wheaton* the original editions were prepared under the direction of an officer of the court—the reporter—and the government received copies for its own use.

These original editions have an official character which may also extend to reprints made under the direction of the reporter. So little is known regarding the arrangement with Dallas and Cranch that it is difficult to say whether their reports can be regarded as official.

It should be noted that the list on pages 608–14 of the *Checklist* includes only the volumes in the Public Documents Library and does not pretend to give all the editions. Most of the volumes listed are reprints made many years after the death of the reporter. These reprints were purchased by the government, not in editions, but as needed to supply new offices. Other editions not listed in the *Checklist* were also purchased by the government. All the volumes prior to 257 were sold to the public through trade channels and must still be obtained in that manner. The question as to what edition is official is largely academic, as it is unlikely that there are any material errors in the reprints. While the reprints probably give the text of the decisions correctly, many of them omit the abstracts of the arguments of counsel, generally prepared by the reporter, and the student does not have the benefit of the cases cited by counsel to support his case. As the reprints generally indicate the original pagination, it is not difficult to ascertain what part of the text has been omitted. The choice of editions depends largely on the format, arrangement, and the additional notes. The notes added by the publisher may be copyrighted, but not the text of the decisions.[5]

No digests have been published by the government, although one covering Volumes 187–202 was prepared by the reporter, Charles Henry Butler. This digest and two others

[5] The right of the reporter to copyright was disposed of in *Wheaton v. Peters* (8 Pet. 591); the matter of copyright of the volumes printed at the Government Printing Office is covered by the act of March 4, 1909 (35 Stat. 1077).

are listed in the *Checklist* (pages 614–15) by reason of the fact that copies were bought by the government for the use of its officers. Nevertheless no complete edition of any of the digests referred to above was purchased by the government, and the circumstance that certain copies were purchased for official use does not seem to make any of these editions government publications. The sale to the public has been through trade channels. Volume 257 was the first official government publication and contained court decisions from October 3, 1921, to February 27, 1922. Volume 388 contains decisions for the October 1966 term (ending June 12, 1967).

As handed down, the decisions are printed in slip form. For many years this printing was done at a commercial establishment, but since the October 1946 term of court, under the authority of Title 28, Section 412, *United States Code,* the slip forms have been printed by the government. They may be purchased from the Superintendent of Documents by subscription for each term of court, or each decision may be purchased individually.

Court of Claims.   The Court of Claims is a special federal court of limited jurisdiction created in 1855 to adjudicate cases involving contractual obligations of the United States. Its decisions have been published by the government since its establishment. From 1855 to 1863 the decisions were printed as a special series of documents of Congress under the title *Reports of the Court of Claims Submitted to the House of Representatives.* These publications do not form part of any of the documents or reports series, but they have the following numbers in the serial number set.

	Serial Number
1855–56	871–72
1856–57	915
1857–58	970–72
1858–59	1021
1859–60	1072–76
1860–61	1108–10
1861–62	1146–47
1862	1173

The decisions since 1862 have been published in numbered volumes beginning with Volume 1 for 1863–65, the present title being *Cases Decided in the Court of Claims of the United States*. Indexes and a digest have been published as follows:

General index of Court of Claims decisions. Vols. 1–29 (published in Vol. 30 and also separately)
Digest of Court of Claims reports from March 1863 to December 1875 [Vols. 1–10]
Index to cases decided in Vols. 1–54 (in Vol. 54)
Index to cases decided in Vols. 55–61 (in Vol. 62)
Index to cases decided in Vols. 1–89 (in Vol. 89)
Index to cases decided in Vols. 90–99 (in Vol. 99)
Index to cases decided in Vols. 100–109 (in Vol. 110)
Index to cases decided in Vols. 110–119 (in Vol. 120)
Index to cases decided in Vols. 120–129 (in Vol. 130)
Index to cases decided in Vols. 130–139 (in Vol. 140)
Index to cases decided in Vols. 140–149 (in Vol. 150)
Index to cases decided in Vols. 150–159 (in Vol. 160)
Index to cases decided in Vols. 160–171 (in Vol. 170)

The latest rules of the United States Court of Claims, made effective October 15, 1953, are contained in Volume 140, with some amendments to rules in Volume 178. The centennial proceedings from 1855–1955 are reported in Volume 132.

The decisions as rendered are published separately by the court but are not available for general distribution.

Court of Customs and Patent Appeals. The Court of Customs and Patent Appeals was created by the act of August 5, 1909, with the title "Court of Customs Appeals," and with jurisdiction over appeals from the Board of General Appraisers, now the Customs Court. By the act of March 2, 1929 (45 Stat. 1475), effective April 1, 1929, the court was given jurisdiction over appeals from the Patent Office, and its name was changed to "Court of Customs and Patent Appeals."[6]

The first 16 volumes, which cover the period 1909–29, bear

---

[6] Prior to April 1, 1929, appeals on cases from the Patent Office lay to the Court of Appeals of the District of Columbia, and all decisions on patent appeals rendered prior to April 1929 appear in the reports of that court, which are not government publications; they have always been printed in the volumes entitled *Decisions of the Commissioner of Patents.*

the title *Court of Customs Appeals Reports*. Each of the later volumes, which bear the title *Court of Customs and Patent Appeals Reports*, is in two unnumbered parts bearing the same volume number, one part devoted to customs cases and one part to patent cases. Volumes 1–15 contain cumulative indexes.

Digests by Jesse C. Weaver covering the customs decisions in Volumes 1 and 22 and the patent and trademark decisions in Volumes 17 and 22 were published in 1936 by Callaghan and Company in two volumes, with titles as follows:

Digest of the customs reports covering decisions of the United States Court of Customs and Patent Appeals (538 pp.)

Patent and trade-mark digest of the decisions of the United States Court of Customs and Patent Appeals (218 pp.)

While these digests are commercial publications and are not sold by any government agency, the compilation was prepared and the printing done under a contract with the court, and the volumes were published under authority of the court.

The decisions on customs matters rendered up to 1916 are abstracted in the volume entitled *Digest of Decisions of United States Courts, Board of General Appraisers, and the Treasury Department under the Customs Revenue Laws*, 1918 (two volumes).

Decisions on customs matters were published in *Treasury Decisions under Customs, Certain Internal Revenue, Narcotic and Other Laws*, until that publication was superseded by *Customs Bulletin*. This is issued weekly and contains regulations, rulings, decisions, and notices concerning customs and related matters, and decisions of the Customs Court and Court of Customs and Patent Appeals. Decisions on patent matters are published in the *Official Gazette of the United States Patent Office*.

Customs Court. The decisions of the Customs Court, known as "Board of General Appraisers" from the time of its creation on June 10, 1890, until May 28, 1926, when it was renamed "United States Customs Court," were published in the semi-annual volume issued by the Treasury Department, which has had several titles over the years (see page 286).

1890. Synopsis of the decisions of the Treasury Department on construction of the tariff, navigation, and other laws
1891–97. Synopsis of the decisions of the Treasury Department and
Board of United States General Appraisers on the construction of the
tariff, immigration, and other laws
1898–99. Treasury decisions under tariff and internal revenue laws, etc.
1900–03. Treasury decisions under tariff and navigation laws, etc.
1904–. Treasury decisions under customs and other laws

Beginning with 1899 the volumes have been numbered
consecutively.

Digests of the decisions of the Board of General Appraisers,
the Customs Court, and the higher courts have been published
by the Treasury Department as follows:

Compilation of customs laws and digest of decisions rendered by the
Courts and the Board of United States General Appraisers [1883–97],
by Thomas J. Doherty, 1908, 1,383 pp.
Digest of decisions of the United States Courts, Board of General Appraisers and the Treasury Department under the Customs Revenue
Laws [1883–1913], 1918, 2 vols.
Digest of customs and related laws and decisions thereunder [1909–34],
by Thomas J. Doherty, 1936 [1935 on back title], 3 vols.,[7] and supplement [1935–40], 1941.

The 1936 digest includes such matter from the 1908 digest
as embodies precedents or principles that are of contemporary
value or historical interest, but it does not contain all the decisions in the 1908 volume.

Originally both administrative decisions of the Treasury
Department on matters pertaining to the Bureau of Customs
and Customs Court decisions appeared in *Treasury Decisions.*
The Tariff Act of 1930 transferred the United States Customs
Court to the Department of Justice, and subsequently, under
the act of August 7, 1939, the court was transferred to the Administrative Office of the United States Courts. Beginning with
Volume 1, July–December 1938, decisions in cases adjudged in
the Customs Court have appeared semiannually in consecutively
numbered volumes under the title *United States Customs Court*

---

[7] It should be noted that the index (Vol. 3) is in two parts: Part I, the
statutory provisions, and Part II, the decisions and rulings.

Reports. These volumes also contain abstracts and reappraisement decisions.

Commerce Court. The Commerce Court was organized in 1910 to pass on railroad litigation which arose under the several acts relating to the Interstate Commerce Commission, a duty which had previously been vested in the United States circuit courts. It was abolished in 1913. One volume of reports and a supplement were issued under the title *Opinions of the United States Commerce Court.*

Tax Court. The Tax Court of the United States (formerly the United States Board of Tax Appeals; name changed to Tax Court by Revenue Act of 1942, 56 Stat. 957) is an independent executive agency. The board was created by the Revenue Act of 1924 (43 Stat. 336) and continued by the Revenue Act of 1926 (44 Stat. 105), the Internal Revenue Code of 1939, and the Internal Revenue Code of 1954. The Tax Court tries and adjudicates controversies involving the existence of deficiencies or overpayments in income, excess profits, estate, gift, and personal holding company surtaxes in cases where deficiencies have been determined by the Commissioner of Internal Revenue; adjudicates applications for refund of excess-profits tax after the rejection by the Commissioner of claims for refund of such taxes under applicable provision of the Internal Revenue Code of 1939. The reports of the Board of Tax Appeals are in 47 volumes, July 16, 1924–October 21, 1942. Tax Court reports begin with Volume 1, October 22, 1942.

Court of Military Appeals. The United States Court of Military Appeals was established pursuant to the act approved May 5, 1950 (64 Stat. 129; 10 U.S.C. 867), as the final appellate tribunal in court-martial convictions. Judicially independent, although it operates as a part of the Department of Defense for administrative purposes, the Court is called upon to exercise jurisdiction as to questions of law in all cases (1) affecting a general or flag officer, or extending to death; (2) certified to the Court by the Judge Advocates General of the armed services and by the General Counsel of the Department of Transportation, acting for the Coast Guard; and (3) petitioned by the accused who have received a sentence of a year or more confinement and/or a punitive discharge. In these cases, the decisions of the Court are final—there is no further direct review.

Court of Military Appeals Digest was published in 1967 (1,036 pages), prepared by R. L. Tedrow. It contains annotated and digested opinions of the Court. *Opinions of the U.S. Court of Military Appeals* is regularly published in the Department of the Army Pamphlet series by the Judge Advocate General's School of the U.S. Army at Charlottesville, Virginia.

Special Compilations

Special compilations have been issued from time to time containing all the decisions on a particular topic. Some of these are confined to decisions of federal courts, but a few include the decisions of state courts. Some of these compilations have been issued only once, but others form continuing series published at both regular and irregular intervals.

Constitution.   The leading cases interpreting the Constitution are abstracted or cited in the volume entitled *The Constitution of the United States of America* (1,693 pages), S. Doc. 39, 1964. This work and others relating to the Constitution are described on page 195. At the end of the volume is a brief résumé of the acts of Congress declared unconstitutional.

Antitrust laws.   The decisions of all United States courts dealing with cases arising under the Sherman Act and related laws have been published by the Department of Justice under the title *Federal Anti-trust Decisions*. Up to 1939 twelve volumes had been published, as indicated below. It should be noted, however, that some of the volumes contain decisions for years earlier or later than indicated by the title.

Federal antitrust decisions . . . 1890–1912 . . . Vol. 1 [1890–99], by
    James A. Finch, 1912, 1,042 pp. (issued also as S. Doc. 111, Pt. 1,

62 Cong. 1 sess.); previously published in 1907 as *Federal Anti-trust Decisions* . . . 1890–1906 . . . Vol. 1 [1890–99]

Same, 1890–1912, Vol. 2 [1900–06], by James A. Finch, 1912, 1,036 pp. (issued also as S. Doc. 111, Pt. 2, 62 Cong. 1 sess.); previously published in 1907 as *Federal Anti-trust Decisions* . . . 1900–06 . . . Vol. 2

Same, 1890–1912, Vol. 3 [1906–10], by John L. Lott, 1912, 984 pp. (issued also as S. Doc. 111, Pt. 3, 62 Cong. 1 sess.)

Same, 1890–1917, Vol. 4 [1910–12], by John L. Lott and Roger Shale, 1917, 912 pp.; this is a revised and enlarged edition of *Federal Anti-trust Decisions* . . . 1890–1912 . . . Vol. 4 [1910–12], by John L. Lott, 1912 (issued also as S. Doc. 111, Pt. 4, 62 Cong. 1 sess.)

Same, 1890–1917 . . . Vol. 5 [1912–14], by John L. Lott and Roger Shale, 1917, 953 pp.

Same, 1890–1917 . . . Vol. 6 [1914–17], by John L. Lott and Roger Shale, 1918, 1,048 pp.

Same [Vol. 7], index digest (Vols. 1–6), by John L. Lott and Roger Shale, 1918, 513 pp.

Same, 1917–23 . . . Vol. 8 [1917–20], by John L. Lott and Thaddeus G. Benton, 1924, 1,174 pp.

Same, 1917–23 . . . Vol. 9 [1920–23], by John L. Lott and Thaddeus G. Benton, 1924, 1,165 pp.

Same, 1923–27 . . . Vol. 10, by John L. Lott and Joseph V. Machugh, 1928, 1,203 pp.

Same, 1927–31 . . . Vol. 11, by Abner J. Swanson, 1934, 913 pp.

Same, 1927–31 . . . Vol. 12, by Abner J. Swanson, 1935, 1,167 pp.

The text of the antitrust laws and a summary of cases are given in the publication of the Department of Justice entitled *The Federal Antitrust Laws, with Summary of Cases Instituted by the United States and Lists of Cases Decided Thereunder,* 1938 (355 pages). The main divisions of this work are as follows:

Antitrust laws and laws relating thereto, pp. 1–80
Summary of cases instituted, pp. 81–269
Indexes, pp. 270–355

The text of the decrees and judgments from July 2, 1890, to January 1, 1918, is given in *Decrees and Judgments in Federal Antitrust Cases,* compiled by Roger Shale, 1918 (860 pages). The Attorney General of the United States appointed a committee to study the antitrust laws on August 27, 1953. This committee, known as the Attorney General's National Committee to Study the Antitrust Laws, submitted its final report (393 pages) on March 31, 1955.

Caustic Poison Act judgments.   Judgments by United States courts under the act regulating interstate commerce in caustic poisons were published by the Food and Drug Administration under the title *Notices of Judgment under Caustic Poison Act,* No. 1, 1931, to No. 160, 1962. This material now appears in *Food and Drug Administration Papers.*

Federal Trade Commission cases.   Court decisions involving the powers of the Federal Trade Commission are assembled in *Statutes and Decisions Pertaining to Federal Trade Commission, 1914–29,* second edition, compiled by Henry Miller, 1935 (1,241 pages).[8] As the laws relating to the commission are not voluminous, practically all of the volume is devoted to the decisions. A substantial part of the volume is devoted to cases which arose out of the Federal Trade Commission Act or the Clayton Act against unlawful restraints and monopolies and to which the commission was not a party. Volumes 2–6, covering the years from 1930 to 1960, were compiled by Harriette H. Esch, 1939 (714 pages), 1944 (785 pages), 1951 (849 pages), 1957 (842 pages), and 1961 (1,068 pages). Volume 7 is entitled *Statutes and Court Decisions, Federal Trade Commission, January 1, 1961–December 31, 1965* (1,633 pages).

Food and Drugs Act judgments.   Judgments of the United States district courts under the Pure Food and Drugs Act have been issued from time to time by the Food and Drug Administration and its predecessors—the Food, Drug, and Insecticide Administration and the Bureau of Chemistry. These are usually issued in pamphlets containing a number of judgments, generally 25 or multiples thereof. The judgments are numbered in a continuous series. These have generally been published in a separate series having the title "Notices of Judgment under Food

[8] This is apparently a reprint of the first edition, which was issued in 1930.

and Drugs Act," but for some time they were issued as supplements to the Service and Regulatory Announcements. The list below indicates the offices publishing them and the series in which they have occasionally appeared.

Nos. 1–122 (1908–09), Office of Secretary of Agriculture, Food and Drug Inspection Board

Nos. 123–2785 (1910–14), Office of Secretary of Agriculture; Nos. 2763–85 were also included in Service and Regulatory Announcements of the Bureau of Chemistry for January, February, and March 1914

Nos. 2786–2985 (1914), in Service and Regulatory Announcements of Bureau of Chemistry for February and March 1914; Nos. 2786–2879 and 2880–2985 were reprinted separately in two pamphlets without title or name of issuing office

Nos. 2986–15,000 (1914–27), Bureau of Chemistry, as supplements to Service and Regulatory Announcements

Nos. 15,001–16,825 (1927–30), Food, Drug and Insecticide Administration

Nos. 16,826–31,157 (1930–1943), Food and Drug Administration

A general index has been issued covering Nos. 1–10,000; separate indexes have been published for each thousand notices thereafter.

These series were replaced during the years 1940–66 by *Notices of Judgment under the Federal Food, Drug, and Cosmetic Act*, with three separate series. One contains notices relating to cosmetics, the second to drugs and devices, and the third to foods. The Food and Drug Administration was under the Department of Agriculture until 1940 when it was placed under the Federal Security Agency, which is currently in the Department of Health, Education, and Welfare. In 1967, these series were replaced by a listing in the monthly publication, *Food and Drug Administration Papers*.

The important court cases have been assembled in *Decisions of Courts under the Federal Food and Drugs Act*, by Otis H. Gates, 1934[9] (1,546 pages). This volume covers the period from March 12, 1908, to February 21, 1933.

As regards court cases, the volume cited above supersedes *Food and Drugs Act, June 30, 1906 and Amendments of Aug.*

[9] The imprint on this volume bears the date of 1934, but the book was not released until 1937.

23, 1912 and Mar. 3, 1913, with the Rules and Regulations for the Enforcement of the Act, Food Inspection Decisions, Selected Court Decisions, Digests of Decisions, Opinions of the Attorney General and Appendix, compiled by C. A. Gwinn, 1914 (857 pages). The material other than decisions is indicated by the title; the appendix contains a legislative history of the act and the amendments, the opinion of the Solicitor General, and the decision of President Taft on the meaning of the term "whisky." The older volume has not been superseded for the material other than the court cases.

Government contracts. The Bureau of the Budget in 1925 issued the following publication: *Digest of the Principal Decisions of the United States Supreme Court, United States District Courts, Court of Claims and Opinions of the Attorney General Relating to Government Contracts* (109 pages).

Housing. Decisions, opinions, and legislation relating to housing were abstracted in the *Housing Legal Digest,* a processed publication which was issued monthly by the Central Housing Committee from January 1936 through December 1941. The Central Housing Committee was abolished in 1942 and its functions were transferred to the National Housing Agency, which later became the Housing and Home Finance Agency and, in 1965, the Department of Housing and Urban Development. The *Digest* was not continued by the latter agencies.

Indian affairs. A digest of federal and state court decisions, by Kenneth S. Murchison, was published by the Office of Indian Affairs in 1901 under the title *Digest of Decisions Relating to Indian Affairs . . . Vol. 1, Judicial.* It was issued also as House Document 538, 56th Congress, 2d session. A second volume containing a digest of the decisions of the executive departments was planned but apparently never completed.

Insecticide Act judgments. The judgments of United States courts under the act to prevent misbranding and adulteration of insecticides have been published under the title *Notices of Judgment under Insecticide Act* by the following offices:

Office of Secretary of Agriculture, Nos. 1–72 (1912–14)
Insecticide and Fungicide Board, in its Service and Regulatory Announcements, Nos. 72–1100 (1914–27)
Food, Drug and Insecticide Administration, Nos. 1101–1175 (1928–30)
Food and Drug Administration, Nos. 1176–1745 (1930–40)
Agricultural Marketing Service, Nos. 1746–1800 (1940–42)
Agricultural Marketing Administration, Nos. 1801–1825 (May–Oct. 1942)
Food Distribution Administration, Nos. 1826–1840 (Feb. 1943)
Distribution Office, Nos. 1841–1910 (1943–44)
Marketing Services Office, Nos. 1911–1925 (April 1945)
Production and Marketing Administration, Nos. 1926–2066 (1946–51)

Since 1950 these judgments have been published under the title *Notices of Judgment under the Federal Insecticide, Fungicide, and Rodenticide Act* by the following offices:

Production and Marketing Administration, Nos. 1–169 (1950–53)
Agricultural Research Service, Nos. 170–515 (1954–65)

Labor. Annual or biennial compilations of both state and federal decisions affecting labor were published as bulletins of the Bureau of Labor Statistics from 1912 to 1932, the last issue (Bulletin 592), containing a consolidated index to preceding publications of this character.

A compilation of court decisions, federal and state, relating to the National Labor Relations Act are contained in *Court Decisions Relating to the National Labor Relations Act.* Volume I, published in 1944, contains cases decided before December 31, 1939. Since that time other volumes have been released, the latest one being Volume XII covering the period January 1, 1961, through February 28, 1962. Most of the cases covered are proceedings under the act to enforce or review orders of the National Labor Relations Board. The remainder are (1) injunction proceedings brought to enjoin action by the board; (2) contempt proceedings brought by the board to compel compliance with court decrees; (3) proceedings brought by the board to compel compliance with its subpoenas; and (4) miscellaneous litigation bearing upon the administration of the act. These volumes are indexed in *Index of Court Decisions Relating to National Labor Relations Act* (through December 31, 1967), 1968 (303 pages).

The Civil Rights Act of 1964 established the U. S. Equal Employment Opportunity Commission, which has issued *First Annual Digest of Legal Interpretations,* July 2, 1965, through July 1, 1966. Most of the interpretations have been made in response to letters of inquiry to the commission.

Mines and mining. From December 1913 to August 1919 the Bureau of Mines published abstracts of decisions on mines and mining in its Bulletin Series. The decisions include those of both state and federal courts. Each bulletin covered a period of several months.

National banks. For some years digests of decisions relating to national banks were reprinted in the annual reports of the Comptroller of the Currency, and assembled digests were published from time to time. The latest compilations are in five volumes published by the Office of the Comptroller of the Currency:

Digest of decisions relating to national banks, 1864–1926, Vol. I, 1864–1912, 1927, 700 pp.; contains digests of decisions printed in the various editions of the digest prior to Oct. 31, 1912, including Vol. 224, *United States Reports,* and Vol. 197, *Federal Reporter* (first series)

Same, 1864–1926, Vol. II, 1913–26, 1927, 400 pp.;[10] contains digests of decisions reported in Vols. 225–271, *United States Reports,* Vols. 198–300, *Federal Reporter* (first series), and Vols. 1–14, *Federal Reporter* (second series)

Same, 1864–1931, Vol. III, 1927–31, 1932, 336 pp.; contains digests of decisions reported in Vols. 272–283, *United States Reports,* and Vols. 15–50, *Federal Reporter* (second series)

Same, 1864–1934, Vol. IV, Pts. 1 and 2, 1932–34, 327 pp.;[11] contains digests of decisions reported in Vols. 284–291, *United States Reports,* and Vols. 51–69, *Federal Reporter* (second series); Pt. 1 also issued separately

Same, 1864–1936, Vol. V, 1933–36, 541 pp.;[11] contains digests of decisions reported in Vols. 292–295, *United States Reports,* and Vols. 70–81, *Federal Reporter* (second series)

National forests. Court decisions on national forests are given in *Laws, Decisions, and Opinions Applicable to the Na-*

[10] A digest covering the years 1921–24 was published in 1925.

[11] Not printed by the government but bears seal of Office of Comptroller of the Currency.

tional Forests, compiled by R. F. Feagans, 1916 (151 pages). This publication is more fully described on pages 240–41.

Patent, trademark, design, label, and copyright cases. Beginning with the issue for 1876 the decisions of United States courts in patent, trademark, design, label, and copyright cases have been published in the annual volume issued by the Patent Office now entitled *Decisions of the Commissioner of Patents and of the United States Courts in Patent and Trademark Cases.* This volume is known by the year covered, and has no series number. The decisions are published currently in the *Official Gazette of the United States Patent Office.*

Compilations of the court decisions under the Copyright Act of March 4, 1909, have been issued in the following publications of the Copyright Office of the Library of Congress.

Decisions of United States courts involving copyright, 1909–14, 1928, 279 pp. (Bulletin No. 17, 2d ed.)

Same, 1914–17, compiled by Richard C. DeWolf, 1918, 605 pp. (Bulletin No. 18)

Same, 1918–24, compiled by Herbert A. Howell, 1926, 477 pp. (Bulletin No. 19)

Same, 1924–[July] 1935, compiled by Herbert A. Howell, 1936, 947 pp. (Bulletin No. 20[12])

Same, [August] 1935–37, compiled by Herbert A. Howell, 1938, 355 pp. (Bulletin No. 21[12])

Same, 1938–39, compiled by Herbert A. Howell, 1939, 327 pp. (Bulletin No. 22)

Same, 1939–40, compiled by Herbert A. Howell, 1943, 391 pp. (Bulletin No. 23)

Same, 1941–43, compiled by Herbert A. Howell, 1944, 683 pp. (Bulletin No. 24)

Same, 1944–46, compiled by Herbert A. Howell, 1947, 459 pp. (Bulletin No. 25)

Same, 1947–48, 1950, 488 pp. (Bulletin No. 26)

Same, 1949–50, 1953, 591 pp. (Bulletin No. 27)

Same, 1951–52, 1954, 587 pp. (Bulletin No. 28)

Same, 1953–54, edited by Wilma S. Davis, 1955, 529 pp. (Bulletin No. 29)

Same, 1955–56, edited by Benjamin W. Rudd, 1958, 652 pp. (Bulletin No. 30)

[12] Earlier bulletins of the Copyright Office on other subjects are also numbered 20 and 21.

Same, 1957–58, 1959, 717 pp. (Bulletin No. 31)
Same, 1959–60, 1961, 732 pp. (Bulletin No. 32)
Same, 1961–62, 1963, 714 pp. (Bulletin No. 33)
Same, 1963–64, 1965, 616 pp. (Bulletin No. 34)
Same, 1965–66, 1967, 950 pp. (Bulletin No. 35)
A cumulative index covering the years 1909–54 (289 pp.), 1956, edited by Wilma S. Davis

Postal Service. Court decisions dealing with the Postal Service are abstracted in the volumes entitled *Digest of Decisions of United States and Other Courts Affecting the Post Office Department and the Postal Service.* These volumes are not generally available, as they have not been distributed to depository or other libraries and are not sold. The Post Office Department states that the *Digest* "contains considerable copyrighted material which was used through the courtesy of the publishers with the understanding that it was for official purposes of the Government only. In view of this the *Digest* is distributed only to officials of the Government."

Prohibition. Abstracts of Supreme Court decisions relating to prohibition were published by the Bureau of Prohibition in the pamphlet of 60 pages entitled *Digest of Supreme Court Decisions Interpreting the National Prohibition Act and the Willis-Campbell Act,* December 1928.

Public health. Many court decisions relating to public health are published in *Public Health Reports,* issued monthly by the Public Health Service since 1878.

Railroads. The federal statutes relating to the regulation of common carriers and annotations to the decisions of the courts and the Interstate Commerce Commission are given in the eight-volume work entitled *Interstate Commerce Acts, Annotated,* prepared by and under the direction of Clyde B. Aitchison, Commissioner, for the Interstate Commerce Commission.

This work originally comprised five volumes issued as Senate Document 166, 70th Congress, 1st session. Volume 5 contains a history of the Interstate Commerce Commission cases reviewed by the courts. It should be noted that this work relates to the regulation of the carriers and does not cover a mass of other legislation, such as the pure food laws, based on the powers of Congress over interstate commerce. Supplements to the original publication have been issued, the latest one being Volume 19, entitled *Interstate Commerce Acts Annotated, 1962 Supplement*. Volume 20, a *Cumulated Index* of the indexes in Volumes 5, 8, 10, and 11 through 19, was issued in 1968.

The court rulings under the several acts relating to safety appliances and hours of service are abstracted in the work entitled *A Digest of Decisions (including dicta) under the Federal Safety Appliance and Hours of Service Acts* (281 pages), by Otis B. Kent, published by the Interstate Commerce Commission in 1915. The volume also contains rulings by the commission.

State laws. State laws declared invalid by the Supreme Court are listed in *United States Supreme Court Cases Declaring State Laws Unconstitutional, 1912–1938*, compiled by Margaret W. Stewart and Agnes M. Brown, 1938 (20 pages), published by the Library of Congress as *State Law Index, Special Report No. 2*. The cases are arranged chronologically with citations to Supreme Court reports and the laws affected. This compilation is a supplement to a similar list on pages 131–58 of *The Supreme Court and Unconstitutional Legislation*, by Blaine F. Moore, 1913 (Columbia University Studies in History, Economics, and Public Law, Vol. 54, No. 2).

Taxation. Abstracts of cases involving limitation on taxation are given in *Taxing Power of the Federal and State Governments*, 1936 (125 pages), published by the Joint Committee on Internal Revenue Taxation.

The Joint Committee on Internal Revenue Taxation has also issued the following publications regarding tax cases:

Federal and state tax cases, decisions of the Supreme Court of the United States, October term 1938, to January 11, 1943, 756 pp., issued in 1943
Tax cases decided by the Supreme Court of the United States, October term 1942–January 1945, 412 pp., issued in 1945

Tax cases decided by the Supreme Court, October term 1944 through October term 1948, 922 pp., issued in 1949

Tax cases decided with opinions by the Supreme Court, October term 1949 through October term 1953, 400 pp., issued in 1955

Tax cases decided with opinions by the Supreme Court, Vols. 348–349, *U. S. Reports*, October term 1954, 123 pp., issued in 1955

Tax cases decided with opinions by the Supreme Court, Vols. 352–354 of the *U. S. Reports*, October term 1956, 126 pp., issued in 1958

Tax cases decided with opinions by the Supreme Court, Vols. 355–357 of the *U. S. Reports*, October term 1957, 206 pp., issued in 1959

Tax cases decided with opinions by the Supreme Court, Vols. 361–364 of the *U. S. Reports*, October term 1959, 223 pp., issued in 1961

Tax cases decided with opinions by the Supreme Court, Vols. 364–367 of the *U. S. Reports*, October term 1960, 163 pp., issued in 1962

Tax cases decided with opinions by the Supreme Court, Vols. 368–370 of the *U. S. Reports*, October term 1961, 107 pp., issued in 1963

Decisions on tariff laws are discussed under "Court of Customs and Patent Appeals" and "Customs Court" (pages 284–87). Those on income and other internal federal taxes are discussed under "Internal revenue" (page 316).

Veterans' insurance.   The Bureau of War Risk Litigation of the Department of Justice has published a *Digest of Veterans' Insurance Cases,* 1936 (371 pages). This volume includes: (1) all decisions by the Supreme Court up to and including Volume 297 of *United States Reports* and of the circuit courts of appeal and Court of Appeals of the District of Columbia up to and including 81 Fed. (2d); (2) reported decisions by the district courts and the Comptroller General and reported opinions of the Attorney General; and (3) other selected decisions. This volume supersedes a loose-leaf digest published in 1934 and two supplements thereto. Volume 2, issued in 1941 (288 pages), covered the period from May 1936 to and including May 1941.

War laws.   Court opinions, charges to the jury, and rulings in cases arising out of the war laws of 1917 and 1918 are given in the series published by the Department of Justice under the title *Interpretation of War Statutes.* This series comprises 204 numbered bulletins. Complete sets are available at the Library of the Department of Justice and at the Public Documents Library.

Water resources. A guide to the decisions relating to water resources is afforded by the publication of the Tennessee Valley Authority described on page 255.

CHAPTER ELEVEN

ADMINISTRATIVE REGULATIONS AND DEPARTMENTAL RULINGS

THE POWERS CONFERRED by Congress upon governmental agencies include the regulation of the conduct of business such as the work of the Interstate Commerce Commission, and the administration of purely governmental activities, such as the disposal of the public lands, in which there may be an adjudication as between the government and the individual, or between two individuals. In some cases the several agencies have power to make regulations within certain defined limits. In almost all cases the initial interpretation of the law is made by the administering agency. In many situations the ruling of the government agency is final, but in an appreciable number an appeal may be taken to the courts.

Almost every agency that has regulatory powers issues rulings and regulations in printed form. These are not always brought together in a numbered series but are often issued as separate pamphlets. Only the regulations and rulings that appear periodically or in a separate series are discussed below. Most of the series are discussed under the name of the office or officer making the rulings, but some are described under the subject matter.

Federal Register. Provision for the assembled contemporaneous publication of regulations of all executive agencies was made by the act of July 26, 1935, authorizing and directing the publication of the *Federal Register*.

The act cited above prescribes publication in the *Federal Register* of—

(1) all presidential proclamations and executive orders, except such as have no general applicability and legal effect or are effective only against federal agencies or persons in their capacity as officers, agents, or employees thereof; (2) such documents or classes of documents as the President shall determine from time to time have general applicability and legal effect; and (3) such documents or classes of documents as may be required so to be published by act of the Congress.

The act specifies that every order prescribing a penalty shall be deemed to have general applicability and legal effect. It also provides that there shall be published such other documents or classes of documents as may be specified in regulations approved by the President.

The particular papers or classes of papers of the several departments and offices required to be published in the *Federal Register* are listed in the issue for May 28, 1938 (daily edition, Volume 3, No. 105, pages 1209–24; bound edition, Volume 3 [Part 1], pages 1013–28). These regulations were not published separately, as were the earlier ones.

Beginning with the issue for June 4, 1938, the rules, regulations, and orders are arranged under 50 titles, which are sometimes parallel to those of the *United States Code*. The notices follow. Indexes are issued monthly, quarterly, and annually.

Until 1938 two bound volumes, with continuous pagination, were issued for each year, but they do not cover six-month periods. The pagination of the bound edition is not the same as that of the daily, as certain informational matter that appeared repeatedly in the daily, and blank and part blank pages, were omitted. Therefore page citations should state specifically whether they are to the bound or daily edition. The bound volumes are printed on better paper.

The bound volumes have a table giving cross references from the pages in the daily edition to the bound edition and a table giving citations to amendments or related documents. These tables appear in Part 2 only of the volumes for 1936 and 1937, but are printed also at the end of the first part of the volume for 1938. The bound volumes were discontinued with Volume 3 in 1938 and replaced by the *Code of Federal Regulations*.

The *Federal Register* was first issued on March 14, 1936. It appears every Tuesday, Wednesday, Thursday, Friday, and Saturday except days following legal holidays. It is published by the National Archives and Records Service, but the distribution to the public is by sale by the Superintendent of Documents. Monthly, quarterly, and annual indexes are issued.

The *Codification Guide* is a list of sections in the *Code of Federal Regulations* which are affected by provisions contained in the *Federal Register*. The *Guide* is published monthly on a cumulative basis from the first of each year. It lists by number the titles, parts, and sections of the *Code* which are amended or otherwise affected. Entries indicate the nature of the changes. Proposed rules are listed at the end of appropriate titles. Daily numerical guides listing parts affected appear following the table of contents of each issue of the *Federal Register* and within-the-month cumulations appear at the end of each issue. A subject index to the daily *Federal Register* is published separately monthly, quarterly, and annually.

A *Weekly Compilation of Presidential Documents* makes available the transcripts of the President's news conferences, messages to Congress, public speeches and statements, and other materials released by the White House up to 5:00 P.M. each Friday.

Code of Federal Regulations.   The legislation which brought about the establishment of the *Federal Register* also laid the foundation for the *Code of Federal Regulations*. Prior to the Federal Register Act of July 26, 1935 (49 Stat. 500; 44 U.S.C. 301–14), and the publication of the *Federal Register* beginning with the issue of March 14, 1936, there were no facilities within the executive branch of the federal government for the central filing and publication of presidential proclamations, executive orders, administrative rules, regulations, and similar documents which have general applicability and the force of law. The lack of such facilities made it extremely difficult and sometimes impossible for interested parties, official and private alike, to inform themselves concerning the rules, regulations, and other documents which implement, interpret, or apply many federal statutes.

Under the provisions of this act, the Archivist of the United States, acting through a division established by him in the National Archives (Division of the Federal Register), was charged with the custody and, together with the Public Printer, with the prompt and uniform printing and distribution of the documents coming within the purview of the act. These provisions included the appointment of the Director of the Division of the Federal Register (now Office of the Federal Register) and the appointment of a permanent Administrative Committee of three members consisting of the Archivist, or Acting Archivist, as chairman; an officer of the Department of Justice designated by the Attorney General; and the Public Printer or Acting Public Printer.

Section 11 of the act required each executive agency to prepare and file with the Administrative Committee of the Federal Register a complete compilation of all documents which had been issued or promulgated prior to the date documents were required or authorized to be published in the *Federal Register*. These compilations were to consist only of the documents which were still in force and effect and relied upon by the submitting agency as authority for, or invoked or used by it in the discharge of, any of its functions or activities. The Administrative Committee was required to report with respect to the documents to the President, who was to determine which of such documents had general applicability and legal effect and to authorize the publication thereof in a special or supplemental edition of the *Federal Register*. Further administrative and legislative study of the problems involved led to the act approved June 19, 1937, which amended Section 11 of the Federal Register Act to provide for a codification rather than a compilation of all existing regulations. The amended Section 11 also provided for complete recodification at the end of five-year periods.

The first edition of the *Code* was compiled as of June 1, 1938. The first supplement covered the remainder of the calendar year 1938. Subsequent separately bound supplements covered the calendar years 1939, 1940, and 1941, respectively.

The national emergency preceding World War II and the war itself resulted in a notable increase in federal administrative documents. Because of this volume of emergency material and the preoccupation of all agencies with the war effort, it was evident that the first recodification scheduled under the Federal Register Act for June 1, 1943, would be impracticable at that time. Section 11 was amended to provide for cumulative supplements instead.

The *Code of Federal Regulations,* 1949 edition, was prepared and published as a special edition of the *Federal Register,* dated January 1, 1949, by the Division of the Federal Register, the National Archives. The publication was made pursuant to Part 2 of the regulations of the Administrative Committee of the Federal Register, approved by the President October 11, 1948.

The contents of the *Federal Register* and *Code of Federal Regulations* are by law prima-facie evidence of the text of the original documents and are required to be judicially noticed (49 Stat. 502, 50 Stat. 304; 44 U.S.C. 307, 311 [c]).

The *Code* is composed of 50 titles and a general index. These titles, which frequently correspond to those of the *United States Code,* are arranged alphabetically beginning with Title 4 and are divided into as many chapters and parts and published in as many volumes as required. The volumes of the *Code* are revised annually, with three exceptions for which supplements are issued. The exceptions are Title 32, Parts 590–699, Title 35, and Title 37.

Agriculture Department. Under various acts the Secretary of Agriculture has been given regulatory powers over certain products and industries which move in interstate commerce. While the regulations, orders, and other information regarding the several subjects are published first in the *Federal Register,* some of them are still published in the Service and Regulatory Announcements issued by the subordinate agencies which administer the laws on behalf of the Secretary.

Beginning in 1942 the decisions of a quasi-judicial character made by the Secretary of Agriculture have been released in a monthly publication entitled *Agriculture Decisions.* These decisions do not include rules and regulations of general applicability, which are required to be published in the *Federal Register.* The principal statutes concerned are:

Agricultural Marketing Agreement Act of 1937 (7 U.S.C. 601 *et seq.*)
Commodity Exchange Act (7 U.S.C. Chap. 1)
Grain Standards Act (7 U.S.C. 71 *et seq.*)
Packers and Stockyards Act, 1921 (7 U.S.C. 181 *et seq.*)
Perishable Agricultural Commodities Act, 1930 (7 U.S.C. 499a *et seq.*)
United States Warehouse Act (7 U.S.C. Chap. 10)

Consumer and Marketing Service. The Consumer and Marketing Service administers broad consumer food, consumer protection, marketing, and related programs and activities of the Department of Agriculture, including some civil defense and defense mobilization activities. The Service issues regulations in connection wth the following acts:

The U. S. Warehouse Act (7 U.S.C. Chap. 10)
The Agricultural Marketing Agreement Act of 1937 (7 U.S.C. 71 *et seq.*)
Cotton Research and Promotion Act of 1966 (7 U.S.C. Chap. 53)
Agricultural Adjustment Act, Section 32 (7 U.S.C. Chap. 26)
Agricultural Act of 1949, Section 416 (7 U.S.C. Chap. 35A)
Food and Agriculture Act of 1965, Section 709 (7 U.S.C. Chap. 26)
Food Stamp Act of 1964 (7 U.S.C. Chap. 51)
National School Lunch Act of 1946 (42 U.S.C. Chap. 13)
Child Nutrition Act of 1966 (42 U.S.C. Chap. 13)
Agricultural Act of 1954 (7 U.S.C. Chap. 42)
Commodity Exchange Act (7 U.S.C. Chap. 1)

Agricultural Research Service. The Agricultural Research Service was established in 1953 and superseded the Agricultural Research Administration. It consolidated most of the physical, biological, chemical, and engineering research in the Department of Agriculture. The Research Service now administers the legal regulation of livestock, which was begun in the Bureau of Animal Industry in 1884. Regulatory workers seek to prevent entry into the United States of animal and plant diseases and pests, and their transmission to other countries in U. S. exports; to control or eradicate many crop and livestock diseases and pests; to assure humane treatment of laboratory animals by dealers, transporters, and research facilities and of livestock moving in interstate commerce; to provide for safe and effective use of veterinary biologics products and pesticidal chemicals and devices by regulating their composition and labeling and by monitoring the effects of pesticidal residues in areas of extensive chemical treatment.

Regulations under these programs are issued in the Service and Regulatory Announcements of the Agricultural Research Service.

Other regulatory announcements are contained in Veterinary Biologics Division Notices; The P.P.C. Series of the Plant Pest Control Division, which contains quarantine notice relating to insects; and the P.Q. Series, quarantine and import restriction notices and regulations relating to plants released by the Plant Quarantine Division. The latter two publications are processed and are issued irregularly.

Army: Opinions of the Judge Advocate General.   The Judge Advocate General of the Army gives opinions on matters of both military law and civil work carried on by officers of the Army. His opinions seem to have been published only from April 1, 1917, to the end of 1919. Volume 1 covers the nine months from April to December 1917 while Volume 2 embraces the year 1918. The opinions for 1919 were published in monthly pamphlets with a separate index for the year.

While the complete opinions were published for only a short period, digests have covered all opinions issued since 1862. Those from 1862 to 1912 are contained in the volume entitled *A Digest of Opinions of the Judge Advocate General of the Army, 1912.* This volume of 1,103 pages contains digests of opinions from September 3, 1862, to January 31, 1912. It was originally issued in 1912 but was reprinted in 1917. Later digests were issued from time to time,[1] but the leading opinions in those digests were republished in *Digest of Opinions of the Judge Advocate General of the Army, 1912–40,* 1942 (1,148 pages), and Supplement I, 1941 (51 pages). Digests for January 1942 through June 1951 were published in the *Bulletin of the Judge Advocate General of the Army* (which was issued monthly January 1942 through June 1946, bimonthly July 1946 through December 1947, and quarterly January 1948 through June 1951). Since July 1951, this material has been included in *Digest of Opinions, the Judge Advocate General of the Armed Forces,* issued quarterly and cumulated annually.

Atomic Energy Commission. The Atomic Energy Commission has issued three volumes of *Opinions and Decisions of the Atomic Energy Commission With Selected Orders.* Volume 1 covers the period October 8, 1956–December 31, 1961, 1962 (1,011 pages); Volume 2 covers January 2, 1962–December 31, 1964, 1966 (909 pages); Volume 3 covers June 1, 1965–June 30, 1967, 1968 (526 pages).

Attorney General. The Attorney General is the official legal adviser of the President and the heads of departments, and important opinions rendered by him are published by the Department of Justice in the series known as *Official Opinions of Attorneys General.* While the publication of the present series did not begin until 1852, the first five volumes contain a compilation going back to 1789. Volume 6 is the first contemporaneous volume. The opinions are also printed as House documents.

Prior to Volume 37 the opinions had also been issued for some time in signature form. The advance prints for Volume 37 were issued in part in signature form and in part in unnumbered separates. Each of the advance prints for Volumes 38 and 39 contains one opinion. After about 50 unnumbered opinions for Volume 38 had been issued, bearing various dates between July 18, 1934, and July 9, 1935, the separates were numbered

---

[1] Monthly digests were published from 1912 to 1917 in the numbered bulletins of the War Department. Later digests were unnumbered: for 1918 to 1920 they were published monthly; for 1921, semiannually; and for 1922 and thereafter, annually.

beginning with No. 1 for an opinion of July 3, 1935. Thereafter, the separates were numbered beginning with No. 1 for each volume. Three additional cumulative volumes have been published. Volume 39 covers the period March 8, 1937–December 31, 1940; Volume 40, December 31, 1940–December 31, 1948; Volume 41, January 1, 1949–December 31, 1960. Opinion No. 1 in Volume 42 is dated April 14, 1961.

Three digests have been published covering the following volumes and years:

> Vols. 1–16, 1789–1881 (published also as
> H. Misc. Doc. 15, 48 Cong. 2 sess.)
> Vols. 17–25, 1881–1906
> Vols. 26–32, 1906–21

An Index to Official Opinions of Attorneys General of the United States (14 pages) is a cumulative supplement which includes all opinions released for publication from January 1, 1941, to August 1, 1958. An index was also prepared for volumes 33–39, inclusive, 1921–40 (26 pages).

Comptroller General. The Comptroller General is the officer who has the final determination of the legality of all payments of most of the public funds of the United States. This function was exercised by the First and the Second Comptroller from 1817 to 1894, by the Comptroller of the Treasury from 1894 to 1921, and by the Comptroller General since 1921.

The publication of the decisions of the First Comptroller was begun in 1880. The set comprises seven volumes, with the title *Decisions of the First Comptroller;* some were issued as congressional documents, some as department publications, and some as both. The seven volumes were published as follows:

Vol. 1, 1880, 2d ed.[2] Issued only as H. Ex. Doc. 81, 46 Cong. 3 sess. The appendix in this volume (pp. 409–704) contains a detailed account of the "organization and duties of the accounting officers in the Treasury Department and of the accounting division of the General Land Office."

Vol. 2, 1881, 1st ed. Issued only as department publication. The second edition (pp. 599–609), issued only as H. Ex. Doc. 219, 47 Cong. 1 sess.,

[2] Only 50 copies of the first edition were printed in the form of loose sheets.

contains an account of the organization of the Office of the Secretary of the Treasury.

Vol. 3, 1882. Issued as department publication and as H. Misc. Doc. 37, 47 Cong. 2 sess. The appendix to this volume (pp. 399–430) contains an account of the "organization and duties of the offices of the Treasurer of the United States and the Register of the Treasury."

Vol. 4, 1883. Issued as department publication and as H. Misc. Doc. 56, 48 Cong. 1 sess.

Vol. 5, 1884. Issued as department publication and as H. Misc. Doc. 22, 48 Cong. 2 sess.

Vol. 6 [January–March] 1885. Issued as department publication and as H. Misc. Doc. 69, 49 Cong. 1 sess.

[Vol. 7], May 1893–September 1894. Issued only as department publication.

The decisions of the Second Comptroller were never published in full, but four volumes containing abstracts were issued under the title *Digest of Decisions of the Second Comptroller,* as follows:

[Vol. 1], 1817–69[3]
Vol. 2, 1869–84
Vol. 3, 1884–93
Vol. 4, Jan. 1, 1893–Oct. 1, 1894

After the establishment of the Office of Comptroller of the Treasury in 1894, the leading decisions were published regularly under the title *Decisions of the Comptroller of the Treasury.* Twenty-seven annual numbered volumes were issued covering the fiscal years ending June 30, 1895, to June 30, 1921. These were succeeded by the *Decisions of the Comptroller General,* issued in annual numbered volumes for fiscal years ending June 30 beginning with Volume 1 for the year ending June 30, 1922. The decisions are also issued monthly in pamphlet form. The March, September, and December issues include an index digest, and the June issue includes cumulative tables and the index digest.

Several digests of the *Decisions of the Comptroller of the Treasury* have been published, the latest covering Volumes 1–26, or the period 1894–1920, the title being *Digest of Decisions of the Comptroller of the Treasury, 1894 to 1920.*

[3] Two earlier editions were published covering the years 1817–52 and 1817–65.

A general index to the 27 volumes of *Decisions of the Comptroller of the Treasury* and to Volumes 1–8 of the *Decisions of the Comptroller General*, covering the years 1894 to June 30, 1929, has been published by the General Accounting Office under the title *Index to the Published Decisions of the Accounting Officers of the United States 1894–1929*, 1931 (857 pages). This volume contains also a list of court decisions cited in the decisions of the accounting officers. The list of decisions is arranged alphabetically by names of cases and not by subject matter.

Six volumes entitled *Index-Digest of Published Decisions of the Comptroller General of the United States* have been published. These volumes cover the following periods:

July 1, 1929–June 30, 1940, 1,078 pp.
July 1, 1940–June 30, 1946, 1,248 pp.
July 1, 1946–June 30, 1951, 766 pp.
July 1, 1951–June 30, 1956, 533 pp.
July 1, 1956–June 30, 1961, 686 pp.
July 1, 1961–June 30, 1966, 770 pp.

Contract appeals. Effective May 1, 1949, the Armed Services Board of Contract Appeals was created by the joint action of the Secretaries of the Army, Navy, and Air Force, each of whom delegated to the board the authority to consider and determine as fully and finally as might each of the Secretaries, appeals by contractors under military contracts from decisions by contracting officers on disputed questions. Earlier contract decisions were contained in *Digest of Decisions of the Army Board of Contract Appeals, 1942–50* (317 pages). Decisions under the present board are found in *Digest of the Decisions of the Armed Services Board of Contract Appeals, 1950–53* (246 pages). Volume 3 of this publication contains decisions for 1953–54 (196 pages). Volume 4 covers the period 1955–56 (142 pages). The decisions are arranged alphabetically by topic.

Customs Bureau. Administrative rulings under the laws governing the collection of duties appeared for many years in the publication known as *Treasury Decisions*. On January 4, 1967, the title was changed to *Customs Bulletin*, a weekly pamphlet. The rulings embrace all the ramifications of the customs law, including classification of merchandise, rates of duty, drawback, and exchange rates.

Employees' compensation. The opinions of the Solicitors of the Department of Commerce and Labor and of the Department of Labor from August 1908 to April 1915 on cases arising under the law granting compensation to employees of the United States injured in the course of their employment are contained in the volume published by the Department of Labor entitled *Opinions of the Solicitor for the Department of Labor Dealing with Workmen's Compensation under the Act of Congress Granting to Certain Employees of the United States the Right to Receive from It Compensation for Injuries Sustained in the Course of Their Employment, Approved May 30, 1908,* 1915 (811 pages). An earlier volume published by the Department of Commerce and Labor contained the opinions to August 1912.

The Employees' Compensation Appeals Board was established in 1946. Since that time its decisions have been published annually in *Decisions of the Employees' Compensation Appeals Board.* However, Volume I contained decisions for the period from July 16, 1946, to June 30, 1948.

Federal Communications Commission. The Federal Communications Commission, established by the act of June 19, 1934 (48 Stat. 1064), to succeed the Federal Radio Commission and, in addition, to exercise control over communications by wire, is publishing its rulings in the series entitled *Federal Communications Commission Reports—Decisions, Reports, and Orders.* . . . The Commission also publishes on an irregular basis *Public Notices,* which are available in advance of the bound volumes of the *Reports.* Another publication, *Rules and Regulations,* is issued in 10 loose-leaf volumes for which supplementary material is provided to keep the volumes current. Rules and regulations are also published in the *Federal Register* and become part of the *Code of Federal Regulations.*

Federal Maritime Commission. Reorganization Plan 7, effective August 12, 1961, abolished the Federal Maritime Board and transferred its regulatory functions to the Federal Maritime Commission and functions relating to subsidization of the merchant marine to the Secretary of Commerce. The Commission has issued *Rules of Practice and Procedure* . . . , 1965 (38 pages).

Federal Power Commission.   Reports, decisions, opinions, and orders of the Federal Power Commission are contained in *Federal Power Commission Reports.* Volume I contained the reports from January 1, 1931, to June 30, 1939. Later volumes were issued annually until 1957, when the change was made to 2 volumes a year. A cumulative digest has been published covering the period 1931–57. The reports are also available as *Preliminary Prints.* The Commission also issues *Reports Under the Natural Gas Act* and *Reports Under the Federal Power Act,* both of which are loose-leaf volumes with supplementary pages supplied to keep them up to date.

Federal Reserve System.   Abstracts of the administrative rulings of the Federal Reserve Board to October 1, 1937, are given in the *Digest of Rulings of the Board of Governors of the Federal Reserve System, from 1914 to October 1, 1937* (683 pages), published by that board. This publication also includes digests of court decisions and opinions of the Attorney General and all textual changes that have been made in the Federal Reserve Act, the words deleted or added being set in appropriate type. Two loose-leaf publications have largely replaced the *Digest of Rulings: Interpretations of the Board of Governors* and *Textual Changes in the Federal Reserve Act.*

Federal Trade Commission.   The rulings and opinions of the Federal Trade Commission in cases involving restraint of trade and unfair competition are published in the volumes entitled *Federal Trade Commission Decisions.* One digest has been published under the title *Index Digest of Vols. I, II, and III of Decisions of the Federal Trade Commission with Annotations of Federal Cases from 1915 to June 1, 1938,* 1940 (60 pages).

The decisions are issued in separate form as they are rendered.

Fish and wildlife. The United States Fish and Wildlife Service was created in the Department of the Interior on November 6, 1956, and replaced the former Fish and Wildlife Service. The activities of this service originally were under the Bureau of Fisheries of the Department of Commerce and the Biological Survey, which had been established in the Department of Agriculture on July 1, 1885. They remained there until their transfer to the Department of the Interior on June 30, 1940.

The functions of this service include responsibility for the prevention of destruction or depletion of the nation's marine and inland fishery resources by conducting research, developing conservation measures, and providing information and aid to commercial fisheries; the conservation of wild birds, mammals, and sports fish and the maintenance of wildlife refuges; the control of predatory animals; and the conduct of activities relating to international agreements concerning fishery resources and migratory birds. Rules and regulations of the service are published in the numbered series entitled *Regulatory Announcements*.

Food and Drug Administration. The name "Food and Drug Administration" was first provided by the Agricultural Appropriation Act of 1931, although similar law-enforcement functions had been carried on under different organizational titles since January 1, 1907, when the Food and Drugs Act of 1906 became effective. It was transferred from the Department of Agriculture to the Federal Security Agency in 1940 and is now part of the Department of Health, Education, and Welfare. The Food and Drug Administration enforces the Federal Food, Drug, and Cosmetic Act; Tea Importation Act; Import Milk Act; Caustic Poison Act; and Filled Milk Act. Its activities are directed mainly toward promoting purity, standard potency, and truthful and informative labeling of the essential commodities covered by the provisions of these five acts.

Until June 1958 all regulations and pertinent information were contained in the Service and Regulatory Announcements, which were divided into three subseries: Food and Drugs, Caustic Poison, and Import Milk. Since 1958 regulations under the Federal Food, Drug, and Cosmetic Act have been issued in loose-leaf form as *F.D.C. Regulations,* which are part of Chapter 21 of the Code of Federal Regulations.

From 1914 to 1923 sundry rulings relating to the administration of the Pure Food and Drugs Act were contained in the Service and Regulatory Announcements of the Bureau of Chemistry of the Department of Agriculture, 28 numbers of this series being issued. The series proper was discontinued in 1923, but the supplements, which contained only notices of judgment (see page 291), continued until the end of the fiscal year 1927. This series contained the rulings known as *Opinions,* which had a separate numbering running from 1 to 394.

The administrative rulings of the Department of Agriculture known as *Food Inspection Decisions* were issued under the imprint of three units of the department. Nos. 1–68 (August 1, 1903–April 18, 1907) were published by the Bureau of Chemistry; Nos. 69–112 (May 14, 1907–January 6, 1910), by the Board of Food and Drug Inspection of the Office of the Secretary; Nos. 113–212 (February 17, 1910–July 19, 1934) with the caption "Office of the Secretary." Decisions Nos. 40–155 were assembled in the volume entitled *Food and Drugs Act, June 30, 1906, and Amendments of August 23, 1912, and March 3, 1913,* compiled by C. A. Gwinn, 1914 (857 pages). No other decisions have been assembled in book form. It should be borne in mind that all of these decisions are administrative rulings of the Secretary of Agriculture. They should not be confused with the decisions of the courts, which are termed *Notices of Judgment.*

One number of the Import Milk subseries has been issued in an English and a French edition. It was published by the Food, Drug, and Insecticide Administration. The most recent publication on this subject is *Federal Import Milk Act and Regulations,* 1963 (10 pages).

Prior to 1920 the enforcement of the act to prevent the importation of impure or unwholesome tea was in the hands of the Treasury Department, and the rulings and regulations were published in the weekly *Treasury Decisions*. From 1920 to 1923 they were published in the Service and Regulatory Announcements of the Bureau of Chemistry and in Department of Agriculture Circular 9. There was no regular publication of rulings between 1923 and 1927, but after the organization of the Food, Drug, and Insecticide Administration in 1927 they were published in the Tea subseries of the Service and Regulatory Announcements of that agency and its successor, the Food and Drug Administration.

The rulings governing the interstate shipment of adulterated or misbranded insecticides and fungicides were first published in several editions of Circular 34 of the Office of the Secretary of Agriculture, the first edition being issued in 1910. From 1914 to 1927 this material was contained in the Service and Regulatory Announcements of the Insecticide and Fungicide Board of the Department of Agriculture. A general index to Nos. 1–52 is given in No. 55. On July 1, 1927, the work of the Insecticide and Fungicide Board was taken over by the Food, Drug, and Insecticide Administration, and the rulings were published by that organization in the Insecticide and Fungicide subseries of the Service and Regulatory Announcements.

Immigration and naturalization. The Administrative Procedure Act of June 11, 1946 (60 Stat. 237), provided that all final opinions or orders in the adjudication of cases which could be cited as precedents should be made available to the public. In accordance with this law, all opinions and orders made by the Attorney General, the Board of Immigration Appeals, the Commissioner of Immigration and Naturalization, and certain designated officials of the Immigration and Naturalization Service in connection with immigration and naturalization matters are contained in *Administrative Decisions Under Immigration and Nationality Laws of the United States*. All precedent-creating decisions are included, beginning with the creation of the Board of Immigration Appeals in August 1940.

Internal revenue. Prior to 1898 the decisions on matters relating to internal revenue are available only in the first digest noted below.

Digest of decisions and regulations made by the Commissioner of Internal Revenue under various acts of Congress relating to internal revenue and abstracts of judicial decisions and opinions of Attorneys General, as to internal revenue cases, from Dec. 24, 1864, to June 13, 1898

Same, from June 13, 1898, to Dec. 31, 1904

Digest of Treasury decisions relating to internal revenue . . . from Sept. 9, 1916, to Dec. 31, 1920

Beginning with 1898 the decisions have been published annually as follows:

Compilation of decisions rendered by the Commissioner of Internal Revenue under the War Revenue Act of June 13, 1898 [Vol. 1, 1898], Vol. 2, Jan. 1, 1899–June 9, 1900

Compilation of decisions rendered by the Commissioner of Internal Revenue, Vols. 3–6, 1900–03

Treasury decisions under internal revenue laws of the United States, Vols. 7–36, 1904–42

Current decisions are included in the *Internal Revenue Bulletin,* which is issued weekly, and in semiannual cumulative bulletins.

The Tax Court of the United States, formerly the Board of Tax Appeals, created in 1924 (43 Stat. 336), is an independent agency in the executive branch of the government to hear appeals from the rulings of the Commissioner of Internal Revenue in cases involving income, excess profits, estate, and gift taxes. Its rulings were previously published in final form under the title *Reports of the United States Board of Tax Appeals* and, since October 1942, under the title *Tax Court Reports.* Decisions on individual cases are published separately and are also assembled in monthly pamphlets. All of these are sold by the Superintendent of Documents.

Rulings on questions arising out of the administration of the income tax are given in the *Internal Revenue Bulletin* and its predecessor, *Income Tax Rulings.* The force of those rulings is described in the *Bulletin* as follows:

The *Internal Revenue Bulletin* is the authoritative instrument of the Commissioner of Internal Revenue for announcing official rulings and procedures of the Internal Revenue Service and for publishing Treasury Decisions, Executive Orders, tax conventions, legislation, court decisions, and other items considered to be of general interest.

It is the policy of the Service to publish in the Bulletin all substantive and procedural rulings of importance or of general interest, the publication of which is considered necessary to promote a uniform application of the tax laws. It is also the policy to publish all rulings and statements of procedures which supersede, revoke, modify, or amend any published ruling or procedure. Except where otherwise indicated, published rulings and procedures apply retroactively. Rulings and statements of procedures relating solely to matters of internal management are not published. However, statements of internal practices and procedures affecting rights or duties of taxpayers, or industry regulation, which appear in internal management documents are published.

Revenue Rulings and Revenue Procedures reported in the *Bulletin* do not have the force and effect of Treasury Department Regulations (including *Treasury Decisions*), but are published to provide precedents to be used in the disposition of other cases, and may be cited and relied upon for that purpose. No unpublished ruling or decision will be cited or relied upon by any officer or employee of the Internal Revenue Service as a precedent in the disposition of other cases.

Since each published ruling represents the conclusion of the Service as to the application of the law to the entire state of facts involved, Service personnel and others concerned are cautioned against reaching the same conclusions in other cases unless the facts and circumstances are substantially the same. In applying rulings and procedures published in the *Bulletin,* personnel of the Service and others concerned must consider the effect of subsequent legislation, regulations, court decisions, rulings and procedures.

Internal Revenue Cumulative Bulletin 1967–1 contains all rulings, decisions, and procedures pertaining to Internal Revenue matters published in the weekly Internal Revenue Bulletins 1967–1 to 1967–26, inclusive, for the period January 1 to June 30, 1967. It also contains a cumulative list of announcements relating to decisions of the Tax Court of the United States published in the Internal Revenue Bulletins.

The first *Bulletin* each month includes an index for the preceding month. These monthly indexes are cumulated quarterly and semiannually.

Cumulative bulletins have been published from time to time. From April 1919 to December 1921, the cumulative bulletins were issued under the title *Income Tax Rulings, Cumulative Bulletin,* the serial numbers and periods being as follows:

No. 1, April to December 1919
No. 2, January to June 1920
No. 3, July to December 1920
No. 4, January to June 1921
No. 5, July to December 1921

For 1922 and later years cumulative bulletins have been published under the title *Internal Revenue Bulletin—Cumulative Bulletin.* Each issue contains the rulings for six months from January to June and from July to December. The two issues for each year bear the same Roman number, beginning with I for 1922. In addition, the issue covering January to June bears the Arabic number 1, and the issue covering July to December bears the Arabic number 2.

Digest of Income Tax Rulings; Digest A, April 1919–December 1930, Inclusive (1,366 pages), covers income-tax matters only. *Digest No. 13* contains abstracts of all rulings published in the *Bulletin* during 1922–24, and *Digest No. 22* those during 1925–27.

Rulings of the Bureau of Internal Revenue on the sales tax are contained in the following publications:

1920, Sales tax rulings, 1–112
1921, January–June, Sales tax rulings, 113–265
1921, July–December, Sales tax rulings, 266–356

Each of these was a cumulative bulletin, as the rulings had been issued earlier in monthly publications.

Index-Digest Supplements have been issued for *Cumulative Bulletins* as follows:

1953–56, 1958, 747 pp.
1957–60, 1961, 1,508 pp.
1961–64, 1965, 1,012 pp.

The *Internal Revenue Looseleaf Regulations System* is divided for distribution into five services: Income Tax, Estate and Gift Tax, Employment Tax, Excise Taxes, and Procedure and Administration. These will include all tax regulations issued by the Internal Revenue Service except those relating to alcohol, tobacco, and certain firearm taxes and those issued under tax conventions.

Interstate Commerce Commission. Since the organization of the Interstate Commerce Commission its decisions have been published in numbered volumes under the title *Interstate Commerce Commission Reports, Vol. . . . , Decisions of the Interstate Commerce Commission of the United States.*[4] The first 11 volumes were printed privately (1–5 by L. K. Strouse and Co. and 6–11 by the Lawyers Co-operative Publishing Company). For some time the decisions were assembled in three groups: Finance Reports, Valuation Reports, and undesignated (which includes all other reports).

The Finance Reports contain decisions relating to stock and bond issues and the abandonment of track; the Valuation Reports cover the valuation of physical property; the undesignated reports include decisions on rates and all other matters. The volume numbering, however, was continuous in one series until 1929, the Finance and the Valuation Reports being as follows:

Finance Reports			Valuation Reports	
65	111	180	75	
67	117	184	84	133
70	124	187	97	134
71	131	189	103	135
72	138	193	106	137
76	145	199	108	141
79	150	202	110	143
82	154	207	114	149
86	158	212	116	
90	162	217	119	
94	166	221	121	
99	170	224	125	
105	175		130	

All other volumes contain traffic reports.

At the present time the decisions are assembled in five

[4] The *Interstate Commerce Commission Reports,* which contain the decisions, must not be confused with the *Annual Reports of the Interstate Commerce Commission,* which are annual administrative reports.

groups: Finance Docket Decisions, Traffic Decisions, Water Carrier and Freight Forwarder Application Decisions, Motor Carrier Decisions, and Motor Carrier Decisions (Finance).

Beginning in July 1929, the Valuation Reports were issued in a separate series entitled *Interstate Commerce Commission Reports, Vol. . . . , Valuation Reports, Decisions of the Interstate Commerce Commission of the United States.* This series begins with Volume 22, the Valuation Reports listed above being regarded as Volumes 1–21. This series was discontinued with Volume 57 covering the period March 1960–March 1964.

The Motor Carrier Act of 1935 (49 Stat. 543) gave the commission regulatory powers over motor carriers engaged in interstate commerce. This gave rise to a new series of reports entitled *Interstate Commerce Commission Reports, Vol. . . . , Motor Carrier Cases, Decisions of the Interstate Commerce Commission.*

The decisions of the commission are also printed in separate form as rendered. The orders of the commission do not form part of the decisions and are issued separately only, not being assembled in book form. Digests and indexes have been published as follows:

Tables of cases and opinions of the Interstate Commerce Commission . . . from April 1887 to June 1913, Vols. 1–27, inclusive, I.C.C. Reports, 1914, 168 pp.

Supplement No. 1 to Table of cases and opinions of the Interstate Commerce Commission from June 1913 to July 1915, Vols. 27–35, inclusive, 1915, 88 pp.

Supplement No. 2 to Table of cases and opinions of the Interstate Commerce Commission from July 1915 to December 1921, Vols. 36–64, inclusive, 1922, 297 pp.

Unreported opinions:[5] Vol. 1, index-digest (Interstate Commerce Com-

---

[5] Beginning November 23, 1909, the commission instituted the practice of formulating unreported opinions. Opinions in the first series were printed and numbered 1 to 752. On or about January 1913, these printed unreported opinions were discontinued and a multigraph series started, being numbered A–1 to A–1064. On March 9, 1915, the multigraph series was discontinued and the printed series resumed. In the resumption of the printing of the unreported opinions, in order to preserve a complete record of the opinions issued, the number of opinions in the first series (752) was added to the number in the "A" series (1064), making a total of 1816; the first number given to the new

mission), 1917, 349 pp.; Vol. 2, Table of cases, table of cases cited, table of commodities, table of localities, 1917, 370 pp.

Table of commodities in the decisions of the Interstate Commerce Commission, 1887–1909, Interstate Commerce Commission reports, Vols. 1–15, 1909, 55 pp.

Same, 1906–12, Interstate Commerce Commission reports, Vols. 12–23, 1912, 146 pp.

Same, 1912–17, Interstate Commerce Commission reports, Vols. 24–42, 1917, 272 pp.

Same, 1917–20, Interstate Commerce Commission reports, Vols. 43–58, 1921, 163 pp.

Labor. Several agencies have been established for the administration and adjudication of various acts relating to labor problems. The published rulings of each of these are discussed below.

Labor Standards. The Walsh-Healey Act of June 30, 1936 (49 Stat. 2036), established labor standards to be followed by government contractors if the amount of the contract exceeds $10,000, and the Division of Public Contracts was created in the Department of Labor to administer the law. On October 15, 1942, this division was consolidated with the Wage and Hour Division to form the Wage and Hour and Public Contracts Divisions. The rulings up to April 30, 1956, have been published in *Rulings and Interpretations under the Walsh-Healey Public Contracts Act* issued as Division of Public Contracts, Rulings and Interpretations No. 3. There were three earlier editions, No. 1 and No. 2, and one without series and number.

National Labor Relations Board. The National Labor Relations Board was a direct outgrowth of the provisions of the

---

series was thus 1817. This practice was continued until the number reached 2249, when the commission decided to discontinue the practice of issuing unreported opinions.

In order to have a complete check of the subjects considered in these unreported opinions, an index-digest, together with a table of cases, table of cases cited, table of commodities, and table of localities was prepared.

It was thought best to separate these indexes into two volumes, the first volume to comprise the index-digest, and the second, the table of cases, table of cases cited, table of commodities, and table of localities. (From Letter of Transmittal.)

National Industrial Recovery Act. A National Labor Board was created on August 5, 1933, and was succeeded on June 29, 1934, by the National Labor Relations Board, both of these being created by executive order. The decisions of these boards were printed as follows:

Decisions of National Labor Board [Pt. 1], August 1933–March 1934, 1934, 98 pp.
Decisions of the National Labor Board, Pt. 2, April 1934–July 1934, 1934, 94 pp.
Decisions of National Labor Relations Board [Vol. 1], July 9, 1934–December 1934, 1935, 223 pp.
Decisions of National Labor Relations Board, Vol. 2, Dec. 1, 1934–June 16, 1935, 1935, 556 pp. (contains index for Vols. 1 and 2)

An act approved July 5, 1935 (49 Stat. 449), created a new National Labor Relations Board to take the place of the existing board of the same name. Its rulings have been published under the title *Decisions and Orders of the National Labor Relations Board.* This series began with Volume 1. Two cumulative issues entitled *Table of Cases Decided* have been published. The first covers Volumes 1–74 (December 7, 1935–August 21, 1947, 508 pages). The second covers Volumes 75–104 (August 22, 1947–May 27, 1953, 1954, 237 pages). In 1965 the the name was changed to *Index of Board Decisions* with the issue covering Volumes 105–150 (May 22, 1953–February 12, 1965, 513 pages). In 1967, an issue covering Volumes 147–166 (May 18, 1964–August 9, 1967, 183 pages) was published. Another publication is *Digest of Decisions of the National Labor Relations Board,* which is a digest of decisions and orders. Starting in 1951, an annual supplement has also been issued with irregular cumulations, the latest of which covers Volumes 116–127 (July 1, 1956–June 30, 1960).

PETROLEUM LABOR POLICY BOARD. The Petroleum Labor Policy Board was established by the Secretary of the Interior, who had been designated by the President as administrator of the petroleum industry. Its rulings were published by the Department of the Interior with the title *Decisions of the Petro-*

leum Labor Policy Board, February 6, 1934–March 13, 1935 (95 pages). The board was terminated on March 31, 1936.

RAILROAD LABOR RULINGS. The rulings of the former Railroad Labor Board have been published in six volumes entitled *Decisions of the United States Railroad Labor Board.* A cumulative index to Volumes 1–5 appears in Volume 5 and has also been published separately. An index-digest to the decisions to July 1, 1923, has also been issued. This digest includes the decisions to about the middle of Volume 4.

The act of June 21, 1934 (48 Stat. 1189), created a National Railroad Adjustment Board, consisting of four independent divisions, to adjust disputes between carriers and employees. The decisions of the board are published in several series, corresponding to the divisions into which it is divided.[6] The titles are as follows:

Vol.   , Awards   to   , First Division, National Railroad Adjustment
Board
Awards of the Second Division, National Railroad Adjustment Board . . .
Vol. , Awards   to   , inclusive
Vol.   , Awards   to   , Third Division, National Railroad Adjustment
Board
Vol.   , Awards   to   , and interpretation with index-digest, Fourth
Division, National Railroad Adjustment Board

The awards are also issued separately with individual pagi-

[6] The jurisdiction of the several divisions is as follows:
First division: Over disputes involving train- and yard-service employees of carriers; that is, engineers, firemen, hostlers and outside hostler helpers, conductors, trainmen, and yard-service employees.
Second division: Over disputes involving machinists, boilermakers, blacksmiths, sheet-metal workers, electrical workers, car men, the helpers and apprentices of all the foregoing, coach cleaners, power-house employees, and railroad-shop laborers.
Third division: Over disputes involving station, tower, and telegraph employees, train dispatchers, maintenance-of-way men, clerical employees, freight handlers, express, station, and store employees, signal men, sleeping-car conductors, sleeping-car porters, and maids and dining-car employees.
Fourth division: Over disputes involving employees of carriers directly or indirectly engaged in transportation of passengers or property by water, and all other employees of carriers over which jurisdiction is not given to the first, second, and third divisions.

nation. Processed indexes to First Division awards 1–2000 (Volumes 1 to 10) and 2001–2645 (Volumes 11 to 14) have been issued, but are not available for distribution.

WAGE AND HOUR RULINGS. The application of the Fair Labor Standards Act of 1938 (52 Stat. 1060) is discussed in a series entitled *Interpretative Bulletin,* issued by the Wage and Hour and Public Contracts Divisions of the Department of Labor. These are not findings on specific cases but are illustrative of typical situations.

Narcotics. Administrative rulings between 1915 and 1917 under the Narcotic Law have been assembled in the publica tion of the Bureau of Internal Revenue bearing the title *Compilation of Treasury Decisions Relating to the Act of December 17, 1914, Known as the Harrison Narcotic Law, Issued during the Period of February 2, 1915, to May 11, 1917.* The administration of this act was in the Bureau of Internal Revenue until April 1, 1927, when it was transferred to the Bureau of Prohibition. The Bureau of Narcotics was created in the Treasury Department by the act of June 14, 1930 (46 Stat. 585). Decisions of the bureau, through December 1966, are found in a weekly publication entitled *Treasury Decisions Under Customs, Certain Internal Revenue, Narcotic, and Other Laws.* In January 1967 the title of the weekly publication changed to *Customs Bulletin.* On April 8, 1968, Reorganization Plan 1 of 1968 transferred the Bureau of Narcotics from the Department of the Treasury, and the Bureau of Drug Abuse Control from the Department of Health, Education, and Welfare, to the Department of Justice and created the Bureau of Narcotics and Dangerous Drugs.

National forests. The more important rulings of the Department of the Interior, the Attorney General, the Comptroller of the Treasury, and the Solicitor of the Department of Agriculture are given in *Laws, Decisions, and Opinions Applicable to National Forests,* compiled by R. F. Feagans, 1916 (151 pages), issued by the Office of the Solicitor of the Department of Agriculture.

National Recovery Administration. The regulations issued by the National Recovery Administration are assembled in *Codes of Fair Competition* in 23 volumes. The arrangement is chronological, but there is a cumulative index in each volume. All the codes had been previously issued in separate form.

Patent Office. Beginning with 1869, decisions relating to patents and trademarks have been printed annually in the publication of the Patent Office now entitled *Decisions of the Commissioner of Patents and of the United States Courts in Patent and Trademark Cases,* issued also as a House document. The first issue was for 1869, but court decisions were not included until the issue for 1876. After 1928 the volumes also include decisions by the Board of Appeals of the Patent Office. Prior to 1946 these reports also included copyright cases. All decisions are published currently in the *Official Gazette of the United States Patent Office.*

In addition to the material indicated by the title, the volume also contains decisions relating to cases involving designs and labels. The material on copyright is limited to court decisions, as the Commissioner of Patents has no jurisdiction over copyright cases.

Pensions and retirement. Regulations and leading cases pertaining to the laws governing pensions of persons in the military and naval services and the retirement of persons in the civil service are given in the following publications (usually referred to as the *Pensions Decisions): Decisions of the Department of the Interior in Appealed Pension and Bounty-Land Claims,* Volumes 1–20; *Decisions of the Department of the Interior in Appealed Pension and Retirement Claims,* Volumes 21–22; and *Decisions of the Administrator of Veterans' Affairs in Appealed Pension and Civil Service Retirement Cases,* Volume 1, July 3, 1930–June 30, 1932. Executive Order No. 6731 of June 5, 1934, transferred the retirement of civilian employees to the Civil Service Commission.

The first 15 volumes of the *Pension Decisions* are covered by the two following digests: *Digest of Decisions and Opinions Relating to Pensions and Bounty Land,* Volumes 1–8, by William L. Chitty and John W. Bixler, and *Digest of Decisions of the Department of the Interior in Appealed Pension and Bounty-Land Claims . . . Contained in Vols. 9 to 15, Inclusive, of the Pension Decisions,* by Eugene B. Payne. The first digest also contains abstracts of opinions made before the publication of the *Pension Decisions.*

Prior to the publication of *Pension Decisions,* the following books, issued at irregular intervals, contained digests of rulings:

Pension laws now in force [with opinions and decisions], 1838, 126 pp. H. Doc. 126, 26 Cong. 1 sess.

Pension laws now in force [with opinions and decisions], 1846, 182 pp. H. Doc. 95, 29 Cong. 1 sess.

Army and Navy pension laws and bounty-land laws . . . from 1776 to 1854 . . . with an appendix containing opinions . . . with decisions, rules, and regulations, by Robert Mayo and Ferdinand Moulton, 2d ed., 1854,[7] 836 pp.

An analytical digest of the pension and bounty-land laws, the decisions of secretaries and opinions of attorneys general thereon . . . by F. F. C. Triplett, 1854, 256 pp.

Decisions [abstracts only] of the Secretary of the Interior, pension and bounty land, 1861 to 1871, 116 pp.

A digest of the laws of the United States governing the granting of Army and Navy pensions and bounty-land warrants; decisions of the Secretary of the Interior, and rulings of the Commissioner of Pensions thereunder . . . , by Calvin B. Walker, 1882, 314 pp.[8]

In all of the foregoing publications the cases pertaining to veterans apply only to persons serving in wars prior to 1917 or in the regular army. Relief of veterans of the world wars has been administered by the Veterans Bureau and its successor, the Veterans Administration. The Veterans Bureau published abstracts of opinions under the title *Digest of Legal Opinions Relating to the United States Veterans Bureau.* Three volumes were issued covering the following periods:

Vol. 1, Oct. 1, 1923–June 7, 1924
Vol. 2, June 7, 1924–June 30, 1925
Vol. 3, July 1, 1925–June 30, 1926

Monthly digests were printed up to November 1926.

[7] First edition published in 1852.
[8] An earlier print in 1881.

Abstracts of important rulings on laws applying to veterans of all wars were contained in the volume entitled *Federal Laws Relating to Veterans of Wars of the United States, Annotated,* published as Senate Document 131, 72d Congress, 1st session (688 pages), and *Supplement I,* issued by the Veterans Administration.

The decisions of the Administrator of Veterans Affairs in cases involving pensions for military service have been published in two volumes entitled *Decisions of the Administrator of Veterans Affairs, Veterans Administration.* Volume I was issued in two parts. Part 1 covered the period from March 1, 1931, to June 30, 1946 (1,502 pages), and Part 2 (308 pages) was an index-digest for Part 1. Decisions from July 1, 1946, to June 30, 1955, are contained in Volume II (1,212 pages). This volume also contains an index-digest. The decisions are now published separately as *Administrator's Decisions.* The latest is dated December 27, 1962.

Post Office Department: Opinions of Solicitor. Opinions on laws affecting the Post Office Department and the Postal Service rendered after 1873 are given in five volumes entitled *Official Opinions of Assistant Attorneys General for the Post Office Department* and in later volumes entitled *Official Opinions of Solicitor for the Post Office Department.* The change in the title was due to a change in the designation of the officer rendering the opinions. These volumes are not distributed to depository libraries and are not sold by any government agency. Although they contain information that apparently is of value to the public generally, the distribution has been limited because the opinions were made for the guidance of officers of the department.

Public lands. All the important regulations and decisions of the Secretary of the Interior relating to the disposition of the public land are published in the series entitled *Decisions of the Department of the Interior.* Prior to Volume 53, this series was entitled *Decisions of the Department of the Interior Relating to Public Lands,* and the contents were limited as indicated by the title. It was generally known under the name *Land Decisions.*

Beginning with Volume 53, which covers the period from January 1, 1930, to June 30, 1932, the volumes include important decisions and opinions relating to all the activities of the department. Probably half the contents of the volume concerns questions other than the disposition of public land. For many years the series included the regulations of the General Land Office (Bureau of Land Management since 1946) and the Department of the Interior relating to public lands. The first volume in this series was issued in 1883. The current volume is issued in signature form. Digests have been issued irregularly.

The digests up to and including the one for Volumes 1–40 are cumulative, and those for Volumes 1–30 and 1–40 are in two parts—the first part containing the digest proper by subjects and the second part containing tables of cases reported and cited, and lists of acts of Congress cited and construed. The digest issued after Volume 50 was published departs from this practice. Part 1 contains the digest proper for Volumes 41–51, instead of for Volumes 1–50, and Part 2 contains the table of cases reported and cited and acts of Congress cited and construed in Volumes 1–50. There is no Part 2 for the digest for Volumes 41–51 and no Part 1 for the digest for Volumes 1–50. The titles of these two volumes and of succeeding cumulative digests are as follows:

Digest of decisions of the Department of the Interior in cases relating to the public lands (Indian matters included), Pt. 1 . . . Vols. 41–51, inclusive, by George A. Warren, 1928, 374 pp.

Same, Vols. 52–61, inclusive, by Elsie M. Kimball, 1962, 505 pp.

Digest of decisions of the Department of the Interior in cases relating to the public lands, also tables of cases reported, cited and overruled, acts of Congress and revised statutes cited and construed; circulars; and rules of practice cited and construed, by Daniel M. Greene, Vols. 1–50, inclusive, Pt. 2, 1927, 366 pp.

Same, Vols. 51–61, inclusive, by Elsie M. Kimball, 1963, 251 pp.

A *Quinquennial Index-Digest, January 1955–December 1959* (460 pages) was published in 1960. There is also a quarterly *Index-Digest,* cumulative with each issue, the latest of which covers the period January–December 1966.

The regulations of the General Land Office governing the disposal of public lands were printed in pamphlet form from time to time, each pamphlet containing the regulations governing a particular type of entry. Those in force at the end of 1929 were compiled by C. G. Fisher, in a volume entitled *Circulars and Regulations of the General Land Office* (1,696 pages).

Later regulations were listed in *Index to Circulars and Regulations of the General Land Office Issued since January 1930*, May 1932, compiled by C. G. Fisher (13 pages). An earlier publication, which preceded the assembled volume of circulars and regulations, is *Index to Circulars and Publications of the General Land Office*, 1928 (48 pages).

Securities and Exchange Commission. The control of traffic in investment securities in interstate commerce was vested in the Federal Trade Commission by the act of May 27, 1933. By the act of June 6, 1934 (48 Stat. 881), this work was transferred to the newly created Securities and Exchange Commission, which was also given power to regulate stock exchanges, the listing of securities, and the operations of members of exchanges. The rulings of the commission to the end of 1936 were published under the title *Securities and Exchange Commission Decisions, July 2, 1934, to December 31, 1936*, Volume 1 (1,036 pages). This volume included four decisions in the same field by the Federal Trade Commission from December 1, 1933, to June 27, 1934. Starting with Volume 2 this publication has been titled *Securities and Exchange Decisions and Reports* and has been published irregularly.

Treasury Department: Opinions of Solicitor. Owing to the fact that the operations of the Treasury Department cover many subjects other than finances and taxes, rulings on many topics are included in the *Digest of Opinions and Briefs of the Solicitor of the Treasury*, by Robert J. Mawhinney. This work is in two unnumbered volumes, one covering the years 1880 to 1910 (510 pages), and the other the years 1911 and 1912. Separate volumes were also issued for each of the years from 1906 to 1909.

CHAPTER TWELVE

PRESIDENTIAL PAPERS

THE PUBLISHED PAPERS of the President vary greatly in content and importance. Some are of a routine nature while others contain important statements of principles and policies.

Messages

The messages of the Presidents include every communication to Congress, whether made in person or transmitted in writing. Prior to the Jefferson administration, annual messages were read in person and others were transmitted in writing. From Jefferson to Wilson probably all messages were transmitted in writing, but since that time some messages on important subjects have taken the form of addresses.

Most presidential messages are printed as documents of Congress. Those not printed separately generally consist of formal transmissions of annual reports, or other papers. The *Congressional Record* always contains the presidential addresses to Congress. It usually includes all other messages except those of a purely routine character, such as the transmittal of a report or the notification of Congress that a bill has been approved. In the case of approved bills, the approval is noted in the *Record*, but not the formal message. All messages are listed in the index to the *Record* under the entry "President of the United States." In the *Monthly Catalog* and the biennial *Document Catalog* the items under "President" include only the messages originating in the Executive Office; a formal transmittal of a report on and an estimate of appropriation for a government agency appears under the name of the agency in which the paper originated or to which it pertains.

An important collection of the writings of the Presidents is the 10-volume work by James D. Richardson entitled *A Compilation of the Messages and Papers of the Presidents, 1789–1897*. . . . This work was also published as House Miscellaneous Document 210, 53d Congress, 2d session. While the title indicates that the work ends with 1897, the appendix in Volume 10 contains what purport to be the messages, proclamations, and executive orders of President McKinley relating to the Spanish-American War, the last being a letter from the President to the Secretary of State dated January 20, 1899. The appendix in Volume 10 contains 115 pages of papers of various dates between 1789 and 1865 that were omitted from Volumes 1–9. These are in three sections under the headings "Special Messages," "Proclamations," and "Executive Orders."

The compilation does not contain all the early messages,[1] nor does it include the accompanying papers, in many cases more important than the messages, which are often mere letters of transmittal. The set is useful if it contains a particular message desired, but the student who wants all the papers would do well to consult the separate documents.

By the concurrent resolution of July 27, 1894 (28 Stat. appendix, p. 15), Congress provided that a complete compilation of "all the annual, special, and veto messages, proclamations, and inaugural addresses" of the Presidents from 1789 to 1894 should be printed, the work to be prepared under the direction of the Joint Committee on Printing. On August 20, 1894, the Joint Committee requested James D. Richardson, a representative from Tennessee and a member of the House Committee on Printing, to make the compilation.[2] The joint resolution of May

[1] See A. W. Greely, *Annual Report of the American Historical Association, 1896*, Vol. 1, pp. 1123–27, for statement of omissions; some of the omitted messages listed by Greely are included in the appendix to Vol. 10.

[2] 56 Cong. 1 sess., S. Rept. 1473, p. 1.

Sec. 5 of the Legislative, Executive, and Judicial Appropriation Act approved Apr. 17, 1900 (31 Stat. 134), gave permission to J. D. Richardson "to compile,

2, 1896 (29 Stat. 473), provided for the distribution to members of Congress and specified that the remainder should be delivered to the compiler. Mr. Richardson stated that about 650 sets were delivered to him.[3]

The act of June 4, 1897 (29 Stat. 62), made further provision for distribution, and authorized and directed the Public Printer to deliver duplicate plates to James D. Richardson, the compiler, "without cost to him." The set comprised 7,052 octavo pages, and the cost of the plates has been estimated at from $3,100 to $3,600.[4] The duplicate plates were delivered to Mr. Richardson, and arrangements were made for the commercial publication of the set and its distribution by subscription.[5]

The official set was issued in two series of 10 volumes each, but there were several prints of some of the volumes. The imprint date on both official sets is 1896 for Volumes 1–3, 1897 for Volumes 4–6, 1898 for Volumes 7–9, and 1899 for Volume 10. The two series are identical in all prints except for the title pages and the copyright notice. The title pages on the plain title set read: "Compilation of the Messages and Papers of the Presidents, 1789–1897, Published by Authority of Congress, by James D. Richardson, a Representative from the State of Tennessee, Vol. 1 [–10], Washington, Government Printing Office." In the other series the title page is the same except that the usual document numbering is added as follows: "53d Congress, 2d Session, House of Representatives, Misc. Doc. No. 210, Pt. 1 [–10]."

---

edit, and publish, without expense to the government, the state papers and diplomatic correspondence" of the Confederate States. It also provided that access to the papers should be given by the heads of the departments having them in charge. There was no official edition of these papers; they were published in two volumes by the United States Publishing Company of Nashville, Tenn., in 1905.

[3] 56 Cong. 1 sess., S. Rept. 1473, p. 11.

[4] Ibid., pp. 11, 25.

[5] The testimony regarding the arrangements, taken by the Senate Committee on Printing in compliance with a Senate resolution, is contained in 56 Cong. 1 sess., S. Rept. 1473 (130 pp.). With the material is an interesting set of instructions to canvassers regarding how to approach "prospects." Similar material is given in amplified form in J. S. Barcus, Science of Selling for Canvassers, Drummers and Clerks, Revised and Specially Adapted to the Sale of Messages and Papers of the Presidents, New York, Bureau of National Literature, Inc., 1917 (418 pp.).

Volumes 1–3 in the plain title set were issued with and without the notation "Copyright, 1897" on the back of the title, but all the volumes in the document set seen by the authors have the copyright notice, although Section 52 of the Printing Act of January 12, 1895, provides that no government publication shall be copyrighted. Moreover, the papers are official and public and not private, and are not subject to copyright, but in a commercial compilation any notes or additional matter could be copyrighted.[6]

In its report on May 22, 1900, the Senate Committee on Printing said in part as follows:

It must be assumed that Congress felt itself to be in Mr. Richardson's debt and undertook to discharge what it regarded as a public obligation in this way. It made a mistake. If anything more than a gracious public acknowledgment of the value of his work was due to Mr. Richardson it should have been paid in money duly appropriated for the purpose. The quasi authority given to Mr. Richardson in this provision of the law to use these plates in his own way for his own benefit led to a series of incidents for which his responsibility may be slight, but which have placed Congress in a false position.

. . . .

Your committee does not see the necessity of new legislation. Congress has it in its own power to avoid a repetition of the false representations of which it has been the victim by not again placing government plates at the disposition of private persons. The language of the statute forbidding the copyrighting of government publications appears to the committee to be as strong as it can be made.[7]

The commercially printed sets are listed on page 334.[8]

[6] In some of the 11-volume sets published commercially, Vols. 1–9 bear the copyright notation, but on the back of the title pages of Vols. 10–11 appears the following statement: "There is no copyright on this work as President [Theodore] Roosevelt considers that his messages and speeches delivered while President have been dedicated to and are the property of the public." In the other commercially printed sets seen the copyright appears on the volumes corresponding to the original set, but not on the volumes giving later messages. In all sets seen the index volumes bear the copyright notice.

[7] 56 Cong. 1 sess., S. Rept. 1473, pp. 3, 4.

[8] The authors are indebted to the Reference Department of the New York Public Library and to the Book Nook, Wortendyke, N.J., for information regarding several sets not seen. The editions are not listed in the *United States Catalog* or in any other compilation that has come to the authors' attention.

COMPLETE SETS

10 vols. published in 1898–99; appear to be an exact reprint of the official sets, except for different title pages and variations in illustrations; probably the first commercial edition printed from the duplicates of the government plates

11 vols. ending with Dec. 5, 1905 (Roosevelt); Vols. 1–9 paged separately; Vols. 10–11 paged continuously; Vol. 11 contains pp. 1131-81 and index; title page of Vol. 1 reads "1789–1908"; title pages of Vols. 2–11 read "1789–1907"

11 vols. ending with Jan. 31, 1908 (Roosevelt); Vols. 1–9 paged separately; Vols. 10–11 paged continuously

11 vols. ending with June 16, 1909 (Taft); Vols. 1–9 paged separately; Vols. 10–11 paged continuously

11 vols. ending with Dec. 7, 1909 (Taft); paged continuously; Vol. 10 contains pp. 6397–7820; Vol. 11 is index

11 vols. ending with Jan. 26, 1911 (Taft); paged continuously; Vol. 10 contains pp. 7205–7966; Vol. 11 is index

11 vols. ending with Nov. 11, 1912 (Taft); paged continuously; Vol. 10 contains pp. 7205–8145; Vol. 11 is index

20 vols. ending with May 13, 1915 (Wilson); Vols. 1–18 paged continuously; Vol. 18 contains pp. 7971–8444; Vols. 19–20 contain index

20 vols. ending with Dec. 15, 1915 (Wilson); Vols. 1–18 paged continuously; Vol. 18 contains pp. 7971–8499, but back title states volume contains pp. 7971–8444; Vols. 19–20 contain index.

20 vols. ending with Dec. 5, 1916 (Wilson); Vols. 1–18 paged continuously; Vol. 18 contains pp. 7747–8187; Vols. 19–20 contain index

20 vols. ending with July 11, 1917 (Wilson); Vols. 1–18 paged continuously; Vol. 18 contains pp. 7811–8316; Vols. 19–20 contain index

20 vols. ending with Dec. 7, 1920 (Wilson); Vols. 1–18 paged continuously; Vol. 18 contains pp. 8417–8887; Vols. 19–20 contain index

20 vols. ending with Mar. 31, 1922 (Harding); Vols. 1–18 paged continuously; Vol. 18 contains pp. 8635–9123; Vols. 19–20 contain index

20 vols. ending with Feb. 25, 1927 (Coolidge); Vols. 1–18 paged continuously; Vol. 18 contains pp. 9077–9675; Vols. 19–20 contain index

SUPPLEMENTS (EACH IN ONE VOLUME)

Mar. 4, 1897 (McKinley), to Aug. 9, 1902 (Roosevelt), 417 pp.
Mar. 4, 1913, to Mar. 4, 1917 (Wilson), pp. 7867–8344
Mar. 4, 1917, to Mar. 4, 1921 (Wilson), pp. 8221–8291

All the commercially printed sets were issued by the Bureau of National Literature or the Bureau of National Literature and Art. These organizations are apparently no longer in existence. Other editions were probably issued.

Mar. 4, 1921 (Harding), to Mar. 4, 1925 (Coolidge), pp. 8292–9480
Mar. 4, 1925, to Mar. 4, 1929 (Coolidge), pp. 9481–9850

The last four volumes listed above in part supplement and in part duplicate various issues of the 20-volume sets.

As the several editions generally bear no distinguishing date and as the same numbered volumes in the several sets do not contain the same material, the work should not be cited by volume numbers.

Most of the commercially printed sets seen by the authors bear on the title page the words "Prepared under the direction of the Joint Committee on Printing, pursuant to an act of the 52d Congress of the United States." Most of those issued later than 1906 also bear the notation "(with additions and encyclopedic index by private enterprise)" but there is no indication of the nature or extent of the additions. Neither the Joint Committee nor Congress had anything to do with the compilation of papers later than those in the original official edition, namely to January 20, 1899, and the papers of a later date were not printed from duplicates of government plates.

The papers between 1789 and 1877 which are given in the appendix in Volume 10 of the official editions, and which had not been included in Volumes 1–9, are not reproduced in any of the later commercial sets seen by the authors.

A 10-volume collection entitled *Presidential Messages and State Papers*, edited by Julius W. Muller, was published by the Review of Reviews Company in 1917. This ends with President Wilson's message of September 9, 1917. It is admittedly a selection and does not pretend to contain all the papers. Its format is different from the set printed from the duplicate government plates, and it apparently has no connection with the enterprise previously described.

In the first half of the 19th century several commercial compilations of presidential papers were published. Several commercial compilations of both the official and personal papers of individual presidents have also been printed. An official collection of personal and official papers is that in *The Writings of George Washington*, prepared under the direction of the

United States George Washington Bicentennial Commission and published by authority of Congress. This series consists of 39 volumes covering the years from 1745 through December 1799 and was printed at the Government Printing Office from 1931 to 1944. Volumes 38 and 39 are general indexes.

Recent commercial publications containing presidential messages that deserve mention are the following:

The state papers and other public writings of Herbert Hoover, collected and edited by William Starr Myers, 1934, Vol. 1, Mar. 4, 1929–Oct. 1, 1931; Vol. 2, Oct. 1, 1931–Mar. 4, 1933

The Hoover administration, a documented narrative, by William Starr Myers and Walter H. Newton, 1936, 553 pp.; contains extracts from the more important messages

The public papers and addresses of Franklin D. Roosevelt, with a special introduction and explanatory notes by President Roosevelt, Vol. 1, 1928–32;[9] Vol. 2, 1933; Vol. 3, 1934; Vol. 4, 1935; Vol. 5, 1936;[10] Vol. 6, 1937; Vol. 7, 1938; Vol. 8, 1939; Vol. 9, 1940; Vol. 10, 1941; Vol. 11, 1942; Vol. 12, 1943; Vol. 13, 1944 through 1945

The publications cited above contain many papers not printed in any government publication and should be consulted for any detailed study of presidential action. The Franklin D. Roosevelt papers in particular include an appreciable number of letters not published elsewhere establishing committees and other agencies advisory to the President. Certain loose documents on presidential papers in the collection of the Library of Congress are being placed on microfilm. These are described further in Chapter 19.

Most of the early messages, as well as the accompanying papers, are contained in the 38 volumes known as *American State Papers*. The annual messages from 1789 to 1814 are in Volume 1 of the subseries relating to foreign relations; later annual messages are in the other volumes of this subseries. Other messages are in the subseries devoted to the subject covered by the message. All the series except the one on Naval Affairs begin with the 1st Congress, but the closing dates range from the 17th (1823) to the 25th (1838) Congress.[11]

---

[9] This volume contains four papers of 1933.

[10] This volume contains fifteen papers of 1937.

[11] For schedule of volumes and dates covered, see pp. 188–89.

Until 1932 the annual messages were generally printed in the publication of the State Department now entitled *Foreign Relations of the United States, Diplomatic Papers*. From 1818 to 1860 this series was published only as a document of Congress; after 1860 it was issued as both a department publication and a document, although the department editions of the volumes for the years 1861–65 do not contain the messages. A list of this series from 1818 to 1909, with references to the serial and document numbers, is given on pages 892–95 of the *Checklist*.

Annual messages from 1848 to 1884 are printed in the series with the back title *Message and Documents*. The messages will be found in the volume dealing with foreign relations. From 1858 to 1920 they also appeared in the series bearing the back title *Abridgment, Message and Documents* or *Message and Documents, Abridgment*. These two series were congressional publications, but they were not numbered and do not form part of the regular congressional series. Additional information regarding them is given on pages 389–90.

The portions of messages relating to the tariff between 1839 and 1857 are given in *Tariff Proceedings and Documents, 1839–57*, 1911, three volumes, published as Senate Document 72, 62d Congress, 1st session.

Veto messages always appear in the *Congressional Record* and in the journal of the house in which the vetoed bill originated.[12] At present they are generally printed as documents of Congress. If so printed they are listed contemporaneously in the *Monthly Catalog* under the headings "House documents" or "Senate documents"; they appear in the annual index of this publication under the entry "President of the United States," subentry "Veto messages." In the biennial *Document Catalog*, they appear under the entry "President of the United States," subentry, subject of bill vetoed.

Veto messages up to August 1886, the second year of Cleveland's first term, are given in *Veto Messages of Presidents of the United States, with the Action of Congress Thereon*, compiled

[12] The Constitution requires that the objections of the President be entered in the journal of the house in which the bill originated. Art. I, Sec. 7, Clause 2.

by Ben Perley Poore, published also as Senate Miscellaneous Document 53, 49th Congress, 2d session (549 pages).

A consolidated compilation entitled *Presidential Vetoes: List of Bills Vetoed and Action Taken Thereon by the Senate and House of Representatives, 1st Congress Through 86th Congress, 1789–1961* (244 pages), which was compiled by Richard D. Hupman and the Senate Library staff, was published in 1961. If the veto was accompanied by a message, the document number is given; if any action was taken, the *Congressional Record* is cited. This publication supersedes the following two publications: *Veto Messages . . . 1889–1938* (95 pages), which covers the 51st to the 75th Congress and was published by the office of the Secretary of the Senate; and *Presidential Vetoes, . . . 51st Congress Through 84th Congress, 1889–1956* (168 pages), compiled by Richard D. Hupman and the Senate Library staff and published in 1956. A list of vetoes for each session may be found in the index of the *Congressional Record*. The messages should be in Richardson's *Messages and Papers of the Presidents*.

Pocket vetoes up to the end of the 70th Congress, 1st session (1928), are listed and notes on the disposition of the bills are given in a pamphlet by Robert P. Reeder entitled *Report on Pocket Veto* (43 pages), published as House Document 493, 70th Congress, 2d session.

A pocket veto is the result of the failure of the President to sign a bill within ten days after it is presented to him after the adjournment of Congress. As Congress is not in session, there is no immediate message on a pocket veto, but occasionally the President brings the matter to the attention of Congress at the next session. Such messages are given in Poore's *Veto Messages* and in Richardson's *Messages and Papers of the Presidents*.

Frequently a President will give his reasons for a pocket veto in a press statement or through the publication of a letter to a correspondent. Such announcements ordinarily are not printed in any official publication. President Franklin D. Roosevelt made it a practice to issue press statements on all pocket vetoes. These were transmitted to the Secretary of the Senate after the adjournment of Congress and were printed in the bound volume of the *Congressional Record* at the end of the

Senate proceedings on the last day of the session. They do not appear in the index. Lists of the pocket veto statements with citations to the *Congressional Record* are given in the biennial *Document Catalog* under the entry "President of the United States," subentry "Veto."

In response to a recommendation of the National Historical Publications Commission (44 U.S.C. 393), which was then incorporated in regulations of the Administrative Committee of the Federal Register issued under Section 6 of the Federal Register Act (44 U.S.C. 306), the Federal Register Division, National Archives and Records Service, General Services Administration, started a series of publications in 1958 entitled *Public Papers of the Presidents of the United States*. Several volumes have been released. The first one to be published contains the public messages and statements of President Eisenhower that were released by the White House during the year 1957. There are now eight volumes covering the Eisenhower administration, eight for President Truman, three for President Kennedy, and six for President Johnson.

The basic text of the volumes consists of oral utterances by the President or of writings subscribed by him. All materials included in these volumes is in the public domain by virtue of White House release or otherwise. The basic text is selected from the official text of communications to the Congress, public addresses, transcripts of press conferences, public letters, messages to heads of state, statements released on miscellaneous subjects, and formal executive documents promulgated in accordance with law. Ancillary text, notes, and tables are from official sources only. The material is presented in chronological order. Each volume contains a subject index.

Speeches

Many speeches of the Presidents made over the radio, television, or to unofficial gatherings contain important announcements of policy. Some are issued as pamphlets, others are printed in the *Congressional Record* or as documents of Congress on the motion of a member of either house, and several have appeared in the *Press Releases* of the State Department. They are also contained regularly in the *Department of State Bulletin* currently and eventually are included in *Public Papers of the Presidents*. These speeches may be found by means of the respective indexes to these publications.

House Document 218, 87th Congress, contains *Inaugural Addresses of Presidents of the United States from George Washington 1789 to John F. Kennedy 1961* (270 pages).

Proclamations and Executive Orders

While proclamations and executive orders are published in separate series, they overlap in content, and for that reason are discussed together.

Under many statutes the President is given specific power to take certain action, and his action is formally expressed in a proclamation or an executive order. There is no hard-and-fast distinction between a proclamation and an executive order, but proclamations are generally used for matters of widespread interest, although some executive orders have had as far-reaching effects as proclamations. In some cases the law specifically says that the President shall "proclaim," and in such cases the proclamation is necessarily used. In other cases, such as a recommendation for the observance of Fire Prevention Week, the proclamation has no legal effect, but is merely an appeal to the public.

Executive orders have a wide scope, ranging from the authorization of the appointment of a charwoman in a local post office (No. 6420) to prescribing rules and regulations under the Trading-with-the-Enemy Act (No. 2796). Most of them relate to the conduct of government business or to organization of the executive departments, but many have a wider significance. Most of the emergency agencies created in 1933 were established by executive order. The codes of fair competition authorized by Title I of the National Industrial Recovery Act (June 16, 1933) were approved by means of executive orders, but the details of the codes were published separately by the National Recovery Administration.

An executive order has never been defined by law or regulation. In a general sense every act of the President authorizing or directing that an act be performed is an executive order, but there are legitimate differences of opinion regarding the papers that should be included in such a classification. In 1907 the State Department began the numbering of executive orders, assigning numbers to those previously issued.[13] As the numbered executive orders by 1936 amounted to less than 8,000, it is evident that all the earlier papers that might fall in this group have not been taken into consideration. On March 31, 1936, the Secretary of the Interior informed the Senate Committee on the Judiciary that there "are estimated to be on file in the General Land Office 12,000 of such executive orders ranging in date from about the year 1806."[14]

Many early papers now classed as executive orders were recommendations by heads of departments which the President approved. On August 5, 1933, the President approved a recommendation of the National Recovery Administration that a National Labor Board be created. Apparently this was not transmitted through the usual office staff, but was presented to the President in person, was approved, and was taken back to the National Recovery Administration. Apparently no copy was sent to the State Department, and this paper does not appear in the printed series of executive orders. But on December 16, 1933, an executive order (No. 6511) providing for the "Continuance of the National Labor Board, etc." was approved.

On December 11, 1933, the President created a committee "to recommend permanent machinery to coordinate all government relations to American foreign trade." No executive order was issued, the only information regarding the creation of the committee being a White House press release. On March 23,

[13] The method of promulgation and the form of executive orders are prescribed in Executive Order No. 10006 of Oct. 9, 1948. Earlier executive orders on the same subject were No. 5220 of Nov. 8, 1929, No. 5658 of June 24, 1931, No. 6247 of Aug. 10, 1933, No. 6497 of Dec. 15, 1933, No. 7081 of June 20, 1935, and No. 7298 of Feb. 18, 1936.

[14] 74 Cong. 2 sess., S. Rept. 1756, p. 2.

1934, the office of Special Adviser on Foreign Trade was created by Executive Order No. 6651, which specifically stated that the committee was "supplanted by the present arrangement." In this case an executive order definitely terminated a unit created without an executive order.

Prior to March 14, 1936, executive orders were issued in separate form only, but beginning with that date the method of publication was changed as is indicated below. Notwithstanding their importance all of them have not been assembled or listed in any government publications. In a few cases the departments have printed collections of executive orders relating to their work, notably the executive orders relating to Indian reservations and the executive orders relating to the Panama Canal. Orders relating to appointments in the classified civil service without examination are generally listed or reprinted in the *Annual Report of the Civil Service Commission* or in the publication of that Commission entitled *Civil Service Act and Rules, Statutes, Executive Orders, and Regulations,* issued at irregular intervals. The text of some is given in the 1934 and later editions of the *United States Code.*

For some years prior to March 14, 1936, each proclamation was issued in separate form, but the method of publication of individual proclamations and executive orders was changed with the first issue of the *Federal Register* on March 14, 1936. Beginning on that date, the *Federal Register* contains all these papers "except such as have no general applicability and legal effect or are effective only against federal agencies or persons in their capacity as officers, agents or employees thereof." The existing series was continued as heretofore, but the separate prints included only such papers as were not published in the *Federal Register.*

Separate prints of the relatively infrequent executive orders without general applicability and legal effect were discontinued after the publication of Executive Order No. 10006 of October 9, 1948. This order requires current publication in the *Federal Register* of *all* proclamations and executive orders.

A *Weekly Compilation of Presidential Documents,* published by the Office of the Federal Register of the General Services

Administration, began with an issue dated August 2, 1965. Published every Monday, it contains transcripts of the President's news conferences, messages to Congress, public speeches, remarks, and statements and other Presidential material released by the White House up to 5 P.M. each Friday. An index of contents precedes the text, and a cumulative index to prior issues is at the end. The cumulations start anew with each quarter. Semiannual and annual indexes are published separately.

Beginning with Proclamation No. 2287 of June 6, 1938, and Executive Order No. 7906 of the same date, proclamations and executive orders have been published by the Office of the Federal Register in the supplements to Title 3 of the *Code of Federal Regulations*. The first of these was published in 1943 and covered the period through June 1, 1943. An additional supplement covered the remainder of 1943. Subsequently, supplements covering calendar years were issued annually. Periodically they are cumulated in larger volumes entitled "compilations." The series is composed of the following volumes:

Title 3—The President, 1936–38 Compilation
Title 3—The President, 1938–43 Compilation
Title 3—The President, 1943–48 Compilation
Title 3—The President, 1949–53 Compilation
Title 3—The President, 1954–58 Compilation
Title 3—The President, 1959–63 Compilation
Title 3—The President, 1964–65 Compilation
Title 3—The President, 1936–65 Cumulated Indexes and Tables

Prior to September 1947 all proclamations and executive orders were listed in the *Monthly Catalog* under the heading "President of United States" with citations to the *Federal Register* if they appear in that publication; in the index they are entered under the subject. In the biennial *Document Catalog* the detailed entry was under the subject matter, subentry "President of the United States." Prior to Volume 12 (1913–15) a detailed entry appeared also under the main entry "President of the United States," with subentry under the subject matter; in Volume 12 and later issues the only detailed entry is under the subject matter. Under the main entry "President of the United

States," subentries "Proclamations" and "Executive orders," were numerical lists of the proclamations and executive orders with cross references to the subject-matter entry.

At present all proclamations are assembled in one section of the *Statutes at Large,* being generally in Part 2 if more than one part is printed. There is probably no volume or series that contains all the proclamations. Some of these papers issued between 1791 and 1855 are given in Volumes 3, 4, 5, 9, 10, and 11 of the *Statutes at Large.*

Each volume subsequent to Volume 10 purports to contain the proclamations issued during the congress or congresses covered by the volume. A note in Volume 11 states that it contains all proclamations not previously published, but this is not true, as President Washington's first Thanksgiving proclamation of October 3, 1789, did not appear in the *Statutes at Large* until 1932, when it was quoted in President Hoover's Thanksgiving proclamation of that year (47 Stat. 2539). It is given by Richardson, who quoted it from Jared Sparks' *Writings of George Washington.* Several other proclamations which are not in the *Statutes at Large* are given by Richardson, but one of March 22, 1880, referred to in an act of June 20, 1890 (26 Stat. 169), is in neither Richardson nor the *Statutes at Large.* The original of the proclamation of March 22, 1880, has not been located, but printed copies are reported at several places.

The files of the General Land Office contain copies of many papers which purport to be proclamations but which were never published in the *Statutes at Large.* Apparently none of these has been countersigned by the Secretary of State, and this circumstance probably accounts for their not appearing in the *Statutes at Large.* There appears to be no law requiring the countersignature of proclamations by the Secretary of State, and the absence of such countersignature apparently does not affect the validity of the instrument.

Richardson's *Messages and Papers of the Presidents* purports to contain proclamations during the period covered by that work, but as has been noted above there are omissions. Proclamations issued prior to 1909 changing rates of duty are given in *Tariff Acts . . . of the United States from 1789 to 1909,* published as House Document 671, 61st Congress, 2d session; an earlier edition was published as House Document 562, 55th Congress, 2d session.

The more important proclamations of Presidents Hoover and Franklin D. Roosevelt are given in the collections of their papers cited on page 336. The Roosevelt papers contain also many of the executive orders. Complete lists of proclamations and executive orders from March 1933 to January 1937 are given on pages 515–624 of Volume 4 (1935) of the *Public Papers and Addresses of Franklin D. Roosevelt.*

There is no assembled index to all the proclamations, but citations to the *Statutes at Large* containing those prior to March 4, 1931, on certain subjects are given in *Index to the Federal Statutes, 1789–1931*, as follows:

Other Papers

While treaties are proclaimed by the President, they are not included in the proclamation series. Forms of publication of treaties are discussed in Chapter 13. Appointments made by and with the advice and consent of the Senate are listed in the *Congressional Record* when the nomination is transmitted to the Senate. As a general rule appointments made during a recess of the Senate or those not requiring confirmation cannot be verified in any official publication. Appointments in the Foreign Service are listed in the *Department of State Bulletin*.[15]

Not all the formal acts of the President are expressed in proclamations or executive orders. While the appointment of a clerk without regard to civil service rules is evidenced by an executive order, the pardon of a prisoner, the commutation of a sentence, and many other acts of the President are evidenced merely by endorsement of the recommendation and without formal publication.

Press statements issued by the White House are given in the published papers of Presidents Hoover and Franklin D. Roosevelt. The Roosevelt papers contain also many transcripts of the questions and answers at the presidential press conferences.

A list showing the places of deposit of the unpublished papers of the Presidents was inserted in the *Congressional Record* on July 13, 1939, during the debate on Senate Joint Resolution 118, which provides for the establishment and maintenance of the Franklin D. Roosevelt Library, where the manuscript papers of Franklin D. Roosevelt are deposited.[16]

Presidential Libraries

Since 1939 five presidential libraries have been established under the sponsorship of the federal government. Only two similar institutions, the Hayes Memorial Library in Ohio and the Hoover Library at Stanford University in California, had been established prior to 1939.

The Franklin D. Roosevelt Library at Hyde Park, New York,

[15] Prior to July 1939 they were published in *Press Releases* issued by the State Department.
[16] *Congressional Record*, daily ed., July 13, 1939, p. 12646.

was established by a joint resolution of Congress passed in 1939, which provided for its acceptance and operation by the Archivist of the United States. Under the act of 1955, generally called the Presidential Libraries Act, the Harry S. Truman Library at Independence, Missouri, the Dwight D. Eisenhower Library at Abilene, Kansas, the Herbert Hoover Library at West Branch, Iowa, and the John Fitzgerald Kennedy Library at Cambridge, Massachusetts, have been established. Public Law 89–169, approved September 6, 1965, authorized the General Services Administration to enter into an agreement with the University of Texas for the Lyndon Baines Johnson Archival Depository.

CHAPTER THIRTEEN

FOREIGN AFFAIRS

PRIOR TO 1929 when the State Department began its present systematic publication program, there were few current publications dealing with foreign relations, the material printed contemporaneously then consisting mostly of the treaties and conventions published separately and in the *Session Law°* and the *Statutes at Large. Papers Relating to the Foreign Relations of the United States*[1] had been printed for some time, but it was many years in arrears.

Publications on foreign affairs have been issued both by the State Department and by Congress, particularly by the Senate Committee on Foreign Relations. The Post Office Department has published postal conventions. All classes of publications are discussed in this chapter, but the publishing office is the State Department unless otherwise noted.

A comprehensive bibliography of all material dealing with foreign relations is contained in the *Guide to the Diplomatic History of the United States, 1775–1921,* by Samuel F. Bemis and Grace G. Griffin (979 pages), published by the Library of Congress in 1935. This valuable work enumerates not only the official printed papers of the United States government, but also publications of other governments, bibliographies, secondary sources, and collections of manuscripts. It contains also a list of the most significant journals and other general works, published both in the United States and foreign countries, a discussion of the nature of the sources, notes on the printed

---

[1] In 1947, the title was changed to *Foreign Relations of the United States: Diplomatic Papers* (occasionally referred to in later chapters as *Foreign Relations*).

state papers of foreign countries, and a discussion of manuscript sources available in the United States and foreign countries.

Treaties[2]

Section 2, Clause 2, of the Constitution provides that the President "shall have power, by and with the advice and consent of the Senate, to make treaties, provided two-thirds of the senators present concur. . . ." The President, through his accredited representative, therefore negotiates and signs treaties, which are then submitted to the Senate for its "advice and consent."

The Senate may reject, give its advice and consent to ratification, with or without amendment, or it may take no action, which is equivalent to rejection for the time being. If it rejects a treaty, the instrument is dead until such action is reversed; if it amends a treaty, the amendments must be accepted by the other party or parties, if the treaty is to be brought into force.

The acceptance of a treaty by the Senate does not make it effective, as both its ratification and proclamation are acts of the President, and he is at liberty to withhold such action. The amendments or reservations made by the Senate may be displeasing to him, or conditions may have changed since the instrument was drafted.

Even after the President ratifies a treaty it may not become effective for some time. The treaty may contain reservations making its effectiveness contingent upon specified conditions; a multipartite treaty is generally not effective until a specified number or all of the signatories have ratified it. Therefore the effective date, so far as the United States is concerned, may be some years later than the date of signing.[3] Ordinarily a treaty is not printed by the United States for public use before it be-

[2] The term "treaties" as used in the following pages includes any international agreement submitted to the Senate for its advice and consent to ratification, whether designated "treaty," "convention," "protocol," "charter," "constitution," or by some other name.

[3] For discussion of controlling dates, see Hunter Miller, *Treaties and Other International Acts of the United States of America*, Vol. 1 (short print), pp. 32-33.

comes effective. The several prints are described in the following pages.

Contemporaneous Print of Treaties

For many years treaties have been published in separate form, but it was not until 1908 that the designation "Treaty Series" was assigned to them. The numbering on the pamphlets begins with 489, a multilateral treaty creating the International Institute of Agriculture, signed June 7, 1905, previous numbers being assigned to the earlier issues. The older treaties which have been reprinted since 1908 generally bear the series designation and number.

The numbering of the Treaty Series is chronological according to the date on which the treaty became effective so far as the United States is concerned. The numbers assigned to issues prior to No. 489 are only partly in chronological order.[4] There is no complete collection of all numbers in print, as some to which numbers prior to 489 have been assigned were never printed. There are fractional numbers or numbers with a letter suffix in issues in the numbered prints, as well as in the unprinted papers to which numbers have been assigned.

The Treaty Series of the Department of State was combined in 1946 with the Executive Agreement Series to form the Treaties and Other International Acts Series, which begins with No. 1501.

A complete numerical list prior to July 1, 1931 (Nos. 1–839), is given in *Treaties and Other International Acts of the United States of America,* edited by Hunter Miller, Volume 1 (short print), pages 100–35. The same list with a subject index is included in *Subject Index of the Treaty Series and the Executive Agreement Series* (214 pages), published by the State Department in 1932. This list is reprinted, with additions bringing it to June 18, 1934, in *List of Treaties Submitted to the Senate, 1789–1934* (138 pages), published by the State Department in

[4] For discussion of the method of numbering prior to No. 489, see *ibid.,* pp. 36–37.

1935, and to December 31, 1939, in *Treaties Submitted to the Senate, 1935–1939* (22 pages), published in 1940. A complete listing to the end of 1937 is included in Volume 4 of *Treaties, Conventions, International Acts, Protocols and Agreements*, described on pages 354–55.

The Treaty Series prior to October 1929 also included some but not all executive agreements. The Treaty Series did not include Indian treaties, which were discontinued in 1871 (16 Stat. 566).

Postal conventions, negotiated by the Post Office Department under express authority of law, are now included in the Treaties and Other International Acts Series published by the State Department,[5] but up until 1939 they were issued in separate form by the Post Office Department, unnumbered and with no series designation.[6] While some of these separate prints of postal

[5] The first print in a State Department series is the postal agreement of 1944 with Palestine (Executive Agreement Series 439).

[6] Postal treaties and conventions are not submitted to the Senate. As early as 1792 the Postmaster General was authorized to "make arrangements with the postmasters in any foreign country for the reciprocal receipt and delivery of letters and packets." This was repeated substantially in various later acts, but the first statutory reference to postal conventions seems to be in the act of Mar. 9, 1868 (15 Stat. 40), which provides for the publication of postal conventions made by the Postmaster General "by and with [the] advice and consent of the President" under the authority of the act of Mar. 3, 1851 (9 Stat. 589). This was repeated in somewhat different form in the joint resolution of Mar. 1, 1869 (15 Stat. 347), which directs the Secretary of State to cause to be published the several postal conventions made with foreign countries, under the provisions of the act of Mar. 3, 1851. The act of Mar. 3, 1851 (9 Stat. 589), does not refer specifically to postal conventions, but gives the Postmaster General power to fix rates of postage in order to make better postal arrangements with other governments. Section 167 of the act of June 8, 1872 (17 Stat. 304; Rev. Stat., Sec. 398), specifically provides that the Postmaster General "by and with the advice and consent of the President may negotiate and conclude postal treaties or conventions." This section was re-enacted by the act of June 12, 1934 (48 Stat. 943), which did not change the portion authorizing the Postmaster General to make postal treaties, but added another clause providing that the construction of a postal treaty by the Postmaster General shall be conclusive upon all officers of the United States. Sec. 20 of the act of June 8, 1872 (17 Stat. 287; Rev. Stat., Sec. 398), which is existing law, provides that the Postmaster General shall send a copy of each postal convention to the Secretary of State, who shall furnish a copy to the Congressional [Public] Printer for publication, the proofs to be revised at the Post Office Department. Similar provisions are in Sec. 3804 of the *Revised Statutes*, which was derived from the act of Mar. 9, 1868 (15 Stat. 40). It appears that the

conventions bore the seal of the Department of State on the title page, all were publications of the Post Office Department.

Ordinarily treaties are made public at the discretion of any party to them, but for many years in the United States the treaties were generally not printed in any government publication prior to removal of the injunction of secrecy by the Senate. For this reason they were often available in foreign publications before any official text was published by the United States. For instance, a multilateral convention for the suppression of the slave trade signed by the United States and other powers at Geneva on September 25, 1926, was printed by the League of Nations (Treaty Series, Volume 60), the British Foreign Office (Treaty Series, 1927, No. 16), and doubtless by other powers in 1927. The first publication by the United States was in the *Senate Executive Documents*, the injunction of secrecy having been removed on February 25, 1929. The earliest print available for general circulation was that in No. 778 of the Treaty Series, available in April 1929. This is not an exceptional example. One instance of publication prior to the removal of the injunction of secrecy is that of the Treaty for the Construction of the Great Lakes-St. Lawrence Waterway, which was published in *Treaty Information Bulletin* No. 34 of the State Department for July 1932 immediately after its signature and before its transmittal to the Senate, Congress having adjourned. On January 19, 1933, the injunction of secrecy was formally removed by the Senate. In making the motion to remove the injunction of secrecy the Chairman of the Committee on Foreign Relations remarked that the motion was a technical one, as the treaty had already been made public. He made no comment

---

seal of the State Department has been inadvertently placed on the title page of some conventions by the Government Printing Office.

Apparently the first formal postal convention negotiated by the Post Office Department was one of 1847 with Bremen. This convention evidently was not ratified; at least it appears not to have been published in any form. However, it is cited in the postal convention with Bremen, Aug. 4, 1853 (16 Stat. 953). A complete list of postal conventions is given in *Index to the Federal Statutes, 1874–1931*, p. 440. A list of postal conventions in force on Dec. 31, 1932, is given in the supplement to *Treaty Information Bulletin* No. 39 for December 1932.

on precedents or propriety. The custom of not publishing treaties prior to the removal by the Senate of its injunction of secrecy is not generally followed today.

Periodic Publication of Treaties

Prior to 1950, treaties, including postal conventions, were printed annually in the *Statutes at Large*.

With the exception of the first six volumes of the *Statutes at Large,* the conventions and treaties were printed in each volume and were for the same period as the volume. Treaties effective between 1778 and 1845 are assembled in Volumes 7–8: Volume 7 contains Indian treaties;[7] Volume 8 includes treaties and conventions with foreign nations.[8] From 1845 to 1863 each volume covered two or more congresses as follows: Volume 9, 29th to 31st Congress (1845–51); Volume 10, 32d to 33d Congress (1851–55); Volume 11, 34th to 35th Congress (1855–59); Volume 12, 36th to 37th Congress (1859–63).[9] Volumes 13–49 (1863–1936) each cover a single congress.[10] Volumes 50–52 each cover a single session of the 75th Congress (1937–38). Volumes 32–50 were published in two parts, the treaties and conventions being in Part 2, except for Volume 44 for the 69th Congress (1925–27), which was published in three parts, the treaties and conventions being in Part 3.[11] Volumes 51 and 52 for the 2d and

---

[7] The following treaties for this period are in Vol. 11: Choctaws and Chickasaws, 1837; Stockbridge and Munsee, 1839; Wyandotte, 1842.

[8] The secret treaty with France of 1778 and a treaty with France of 1783 are in Vol. 17.

[9] The following treaties for this period are in later volumes: Sac and Foxes of the Mississippi 1800, Vol. 15; Venezuela 1861, Vol. 17; Denmark 1861, Ottoman Empire 1862, and Kickapoo Indians 1863, Vol. 13.

[10] The modification of the treaty of 1856 with Siam, proclaimed in 1868, which should be printed in Vol. 15, appears in Vol. 17.

[11] The volume sometimes cited as "Vol. 18, Pt. 2," or "18(2)," contains the treaties in force on Dec. 1, 1873. This is Vol. 2 of the *Revised Statutes,* although the volume number does not appear on the title page, which reads as follows: *Revised Statutes of the United States Relating to the District of Columbia and Post Roads Passed at the 1st Session of the 43d Congress 1873–74, together with the Public Treaties in Force on the First Day of December 1873,* 1875 (201 + 345 + 902 pp.). Each of the three parts has a separate title page. The part relating to treaties has the following title page: "Public Treaties of the United States in Force on the First Day of December 1873."

3d sessions of the 75th Congress are in one part. Printing in the *Statutes at Large* was discontinued in accordance with the act of September 23, 1950, Section 2 (64 Stat. 979), which provides that beginning as of January 1, 1950, all treaties and other international agreements shall be contained in a compilation entitled *United States Treaties and Other International Agreements.*

The *Statutes at Large* did not contain many papers included in the numbered Treaty Series, but the new *United States Treaties and Other International Agreements* volumes contain all material included in the numbered Treaties and Other International Acts Series.

A few treaties were perhaps inadvertently omitted, such as No. 243 of December 22, 1898, with Mexico extending the convention of March 1, 1889 (No. 232), relating to the boundary (26 Stat. 1512); and No. 421 of June 25, 1902, with Mexico relating to extradition. Most of the numbers in the Treaty Series omitted from the *Statutes at Large* are executive agreements, which were not submitted to the Senate.

Compilations of Treaties

There have been numerous compilations of treaties, some including all treaties and some only treaties in force. One compilation which includes all treaties, except for Indian treaties and postal conventions, is contained in the following volumes:

Treaties, conventions, international acts, protocols, and agreements between the United States of America and other powers, 1776–1909, by William M. Malloy, 2 vols. (S. Doc. 357, 61 Cong. 2 sess.)

Same, 1910–23 . . . Vol. 3, compiled by C. F. Redmond, pp. 2493–3918 (S. Doc. 348, 67 Cong. 4 sess.)[12]

Same, 1923–37 . . . Vol. 4, compiled by Edward J. Trenwith, pp. 3919–5755 (S. Doc. 134, 75 Cong. 2 sess.)[13]

Volume 4 of the compilation cited above contains, in addition to the treaties, the following material:

[12] This is often cited as *Malloy*, Vol. 3. An earlier edition by Garfield Charles was printed in 1913 as S. Doc. 1063, 62 Cong. 3 sess.

[13] This has been cited as *Malloy*, Vol. 4.

A chronological list of the treaties in the four volumes
A list, by countries, of treaties in Volumes 3 and 4
List of treaties submitted to Senate, 1789–1937, with indication of action
    and citations to the Treaty Series
Numerical list of the Treaty Series with citations to the *Statutes at Large*
An index to Volumes 1 to 4

The State Department will publish in the near future *Treaties and Other International Agreements of the United States of America, 1776–1949.* This series will be published in 15 volumes.

The *United States Treaties and Other International Agreements,* compiled by the Department of State, contains all treaties to which the United States is a party that have been proclaimed during each calendar year, and all international agreements other than treaties to which the United States is a party that have been signed, proclaimed, or with reference to which any other final formality has been executed, during each calendar year. The treaties and agreements contained in these volumes are printed in the language or languages appearing in the original treaties, the foreign texts being almost invariably as authentic as the English text.

In 1931, the State Department started a new compilation, edited by Hunter Miller, entitled *Treaties and Other International Acts of the United States of America.* As originally planned, this compilation was to have included all treaties that have ever been in force except those with Indian tribes and postal conventions. However, owing to lack of funds, no work has been done on this project since June 30, 1948.

Only a preliminary edition of Volume 1 and the final editions of Volumes 2–8 have been issued. The final edition of Volume 1 was not to have been issued until all the document volumes covering the period ending December 31, 1930, were off the press. The periods covered by Volumes 2–8 are as follows: Volume 2, 1776–1818; Volume 3, 1819–35; Volume 4, 1836–46; Volume 5, 1846–52; Volume 6, 1852–55; Volume 7, 1855–58; Volume 8, 1858–63.

This edition comprises complete and literal copies of the

texts, in chronological arrangement according to date of signature, of all the treaties and other acts of the United States of an international character which have at any time gone into force, whether now in force or not. Following the text of each treaty are notes of a textual and procedural nature.

No one of the compilations described above includes the postal conventions and treaties with Indian tribes. It appears that no complete collection of postal conventions has ever been printed. The editions of *Postal Laws and Regulations* for 1887, 1893, and 1902 contain appendixes which appear to be compilations of postal conventions, but none of them includes all the conventions made, and it is doubtful if any of them contains all in force.

Prior to 1871 formal treaties were made with Indian tribes, which were regarded as "domestic dependent nations." These have been assembled in *Indian Affairs, Laws and Treaties*, by Charles J. Kappler. Volume 2 of this work, published as Senate Document 319, 58th Congress, 2d session, contains all ratified treaties; Volume 4, published as Senate Document 53, 70th Congress, 1st session, contains the texts of unratified treaties negotiated at various times. Volumes 1 and 3 contain laws. *List of Indian Treaties,* with memorandum and accompanying information from the chairman to members of the House Committee on Interior and Insular Affairs, was published in 1964 as a committee print of the 88th Congress (45 pages). *Federal Opinion on Need for Indian Treaty Study* was published in 1965 by the same committee as House Report 1044, 89th Congress (130 pages).

Digests of the commercial treaties of the United States, and some of those of other powers to which the United States was not a party, are contained in the volume published by the Tariff Commission in 1922 entitled *Handbook of Commercial Treaties* (899 pages). The same body in 1919 issued *Reciprocity and Commercial Treaties* (535 pages), which discussed the effects but did not contain the texts of treaties of this character to which the United States was a party.

Certain treaties relating to the Canal Zone and the Panama Canal are given in the volume entitled *Canal Zone Code, an Act of Congress of the United States to Establish a Code of Laws for the Canal Zone, Approved June 19, 1934, together with an Appendix Containing Certain Treaties and General Laws of the United States Applicable in or Relating to the Canal Zone or the Panama Canal,* 1934 (1,237 pages). A later volume, *1962 Canal Zone Code,* does not contain treaties.

Air Laws and Treaties of the World, in three volumes, prepared by the staff of the Law Library of the Library of Congress, has been issued as a committee print of the 89th Congress, 1st session, and replaces *Air Laws and Treaties of the World, Annotated Compilation,* prepared by William S. Strauss, Assistant to the General Counsel, Library of Congress, which was issued as a committee print of the 87th Congress, 1st session.

Treaties and Other International Agreements Containing Provisions on Commercial Fisheries, Marine Resources, Sport Fisheries, and Wildlife to Which the United States Is a Party, compiled by Virginia W. Brewer and Marjorie Ann Browne of the Library of Congress, has been issued as a committee print of the 89th Congress, 1st session, 1965 (410 pages).

Another committee print, *Collective Defense Treaties,* prepared by Helen Mattas (514 pages), has been issued during the 90th Congress, 1st session (1967). Included are maps, texts of treaties, chronology, status of forces agreements, and a comparative chart.

General Agreement on Tariffs and Trade, a report on United States negotiations at the 1964–67 Trade Conference at Geneva, Switzerland, has been published in two volumes. Volume 1 contains four parts, two of which were published in 1967 (184 pages). Part 1 is *Concessions by Country* and Part 2 is *Special Multilateral Negotiations.* Parts 3 and 4 were published in 1968 (206 pages). Part 3 is *Concessions Granted on Principal Products* and Part 4 is *Concessions Granted on Principal Products by the United States.* Volume 2, in 2 parts, appeared in 1967 (632 pages). Part 1 is *List of Tariff Schedules Granted by the United States,* TSUS schedules 1–4; Part 2 contains TSUS schedules 5–7.

Lists of Treaties

Several lists of treaties are described below, but no complete list of all treaties and international acts of the United States has been published, and the State Department is authority for the statement that "there is not even available a complete list of all treaties and other international acts [of the United States] that went into force."[14]

In 1933, *A List of Treaties and Other International Acts of the United States in Force December 31, 1932,* Publication 436 (172 pages), was issued as a supplement to *Treaty Information Bulletin* No. 39, and a further revision of this compilation was published under the title *Treaties in Force: A List of Treaties and Other International Acts of the United States in Force on December 31, 1941,* Publication 2103. Information regarding treaties and other international acts is classified under five principal headings, namely: Promotion of peace, Political, Humanitarian, Economic, and Miscellaneous. Included are executive agreements and other papers not published in the *Statutes at Large* and some multilateral treaties signed but not in force. The dates of signature, of exchange of ratifications, of proclamation, and of going into effect are given for each treaty. Where applicable, references are given under each paper to the place of publication in the *Statutes at Large;* the Treaty Series; the Executive Agreement Series; the Malloy, Redmond, and Trenwith compilations; the League of Nations Treaty Series; or other sources if the paper does not appear in the volumes listed above.

The next revision of *Treaties in Force* was dated October 31, 1955. Subsequent revisions were issued as of October 31, 1956, and as of January 1 for the years 1958, 1959, 1960, 1961, 1962, 1963, 1964, 1965, 1966, 1967, and 1968. This publication

[14] *List of Treaties Submitted to the Senate, 1789–1934,* p. 13.

lists treaties and other international agreements of the United States on record in the Department of State on a given date, which have not expired by their terms or which have not been denounced by the parties, replaced or superseded by other agreements, or otherwise definitely terminated. The title *Treaties in Force* uses the term "treaties" in its generic sense as referring to all international agreements of the United States. In addition to listing such "treaties," the publication lists agreements in force between the United States and foreign countries which have been made by the Executive (a) pursuant to or in accordance with existing legislation or a treaty, (b) subject to congressional approval or implementation, or (c) under and in accordance with the President's constitutional power. The list is arranged in two parts, followed by an appendix. Part I includes bilateral treaties and other agreements listed by country or other political entity, with subject headings under each country or other entity. Postal agreements with territorial possessions of a country appear at the end of the appropriate country listing. Part II includes multilateral treaties and other agreements, arranged by subject headings, together with a list of the states which are parties to each agreement. In some cases status charts covering a number of closely related agreements are included together with the states which are parties. A consolidated tabulation of documents affecting international copyright relations of the United States is given in the appendix. This tabulation includes, in addition to treaties and conventions listed under appropriate country and subject headings in the main list, proclamations issued with respect to copyright relations. Exchanges of notes which preceded or accompanied various proclamations are included in the main list only.

A numerical list and index of the papers published in the Treaty Series up to July 1, 1931, with citations to the *Statutes at Large,* have been published by the State Department under the title *Subject Index of the Treaty Series and the Executive Agreement Series,* Publication 291 (214 pages). The list appears also in Miller's *Treaties and Other International Acts of the United States of America,* Volume 1 (short print). *List of*

Treaties Submitted to the Senate, 1789–1934, Publication 765 (138 pages), and *Treaties Submitted to the Senate, 1935–1944,* Publication 2311 (28 pages), supplement this information. As indicated by the title, *List of Treaties Submitted to the Senate,* this list includes treaties which did not become effective as well as those which went into force. It is arranged chronologically according to date of signature and shows the country, the subject or title, the date submitted to the Senate, the number of the Senate executive document containing the treaty, the Treaty Series number if published in that series, and a classification according to the following categories:

1. Treaties accepted by the Senate
2. Treaties accepted by the Senate but subject to amendment, reservation, or qualification
3. Treaties rejected by the Senate
4. Treaties withdrawn by the President
5. Treaties on which no final action has been taken by the Senate
6. Treaties which were not submitted for advice and consent to ratification but which were sent to the Senate for its information

In 1950 the Department of State issued Publication 3787, a numerical list of the Treaty Series, the Executive Agreement Series, and the Treaties and Other International Acts Series. This is a reprint from *United States Treaty Developments,* Publication 2851 (see page 339) and contains material included in Appendix II of that publication through the June 1949 release thereof.

Two publications issued by the State Department in 1919, but perhaps not generally available in libraries owing to the fact that they were originally confidential publications, are *Tentative List of Treaty Collections* (103 pages) and *Catalogue of Treaties 1814–1918* (716 pages). Both of these apply to treaties of all countries. The catalog is not a mere enumeration, but for each treaty indicates where the printed text may be found and in what language the treaty is printed.

The volume entitled *Index to the Federal Statutes, 1874–1931* contains the following lists of treaties which have been printed in the *Statutes at Large* and gives citations to that source.

Treaties, exclusive of Indian treaties, which were submitted to the Senate prior to March 4, 1931, but which did not go into force prior to October 1, 1932, are enumerated in *List of Treaties Submitted to the Senate 1789–1931 Which Have Not Gone into Force*, Publication 382 (25 pages), published by the State Department in 1932. This list includes 228 treaties, but only 12 were formally rejected by the Senate. The Senate accepted or amended 102 treaties which did not become effective because they were not ratified by the President; 17 were withdrawn; 6 were transmitted for information only; and 91 received no action. The list is preceded by a brief discussion of the principal features affecting the treaties enumerated.

The treaties which did not become effective are not assembled in any collection and it is probable that some were never printed. Many were printed as Senate executive documents and some have doubtless been issued as regular documents. What is probably an incomplete list of those which were printed as Senate executive documents up to the end of the 2d session of the 61st Congress and from which the injunction of secrecy had been removed is given on pages 1476–91 of the

Checklist. Later issues from which the injunction of secrecy has been removed are listed in the biennial *Document Catalog* and the *Monthly Catalog.* It should be noted, however, that the document is listed when the injunction of secrecy is removed and not when the treaty is printed.

Senate Document 216, 72d Congress, 2d session, entitled *Treaties Ratified by the Senate,* contains a list of treaties approved by the Senate between December 1, 1924, and February 18, 1933. The information given includes the date of reference to the Committee on Foreign Relations, a citation to the Senate executive document, the subject, the date reported by the committee, and the date approved.

Current Treaty Information

A monthly publication containing current information regarding treaties was issued by the State Department beginning with October 1929, under the title *Treaty Information Bulletin.* From March to September 1929, a processed publication was issued bearing the titles *Monthly Bulletin of Treaty Information* and *Bulletin of Treaty Information.* This publication contained condensed information regarding steps and publications relating to treaties, the meetings of international conferences, appointments to international bodies, decisions dealing with the interpretation of treaties, and notes regarding conventions and agreements to which the United States is not a party. It was a useful publication for keeping currently informed. An index to this publication was issued under the title *Treaty Information, Cumulative Index, Bulletins 1–69, Inclusive, October 1929–June 1935* (133 pages).

The *Treaty Information Bulletin* and the weekly pamphlet *Press Releases* were discontinued with the issues for June 1939. They were replaced by the *Department of State Bulletin,* a weekly publication, indexed semiannually, which contains the texts of press releases, information regarding treaties, and other material on current developments in American foreign relations and the work of the Department of State.

The texts of international agreements entered into by the United States are available in a number of publications. However, up-to-date factual information on the subsequent status of such agreements and on subsequent developments affecting them was not available in any one publication. To meet the need for such a compilation a loose-leaf publication (No. 2851) entitled *United States Treaty Developments* (514 pages) was issued by the Department of State. The first volume was released in 1948, and six transmittal sheets, through December 1950, were issued. It has been discontinued temporarily owing to lack of funds. The volume does not contain comprehensive notes, digests, or critical commentaries but serves as a guide to materials of an authoritative nature. It is a combination and extension of such previous publications of the Department of State as *Treaties Submitted to the Senate, Treaty Developments 1944,* and *A List of Treaties and Other International Acts of the United States in Force on December 31, 1941.*

Before 1929 the denunciation of a treaty by the United States was not a matter of record in any official publication. The fact may have been noted in the papers and journals, or some reference may have been made to it in the *Congressional Record,* but official confirmation could be obtained only by writing to the Secretary of State. Since 1929 treaties which have been either denounced or superseded by new agreements have been listed in *Press Releases,* a publication of the Department of State, or in the *Department of State Bulletin.*

Executive Agreements

The use of the term "executive agreement" as a designation for a paper relating to foreign affairs dates only from 1929, but the papers themselves existed under various designations for many years. While an exact definition is not possible, it may be said in general that an executive agreement, in the sense that the term is used by the United States, is an international arrangement made by the Executive without the advice and consent of the Senate and is based upon the constitutional authority of the President, legislation enacted by the Congress, the provisions of a treaty approved by the Senate, or a combination of two or more such bases. Such agreements usually consist of an exchange of notes between the Secretary of State and the head of the diplomatic mission of a foreign power or between the chief diplomatic officer of the United States in a foreign country and the head of the Foreign Office. At least one agreement, however, has been signed by the President and by the head of the foreign state.[15] Not every interchange of notes constitutes an executive agreement. One essential element to bring the paper within the classification is that each government binds itself to take or not to take a specified action.

The Executive Agreement Series, which consists of separate numbered prints of the agreements, was begun in 1929 and terminated in July 1946 with issue No. 506. Prior to that time the separate prints of executive agreements were generally published in the Treaty Series, but some were not so issued.

Executive agreements are currently included in the Treaties and Other International Acts Series, which began in 1946 with No. 1501 in order to avoid conflict with the numbers in the Treaty Series and the Executive Agreement Series which it replaced.

Such of the executive agreements as had been published in the Treaty Series were also printed in the *Statutes at Large*, and beginning with Volume 47 the executive agreements are brought together as a section of this publication. Although in general this volume covers the period 1931–33, the collection of executive agreements goes back to the beginning of the Executive Agreement Series in 1929.

[15] For a discussion of executive agreements, see John Bassett Moore, *Digest of International Law*, 1906, Vol. 5, pp. 210–18; "Treaties and Executive Agreements," *Political Science Quarterly*, 1905, Vol. 20, pp. 385–420; James T. Barnett, "International Agreements without the Advice and Consent of the Senate," *Yale Law Journal*, 1905, pp. 18, 63.

For criticism by Senator Oscar W. Underwood of action of the President in making arrangements through executive agreements, see *Congressional Record*, Vol. 62, Pt. 12, pp. 13050-71.

There is no complete collection of executive agreements, and it is probable that some of them have not been printed in any of the regular series issued by the State Department. Some may be found in *Foreign Relations of the United States;* and some, not elsewhere readily available, in the Malloy, Redmond, and Trenwith compilations listed on page 354.

Such of the executive agreements as were included in the Treaty Series are indexed in *Subject Index of the Treaty Series and the Executive Agreement Series,* which covers all issues in these series to July 1, 1931.

The act of June 12, 1934 (48 Stat. 943), as extended by subsequent legislation, authorized the President to enter into foreign trade agreements for the reciprocal reduction of tariff rates. The first of these agreements, with Cuba, was signed on August 24, 1934, and was published as Executive Agreement Series No. 67.

Diplomatic Correspondence

The collections of official papers relating to the foreign relations of the United States include communications both to and from foreign governments and their representatives and to and from American representatives in foreign countries.

Prior to 1861 this material was contained in annual congressional documents, which are listed on pages 892–93 of the *Checklist.* Beginning with 1861, one or more volumes have been issued by the Department of State for each calendar year, with the exception of 1869, in a series now entitled *Foreign Relations of the United States—Diplomatic Papers.* These volumes are also published as congressional documents.

From 1861 to 1868, this series was entitled *Papers Relating to Foreign Affairs, Accompanying the Annual Message of the President.* In 1869 there was no volume devoted to diplomatic correspondence, but some papers are given in House Executive Document 1, Part 1, 41st Congress, 2d session, containing the messages of the President and the annual reports of the Postmaster General and the Secretary of the Navy. Up to 1896 these papers were also printed in the series known as *Message and Documents,* described on pages 389–90.

The 1932 volumes, published in 1947 and 1948, were the first to bear the present title. Owing to the increase in material since World War I, several volumes are now issued for each year, with subtitles designating the country or area of the world to which they relate, such as "The American Republics," "The Soviet Union," etc. Publication of a special series of volumes relating to China was started in 1956. *Foreign Relations of the United States, Diplomatic Papers: 1942, China* (782 pages), also issued as House Document 117, 84th Congress, 1st session, and *Foreign Relations of the United States, Diplomatic Papers: 1943, China* (908 pages), also issued as House Document 118, 84th Congress, 1st session, have been published in this series. A two-volume series entitled *Foreign Relations of the United States, Japan 1931–1941,* was published in 1943.

The diplomatic correspondence is ordinarily not printed until some years have elapsed. For example, two volumes entitled *The Lansing Papers, 1914–1920,* were not published until 1939 and 1940; thirteen volumes entitled *The Paris Peace Conference, 1919,* were published in 1942–47; and a volume entitled *The Soviet Union, 1933–1939* was published in 1952. The latest volumes to be published are:

1940 (in five vols.), Vol. I: General, 1959, 832 pp.; Vol. II: General and Europe, 1957, 915 pp.; Vol. III: The British Commonwealth, the Soviet Union, the Near East, and Africa, 1958, 1,028 pp.; Vol. IV: The Far East, 1955, 1,022 pp.; Vol. V: The American Republics, 1961, 1,202 pp.

1941 (in seven vols.), Vol. I: General, the Soviet Union, 1958, 1,048 pp.; Vol. II: Europe, 1959, 1,011 pp.; Vol. III: The British Commonwealth, the Near East, and Africa, 1959, 998 pp.; Vol. IV: The Far East, 1956, 1,044 pp.; Vol. V: The Far East, 1956, 938 pp.; Vol. VI: The American Republics, 1963, 622 pp.; Vol. VII: The American Republics, 1962, 627 pp.

1942 (in seven vols.[16]), Vol. I: General, the British Commonwealth, and

---

[16] The seventh volume has also been issued but bears no volume number. It is State Department Publication 6353, *Foreign Relations, 1942, China.*

the Far East, 1960, 963 pp.; Vol. II: Europe, 1962, 863 pp.; Vol. III: Europe, 1961, 869 pp.; Vol. IV: The Near East and Africa, 1963, 854 pp.; Vol. V: The American Republics, 1962, 838 pp.; Vol. VI: The American Republics, 1963, 773 pp.

1943 (in six vols.), Vol. I: General, 1963, 1,189 pp.; Vol. II: Europe, 1964, 1,069 pp.; Vol. III: The British Commonwealth, Eastern Europe, and the Far East, 1963, 1,151 pp.; Vol. IV: The Near East and Africa, 1964, 1,188 pp.; Vol. V: The American Republics, 1965, 932 pp.; Vol. VI: The American Republics, 1965, 869 pp.

1944 (in seven vols.), Vol. I: General, 1966, 1,554 pp.; Vol. II: General, Economic and Social Matters, 1967, 1,129 pp.; Vol. III: The British Commonwealth and Europe, 1965, 1,478 pp.; Vol. IV: Europe, 1966, 1,473 pp.; Vol. V: The Near East, South Asia, Africa, and the Far East, 1965, 1,345 pp.; Vol. VI: China, 1967, 1,206 pp.; Vol. VII: The American Republics, 1967, 1,710 pp.

1945 (in five volumes), Vol. I: General, The United Nations, 1967, 1,611 pp.; Vol. II: General, Political and Economic Matters, 1967, 1,577 pp.; Vol. III: European Advisory Commission, Austria and Germany, 1968, 1,624 pp.; Vol. IV: Europe, 1968, 1,356 pp.; Vol. V: Europe, 1967, 1,349 pp.

Volumes published prior to 1925 do not usually contain documentation relating to the negotiation of treaties. In that year the policy of including the record of such negotiations in *Foreign Relations* was established. The plan of compilation adopted in 1925 and slightly amended in 1955 provided for the publication, subject to necessary security regulations, of "all documents needed to give a comprehensive record of the major foreign policy decisions."

Previously unpublished communications from friendly foreign governments are not printed unless the government concerned gives its consent to publication. As correspondence relating to a particular year may be withheld for the time being and appear in a later volume, it is advisable to consult the subsequent volumes in the series.

The Department of State exercises its own discretion as to what correspondence originating with officers of the United States government should be published, being guided by principles of "historical objectivity." According to the 1955 amendment of the plan of compilation, nothing shall be omitted from the *Foreign Relations* volumes "for the purpose of concealing or glossing over what might be regarded by some as a defect of policy." However, certain omissions are permitted for the following reasons:

(a) To avoid publication of matters which would tend to impede current diplomatic negotiations or other business.

(b) To condense the record and avoid repetition of needless details.

(c) To preserve the confidence reposed in the department by individuals and by foreign governments.

(d) To avoid giving needless offense to other nationalities or individuals.

(e) To eliminate personal opinions presented in despatches and not acted upon by the department. To this consideration there is one qualification—in connection with major decisions it is desirable, where possible, to show the alternatives presented to the department before the decision was made.

The volumes for the years 1861–99 are indexed in *General Index to the Published Volumes of the Diplomatic Correspondence and Foreign Relations of the United States, 1861–1899* (945 pages), published by the State Department in 1902. Later volumes are indexed in *Papers Relating to the Foreign Relations of the United States, General Index, 1900–1918,* 1941 (507 pages).

Many papers relating to foreign affairs have been published as separate documents. All material relating to foreign affairs published from 1828 to 1861, whether in House and Senate documents and reports, the journals of the two houses, the *Congressional Globe* and its predecessors, or executive publications, is indexed in *Index to United States Documents Relating to Foreign Affairs 1828–61,* prepared by Adelaide R. Hasse and issued by the Carnegie Institution of Washington (Publication No. 185, three volumes, 1914–21).

Several compilations of correspondence have been issued under authority of the government. The printing of correspondence relating to foreign affairs during the Revolution was ordered by Congress by the joint resolution of March 27, 1818 (3 Stat. 475). This resulted in the work entitled *Diplomatic Correspondence of the American Revolution . . .* edited by Jared Sparks and first printed in twelve volumes in 1829–30 by

Nathan Hale and Gray Bowen of Boston and G. & C. & H. Carvill, New York. A second edition in six volumes was printed by John C. Rives of Washington in 1857. A joint resolution of August 13, 1888 (25 Stat. 629), provided for a revised edition to be prepared by Francis Wharton. This was published in six volumes under the title *Revolutionary Diplomatic Correspondence,* and also as House Miscellaneous Document 603, 50th Congress, 1st session.

On May 5, 1832 (4 Stat. 513), an appropriation was made for printing the correspondence between the peace of 1783 and March 4, 1789. This resulted in the work entitled *Diplomatic Correspondence . . . from . . . 10th September, 1783 to . . . March 4, 1789.* It appeared in a seven-volume edition published in 1833–34, by Francis P. Blair, a seven-volume edition by Blair and Rives in 1837, and a three-volume edition by John C. Rives in 1855.

The more important correspondence between 1789 and 1828 and many congressional reports and documents were reprinted in the six volumes of *American State Papers* bearing the subtitle *Foreign Relations,* published by Gales and Seaton between 1832 and 1859 under authority of the act of March 2, 1831 (4 Stat. 471), the resolution of March 2, 1833 (4 Stat. 669), and the act of June 12, 1858 (11 Stat. 328).

The volume entitled *Diplomatic History of the Panama Canal,* published as Senate Document 474, 63d Congress, 2d session (602 pages), contains correspondence and related papers transmitted by the Secretary of State in April 1914 in response to a Senate resolution. It consists entirely of letters and treaties and therefore embraces original sources for a history instead of a narrative.

While not government publications, it seems desirable to mention two collections of official papers published under the auspices of the Carnegie Endowment for International Peace, both selected and arranged by William R. Manning of the State Department. The first of these, entitled *Diplomatic Correspondence of the United States Concerning the Independence of the Latin-American Nations,* three volumes, 1925, covers the period 1810–30; the second, entitled *Diplomatic Correspondence of the United States: Inter-American Affairs, 1831–60,* is made up of the following twelve volumes: Volume 1, Argentina; Volume 2, Brazil and Bolivia; Volume 3, Central America up to 1850; Volume 4, Central America, 1851–60; Volume 5, Chile and Colombia; Volume 6, Dominican Republic, Ecuador, and France; Volume 7, Great Britain; Volumes 8 and 9, Mexico; Volume 10, Netherlands, Paraguay, and Peru; Volume 11, Spain; Volume 12, Texas and Venezuela. These publications also include correspondence with European nations on Latin American affairs. The assembling of the material in the several volumes is alphabetical by countries. Each volume is indexed separately.

Current Developments in Foreign Relations

The weekly *Department of State Bulletin,* published since July 1939, contains information on current developments in the field of foreign relations and the work of the Department of State and the Foreign Service, including press releases, official statements of policy, texts of important documents, the United States position in the United Nations, and authoritative articles by department officials. This periodical is indexed semiannually. It replaced *Press Releases,* a weekly publication issued from October 1929 to June 1939, which made available in printed form the processed statements regarding foreign policy issued daily to the press. *Press Releases* was also indexed at intervals of six months, with a cumulative index for the period October 5, 1929, to December 29, 1934.

Foreign Policy Briefs, a biweekly news issue, offers concise authoritative coverage expressed in layman's language.

Conferences

The publications of the State Department and of Congress include many reports on international conferences and congresses, but it was not until 1929 that a special series relating to conferences was started by the State Department. Generally each number in the Conference Series relates to a particular conference or to some development resulting from a conference. Beginning with 1948 this material was included in a new series entitled International Organization and Conference Series. This series was divided into four groups: General, Regional, United Nations, and Specialized agencies. These groups were discontinued in the spring of 1959, and publications on international organizations and conferences are now numbered in one sequence.

The record of participation of the United States government in international conferences for the period since July 1, 1932, may be found in the volumes of two series of Department of State publications: (1) *American Delegations to International Conferences, Congresses, and Expositions and American Representation on International Institutions and Commissions, with Relevant Data*, a series which covers the period from July 1, 1932, through June 30, 1941; and (2) *Participation of the United States Government in International Conferences*, a series which covers the period since July 1, 1941.

Other valuable sources of both background and current information concerning international conferences and organizations are the weekly *Department of State Bulletin; International Organizations in Which the United States Participates, 1949* (335 pages), which contains data on such topics as the origin and development, membership, functions, structure, finances, and status of a number of international bodies; and the annual *United States Participation in the United Nations*.

A volume containing records of the conferences at Malta and Yalta, as well as preconference background material, was issued in 1955 in a special series of *Foreign Relations* volumes and as House Document 154, 84th Congress, 1st session. It is entitled *The Conferences at Malta and Yalta, 1945* (lxxviii + 1,032 pages). Two other publications in this series are *The Conferences at Cairo and Teheran, 1943*, 1961 (932 pages), and *The Conference of Berlin* [the Potsdam Conference], *1945*, 1960 (Vol. 1, 1,088 pages; Vol. 2, 1,645 pages).

Arbitrations

The most voluminous publications issued by the State Department, with the exception of the volumes of *Foreign Relations,* are those dealing with international arbitrations to which the United States has been a party. Prior to 1929 these did not appear in a regular series, the papers relating to each arbitration being published as a unit. These publications generally contain, for both parties, the testimony, exhibits, arguments, and awards. A list of such publications to the end of 1909 is given on pages 909–21 of the *Checklist.* Issues from 1909 to 1929 may be found in the catalogs issued by the Superintendent of Documents. Beginning with 1929, these were published in the numbered Arbitration Series. The last one which has been published was No. 9 in 1948, which dealt with Mexican Claims.

In 1898 the State Department issued *History and Digest of International Arbitrations to Which the United States Has Been a Party,* by John Bassett Moore, which was published also as House Miscellaneous Document 212, 53d Congress, 2d session.

Regional Problems

The Department of State publishes five series which give information on questions relating to limited areas. These are the East Asian and Pacific Series, the Inter-American Series, the European and British Commonwealth Series, the Near and Middle Eastern Series, and the African Series.

Congressional Publications on Foreign Relations

As all treaties are transmitted to the Senate, the publications of that body and its Committee on Foreign Relations contain a mass of material dealing with foreign affairs. The *Executive Journal* (see pages 145–46) indicates the action of the Senate and contains many of the shorter reports of the Committee on

Foreign Relations, but it does not include any debates in executive session. Many of the executive sessions, however, are open and the debate is reported in the *Congressional Record*.

The series entitled *Senate Executive Documents* contains the English language version of treaties submitted to the Senate for its advice and consent to ratification, together with the President's message of transmittal, the report on the treaty by the Secretary of State, and all accompanying papers. Through the 79th Congress, the *Senate Executive Documents* were almost invariably printed as confidential documents. However, since the beginning of the 80th Congress in 1945 the Senate has removed its injunction of secrecy from the documents at the time of the first reading of the treaty in the Senate and has ordered the printing of them without the confidential classification.

Committee reports on treaties are printed in a special series known as *Senate Executive Reports*, which are not generally available (see page 166). All of the reports of the Senate Committee on Foreign Relations to the end of the 56th Congress (1789–1901) have been assembled in eight volumes and published as Senate Document 231, 56th Congress, 2d session. This compilation includes the reports printed in the *Executive Journal*, those issued as Senate executive reports, and papers printed as regular reports and documents. The contents of the several volumes are given on page 176.

The Senate has also ordered the publication of several compilations dealing with treaties. One of these is *Compilation of Treaties between the United States and Certain Foreign Powers with Amendments, Modifications or Reservations Adopted by the United States Senate, and the Action of Foreign Governments Thereon*, 1921 (317 pages), issued as Senate Document 72, 67th Congress, 1st session. This is a poorly arranged collection, with no table of contents or index. The material includes excerpts from the *Senate Journal*, texts of treaties, correspondence with foreign powers, reports of the Senate Committee on Foreign Relations, and extracts from newspapers. There is no uniformity in the material relating to the several treaties.

Treaty reservations made by the Senate are enumerated in

Compilation of Treaty Reservations . . . Made . . . by the Senate . . . 1919 (12 pages), issued as Senate Document 148, 66th Congress, 1st session. The treaty reservations included in this publication are those in the following treaties:

Treaty of peace, amity, commerce, and navigation with Korea concluded May 22, 1882
General act for the repression of African slave trade signed July 2, 1890
Supplementary industrial convention concluded Apr. 15, 1891
Agreement with Russia regulating the position of corporations and other commercial associations signed June 25, 1904
Algeciras convention of 1906
Convention for the settlement of international disputes signed at The Hague, 1907
Convention concluded at the Second Hague Peace Conference held at The Hague, 1907, concerning the rights and duties of neutral powers in naval war
Convention respecting the limitation of the employment of force for the recovery of contract debts signed at The Hague, 1907
Extradition convention with Portugal signed May 7, 1908
Ship canal treaty with Panama signed Jan. 9, 1909
Arbitration treaty with Great Britain signed Aug. 3, 1911
International wireless telegraph convention concluded July 5, 1912
Convention signed at Paris on Jan. 17, 1913, modifying the international sanitary convention of Dec. 3, 1903
Nicaragua canal route, convention with Nicaragua signed Aug. 5, 1914
Convention with Denmark ceding the Danish West Indies to the United States signed Aug. 4, 1916

An earlier edition was issued as Senate Document 138, 66th Congress, 1st session (10 pages).

The basic documents on American foreign policy covering the years 1941–49 were published in 1950 under the title *A Decade of American Foreign Policy: Basic Documents, 1941–49*, as Senate Document 123, 81st Congress, 1st session. To supplement this publication the Department of State issues annual volumes (see page 377).

Background Information on the Soviet Union in International Relations was published as House Report 3135, 81st Congress, 2d session. This is a compilation of material, based on published documents, on the record of the Soviet Union in international relations and indicates some of the main currents of Soviet policy, such as treaty violations, obstructionism in the solution of international problems, and territorial expansion.

The Legislative Reference Service of the Library of Congress prepared a study of conditions in the Soviet Union that were purportedly leading the Russian people to oppose more and more strongly the Communist oppression. That study, *Tensions Within the Soviet Union,* was published as Senate Document 41, 82d Congress, 1st session, and a revision as Senate Document 69, 83d Congress, 1st session. Later, a companion study was authorized which was published under the title *Tensions Within the Soviet Captive Countries.* This study, published as Senate Document 70, 83d Congress, 1st session, is in seven parts, as follows: Part 1, Bulgaria; Part 2, Rumania; Part 3, Soviet Zone of Germany; Part 4, Czechoslovakia; Part 5, Poland; Part 6, Albania; Part 7, Hungary.

Miscellaneous Publications on Foreign Relations

Three digests of international law have been published by the government, one by Francis Wharton in 1886 and 1887, one by John Bassett Moore in 1906, and the third by Green Haywood Hackworth between 1940 and 1944.

The Wharton digest is in three volumes and appears in two editions, the second being printed also as Senate Miscellaneous Document 162, 49th Congress, 1st session.

The Moore digest, in eight volumes, absorbing for all practical purposes the three volumes by Wharton, was issued also as House Document 551, 56th Congress, 2d session.

The Hackworth digest is in eight volumes issued by the State Department and covers documents accumulated in the Department roughly from 1906 to 1940. The material contained in Moore's digest is not duplicated in the Hackworth volumes. The contents of the Hackworth volumes is as follows:

Vol. 1. International law; states, territories, and governments; recognition; territory and sovereignty of states; national jurisdiction and territorial limits

Vol. 2. National jurisdiction; exemptions from territorial jurisdiction; high seas and interoceanic canals

Vol. 3. Nationality; passports and registration; aliens

Vol. 4. Extradition; international communications; intercourse of states; consuls

Vol. 5. Treaties, hemispheric security; state responsibility; and international claims

Vol. 6. Modes of redress; war; maritime war

Vol. 7. Interference with neutral commerce; prize; neutrality

Vol. 8. General index; list of cases

A further *Digest of International Law* to cover the period from 1940 is being produced by Marjorie M. Whiteman in the Department of State. Volume 1 appeared in 1963, Volume 8 in 1967, and Volume 2 in 1968. Volume 9 is expected to be published in 1969 and Volume 7 in 1970. Miss Whiteman is also the author of the three-volume work entitled *Damages in International Law,* published in 1937 and 1943.

Publications on various subjects have been issued from time to time, such as *Digest of the Published Opinions of the Attorneys General and the Leading Decisions of the Federal Courts with Reference to International Law, Treaties, and Kindred Subjects,* 1877 (290 pages). Two editions were published in the same year, the second being issued also as Senate Executive Document 46, 44th Congress, 2d session.

The Senate Committee on Foreign Relations and the House Committee on Foreign Affairs have for many years published the transcripts of extensive hearings on matters relating to foreign relations. The hearings of the House committee deal with domestic legislation arising from international affairs, while those of the Senate committee pertain both to legislation and to the ratification of treaties. The hearings before the appropriations committees of the two houses on the annual appropriations for the State Department also contain many sidelights on the subjects coming within the range of activities of the Department. The State Department at times also issues special publications not falling into the classes described above.

Its current documentation program includes numerous pamphlets and leaflets dealing with the organization of the department and various aspects of foreign affairs, many of them written for the nonexpert, but interested, student of international relations. All of these may be located by means of the catalogs issued by the Superintendent of Documents.

The Historical Office of the Bureau of Public Affairs of the Department of State has published *American Foreign Policy: Current Documents, 1956,* Publication 6811, 1959 (1,495 pages). This is an annual one-volume collection of the principal messages, addresses, statements, reports, diplomatic notes, and treaties made in a given calendar year which indicate the scope, goals, and implementation of the foreign policy of the United States. Earlier publications were Senate Document 123, 81st Congress, 1st session, entitled *A Decade of American Foreign Policy: Basic Documents, 1941–49,* 1950, and *American Foreign Policy, 1950–1955: Basic Documents,* in two volumes, Department of State Publication 6446, 1957 (3,245 pages).

A record of our relations with China, with special emphasis on the years from 1944–49, is contained in Far Eastern Series 30 entitled *United States Relations with China,* 1949 (1,054 pages). While this publication covers a relatively small part of the relations between China and the United States, it does present a record which reveals the salient facts determining our policy toward China during this period and which reflects the execution of that policy.

Another publication in the International Organization and Conference Series is entitled *The Suez Canal Problem, July 26–September 22, 1956* (370 pages). The material contained in this publication refers to the events occurring during the time that the Egyptian government proposed the nationalization of the Universal Suez Maritime Canal Company.

In June 1946 the British Foreign Office and the United States Department of State agreed to publish jointly documents from captured archives of the German Foreign Ministry and the Reich Chancellery. Although the captured archives went back to the year 1867, the publication was limited to papers relating to the years after 1918, since the object of the publication was to establish the record of German foreign policy preceding and during World War II. The French government also participated in the project. This publication began with Series D, of which 13 volumes (1937–45) have been published. Series C (1933–37) will be completed in six volumes. The first 5 volumes have been published to the present time. The latest to be issued is *Documents on German Foreign Policy, 1918–1945, Series C (1933–1937), the Third Reich: First Phase, Vol. V,* March–October 1936, 1966 (1,208 pages).

The Department of State publishes a geography series comprised of *Geographic Bulletin* (7 numbers published), *Geographic Report* (11 numbers published), and the *International Boundary Studies* (73 numbers published).

CHAPTER FOURTEEN

REPORTS ON OPERATIONS

THE ANNUAL EXECUTIVE BRANCH administrative reports constitute the oldest series of government publications and are the sources where one is usually able to find full information regarding the operations of the several departments and agencies of the government. Unfortunately they have never been prepared according to a uniform plan. Data on operations of constituent units of an organized executive department may be found in the annual report of the head of the department, the annual report of the bureau, and the annual report of the department.

Reports of Heads of Departments

The annual report of the Secretary generally contains a review of the work of the department as a whole, but as a rule it touches on only the outstanding features of the operations of the subordinate units. In some cases, abstracts of the reports of the bureaus are appended. All heads of departments have issued reports each year except the Secretary of State, who made only one annual report—that for the fiscal year 1896.[1]

The annual reports prior to 1910 are listed in the *Checklist*, which also indicates for each report whether it was issued as a separate document of Congress, as part of a document, or as both a departmental and a congressional publication. For 1910

[1] The annual volume entitled *Foreign Relations* contains diplomatic correspondence for the year covered, but it is not an administrative report.

and later years recourse must be had to the biennial *Document Catalog* and the *Monthly Catalog*. The *Tables and Index* also lists the reports prior to 1893 that were issued as documents.

Bureau Reports

The report of the head of a bureau is the place where the most detailed account of bureau activities may be found. Annual reports of bureaus as a rule deal with operations, although there are a few which contain technical contributions to knowledge.

The reports of bureaus in the same department vary considerably in content, owing to the lack of uniform conceptions of what should appear. President Theodore Roosevelt in 1906 issued an executive order regarding annual reports which was confined mostly to an enumeration of what should not be included. So far as known, no subsequent official attempt has been made to lay down definite government-wide rules.

Owing to lack of money for printing, the tendency has been to curtail the contents of annual reports, and in some cases to omit the printing. Some are available in processed form. Some few services have never published an annual report and all the information concerning their operations must be sought in the annual report of the Secretary. An outstanding example of this is the Customs Bureau of the Treasury Department.

At times gaps will be found in the series of annual bureau reports. Notable examples of this unfortunate condition are offered by the reports of the Office of Indian Affairs, the General Land Office, the National Park Service, and the Bureau of Reclamation. These were issued regularly up to and including the ones for the fiscal year 1926. They were then discontinued by order of the Secretary of the Interior, and for the fiscal years 1927 and 1928 the only material available is that in the annual report of the Secretary. For these years, however, the appropriate pages in the annual report of the Secretary were reprinted in a separate pamphlet for each bureau and with independent pagination under the title *Extract from Annual Report of the Secretary of the Interior . . . Relating to . . . .* From 1929 to 1932 they were again issued as separate reports, but for 1933 to 1938 the only account of the work of these bureaus is that given in the report of the Secretary. Since 1938 some of the bureaus have reprinted their reports with the pagination contained in the annual report of the Secretary. The 1963 reports of the Department of Interior and the Bureau of Reclamation were the last ones to be issued. Beginning in 1964, the annual reports were replaced by Interior Conservation Yearbooks. The first yearbook was published in 1965 and is entitled *The Quest for Quality.* Succeeding volumes are as follows: *The Population Challenge* (1966), *The Third Wave* (1967), *Man . . . An Endangered Species?* (1968), and *It's Your World* (1969).

Department Reports

Consolidated reports of the older executive departments generally antedate the separate reports of the bureaus, or at least the consolidated reports are more generally available. The department reports as a rule consist of the report of the Secretary and the reports of the several officers reporting directly to the Secretary. Most of the department reports were discontinued with the reports for 1920. In the years immediately prior to their discontinuance, the department reports were duplicated by the separate reports of the several bureaus, although occasionally the department volume contained reports not issued separately. In many libraries the annual reports of the bureaus may be found only in the department compilation.

Up to and including 1931 the annual report of the Secretary of the Treasury had been issued in two forms, the shorter report bearing the title *Annual Report of the Secretary of the Treasury . . .* and the longer having the title *Annual Report of the Secretary of the Treasury . . . with Appendices.* The longer report was generally regarded as a department report, but it did not include the complete annual reports of some of the bureaus. For some offices, the annual report of the Secretary contained abstracts, and for some, what appeared to be the complete bureau reports. However, some of the bureau reports accompanying the Secretary's report were incomplete. Therefore, the reader would do well to consult the separate bureau reports if all the statistical data are desired. Some of the subordinate units of the Treasury do not issue separate annual reports, and for such units the material in the report of the Secretary is all that is available. For 1932 and thereafter only the shorter report, without the appendixes, was issued. This report was printed as a document of Congress in place of the report with appendixes, which had previously been the volume issued in the documents series.

The Post Office and Justice Departments are unifunctional, and as a rule printed reports are not issued for their subordinate units. The reports of the Postmaster General and of the Attorney General are equivalent to reports for the two departments.

Reports of Independent Establishments

The several commissions, boards, and other independent establishments are largely unifunctional, and as a rule do not issue separate reports for subordinate units. An exception is the Tennessee Valley Authority, which has annual reports for the Division of Agricultural Relations, the Division of Forestry Relations, Distributors of TVA Power, and the National Fertilizer Development Center.

Annual Reports Issued as Documents

The department reports were generally issued also as documents of Congress, and for many years they were printed only in that form.[2] Some of the bureau reports have been issued in both departmental and document editions. The reports of the

[2] The duplication is discussed in detail on pp. 109–16.

independent establishments show the following variation in plan of publication: (1) a single edition with document number, (2) a single edition without document number, and (3) two editions, one with and one without document number.

For instance, of the reports for 1932, that of the Alien Property Custodian was issued in a single edition as House Document 425, 72d Congress, 2d session; that of the Federal Radio Commission was issued in a single edition without document number; and that of the Federal Power Commission was issued in two editions—one without document number and one as House Document 435, 72d Congress, 2d session. The *Monthly Catalog* indicates the form of publication. Many of the older annual reports are available only as Senate or House documents. Citations to the document numbers will be found in the following publications:

Prior to 1881, in *Poore's Catalogue.* The index in Poore will not be of great assistance, as many citations under a subject are grouped without differentiation. In the catalog portion the items are arranged chronologically regardless of numerical sequence or series, and it may take some time to find the item desired. In some cases the citation is "Senate Document" or "House Document" without indication as to whether the publication is an executive or a miscellaneous document. In other cases, the citation is "Executive Document" without indication as to whether it is a House or Senate document.

1881–93, in the *Ames Index.* In this work some of the reports are listed under the name of the officer instead of the establishment, without cross reference. Thus the annual report on operations of the Government Printing Office will be found under "Public Printer."

Prior to 1893, in *Tables and Index.* The serial number and the document number are given after each entry.

Prior to 1896, in Senate Document 103, 54th Congress, 2d session. Only the more important reports are included.

Prior to 1910, in the *Checklist.* The serial number and the document number are given after each entry.

Prior to 1921, in the 1924 edition of the *Senate Catalogue,* pages 653–933. This list gives the document number and the volume number, but does not give the serial number.

1895–1932, in the annual *Document Index.*

1893–1940, in the biennial *Document Catalog.*

Current publications, in the *Monthly Catalog.*

Statistical Appendixes

Some agencies issue separate statistical appendixes to their annual reports. The Forest Service had a Statistical Supplement from 1942 to 1953. Other such appendixes are issued by the Rural Electrification Administration, the Bureau of Reclamation and the Bureau of Land Management.

Other Reports on Operations

Considerable information on the work of the several offices may often be found in the annual hearings on the appropriation bills. While the hearings deal primarily with future operations, much of the work is of a continuing character, and the hearings disclose many facts regarding the past which are not brought out in the annual reports.

Hearings on the regular appropriations bills have been held before the Appropriations Committees of the House and Senate beginning with those for the fiscal year 1923.[3]

Prior to the fiscal year 1922 the hearings on appropriations were held before both the Appropriations Committees and the several committees dealing with substantive legislation, different items for the same departments being considered by different committees.

When the hearings for the fiscal year 1922 were held, the system was in a transition stage and was different from that of earlier and later years. The important regular appropriation bills and the committees holding the hearings for the fiscal year 1922 and prior years were as follows:

[3] Hearings on annual appropriation bills are held and published some time in advance of the fiscal year to which they relate. Hearings on deficiency and supplemental appropriation bills are generally held in the calendar year which has the same number as the fiscal year. The fiscal year ends on June 30 and is designated by the year in which it ends; thus the fiscal year ending June 30, 1960, is known as the fiscal year 1960.

Deficiency appropriation bills[4] (carrying appropriations for all agencies
needing additional funds)

District of Columbia appropriation bill

Fortifications appropriation bill; for years after 1922 in War Department
bill[5]

Legislative, executive, and judicial appropriation bill (carrying some appropriations for almost all agencies); for years after 1922 in the bills
relating to the several departments and independent offices

Sundry civil appropriation bill (carrying some appropriations for almost
all agencies); for years after 1922 in the bills relating to the several
departments and independent offices

Agriculture appropriation bill: Fiscal year 1922, House Committee on
Appropriations; fiscal years prior to 1922, House Committee on Agriculture and Senate Committee on Agriculture and Forestry; for years
after 1922 included in Agriculture Department bill

Army appropriation bill: Fiscal year 1922, House Committee on Appropriations and Senate Committee on Military Affairs; fiscal years prior
to 1922, House and Senate Committees on Military Affairs; for years
after 1922 included in War Department bill

Diplomatic and consular appropriation bill: Fiscal year 1922, House
Committee on Appropriations; fiscal years prior to 1922, House Committee on Foreign Affairs and Senate Committee on Foreign Relations;
for years after 1922 included in State Department bill

Indian appropriation bill: Fiscal year 1922, House Committee on Appropriations; fiscal years prior to 1922, House and Senate Committees

[4] There are generally several deficiency bills at each session. In earlier years
they were called "Urgent deficiency bills" and "General deficiency bills"; for
many years they have generally been called "First deficiency bill," etc.

[5] The Department of War was incorporated in the National Military Establishment and redesignated Department of the Army by the National Security Act
of 1947 (61 Stat. 499). The National Security Act amendments of 1949 (63 Stat.
578) redesignated the National Military Establishment as the Department of
Defense and established it as an executive department of the government which
includes the military departments of the Army, Navy, and Air Force.

[6] Hearings have not been published for every year.

on Indian Affairs; for years after 1922 included in Interior Department bill

Military Academy appropriation bill: Fiscal year 1922, included in Army appropriation bill; fiscal years prior to 1922, House and Senate Committees on Military Affairs; for years after 1922, included in War Department bill

Naval appropriation bill: Fiscal year 1922, House Committee on Appropriations and Senate Committee on Naval Affairs; fiscal years prior to 1922, House and Senate Committees on Naval Affairs; for years after 1922 included in Navy Department bill[7]

Pension appropriation bill: Fiscal year 1922 and prior years, House Committee on Appropriations; for the years 1923 to 1931 in Interior Department bill; for later years in Independent Offices bill

Post Office appropriation bill: Fiscal year 1922, House Committee on Appropriations and Senate Committee on Post Offices and Post Roads; fiscal years prior to 1922, House Committee on Post Offices and Post Roads and Senate Committee on Post Offices and Post Roads; for years after 1922 included in Post Office Department bill

Rivers and harbors appropriation bill: Fiscal year 1922, House Committee on Appropriations and Senate Committee on Commerce; fiscal years prior to 1922, House Committee on Rivers and Harbors and Senate Committee on Commerce; for years after 1922, included in War Department bill for 1923 to 1937, and in War Department civil appropriation bill after 1937.

When the consideration of appropriations was centered in the two committees beginning with the consideration of the bills for the fiscal year 1923, the contents of the bills were rearranged and all the annual items pertaining to a particular agency were placed in one bill. There are now bills for the executive departments, either individually or in groups,[8] a bill for the Executive Office (White House) and independent establishments, a bill for the legislative branch, including the Li-

[7] The Department of the Navy was incorporated in the National Military Establishment by the National Security Act of 1947 (61 Stat. 499). It was made a military department within the Defense Department by the National Security Act amendments of 1949 (63 Stat. 578).

[8] If an act appropriates for more than one executive department the portion for a particular department is generally called "Title I," etc., and it is provided that each title may be cited as "Department of . . . Appropriation Act. . . ." The term "fiscal year" is not used in the authorized citation, but the single year given indicates the fiscal year.

brary of Congress and the Government Printing Office, and a bill for the District of Columbia.

As a rule, if more than one executive department is covered by an appropriation bill, the House hearings on each department are published in separate volumes while the Senate hearings are likely to be in one volume devoted to all the departments included in the bill. However, the practice is not uniform. Deficiency bills and hearings thereon still cover all agencies.

It should be noted, however, that all appropriations are not carried in a law that is entitled an "appropriation act." Occasionally a substantive law makes an appropriation for carrying it into effect. This happens generally when a new agency is established. For example, the Budget and Accounting Act of June 10, 1921, which created the new Bureau of the Budget, also appropriated the money for the operation of the Bureau for the balance of the fiscal year 1921 and for the fiscal year 1922.

The regular printing of the hearings on appropriation bills is a development dating from 1923. Earlier transcripts of hearings were sometimes printed in the committee reports on the bills. Reports on appropriation bills are ordinarily short, so that if the catalogs show that the report exceeds 25 pages, it is safe to assume that some testimony or other material dealing with the operations of the government is included.

The reports as a rule contain brief statements of reasons for any material changes that may be recommended in the amounts to be appropriated. The debates on appropriation bills often contain criticisms by individual members of the agencies under consideration.

Sporadic publications giving information on operations often result from a congressional investigation or a resolution of inquiry by either house of Congress. The testimony taken during investigations generally appears in the hearings before the committee making the investigation. If a report is made by the committee, it appears in the report series; occasionally the testimony is appended to the report and at times it is printed as a document. If information is supplied in response to a resolution and is printed, it generally appears as a document of the house ordering it. Thus Senate Resolution 351 of the 72d Congress directed the heads of all departments, independent establishments, and government corporations to report on the functions performed. The replies were printed as received, each as a separate document, and were not assembled in one publication.

What purports to be a "Bibliography of Congressional Inquiries into the Conduct of the Business of Executive Departments other than by Standing Committees of Congress, 1789–1911" is given on pages 477–85 of the report of the Commission on Economy and Efficiency entitled *The Need for a National Budget*, issued as House Document 854, 62d Congress, 2d session. Notwithstanding its title, this list does include some inquiries by the standing committees. Its brevity suggests that it might be incomplete.

Certain reports are required by law to be submitted annually to Congress. A list of the reports required in 1912 is given on pages 434–68 of *The Need for a National Budget*, cited above. Many of the laws requiring these reports were repealed by the act of May 29, 1928 (45 Stat. 986–96); some reports have been discontinued under authority of the act of May 13, 1926 (44 Stat. 552); some laws requiring reports have doubtless been repealed by other acts, but on the other hand later legislation has required the submission of additional reports.

At times the executive agencies issue publications describing their field of operations or a special branch of their activities. Examples of these are *United States Lighthouse Service*, by John S. Conway, 1923 (115 pages), *Conservation in the Department of the Interior*, by Ray Lyman Wilbur and William A. DuPuy, 1934 (253 pages), *United States Department of Commerce, How It Serves You on Land and Sea, and in the Air*, compiled by Vincent Vasco, 1946 (118 pages), *Bureau of the Census, Fact Finder for the Nation*, 1965 (58 pages), *Partners in Economic Progress*, published by the Office of Field Services, Department of Commerce, 1966 (30 pages), *Programs and Services of the Department of Health, Education, and Welfare,* 1966 (374 pages), and *The Federal Reserve System,* 1963 (297 pages).

Approximately 150 publications have been issued by government departments and agencies describing their work and the career opportunities available. These are a part of a program to recruit college graduates for jobs in the federal service.

Message and Documents

For many years the department annual reports were issued also in a congressional publication entitled *Message and Documents.* This was generally a straight duplication of the material in the department reports, except that the reports of the Secretary of the Treasury and the subordinate units of the Treasury Department were never included. However, the contents varied considerably. Although congressional publications, these volumes were not part of the congressional series and were not numbered in the document series. They were designated by congress, session, date, and department and by volume and part numbers if the reports for any department made more than one volume. The following are typical:

Message and documents, 38th Congress, 1st session, 1863–64,[9] War Department
Message and documents, 54th Congress, 2d session, 1896–97, Interior Department, Vol. 4, Pt. 1

The publication of *Message and Documents* was discontinued with the volume for the 2d session of the 54th Congress containing the reports for the fiscal year ending June 30, 1896. These books should be used only if no other edition of the annual reports is available. It is doubtful if they are to be found in many libraries.

The author has never seen a complete list indicating what might be found in the *Message and Documents.* On page 1667

---

[9] It should be noted that, contrary to the usual custom, the reports are for the year corresponding to the first of the double dates.

of the *Checklist* the compiler of that publication has a half-page note which disposes rather summarily of the set with the statement that it "had no value because it was merely a duplication (except for binding) of some of the volumes which appeared in the congressional set." As has been pointed out in Chapter 4, there are hundreds of duplications, and that fact alone does not justify such summary dismissal.

Abridgment of Message and Documents

The *Abridgment, Message and Documents,* or *Message and Documents, Abridgment,* was issued by the Joint Committee on Printing for each year from 1858 to 1920. While this purported to be an abridgment of *Message and Documents,* it contained abstracts of reports not in the more extensive set, notably of the reports of the Secretary of the Treasury and of the Treasury bureaus. Like *Message and Documents,* the *Abridgment* is not included in the document series. The several issues are designated by the dates, the earlier ones carrying a double date, such as 1901–02, the reports being for the year corresponding to the first of the double dates. Beginning with 1902 each issue bears a single date. Volume numbers subordinate to the date were used if the abridgment for the year made more than one volume.

The *Abridgment* should not be used if the complete annual reports are available. Its only value is as a substitute for the complete reports. The volumes issued up to 1909 are listed on pages 1621–23 of the *Checklist.*

CHAPTER FIFTEEN

ORGANIZATION AND PERSONNEL

As INFORMATION REGARDING the organization and personnel of the federal government is generally given in the same publication, these topics will be considered together. A brief discussion of the methods of creating the several government units will be included, as these facts have an important bearing on the ease with which contemporaneous information may be obtained. No publication giving the complete organization of the government to its lowest unit is issued, but information regarding the major agencies is available in several series. The legislative, judicial, and executive branches will be discussed separately.

Legislative Branch

The divisions of the legislative branch as established by the Constitution are the Senate and the House of Representatives. The other agencies of the legislative branch are established by a resolution of either house, by concurrent resolution of the two houses, or by statute.

The Senate and the House of Representatives each creates its committees and defines their jurisdiction. Joint committees of the two houses are established by concurrent resolution or by statute. The units which are concerned with the routine business of the houses are created by substantive law or by simply appropriating for the position.

The Library of Congress and the Government Printing Office

at one time were listed in some official publications as independent establishments but now are generally considered to be a part of the legislative branch.

Originally these agencies were concerned solely with matters pertaining to Congress, but their present functions are much broader. However, certain duties in regard to them are exercised by the Joint Committee on the Library and the Joint Committee on Printing, respectively.

Information regarding the organization and personnel of Congress and its agencies is given in the *Congressional Directory*, which is described in detail on page 183. This contains the names and membership of committees, but not their duties. The jurisdiction of each committee is outlined in the *Senate Manual* (see page 186) and the *House Manual* (see page 185). The *House Manual* also contains information on the origin and development of House committees. The names of senators and representatives are also given in the *United States Government Organization Manual* (see page 399). The *Biographical Directory of the American Congress* contains sketches of all members of Congress prior to 1961 (see page 184).

Judicial Branch

The territorial jurisdiction of the Supreme Court, the Court of Customs and Patent Appeals, the Court of Claims, and the Customs Court is nation wide, but that of the several circuit courts of appeals and of the district courts has definite territorial limits.

The several circuit courts of appeals have jurisdiction over a group of states. No district court has jurisdiction beyond the boundary of the state in which it is located. Many district courts have jurisdiction over a portion of a state, as some of the states are divided into several districts. The territorial jurisdiction is defined in the *Statutes at Large* and the *United States Code*.

Executive Branch

In order better to understand the discussion of sources of information, the classification and nomenclature of government agencies will be described. This will be followed by accounts of the contemporaneous, annual, and other sources. It will be noted that there is little uniformity either in nomenclature or method of creation.

Classification of Agencies

The major agencies of the executive branch of the government are the twelve executive departments and the "independent establishments," which are agencies that report directly to the President.[1]

The heads of the executive departments form the President's Cabinet, although that body has no legal status, and the President may designate any person to be a member of it.[2]

The independent establishment is largely a product of the present century, there being in this group in 1910 only nine agencies, including the Library of Congress and the Government Printing Office, which are now considered to be in the legislative branch. With the creation of additional regulatory boards and commissions the independent establishments gradually increased in number.

There have been various suggestions and recommendations made to bring about a more uniform terminology for the several organizational units in the executive departments. For many years the word "bureau" was used to indicate the major subdivision of an executive department. However, the words "service" and "office" were also used to indicate governmental

[1] The term "independent establishment" has never been defined by statute, but it has been used in many laws containing general legislation relating to government services.

[2] See Henry B. Learned, *The President's Cabinet*, Yale University Press, 1912.

units of the same rank as bureaus and, in at least one case, the former Procurement Division of the Treasury Department, a major unit was called a division, a term generally used for a unit of a bureau. The first Hoover Commission recommended the following organizational structure: department, service, bureau, division, branch, section, and unit.[3]

There is still little uniformity to be found among the major units within various departments. For example, among the major units of the Department of Commerce are the Census Bureau, the Maritime Administration, the Patent Office, the Coast and Geodetic Survey, and the National Bureau of Standards. In the Department of the Interior are the National Park Service, the Bureau of Mines, and the Geological Survey. Other government agencies also use the words "bureau," "service," "administration," and "office" interchangeably.

The greatest confusion exists in the use of the terms "commission," "board," "committee," "council," and "authority." The name itself indicates nothing regarding the scope of activities of the unit.

There is likewise no uniformity in the use of the terms "federal," "national," and "United States" as part of the name of a unit established either by law or by executive order.

Field installations are called regional offices, area offices, district offices, or stations.

Some agencies are commonly referred to only by their initials; for example, TVA, NASA, HUD, and FAA.

Contemporaneous Information on Creation of Executive Agencies

Executive departments are always created by act of Congress, and the instruments creating them will always be found in the laws. Prior to March 4, 1933, administrations and independent establishments were generally created by statute, but the broad powers conferred on the President by legislation sub-

[3] *First Report of the Commission on Organization of the Executive Branch of the Government—Relating to the General Management of the Executive Branch,* 1949, Recommendation No. 21, H. Doc. 55, 81 Cong. 1 sess., p. 41.

sequent to March 4, 1933, enabled him to create new units under these laws and to change existing ones by executive order. Therefore the instruments creating administrations and independent establishments must be sought both in the laws and in the executive orders. However, agencies created under authority of the Reorganization Act of 1939 (53 Stat. 561), the Reorganization Act of 1945 (59 Stat. 613), and the Reorganization Act of 1949 (63 Stat. 203) are found in neither of these places. These agencies were created by what are called "Reorganization Plans." When submitted these are printed in the *Congressional Record*, those heretofore submitted being also printed as *Documents*. The Reorganization Acts provide that if a reorganization plan takes effect it shall be printed in the volume of the *Statutes at Large* containing the public laws and in the *Federal Register*.

Executive agencies and functions of the federal government abolished, transferred, or terminated subsequent to March 4, 1933, are listed in Appendix A of the *United States Government Organization Manual*.

Occasionally Congress appropriates for a new activity, and the resulting unit selects its name, which does not appear in the appropriation acts or other laws, in executive orders, or in any other contemporaneous official publication. The first publication of the name is generally in the newspapers. It then appears on the letterhead and on the publications of the unit, usually in the next edition of the *Congressional Directory*, and in the *United States Government Organization Manual*.

The National Commission on Law Observance and Enforcement, also known informally as the Wickersham Commission, offers an example. The Urgent Deficiency Appropriation Act of March 4, 1929 (45 Stat. 1613), made an appropriation to be expended under the direction of the President to make a thorough inquiry into the problem of the enforcement of prohibition and other laws. The President did not establish a commission by executive order, but apparently merely appointed certain persons to make the investigation.

The appointments were announced on May 20, and on May

31 the newspapers carried a statement that the group appointed had adopted the name National Commission on Law Observance and Enforcement. There is no official printed record of the appointments or the adoption of the name. A subsequent appropriation made July 3, 1930 (46 Stat. 862), does not mention the name of the commission, but appropriates for the activity. Apparently the only official printed order relating to the commission is Executive Order No. 5716 of September 16, 1931, issued after the commission had ceased to exist, directing that its records be transferred to the Department of Justice.

The major subdivisions of the departments are usually created by law. As a rule such a law specifically establishes the agency and describes its functions. Occasionally, however, a new agency is created simply by a change in the wording of the act making appropriations for it. An example of this was the creation of the Bureau of Entomology and Plant Quarantine in the Department of Agriculture by the consolidation of the Bureau of Entomology and the Bureau of Plant Quarantine. This was accomplished in the appropriation act for the fiscal year 1935 (48 Stat. 486) by appropriating for the work of the two former agencies under a new heading reading "Bureau of Entomology and Plant Quarantine." There is no other intimation in the act that a new unit was established.

Bureaus have been transferred or created by executive order under authority of two acts—that of February 14, 1903 (32 Stat. 825), creating the Department of Commerce and Labor, and that of June 30, 1932 (47 Stat. 413), as amended by the acts of March 3 and 20, 1933 (47 Stat. 1517 and 48 Stat. 16). On June 2, 1925, the Attorney General held that the authority in the act of February 14, 1903, was a continuing one,[4] and thereafter the Patent Office and the Bureau of Mines were transferred from the Department of the Interior to the Department of Commerce (Executive Orders Nos. 4175 and 4239); later, however, the Bureau of Mines was transferred to the Interior Depart-

[4] 34 Op. Att. Gen. 500.

ment by executive order under the act of June 30, 1932 (Executive Order No. 6611 of February 22, 1934).

Numerous transfers were made by executive order under authority of the act of June 30, 1932, as amended,[5] but that authority expired on March 20, 1935. From that date to April 3, 1939, bureaus created by law could not be transferred by executive order, with the exception that units "engaged in statistical or scientific work" could be transferred to the Department of Commerce from the Departments of State, Treasury, War, Justice, Post Office, Navy, or Interior. However, the emergency agencies established by the President could be discontinued and their duties transferred to other units.

Under the provisions of the Reorganization Act of 1939 the President had authority until January 21, 1941, to transfer agencies, with specified exceptions. These transfers were set forth in Reorganization Plans.

Reorganization Plan No. 1 was published in House Document 262, 76th Congress, 1st session, and in the *Congressional Record* for April 25, 1939 (daily edition, 76th Congress, 1st session, Volume 84, No. 82, pages 6576–81). It is abstracted in the *American Political Science Review* for June 1939. Reorganization Plan No. 2 was published in House Document 288, 76th Congress, 1st session, and in the *Congressional Record* for May 9 (daily edition, 76th Congress, 1st session, Volume 84, No. 91, pages 7423–27). It was abstracted in the *American Political Science Review*.

Five Reorganization Plans were formulated under the Reorganization Act of 1939.

Three Reorganization Plans were proposed under the Reorganization Act of 1945. However, House Concurrent Resolution 155 (60 Stat. 1329) against the adoption of Reorganization Plan No. 1, 1946, passed both the House and the Senate and

[5] For transfers made under authority of this act, see Lewis Meriam and Laurence F. Schmeckebier, *Reorganization of the National Government*, Brookings Institution, 1939, pp. 200–12. This volume contains also a discussion of the general problem of reorganization and a history of reorganization and attempted reorganization from 1932 to 1938.

therefore Reorganization Plan No. 1 did not go into effect. This Reorganization Act expired by its own terms on April 1, 1948.

To give the President the authority to examine and reexamine the organization of all agencies and to determine what changes should be made, the Reorganization Act of 1949 (63 Stat. 203) was passed. The terminal date was later extended to December 31, 1968. Reorganization plans are published in the *Federal Register* and the *Statutes at Large*. Plans carry a consecutive number and the year in which they became effective. The largest number of plans was put forth in the year 1950. Of the 27 plans of that year, 6 were disapproved, leaving 21 which became effective. The number of plans in succeeding years is as follows: 1951, 1; 1952, 5 (3 disapproved); 1953, 10; 1954, 2; 1955 and 1956, 0; 1957, 1; 1958, 1; 1959 and 1960, 0; 1961, 6 (3 disapproved); 1962, 2; 1963, 1; 1964, 0; 1965, 5; 1966, 5; 1967, 3 (1 disapproved); 1968, 4.

The subordinate units of bureaus and independent establishments are generally established by the head of the particular organization, although some have been created by law or executive order. For instance in 1929 the Division of Narcotics in the Public Health Service, a bureau of the Treasury Department, was created by law (45 Stat. 1086), and its name later changed by law to Division of Mental Hygiene (46 Stat. 586). In 1935 in the independent establishments a division of the National Archives for the publication of the *Federal Register* was established by law (49 Stat. 500), while the Consumers' Division of the National Recovery Administration was established by executive order (No. 7120). It is doubtful whether any divisions in bureaus have been created by executive order, but the Division of Industrial Economics in the Office of the Secretary of Commerce was created by Executive Order No. 7323 of March 21, 1936.

As the organization of major units, such as independent establishments, services, and bureaus, is usually not prescribed by law, and as appropriations are generally made for activities and not for minor organization units, the heads of the major units use discretion as to the method of organization, and changes are made frequently. Information regarding the establishment or discontinuance of subordinate units is usually not printed contemporaneously in any official publication, and it may not find its way to the newspapers.

Field areas and offices are generally created by the head of the agency under which they operate, and there is usually no contemporaneous official printed record of their creation. Some of the field units of the Bureau of Customs offer an exception to this general rule, as executive orders are used to establish the boundaries of customs districts and to designate ports of entry. Prior to 1913 customs districts were established by act of Congress. Detailed information regarding many of the field operations of the Department of Agriculture is given in Carleton R. Ball, *Federal, State and Local Administrative Relationships in Agriculture*, 2 volumes, University of California Press, 1938.

Annual and Other Publications on Organization and Personnel

In addition to such contemporaneous printing as has been noted above, there are several publications which give information on organization and personnel at varying intervals.

Some of the annual reports contain information or charts showing the organization at the end of the year, and some give an account of changes. The practice is not uniform in this respect, and the annual reports cannot be depended upon for information on organization. Few annual reports give data on personnel.

A publication entitled *Federal Commissions, Committees and Boards . . . Created . . . Sept. 14, 1901 to March 4, 1929* (147 pages), compiled in the Division of Bibliography of the Library of Congress, was issued as Senate Document 174, 71st Congress, 2d session.

The functions and organization of the departments and independent establishments are given in the *United State Government Organization Manual,* published annually by the Federal Register Division, National Archives and Records Service,

General Services Administration. This volume contains organization charts of some of the more complex agencies. The bureaus and other subordinate units as a rule are discussed in a short paragraph in connection with the description of the departments. The functions of the bureaus are described briefly, but there is no enumeration of their subordinate units. The volume gives the names of the principal officers directing each department and independent establishment.

The provisions of the Legislative Reorganization Act of 1946 directed the Committee on Government Operations to evaluate the effects of laws enacted to reorganize the executive branch of the government. From 1947 to 1952 this committee was called the Committee on Expenditures in Executive Departments, when its name was changed to Committee on Government Operations, United States Senate. The first report entitled *Organization of Federal Executive Departments and Agencies* was issued as a Senate committee report in 1947 and has been issued annually since that time. Accompanying this report is a chart, *Organization of Federal Executive Departments and Agencies,* which outlines the organization of the agencies and also shows personnel assignments to each major operating unit down to the division level as of the date of the report.

A comprehensive discussion of the functions of the United States government and their distribution among the several agencies is contained in a report prepared by the Brookings Institution for the Senate Select Committee to Investigate the Executive Agencies of the Government entitled *Investigation of Executive Agencies of the Government* (1,229 pages), Senate Report 1275, 75th Congress, 1st session.

Some of the problems involved in the proposed reorganization of 1938 are discussed by the President's Committee on Administrative Management in the *Report of the Committee with Studies of Administrative Management in the Federal Government,* 1937 (382 pages).

In accordance with an act approved July 7, 1947 (61 Stat. 246), the Commission on Organization of the Executive Branch of the Government, popularly known as the Hoover Commission, was established for the purpose of studying the operation, organization, and policies of the government in certain broad areas of governmental functions. The areas studied included budget and accounting, intelligence activities, legal services and procedure, lending agencies, medical services, overseas economic operations, paperwork management, personnel and civil service, procurement, real property, subsistence services, surplus property, water resources and power, and several phases of the operation of the Department of Defense.

After the recommendations of this commission had been presented to the Congress, a second Commission on Organization of the Executive Branch of the Government was established in accordance with an act approved July 10, 1953 (67 Stat. 142), for the purpose of continuing the studies made by the first commission and submitting additional recommendations to Congress.

The Commission on Intergovernmental Relations (Kestnbaum Commission) was established by the act of July 10, 1953 (67 Stat. 145), to examine the role of the national government in relation to the states and their political subdivisions. Sixteen reports were issued by the commission through the Government Printing Office in 1955.

Other publications on intergovernmental relations are *The Condition of American Federalism*, a committee print of the Subcommittee on Intergovernmental Relations of the Senate Committee on Government Operations published in 1966 (26 pages); *The Federal System as Seen by AID Officials*, another committee print of the same subcommittee giving the results of a questionnaire dealing with intergovernmental relations, 1965 (215 pages); and *Catalog of Federal Aids to State and Local Governments*, prepared for the same subcommittee by the Library of Congress, 1964 (154 pages). Two supplements to the last publication have been issued: 1965 (65 pages) and 1966 (257 pages).

Civilian nominations requiring confirmation by the Senate have been listed from 1913 to 1916 and from 1933 to 1937 in a series of publications compiled by the office of the Secretary of the Senate, published without document number. The short titles for the several issues are as follows:

63d Congress, 1st session (1913), Nominations made by the President, 212 pp.
63d Congress, 2d session (1913–14), Nominations sent to the Senate, 265 pp.
63d Congress, 3d session (1914–15), Nominations sent to the Senate, 95 pp.
64th Congress, 1st session (1915–16), Nominations to office, 447 pp.
73d Congress, 1st session (1933), Civilian nominations, 47 pp.
73d Congress, 2d session (1934), Civilian nominations, 456 pp.
74th Congress, 1st session (1935), Official civilian nominations, 499 pp.
74th Congress, 2d session (1936), Official civilian nominations, 424 pp.
75th Congress, 1st session (1937), Civilian nominations, 121 pp.

A list showing civilian nominations was published for each session of Congress from 1937 to 1958.

The *Congressional Directory,* issued for each session of Congress, contains information on the directing personnel and the organization of the executive departments and their subdivisions and the independent establishments. The amount of detail is not the same for all units, and it is necessary at times to use other sources for details regarding some of the agencies. This publication is described in more detail on pages 183–84.

Lists generally published annually, but limited to a single department or bureau, are the following:

Combined Lineal List of Officers on Active Duty in Marine Corps
Lineal List of Commissioned and Warrant Officers of Marine Corps Reserve
Official Army National Guard Register
Air National Guard Register
Official Army Register
Register of Commissioned and Warrant Officers of the Navy and Marine Corps and Reserve Officers on Active Duty
Naval Reserve Register
Register of Retired Commissioned and Warrant Officers, Regular and Reserve, of the Navy and Marine Corps
Annual Register of the Naval Academy
Official Register of Officers and Cadets of the Military Academy

Register of Commissioned and Warrant Officers and Cadets and Ships and
Stations of Coast Guard
Air Force Register
Biographic Register [of the Department of State[6]]
Foreign Service List
Professional Workers in State Agricultural Experiment Stations and Co-
operating Institutions
Directory of the Agricultural Research Service
Directory of Local Health Units
Directory of State and Territorial Health Authorities
Education Directory[7]
Register of the Department of Justice and the Courts of the United States
OAR [Office of Aerospace Research] Directory of Key Staff Offices and
Laboratories
DSA [Defense Supply Agency] Field Establishment Directory
Peace Corps Program Directory
Directory, United States Government Inspection Services and Testing
Laboratories
Directory, Interagency Boards of the United States Civil Service Examiners
Roster of Members of PHS [Public Health Service] Public Advisory Groups,
Councils, Committees, Boards, Panels, Study Sections
National Institutes of Health, Scientific Directory
Directory of AEC [Atomic Energy Commission] Specialized Information
and Data Centers
Field Directory, Department of Health, Education, and Welfare

Some of the above have been published for long periods, and
the earlier volumes have historical value. Other agencies which
formerly published registers of employees but which have not
done so for some years are the Post Office Department and the
Department of the Interior. The Department of Commerce
published a register for 1908 only.

[6] Contains a biographical sketch of each employee of the Department, the
United States Mission to the United Nations, the Agency for International
Development, the Peace Corps, the Arms Control and Disarmament Agency,
and the United States Information Agency in grades GS–12 and above. In the
Foreign Service groups, biographies are included for ambassadors, ministers,
Foreign Service Officers, Foreign Service Reserve Officers classes 1–8, and For-
eign Service Staff Officers classes 1–4. Chiefs of overseas missions and employees
of comparable grades of the Agency for International Development, the Peace
Corps, the United States Information Agency, and the Foreign Agricultural
Service of the Department of Agriculture are also included.
[7] This publication is in four parts: Federal Government and States; Counties
and Cities; Higher Education; and Education Associations.

Other volumes of this character which have historical interest are the following:

Executive register of the United States, 1789–1902, by Robert Brent Mosher, 1905, 351 pp. (published also as S. Doc. 196, 58 Cong. 3 sess.). This volume contains lists of heads of departments in each administration, with dates of nomination, confirmation, entrance on duty, and termination of service.

Historical register and dictionary of the United States Army, from its organization, Sept. 29, 1789, to Mar. 2, 1903, 1903, 2 vols. (published also as H. Doc. 446, 57 Cong. 2 sess.). The work contains much detailed information regarding officers thanked by Congress, killed, wounded, or taken prisoner, as well as other information. It also contains a list of officers of the United States Army who joined the Confederate service. It was not compiled under official supervision. The purchase of the manuscript was authorized and provision made for publication in the act of Mar. 2, 1903 (32 Stat. 928).

Official Army register of the Volunteer Force of the United States Army, 1861–65, 8 vols. (Office of the Adjutant General, 1865 and 1867). The offices of the Secretary of War and of the Adjutant General have also issued publications of more limited scope dealing with the personnel of the Army.

Army list and directory. Published at varying frequencies from 1891 to 1943. Contains information regarding the organization of the Army and the commanding personnel of each unit of the military establishment.

Statement showing rank, duties, and addresses of officers of the Corps of Engineers, United States Army. Issued quarterly from July 1, 1899, to October 1, 1921, and semiannually from April 1, 1922, to October 1, 1941.

Navy directory. Officers of the Navy and the Marine Corps, including officers of the Naval Reserve (active), the Marine Corps Reserve (active), and foreign officers serving with the Navy. Published at varying frequencies from 1908 to 1942.

Other agencies, particularly those with field offices, at times issue directories.

Number of Employees

The United States Civil Service Commission issues a monthly processed publication entitled *Federal Employment Statistics Bulletin,* which gives a comparison, by selected agency, of employment for the continental United States and the Washington, D. C., metropolitan area. Separate tables give statistics on paid civilian employment, accessions, separations, full-time employees, citizenship of employee accessions and separations by place of residence, and accessions and separations by citizenship. Special statistical studies on employment are also contained in this publication. This report is intended primarily for administrative use of the federal departments and agencies.

Another processed publication issued by the Civil Service Commission is entitled *Monthly Report of Federal Employment*. This publication gives a comparison for the current month with the preceding month of paid civilian employment for all federal agencies.

CHAPTER SIXTEEN

MAPS

MAPS HAVE BEEN PUBLISHED both independently and in connection with reports since the early days of the government, but extensive systematic map publishing in series was developed only in the last quarter of the 19th century.[1]

The early series which have been continued to the present time were devoted to navigation. The Navy started publishing charts of foreign waters for public use about 1837; the Coast and Geodetic Survey began the publication of charts of coastal waters in 1844; and the Lake Survey, under the Corps of Engineers of the Army, issued the first chart of the Great Lakes in 1852.

For many years, the maps of land areas resulted almost entirely from exploring expeditions or from surveys made for a

---

[1] For a discussion of the work of the government agencies making maps (but not a description of the maps) and recommendations for reorganizing the map work of the government, see *Second Report of the Science Advisory Board, September 1, 1934, to August 31, 1935*, pp. 129–306; also *Investigation of Executive Agencies of the Government, Report of the Senate Select Committee to Investigate the Executive Agencies of the Government*, S. Rept. 1275, 75 Cong. 1 sess., pp. 244–49, 253. For printed catalogs of map collections and bibliographies of maps, see *Guide to the Diplomatic History of the United States, 1775–1921*, by Samuel F. Bemis and Grace G. Griffin, pp. 748–50. For a listing of official maps in an early period, see Martin P. Claussen and Herman R. Friis, *Descriptive Catalog of Maps Published by Congress, 1817–1843*, 1941 (104 pp.). For a compilation of maps and surveys prepared by various federal agencies, see J. O. Kilmartin, "Federal Surveys and Maps," *The American Yearbook*, 1950. For information on current mapping, see the map information sections of the *Journal of the Society of American Military Engineers*, Washington, D.C., and the *Journal of the American Congress on Surveying and Mapping*, Washington, D.C. *The Geographical Review*, 1916 to date, and the *Bulletin*, 1852–1915, both published by the American Geographical Society of New York, constitute other excellent nongovernment sources.

specific object and confined to limited areas. The maps generally formed part of the textual reports of the explorations or surveys.[2]

Many of the older volumes containing maps may be located by means of the tables beginning on page 5 of the *Checklist*. The "Notes" column generally indicates a book composed entirely of maps, although it does not always indicate their character. Maps are found in many other volumes for which there is no such notation, particularly in the reports on explorations and surveys.

After the Civil War, four organizations were developed to engage in topographic and geologic surveys of the West. They were the Geological and Geographical Survey of the Territories (Hayden Survey, Interior Department), the Geographical and Geological Survey of the Rocky Mountain Region (Powell Survey, Interior Department), Geographical Surveys West of the 100th Meridian (Wheeler Survey, War Department), and Geological Exploration of the 40th Parallel (King Survey, War Department).[3] All of these organizations were engaged in topographic mapping, but without coordination of activities. In fact, no comprehensive plan for mapping the entire country existed until, in 1879, the United States Geological Survey succeeded the four earlier organizations and developed one.

Between 1879 and the close of World War I, many overlapping functions developed. To coordinate federal surveying and mapping the President created by executive order on December 30, 1919, the Board of Surveys and Maps of the Federal Government, later known as the Federal Board of Surveys and Maps. This board was directed to establish a central informa-

[2] The reports are listed in *Report of Explorations Printed in the Documents of the United States Government* . . . compiled by Adelaide R. Hasse and published by the Office of the Superintendent of Documents, Government Printing Office, 1899 (90 pp.) There is also a less comprehensive list of the reports under the entry "Explorations and Surveys" in the *Senate Catalog*.

[3] The publications of these surveys appeared under their own names, with the exception of the Survey of the 40th Parallel, which appeared as Vol. 18 of the *Professional Papers of the Engineer Department of the Army*. For list and index of publications and maps, see *Catalogue and Index of the Publications of the Hayden, King, Powell, and Wheeler Surveys*, by Laurence F. Schmeckebier (Geological Survey Bulletin 222, 1904, 208 pp.).

tion office in the Geological Survey for the purpose of collecting, classifying, and furnishing to the public information concerning all map and survey data available in the several government departments and from other sources. The Federal Board was abolished in 1942 and its functions transferred to the Bureau of the Budget and the Map Information Office, Geological Survey, Department of the Interior, which is now composed of three specialized units—the Topographic Maps Section, the Aerial Photography Section, and the Geodetic Control Section.

The Topographic Maps Section carries on continuous research for all topographic data pertaining to the United States, its territories and possessions, produced by federal, state, or commercial organizations.

The Aerial Photography Section is primarily responsible for the assembly of information on the aerial photography of the United States, its territories and possessions, taken by federal and state agencies and by commercial organizations. This unit has the most complete record of aerial photography in existence for the United States, its territories and possessions, showing the film-holding agency for all photography, the date, the flight altitude, the scale, and the focal length of the aerial camera lens.

The Geodetic Control Section is responsible for maintaining records of all horizontal and vertical control data produced by the Geological Survey, the Coast and Geodetic Survey, and other federal agencies. The section maintains records of the latitude, longitude, and elevation above sea level of about five million bench marks scattered throughout the country.

The best single source for the official mapping activities of the government is the National Archives, which has on file in its Cartographic Branch in Washington over 1,000,000 map record items representing some 500 offices of the federal government since 1776. Inventories, special lists, and descriptive catalogs of these have been published and are available from the National Archives. Photo reproductions of maps are also obtainable for a fee.

The Library of Congress also has a large collection of maps published by the government, but doubtless many of the early maps are missing. Other early collections were listed in the processed pamphlet issued by the Board of Surveys and Maps entitled *Map Collections in the District of Columbia.*

No complete list of the maps contained in publications or issued separately has ever been published. In 1901 the Library of Congress issued *A List of Maps of America in the Library of Congress* . . . by Philip Lee Phillips (1,137 pages), which was also published as House Document 516, 56th Congress, 2d session. This list comprises maps of states and portions of states as well as general maps. It does not pretend to include all maps, its scope being limited to those in the Library. Maps in the Library of Congress are further listed in *List of Geographical Atlases in the Library of Congress,* by Philip Lee Phillips, Volumes 1–4, 1909–20, and Volume 5, with bibliographical notes, 1958, compiled by Clara Egli LeGear.

A Library of Congress publication which is not a map in itself is entitled *Marketing Maps of the United States,* 3d edition, 1958 (147 pages), compiled by Walter W. Ristow.

The semiannual publication of the Library of Congress, the *Catalog of Copyright Entries,* Part 6, contains a list of maps and atlases published in the United States and registered under the copyright laws.

Maps sold by the Superintendent of Documents are listed in the annual index of the *Monthly Catalog of United States Government Publications* under the entry "Maps and charts." These entries give the names of areas, etc., as well as citations to the pages on which maps issued by the several units are listed. *Price List 53* lists maps currently available.

In the biennial *Document Catalog* the detailed entry for each map was given under the publishing office, the maps being segregated after all other entries. There was no other detailed listing of maps, but there were cross references to the publishing offices from the names of states or specific areas.

The notations below apply only to maps which are published in specific series, although a few individual maps or collections that may be of interest are cited. New maps published separately are generally listed in the current government catalogs described in another chapter. Maps generally accompany detailed surveys or studies in the field of engineering or the natural sciences and are often found in reports on social and economic subjects. Maps accompanying reports are not listed separately in the catalogs unless available for distribution separately. Most of the agencies selling maps issue lists or index maps. As a rule maps are sold by the agencies that publish them; however, some are sold by the Superintendent of Documents. Information regarding maps may also be obtained from the Map Information Office, Geological Survey, Department of the Interior. In the descriptions below, appropriate notations are made regarding the office from which the maps may be obtained.

United States Maps

In accordance with a recommendation from the National Academy of Sciences—National Research Council, the Geological Survey has undertaken the preparation and publication of *The National Atlas of the United States,* scheduled for 1970. The objective is to create a reference tool of high quality for use by members of Congress, government agencies, business and industrial organizations, libraries, educational institutions, and scholars throughout the world who wish to become better informed about the United States. *The National Atlas* will be a volume of approximately 475 pages, 19 by 14 inches, with about 30 percent of the maps opening to double-page spreads of 19 by 28 inches. There will be a few introductory pages of general reference maps and 40 pages of detailed and carefully indexed sectional maps. The real substance of *The National Atlas* will be thematic maps covering the country's salient physical characteristics (relief, geology, climate, water resources, soils and vegetation), its history (discovery, exploration, territorial growth, settlement, battlefields, and scientific expeditions), economic status (agriculture, industry, resources, transportation, and finance), social conditions (population distribution and structure, educational achievement, centers of art, culture, and scientific research), administrative subdivisions (counties, judicial and election districts, time zones), and status of coverage by aerial photos and map or chart series. There will also be a few world maps to show the place of the United States in world affairs and a detailed index. Text in *The National Atlas* will be limited, with a few exceptions, to map captions and explanations, but references will be provided to more detailed maps and documentation. Many of the maps will be sold separately by the Branch of Distribution, United States Geological Survey, Washington, D.C. 20242. The following are now available:

Sheet Number	*Subject*
59	Physiographic divisions (physiography)
62–63	Classes of land-surface form (map of conterminous United States with inset showing principal islands of Hawaii)
64–61	Land-surface form (map of Alaska. Text on classes of land-surface form in the United States with map showing physical subdivisions)
69	Tectonic features (map of Alaska; text on tectonic features of the United States)
70	Tectonic features (map of conterminous United States with inset showing principal islands of Hawaii)
74–75	Geology (map of conterminous United States with inset showing the principal islands of Hawaii)
86	Soils
89	Potential natural vegetation of Alaska and Hawaii (maps of Alaska and the principal islands of Hawaii)
90	Potential natural vegetation (maps of conterminous United States showing forests and grasslands)
94–95	Monthly sunshine (thirteen maps on one sheet)
97	Annual sunshine, evaporation, and solar radiation
106	Monthly average temperature
108	Monthly maximum temperature
110	Monthly minimum temperature
117	Surface water resources
126	Productive aquifers and withdrawals from wells
127	Water use
142	Territorial growth

270–271   Population distribution, urban and rural, 1960
309   Population trends
360   Congressional districts

There are many kinds of maps of the United States, issued separately or accompanying reports. Most of these have special data superimposed on one of the regular base maps. Listed below are general maps that are likely to be of interest. As a rule these general maps do not show county boundaries.

Bureau of Land Management. The bureau issues a wall map of the United States, including territories and insular possessions, showing extent of public surveys, national parks, national forests, Indian reservations, national wildlife refuges, and reclamation projects. The latest one, issued in 1965, is a 12-color map, printed on two sheets of heavy map paper. It is not folded or mounted for hanging. It is on a scale of 40 miles to the inch and has an over-all dimension of approximately 5 by 7 feet. It is for sale by the Superintendent of Documents. A smaller wall map, issued in 1964, is printed on one 42 by 65 inch sheet.

Geological Survey. Most maps and charts published by the Geological Survey may be found listed in *Publications of the Geological Survey,* 1961, with annual supplements.

Certain other index maps, or status maps, published by the Geological Survey are listed below, together with base maps, outline maps, and a map of physical divisions of the United States. The status maps are usually on a scale of 1:5,000,000.

STATUS MAPS

Status of aerial mosaics. Shows all areas in the United States for which mosaics have been compiled by or for federal, state, and commercial agencies. Gives scale of negatives, dates of photography, and names and addresses of agencies holding mosaic negatives.

Status of aerial photography. Shows areas in the United States that have been mapped by aerial photographs. The legend block shows by color symbols the agency holding primary photography.

Status of geologic mapping in Alaska. Shows by color symbols the areas of published geologic maps on scales larger than 1:100,000 and 1:100,000 to 1:250,000. These maps are available to the public in bulletins, mimeographed reports, or on open file for consultation. Also shown are areas in which mapping has been completed but not yet published and areas in which mapping is in progress.

Status of topographic mapping and progress of operations. Shows areas of the United States not yet mapped and indicates the areas in which new mapping is authorized or in progress. Published semiannually.

BASE MAPS OF THE UNITED STATES

Shows state and county boundaries and county seats with names in black; water features with names in blue; railroads in brown. Insets show Alaska, Hawaii, Canal Zone, Puerto Rico, and the Virgin Islands. Scale, 1:2,500,000. 2 sheets. 54 by 80 inches.

Shows state boundaries and names, capitals and principal cities in black; water features in blue. Insets. Scale, 1:3,168,000. 42 by 65 inches.

Shows state and county boundaries and names; water features in black. Insets. Scale, 1:5,000,000. 27 by 41 inches.

Same, water features in blue.

Shows state boundaries and names in black; county boundaries and names and water features in blue. Scale, 1:5,000,000. 27 by 41 inches.

Shows state boundaries and principal cities in black; water features in blue. Scale, 1:7,000,000. 20 by 30 inches.

Same, except scale, 1:11,875,000. 13 by 20 inches.

Same, except scale, 1:16,500,000. 9 by 13 inches.

CONTOUR MAP OF THE UNITED STATES

Shows state boundaries and principal cities in black; water features in blue; contours in brown. Scale, 1:7,000,000. 20 by 30 inches.

OUTLINE MAP OF THE UNITED STATES

Shows only state boundaries and names in black. Scale, 1:5,000,000. 27 by 42 inches.

PHYSICAL DIVISIONS

Physical divisions of the United States. Scale, 1:7,000,000. 28 by 32 inches.

Coast and Geodetic Survey. The outline maps listed below are published and sold by the Coast and Geodetic Survey:

Conterminous United States, 9 by 13 inches, on a scale of 1:17,800,000
Conterminous United States, Murdoch's projection on intersecting cone, 20 by 30 inches, on a scale of 1:7,000,000

North Atlantic Ocean with Eastern North America and Europe, Lambert
conformal conic projection, 27 by 48 inches, on a scale of 1:10,000,000
North Pacific Ocean on transverse polyconic projection, 17 by 43 inches,
on a scale of 1:20,000,000
United States on Lambert conformal conic projection, 29 by 42 inches,
on a scale of 1:5,000,000,[4] or approximately 80 miles to the inch
United States on Lambert conformal conic projection, 48 by 70 inches,
on a scale of 1:3,000,000
United States on Lambert zenithal area projection, 22 by 28 inches, on
a scale of 1:7,500,000, or approximately 120 miles to the inch
World on Mercator projection, 35 by 47 inches, on a scale of 1:38,000,000

The following maps are also sold by the Coast and Geodetic
Survey:

Base map of Alaska on Lambert conformal conic projection, 29 by 45
inches, on a scale of 1:5,000,000
Base map of the conterminous United States with gradient tints, 36 by
47 inches, on a scale of 1:3,000,000
Outline map for construction of a model of the world, produces a "Lambert Globe" 9 inches in diameter, 22 by 30 inches, on a scale of
1:55,800,000
Physical-political global chart of the world on stereographic projection,
100 by 114 inches, on a scale of 1:10,500,000

Federal Power Commission. The commission issues a series
of regional maps of *Principal Electric Facilities.* The 1966 series
consists of 8 maps on a scale of 32 miles to the inch with insets
on enlarged scales for congested areas. The maps show generating stations and transmission lines and include lists indicating
the number and name of the plants, MW capacity and type,
utility abbreviation, and name and type of owner. The maps
are sold by the Superintendent of Documents. Another map,
entitled *Principal Electric Facilities in the United States,* on a

[4] The scale of a map expressed as a proportion or fraction represents the
relation of a line on map to a line on the ground. Thus, in case of a map with a
scale of 1:62,500 (sometimes expressed $\frac{1}{62,500}$), a line one inch long on a map
represents a line 62,500 inches long on the ground. To reduce a proportional
scale to miles to the inch, divide the scale by the number of inches in a mile
(63,360). Thus, if the map is on the scale of 1:62,500 and 62,500 is divided
by 63,360, the quotient is 0.99–, which represents miles to the inch. To obtain
inches to the mile, divide 63,360 by the scale.

scale of 55 miles to the inch, printed in 8 colors, shows high voltage lines and generating stations, and includes a list of power plants by states, 44 by 64 inches. A 1967 issue is *Major Natural Gas Pipelines*, 55 miles to the inch, 5 colors, showing major pipelines, those under construction or authorized, 13 by 18 inches.

Bureau of Public Roads. The short title *Federal Aid Highways* identifies a map published by the Bureau of Public Roads which shows the United States system of highways on a scale of 1:3,168,000, 42 by 65 inches, in 8 colors. Many of the interstate roads are not yet built, and the map is not for touring. It is for sale by the Superintendent of Documents.

County outline maps. A series of 21 by 33 inch maps of the United States, showing boundaries of counties at each census from 1840 to 1920, was published by the Department of Agriculture in 1921. A separate map, 16 by 25 inches, shows the boundaries of counties in 1931.

Two outline maps of the United States showing the boundaries of counties in 1940 were published by the Department of Agriculture. One of these, measuring 24.2 by 38.6 inches, is on the scale of 1:5,000,000, or approximately 80 miles to the inch; the other, measuring 16.1 by 25.8 inches, is on the scale of 1:7,500,000, or approximately 120 miles to the inch.

An outline map showing counties is also published by the Census Bureau. The latest map shows boundaries as of April 1, 1960. It is 26 by 41 inches on a scale of 3.8 inches representing 300 miles. It is published in two forms: (1) with names and state and county boundaries in black, and (2) with state names and boundaries in black and county boundaries in blue. It may be purchased from the Superintendent of Documents.

Highway maps. Official state highway maps of the folded tourist-type may usually be obtained from the Department of Highways of the state concerned. These departments also issue general highway county maps, usually on a scale of one inch to the mile which show roads, road types, streams, lakes, railways, national and state parks, cities, and villages.

State Maps

Maps of single states frequently accompany publications, the reports of the recent decennial censuses having contained small-scale outline maps of the states showing only county boundaries. The maps enumerated below comprise only those which are now issued in regular series.

Geological Survey. Two series of base maps of states are published by the United States Geological Survey, the essential difference being in the scale. Maps on the scale of 1:500,000 or approximately 8 miles to the inch are available for each of the states except Hawaii.

These maps shows counties, cities, towns, railroads, streams, and public-land lines. They are printed in black or black and blue, with various editions overprinted in multicolor to show highways, contours, and other features. The larger states are printed on more than one sheet, and the smaller states are combined as follows: New Hampshire and Vermont; Massachusetts, Rhode Island, and Connecticut; and Delaware, Maryland, and the District of Columbia.

Maps from the same bases as those described above, but on the scale of 1:1,000,000, or approximately 16 miles to the inch, are available for each of the states except Alaska and Hawaii. Each state is shown on a separate map, with the exception of the following combinations: New Hampshire and Vermont; Massachusetts, Rhode Island, and Connecticut; and Delaware, Maryland, and the District of Columbia.

Shaded relief maps with topographic features emphasized by simulating in color the appearance of sunlight and shadows on the terrain to create the illusion of a solid, three-dimensional model are available for many states. The shading is overprinted on a simplified base map which shows only county boundaries and county seats in black and water features in blue. Contours are not shown. The scale is 1:500,000 except as noted. State maps are available for Alaska (1:2,500,000), Arizona, California (1:1,000,000), Colorado, Connecticut (1:125,000), Kentucky,

Maine, Missouri, New Hampshire and Vermont, New Jersey, New York, North Carolina, North Dakota, Ohio, Pennsylvania, South Dakota, Tennessee, Vermont, Virginia, and Washington, D.C. The map for Puerto Rico and adjacent islands is on a scale of 1:240,000. The Geological Survey also publishes many shaded relief maps of areas of special interest including some national parks, mountains, canyons, and national monuments.

Topographic maps portraying the shape and exact ground elevation by contours are available for nearly all states, usually on a scale of 1:500,000. Highways are usually shown in purple, contours in brown, and national parks, monuments, and forests in color patterns.

The results of studies of mineral resources have been released in various map and chart series. These pertain to the Missouri Basin Studies, Tennessee River Basin Studies, Oil and Gas Investigations, Mineral Investigations, and Geophysical Investigations.

The Geological Survey publishes a list of geologic and water-supply reports and maps for each state. Included are maps and reports relating to the geology and mineral and water resources of the state.

Federal Power Commission. The Federal Power Commission has prepared a set of 8 regional maps entitled *Principal Electric Facilities*, 1965. The maps list the plant and ownership; each generating station is numbered; and each operating utility has a letter code for identification. High voltage lines of 22 kv and above and generating stations exceeding 1,000 kw are shown, and congested areas appear on enlarged inserts.

Post route maps. For many years the Post Office Department has published post route maps of the states and territories. These maps, which are revised frequently, show all post offices and all surface routes—railroad, highway, and water—over which mail is carried to post offices.[5] They indicate the frequency of service over all routes and show distances between

---

[5] They do not show rural-free-delivery routes. Some routes indicated as "rural routes" on the maps show the movement of mail between post offices only.

post offices. As the maps are prepared primarily for the use of postal employees, they do not show railroad lines over which no mail was carried.

As a rule each state is represented on a separate sheet, the states or subdivisions shown together on one sheet being as follows: New Hampshire and Vermont; Massachusetts, Rhode Island, and Connecticut; Maryland, Delaware, and the District of Columbia; California and Nevada; Puerto Rico and the Virgin Islands. Maps requiring two sheets are those for New York, Pennsylvania, Texas, and California-Nevada.

Transportation facilities.   A wall map of the United States on a scale of 1:2,500,000 is issued in four sections. The over-all size is 84 by 88 inches. This map, sold by the Army Map Service, identifies railways by name or initials and classifies them as to single track, two or more tracks, narrow gauge, or under construction. Insets show principal railways in the vicinity of San Francisco, New York City, and Brownsville, Texas.

Minor civil divisions.   A series of state maps, including Alaska, Hawaii, and Puerto Rico, first issued by the Bureau of the Census late in 1934, shows counties and civil divisions smaller than counties which were in existence in 1930 and for which separate figures are given in the detailed census reports. A later series was published in 1960. These maps are printed in one color, black, and show only the boundaries, the names of counties, and the names and/or numbers of subordinate divisions. They show all incorporated places, but do not show unincorporated towns and villages which are not recognized as minor civil divisions by the Bureau of the Census.

This series is of great value in interpreting the detailed data given in the census reports. As the maps do not contain a mass of detail, they are useful as base maps for plotting other data.

While the maps show the names and/or numbers of the minor divisions, they do not give their generic names, such as towns, townships, boroughs, districts, etc. These generic designations may be obtained from the reports of the Fifteenth Census.[6]

[6] Lists of the subdivisions are given in the following volumes: *Population,*

The size and scale vary with the area of the several states. The scale ranges from approximately 4 miles to the inch for New Jersey to approximately 50 miles to the inch for Alaska. A complete list giving scale and size may be obtained from the Superintendent of Documents.

Congressional districts. Small-scale outline maps showing the counties included in each congressional district are printed in the *Congressional Directory*. These maps are of little assistance if a county or city is divided among several districts, but in such cases the wards, precincts, townships, etc., included in each district may be obtained from the biographical section of the *Congressional Directory*, where the minor civil divisions in each district are listed preceding the sketch of the member of Congress.

The Census Bureau issues a *Congressional District Atlas* (1966, 137 pages), the latest issue of which covers redistricting legislation effective for the 90th Congress. The atlas presents maps showing boundaries of the congressional districts. The maps are larger than the ones in the *Congressional Directory*, and separate maps show district boundaries in congested areas. It is sold by the Superintendent of Documents.

Also issued by the Census Bureau and sold by the Superintendent of Documents is a map entitled *Congressional Districts for the 90th Congress*, 1966. This map includes redistricting actions to September 1, 1966, and is on a scale of 6.2 inches to 500 miles.

County Maps

Practically all the state maps described on previous pages show county boundaries. For each of the maps described below the county is the unit of representation.

Soil surveys. The most extensive series of county maps occurs in the reports on soils issued by the Soil Conservation Serv-

---

Vol. 1, Table 4, for each state, or Vol. 3, Pts. 1 and 2, Table 21, for each state. Descriptions of the subdivisions in the several states are given in the report on *Agriculture*, Vol. 1, pp. 2–3.

ice and its predecessors in this work, the Bureau of Soils, the Bureau of Chemistry and Soils, the Bureau of Agricultural Chemistry and Engineering, and the Bureau of Plant Industry, Soils, and Agricultural Engineering of the Department of Agriculture. While most of the maps represent complete counties, many show parts of several counties, and later surveys have many map sheets for one county. An appreciable part of the United States has been mapped.

These maps, which show the several types of soil, are not issued separately, but accompany the textual report giving the results of the surveys.

The maps in this series were first issued in 1899, and to 1922 formed part of the annual publication entitled *Field Operations of the Bureau of Soils.* Each volume included reports on a number of counties, although each county report, accompanied by the map, was issued separately. Beginning with 1923 each report, accompanied by the map, has been issued in separate form only, the issues for each year forming a separate series by the year and being numbered beginning with 1. The year designated in the series represents the year in which the survey was made and not the year of publication. Soil survey, Tippah County, Mississippi, Series 1963, No. 1, was the last soil survey report to be assigned a series and number. It was issued February 15, 1966. Later reports show Soil Survey (name of county), (name of state), and issue (month and year). As methods were largely in process of development up to 1907, the maps issued prior to 1907 are inferior to the later ones. Detailed instructions for this mapping are contained in *Soil Survey Manual,* 1951, Department of Agriculture Handbook 18 (503 pages).

Reports containing the maps are distributed by the Soil Conservation Service, which has lists by states showing reports available for free distribution, maps that may be obtained only by purchase from the Superintendent of Documents, maps no longer available for distribution, and lists of libraries where the maps may be consulted. The bureau has also issued a general map of the United States showing areas included in soil surveys, but the map does not contain citations to the reports. The separate state lists should be used for locating the publications. The Superintendent of Documents also publishes a list of reports sold by him.

Topographic Maps

The most comprehensive and detailed series of topographic maps is that issued by the United States Geological Survey, the first maps being issued in the early eighties. As these maps were planned to form part of a topographic atlas of the United States, the standard maps, known as "atlas sheets," have always represented a quadrangular area bounded by parallels of latitude and meridians of longitude. The standard maps are of uniform size, but the area mapped and the scale have varied.

The first maps represented a degree of latitude and longitude, and were on the scale 1:250,000, or approximately 4 miles to the inch. These were followed by the sheets representing 30' of latitude and longitude, on a scale of 1:125,000, or approximately 2 miles to the inch. Under the general plan adopted, the unit of survey is a quadrangle bounded by parallels of latitude and meridians of longitude. Quadrangles covering 7½' of latitude and longitude are published on the scale of 1:24,000 (1 inch equals 2,000 feet). Quadrangles covering 15' of latitude and longitude are published on the scale of 1:63,360 (1 inch equals about 1 mile), and quadrangles covering 30' of latitude and longitude are published on the scale of 1:125,000 (1 inch equals about 2 miles). In certain western states a few quadrangles covering 1° of latitude and longitude have been published on the scale of 1:250,000 (1 inch equals about 4 miles). A few special maps are published on other scales.

On these maps the relief is represented by brown contour lines (or lines of equal elevation), the drainage is in blue, and the culture (towns, roads, railroads, and other works of man) and the lettering in black. Each map is named for some town or natural feature in the area represented. All standard quadrangle maps of the United States areas are published on sheets about 17 by 21 inches, except for the 1:24,000-scale maps, which are 22 by 27 inches.

These maps are sold by the United States Geological Survey. Separate index maps for each state may be obtained free.

Topographic maps of 80 metropolitan areas are produced on a scale of 1:24,000, mostly in single sheets but some in two or three sheets. The compilations include all cultural and physical data contained on the several 7½′ quadrangle maps originally prepared from aerial photographs and ground surveys. Included on these maps are all main highways, city streets and railroad lines; also parks, reservoirs, principal public buildings, historic sites, and many locations and landmarks of interest. These are available from the Geological Survey.

For the alluvial basin of the Mississippi River between Cairo and the Gulf of Mexico, detailed topographic maps may be obtained from the Mississippi River Commission, Vicksburg, Mississippi, and from the Geological Survey. Each of these maps represents 15′ of latitude and longitude. Most of them are on the scale of 1:62,500, or approximately one mile to the inch, although some are on the scale of 1:48,000, or approximately three-quarters of a mile to the inch.

For some years a group of governments have been cooperating in the preparation of a uniform series of relief map sheets on the scale of 1:1,000,000, or approximately 16 miles to the inch, each map representing 4° of latitude and 6° of longitude. These sheets, together comprising the International Map of the World, show principal cities, railroads, highways, streams, and political boundaries. Contour lines indicate the shape of the land surface and of the ocean floor. Gradations of color indicate the heights of land and depths in the ocean in meters. For the United States the Geological Survey started the IMW series and then also issued a second edition based on maps compiled by the Army Map Service for military use. The second edition maps usually contain more recent information than the IMW edition. Although they do not conform to IMW specifications in all respects, they satisfy the same general purpose. These maps may be obtained from the United States Geological Survey.

Township plats issued by the Bureau of Land Management will be found useful for many purposes, particularly when the more detailed topographic maps are not available. These maps are on the scale of one-half mile to the inch; the relief is indicated roughly by hachures and, in some cases, contours. These are official township plats of surveys of the public-domain lands from the time of the original surveys to the present date, including public lands in Alaska. They show the boundaries, subdivisions, acreage, improvements, and other features of an area included in a cadastral survey.

Geologic Maps

Geologic maps are issued by the United States Geological Survey, but for many years there were only a few issued separately from the printed reports describing the geology of the area mapped. The printed reports appear in the five series known as Monographs, Professional Papers, Bulletins, Geologic Folios, and Water-Supply Papers. The annual report of the Director of the Geological Survey prior to the one for 1902 (twenty-third) contained treatises on geology and ore deposits, accompanied by maps, but the later annual reports have included mostly administrative material. The series of Monographs was discontinued in 1929 with Number 55, *Titanotheres of Ancient Wyoming, Dakota, and Nebraska,* by Henry Fairfield Osborn.

The Geologic Folios were planned to produce a map of the entire United States in quadrangular sections similar to the topographic maps. However, only a small portion of the country is mapped in the series. Each folio contains a topographic base map and maps showing areal geology, underground structure, and mineral deposits. All the folios have been issued in what is known as the "library edition," which measures 18.5 by 22 inches. Some have also been issued in octavo size. Each folio contains a text description of the geology of the area represented. Publication of this series has been discontinued.

In 1921 the Geological Survey published *World Atlas of*

Commercial Geology in two parts. Part 1 is "Distribution of Mineral Products" (72 pages), and Part 2 is "Water Power of the World," by Herman Stabler, B. E. Jones, O. C. Merrill, and N. C. Grover (39 pages). Both parts are out of print.

Agricultural Maps

For some years the Department of Agriculture published advanced sheets of an *Atlas of American Agriculture.* The following parts have been published:

Pt. 1, Physical basis of agriculture, natural vegetation: Grassland and desert shrub, by H. L. Shantz . . .; Forests, by Raphael Zon, 1924, 29 pp. (Advance sheets 6)

Pt. 2, Climate, Sec. 1, Frost and the growing season . . . by W. G. Reed, 1918, 12 pp. (Advance sheets 2)

Pt. 2, Climate, Sec. A, Precipitation and humidity . . . by J. B. Kincer, 1922, 48 pp. (Advance sheets 5)

Pt. 2, Climate, Sec. B, Temperature, sunshine, and wind . . . by J. B. Kincer, 1928, 34 pp. (Advance sheets 7)

Pt. 3, Soils of the United States, by C. F. Marbut, 1935, 98 pp. (Advance sheets 8)

Pt. 5, The Crops, Sec. A, Cotton, by O. C. Stine and O. E. Baker, 1918, 28 pp. (Advance sheets 4)

Pt. 9, Rural population and organizations, Sec. 1, Rural population, by E. A. Goldenweiser, 1919, 19 pp. (Advance sheets 3)

Each part consists of text, list of selected references, and maps. Advance Sheet 1 is a single sheet map which shows precipitation and which is superseded by Part 2, Climate. Part 1, the three sections of Part 2, Part 3, and an additional section on land relief, by F. J. Marschner, have been issued as a bound volume with the title *Atlas of American Agriculture: Physical Basis, Including Land Relief, Climate, Soils and Natural Vegetation of the United States,* 1936.

Part 5 relating to cotton and Part 9 relating to rural population and organizations were published some years ago and do not represent present conditions. The cotton section contains some useful historical maps, and the rural population section contains a series of maps, based on the census of 1910 and not published elsewhere, showing rural population of foreign birth and parentage classified by country of birth and origin.

In 1917 the Department of Agriculture also published the *Geography of the World's Agriculture*, by V. C. Finch and O. E. Baker (149 pages).

As a contribution to *The National Atlas of the United States*, a total of 41 loose-leaf sheets were prepared and published in 1957 from information obtained in the 1954 Census of Agriculture. Each sheet is 16 by 22 inches and includes maps on scales of 1:20,000,000 or 1:30,000,000. Many sheets also have statistical charts. The descriptive text and statistical tables accompany each sheet. The sheets are not bound and each can be ordered separately from the Superintendent of Documents.

The Aerial Photography Division of the Agricultural Stabilization and Conservation Service, Department of Agriculture, issues an annual list of *Aerial Photography Status Maps* (63 leaves) showing areas of the country for which aerial status maps are available.

National Parks and Forests

Detailed topographic maps covering most of the national parks, monuments, and historic sites are published by the Geological Survey. Many of the maps are published with a descriptive text. Some are available in a shaded-relief edition.

The important national forests having recreation facilities are shown on a series of maps issued by the Forest Service. As a rule these maps are not based on detailed topographic surveys, and most of them have been compiled from such data as were available. They show roads, trails, camp sites, and other features of interest to the tourist and generally have descriptive text on the back. They may be obtained free from the Forest Service regional offices or from forest supervisors.

In 1966 the Forest Service issued *Geographic Distribution of the Pines of the World,* by W. B. Critchfield and E. L. Little (Miscellaneous Publication 991), which contains 64 maps. *Silvics of Forest Trees of the United States* (Agricultural Handbook 271) 1965, contains maps of the distribution of 125 important trees and generalized maps of climate, plant hardiness zones, forest vegetation, and the great soil groups.

Weather Maps

For many years the Weather Bureau issued a *Daily Weather Map,* which consisted of a group of five charts with data taken from hundreds of observation stations. In 1968, this was changed to a weekly series entitled *Daily Weather Maps,* with four charts for each day of the week. The new series is published by the Environmental Data Service of the Environmental Science Services Administration of the Department of Commerce. The Surface Weather Map presents data from approximately 200 stations for 7:00 A.M., E.S.T. Areas of precipitation are shown by shading. The 500-Millibar Chart shows the height contours and temperature isotherms of the 500-millibar surface. Arrows show the wind direction and speed. The Highest and Lowest Temperature Chart presents the maximum and minimum values for the 24-hour period ending at 1:00 A.M., E.S.T. The Precipitation Areas and Amounts Chart gives the amount of precipitation to the nearest hundredth of an inch during the 24-hour period ending at 1:00 A.M., E.S.T. Subscriptions may be placed with the Superintendent of Documents.

The Environmental Data Service publishes an atlas entitled *Climatic Maps of the United States,* 1968 (80 pages). These maps present in a uniform format a series of analyses showing the national distribution of mean, normal, and extreme values of temperature, precipitation, wind, barometric pressure, relative humidity, dew point, sunshine, sky cover, heating degree days, solar radiation, and evaporation. The maps occupy 40 large sheets containing 271 climatic maps and 15 tables. The atlas and individual maps may be purchased from the Super-

intendent of Documents. The titles of the individual charts
are as follows:

Normal daily maximum, minimum, average, and range of temperatures
  (°F), monthly and annual
Mean number of days maximum temperature 90°F and above
Mean number of days minimum temperature 32°F and below
Mean dates of last 32°F temperature in spring
Mean dates of first 32°F temperature in autumn
Mean length of freeze-freeze period (days)
Mean length of period between last in spring and first in autumn of 32°F,
  28°F, 24°F, 20°F, and 16°F, respectively, for selected stations, and
  mean freeze dates
Normal total heating degree days, monthly and annual
Normal total precipitation, monthly and annual
Mean total precipitation (inches) by state climatic division, monthly and
  annual
Mean annual precipitation in millions of gallons of water per square mile
  by state climatic divisions
Mean annual precipitation in millions of gallons of water per capita by
  state climatic divisions
Mean total snowfall (inches)
Mean number of days with 0.01 inch or more of precipitation, monthly
  and annual
Mean daily dewpoint, monthly and annual
Maximum persisting 12-hour 1000-mb dewpoint (°F), monthly and
  record
Mean relative humidity (%), monthly and annual
Pan and lake evaporation
Mean percent of possible sunshine, monthly and annual
Mean total hours of sunshine, monthly and annual
Mean daily solar radiation, monthly and annual
Mean sky cover, sunrise to sunset, monthly and annual
Prevailing direction, mean speed (mph), and fastest mile of wind,
  monthly and annual
Surface wind roses, monthly and annual; resultant surface winds, mid-
  seasonal
Normal sea-level pressures, monthly and annual

Maps showing prevailing weather conditions over a series of
years are contained in the *Atlas of American Agriculture* described on pages 424–25.

Aeronautical Charts

Department of Commerce.   In 1927, soon after its organiza-tion, the Aeronautics Branch of the Department of Commerce (afterwards the Air Commerce Bureau, the Civil Aeronautics Administration, the Federal Aviation Agency, and now the Federal Aviation Administration) began the issuance of strip maps showing the principal features of the terrain along estab-lished airways,[7] as well as aids to air navigation, landing fields, and other pertinent data. These maps were not bounded by meridians and parallels but represented a tract extending about 40 miles on each side of the established airway, with a length ranging from 200 to 400 miles. The scale was 1:500,000, or ap-proximately 8 miles to the inch. Each map was named for an important city in the area represented.

With the development of air transportation it was deemed advisable to represent areas other than those along established airways. The publication of a series of sectional maps embrac-ing the entire United States was therefore begun in December 1930, and the strip maps were superseded by sectional maps. The first Sectional Air Navigation Charts were produced, on a scale of 1:500,000, by the Coast Survey in 1930 as part of the series designed to cover the entire United States. In 1935 a series of regional charts (M series) was produced on a scale of 1:1,000,000. The tendency to develop all-purpose aeronau-tical charts for use in any type of flight reached its climax in 1945 with the production of the World Aeronautical Chart series. From that time forward there has been a marked tend-ency to produce many special-purpose charts. Along with the general trend in our civilization, aviation had reached the age of specialization, and aircraft were of many designs and pur-poses. It was therefore essential that aeronautical charts be designed to satisfy the various requirements as the type of flying and navigation equipment dictated. The Coast and Geodetic

[7] An airway is a route marked by beacons and other aids to air navigation.

Survey now publishes 9 series of charts in order to satisfy all segments of aviation for both instrument and visual flight operations.

In 1967, the Coast and Geodetic Survey started a new series of sectional areonautical charts which will eventually replace the present series. Each issue of the present series, with the exception of some of the maps of areas adjacent to the coast and Mexican border, represents 2° of latitude and 6° of longitude. Owing to the irregularity of the coast and the Canadian and Mexican borders, some of the maps of these regions are not uniform as regards the area shown. The scale is 1:500,000, or approximately 8 miles to the inch. The maps bear the name of a city or important natural feature.[8]

These maps show generalized topography and outstanding landmarks in each locality.

Altitudes are indicated by means of tints, the amount of differentiation varying on the maps according to the character of the terrain. As each tint shows a difference of some hundreds of feet, the maps necessarily give only a generalized picture of the relief and do not afford the detailed information regarding slope such as may be obtained from a contour map.

As each map represents an area of approximately 300 miles from east to west and 140 miles from north to south, the series is an extremely useful one for general reference. It comprises 88 maps covering continental United States and Hawaii. Each sheet measures approximately 24 by 42 inches, the width varying with the latitude.

[8] The early maps in this series have also a combined letter and number designation similar to that used on the sheets of the map of the world on the scale of 1:1,000,000 being issued by a number of governments. On the sheets of that map the letter indicates the latitude; the A sheets show the areas from the equator to 4° latitude, B from 4° to 8°, etc. The number indicates the longitude; those numbered 1 represent the areas from 180° west to 174° west, those numbered 2 from 174° to 168°, etc. Thus sheet K 18 of the map on the scale of 1:1,000,000 shows the area between 40° and 44° of latitude and 72° and 78° of longitude. As the airway maps show only 2° latitude, or half that shown on the 1:1,000,000 map, the two airway maps equivalent to K 18 are designated "Upper K 18" and "Lower K 18" in addition to the place designations (Albany and New York). On the 1:1,000,000 maps the areas north and south of the equator are indicated by the prefixes "North" and "South." These prefixes were omitted from the airway maps.

These maps are sold by the Coast and Geodetic Survey. An index-map showing published sheets is distributed free.

Another series available from the Coast and Geodetic Survey is the World Aeronautical Charts. Because of the reduced scale, some of the landmarks and topographic data shown on the sectional charts are omitted. These charts are intended for longer flights and higher speeds.

Other charts of widely varying scales are issued to meet the different needs of air navigation. These are: Planning Charts, Instrument Approach and Procedure Charts, and Jet Navigation Charts. Also issued are Aircraft Position Charts, Global Navigation Charts, Enroute Low Altitude Charts, Enroute High Altitude Charts, Alaska Aeronautical Charts, and Alaska and Hawaii Enroute Charts.

The Civil Aeronautics Board has issued the following maps: *Routes to the United States,* 1967, showing routes authorized to foreign carriers of the Eastern Hemisphere; *United States Air Transportation System,* 1967, showing routes certified to trunkline carriers; *Routes to the United States,* 1967, showing routes authorized to foreign air carriers of Western Hemisphere countries; *Routes Certified to Local Service Carriers,* 1967; *Certificated Cargo Carriers,* 1967, showing domestic, international, and overseas routes; *Certificated Alaska Air Routes,* 1967; and *International and Overseas Air Routes* of United States Carriers, 1967.

Navy Department. Aeronautical charts are published by the Naval Oceanographic Office of the Navy Department, from which they may be obtained. Some of these are strip maps and some sectional.

Waterways

Charts showing depth of water, boundaries of channels, shore lines, and aids to navigation constitute the oldest published series of government maps. The land features shown on these charts are limited to the topography of the immediate shore line. The charts fall into six distinct classes showing (1) the waters of the coast, (2) the Great Lakes, (3) foreign waters, (4) river surveys, (5) harbors, and (6) oceans.

Charts of the coast. There are four classes of charts pertaining to the coastal waters. The *Coast Charts* are on scales of 1:50,000 and 1:100,000 and are designed for inshore coastwise navigation, for entering bays and harbors of considerable width, and for navigating large inland waterways. The *Harbor Charts* are planned for harbors, anchorage areas, and the smaller waterways and are on scales larger than 1:50,000. A special series of charts on a scale of 1:40,000 are called the *Intracoastal Waterway (inside route) Charts*. The fourth class of charts is the *Sailing Charts*. These are on scales of 1:600,000 and smaller. They are intended primarily for use in fixing the mariner's position as he approaches the coast from the open sea, or for sailing between distant coastwise ports. The shoreline and topography are generalized, and only offshore soundings, the principal lights, outerbouys, and landmarks visible at considerable distance are shown. The *Nautical Chart Catalogs* index these and other charts. They may be obtained from the Coast and Geodetic Survey.

Charts of the Great Lakes. The United States Lake Survey, Army Engineers, publishes navigational charts of the Great Lakes and their connecting waters, the International Section of the St. Lawrence River, Lake Champlain, the New York State Barge Canal System, and the Minnesota-Ontario border lakes from Lake Superior to and including the southern portions of Rainy Lake and Lake of the Woods. Standard charts are of three main types—general, coast, and harbor—with scales varying to suit particular purposes. In addition, seven large-scale recreational charts, 11 by 17½ inches, in spiral-bound book form are now available for the pleasure boater. An approximately 600-page Great Lakes Pilot to complement the information on the charts is also available. For a free catalog, write to the United States Lake Survey, 630 Federal Building, Detroit, Michigan 48226.

Bathymetric maps. Published by the Coast and Geodetic Survey, these maps are graphic representations of the topography of the ocean floor by the use of depth contours. They serve as a foundation upon which future exploratory efforts and other geophysical measurements relating to the economic potential and scientific evaluation of the continental shelf can be recorded. They serve the marine environment in the same way that a topographic map serves on land and are basic to an orderly investigation and development of a region.

The following bathymetric maps are available from the Coast and Geodetic Survey, Rockville, Maryland 20852, or from Coast and Geodetic Survey chart distribution centers at 121 Customhouse, San Francisco, California 94126; and 602 Federal Office Building, 90 Church Street, New York, New York 10007.

1. Four maps of the southern coast of California on a scale of 1:250,000.
2. Fifteen maps of the North Atlantic coast of the United States.
3. Six maps of the Aleutian Arc on a scale of 1:400,000.

Foreign waters. For many years the Naval Oceanographic Office of the Navy Department has been publishing charts of foreign waters used by deep-sea shipping. Some of these charts result from surveys made by naval vessels, but most of them, particularly those of the waters adjacent to the principal maritime nations, are reproductions of charts published by foreign countries, with such changes as have been reported by both naval and merchant vessels. A detailed catalog may be obtained on application.

Basic topographic and city maps produced by official and other agencies in Europe, Asia (except India, Pakistan, Afghanistan, and Western China), Greenland, North Africa, Ethiopia, and the Somalilands are discussed briefly in *Foreign Maps,* 1956 (210 pages), United States Department of the Army, TM 5–248. The names of the agencies publishing the maps, the scales of the maps, physical description, and an estimate of reliability and usefulness are given.

Rivers. The rivers in the Atlantic coastal plain, which are really estuaries, are generally shown on the navigation charts of the Coast and Geodetic Survey described above.

The field offices of the Corps of Engineers of the Army have charge of the improvement of rivers and harbors, and many of them have issued maps of the waterways on which work has been done. As a rule these maps show only the topography immediately adjacent to the stream. For the navigable streams, such as the Mississippi, Ohio, Tennessee, Cumberland, etc., these maps show depth of water and aids to navigation.

They are issued in a variety of forms. Some are lithographed, while others are blue prints, blue line prints, or black line prints made on order from the tracings on file. As the prints are not generally issued in editions, they can hardly be regarded as publications, but they are mentioned because of their possible interest.

As a rule, the large rivers are shown on a series of maps. For some rivers the maps are sold in sets only, while for others single maps of a portion of the stream are available. None of these maps is available for free distribution.

A descriptive price list of maps and charts suited for navigation of the Illinois Waterway and of the Mississippi River between Cairo, Illinois, and Minneapolis, Minnesota, may be obtained from the Corps of Engineers, 536 S. Clark Street, Chicago, Illinois 60605; of the Mississippi River from Cairo to the Gulf of Mexico, from the Corps of Engineers, P.O. Box 60, Vicksburg, Mississippi 39181; and of the Ohio River between Pittsburgh and the Mississippi River, from the Corps of Engineers, P.O. Box 1159, Cincinnati, Ohio 45201.

The Corps of Engineers, 536 S. Clark Street, Chicago, Illinois 60605, has available a series of *Division Bulletins* which give information concerning various other maps and charts of rivers, the source from which they may be obtained, and the prices.

Under the acts of January 21, 1927 (44 Stat. 1015), and May 15, 1928 (45 Stat. 538), the Corps of Engineers is making surveys of navigation, flood control, power, and irrigation on a number of rivers. These reports contain maps in addition to elaborate text dealing with the physical and economic features of the several basins. The volumes published to July 1, 1938, are listed in the annual report of the Chief of Engineers of the Army, the list being on pages 1953–57 of Part 1, Volume 2, of the report for 1938. A supplemental list will be found on page 15 of Part 1, Volume 2, of the annual report of the Chief of Engineers of the Army for 1953.

The preliminary reports of the Chief of Engineers on river and harbor projects generally contain maps. There is no general index to these, but they may be located by means of the biennial *Document Catalog* and the *Monthly Catalog,* the entries indicating whether the report includes a map.

Formerly some maps of rivers and harbors were published in the annual reports of the Chief of Engineers. The maps in the annual reports prior to 1918 may be found by means of the *Index to the Reports of the Chief of Engineers, U. S. Army,* Volume 1 (1866–1912) and Volume 3 (1913–17). The maps are referred to at the end of the entries for surveys. There is no index to the reports issued after 1917, but the later annual reports include few maps.

The Geological Survey has also issued a number of river maps. As these maps accompany reports on water power and water resources, they are confined mostly to non-navigable streams. They usually show only the course of the stream and the topography of the banks.

All the published reports of the Geological Survey may be located by means of the catalog entitled *Publications of the United States Geological Survey.* In the index to this pamphlet the citations will be found under the names of the states (subentries "Power," "River surveys," and "Water resources") instead of under the names of the streams. An index of river surveys made to 1947 is contained in *Index to River Surveys Made by the United States Geological Survey and Other Agencies,* by Benjamin E. Jones and Randolph O. Holland, published as Geological Survey Water-Supply Paper 995 (145 pages).

Harbor facilities.   Maps and detailed information on harbor facilities are contained in two series of publications issued by the Corps of Engineers of the Army and sold by the Superintendent of Documents. These are the Port Series and the Lake Series. Forty-nine volumes have been issued in the Port Series and nine in the Lake Series.

The *World Port Index*, 2d edition, 1957 (201 pages), Publication No. 950 of the Hydrographic Office (now the Naval Oceanographic Office), Navy Department, contains the locations and general descriptions of maritime ports and shipping places, with references to appropriate sailing directions and charts.

Oceans. The Naval Oceanographic Office of the Navy Department issues *Catalog of Nautical Charts and Publications, Region 8, Oceania,* which lists charts for the Atlantic Ocean, the Pacific Ocean, the Indian Ocean, and the Polar regions. That office has also issued, as Publication No. 705, *Oceanographic Atlas of Polar Seas,* Part 1, Antarctic, 1957 [1958] (70 pages); Part 2, Arctic, 1958 (149 pages).

The weather of oceans is of interest to several agencies. The Fish and Wildlife Service issued *Wind Atlas of North Pacific,* by James W. McGary and Thomas M. Naito, Special Scientific Report, Fisheries, No. 243, 1957 (35 pages). *U. S. Marine Climatic Atlas of the World* has been published by direction of the Chief of Naval Operations, Navy Department, as follows: Volume 1, North Atlantic Ocean [1956] (275 pages); Volume 2, North Pacific Ocean [1956] (275 pages); Volume 3, Indian Ocean, 1957 (267 pages); Volume 4, South Atlantic Ocean, 1958 (267 pages); Volume 5, South Pacific Ocean, 1959 (267 pages); Volume 6, Arctic Ocean, 1963 (293 pages); and Volume 7, Antarctic Ocean, 1965 (361 pages).

International Boundaries

Surveys of international boundaries have involved both topographic mapping and the provision for permanent marks and vistas by which the boundary may be easily located on the ground. The results of boundary surveys have been published as separate maps, as atlases or attached maps accompanying reports, and as detailed descriptions of the courses of boundaries. The Department of State has a series entitled *International Boundary Studies* which began in 1963. Maps are included to illustrate the text of these reports. There have been several surveys of each boundary, but only the latest are discussed below. The earlier ones are listed on pages 909–21 of the *Checklist*.

Canadian boundary. The International Boundary Commission, United States and Canada, has published a series of maps of the boundary between the United States and Canada from the Atlantic to the Pacific. It has also mapped the boundary between Alaska and Canada. Except for the maps of the St. Lawrence River and the Great Lakes section, these maps show the topographic features immediately adjacent to the boundary and indicate the location of the monuments.

The boundary along the St. Lawrence River and through the Great Lakes and connecting waterways to the mouth of Pigeon River at the head of Lake Superior was surveyed by the International Waterways Commission, whose report was published by the Canadian government under the title *Report of the International Waterways Commission upon the International Boundary between the Dominion of Canada and the United States, through the St. Lawrence River and Great Lakes*, 1916 (286 pages). The charts were issued separately by the Canadian government in two editions with different scales. The large-scale maps, which are listed on page 118 of the report cited above, are no longer available for distribution. The smaller-scale maps may be purchased from the International Boundary Commission, Ottawa, Canada. They are listed in *Catalogue of Nautical Charts*, published by the Hydrographic Service of Canada, Ottawa.

The several arbitrations relating to the Canadian and Alaskan boundary contain maps of historical interest. The reports are listed on pages 909–21 of the *Checklist*. Other official and commercial publications containing maps of the Canadian boundary are listed in *Guide to the Diplomatic History of the United States, 1775–1921*, by Samuel F. Bemis and Grace G. Griffin, Library of Congress, 1935 (979 pages).

Mexican boundary. The boundary between the United States and Mexico west of the Rio Grande was last surveyed and marked between 1891 and 1898 and the results were published in 1898 in three volumes with the general title *Report of Boundary Commission upon Survey and Re-marking of Boundary between United States and Mexico West of the Rio Grande, 1891–96,* issued also as Senate Document 247, 55th Congress, 2d session. Volume 1 contains the text of the report, Volume 2 contains views of monuments and characteristic scenes, and Volume 3 is an atlas of maps showing the topography adjacent to the boundary and the location of the monuments.

The stream beds of the Rio Grande and the Colorado River originally formed part of the international boundary, but as the rivers changed their courses there was a continual transfer of territory from one country to the other. The areas between the abandoned channel and the new channel are known as *bancos.* A series of conventions provided for the determination of the boundary adjacent to the *bancos* by an international commission, and description and maps of the *bancos* considered up to 1929 are given in the four reports listed below, each of which has the main title *Proceedings of the International Boundary Commission, United States and Mexico:*

Elimination of 57 old *bancos* specifically described in the treaty of 1905, 1910
Elimination of *bancos,* treaty of 1905, 2d ser., Nos. 59–89 [no date]
Elimination of *bancos* under the convention of Mar. 20, 1905, Colorado River Nos. 501–02, Rio Grande Nos. 90–131, inclusive . . . 1929
Elimination of *bancos* under convention of Mar. 20, 1905, El Paso-Juarez Valley, Rio Grande Nos. 301–19, inclusive . . . 1931

In 1967 the Department of State published *Demarcation of the New International Boundary (Chamizal),* Treaties and Other International Acts Series 6372 (11 pages).

Historical Maps

With the lapse of time every map has some historical value, although care must be taken to differentiate between errors in mapping and changes that have actually taken place.

Campaigns and battlefields.   While some single maps of campaigns and battlefields have been published, the only comprehensive collection of such maps is the *Atlas to Accompany Official Records of Union and Confederate Armies [Rebellion Records].* It was published by the War Department and issued in 35 numbered and 2 unnumbered parts, and in bound editions in two volumes and three volumes. It was also issued as House Miscellaneous Document 261, 52d Congress, 1st session. No parts of the atlas are now available for distribution by any government office.

The Chickamauga and Chattanooga National Military Park Commission has issued an *Atlas of Battlefields of Chickamauga, Chattanooga and Vicinity* (6 pages, 14 plates). This atlas was also published as House Document 514, 46th Congress, 2d session.

Small maps of campaigns and battles from the colonial period to the Spanish-American War are contained in *American Campaigns,* by Matthew Forney Steele, in two volumes, published by the Office of the Chief of Staff in 1909 (War Department Document 324).[9] Volume 1 contains descriptive text and Volume 2 the maps; most of these are reproduced from commercial publications and do not represent new compilations.

The National Archives has issued a list entitled *Civil War Maps in the National Archives,* 1964 (127 pages). The Library of Congress has published an annotated list of maps and atlases in its collections entitled *Civil War Maps,* 1961 (138 pages).

George Washington Atlas.   In 1932 the George Washington Bicentennial Commission issued the *George Washington Atlas,* edited by Lawrence Martin, chief of the Division of Maps of the Library of Congress. This atlas contains a "collection of 85 maps including 28 made by George Washington, 7 used and annotated by him, 8 made at his direction or for his use or otherwise associated with him, and 42 new maps concerning his activities in peace and war and his place in history."

Cities.   An interesting collection of small maps of cities, with

[9] This work was reprinted in 1922 by the United States Infantry Association.

some maps of historical significance, is contained in Volumes XVIII and XIX of the Tenth Census (1880), entitled *Social Statistics of Cities*. Some of the maps show the extent of special municipal undertakings, such as parks and sewerage systems.

World Maps

An International Map of the World on a scale of 1:1,000,000 is published by the Geological Survey. This map contains 34 sheets published for the United States. It shows principal cities, railroads, highways, streams, and political boundaries. Contour lines indicate the shape of the land surface and of the ocean floor, and gradations of color indicate the height of the land and the depth of the ocean.

A *Physical Political Global Chart of the World* is a stereographic projection on a scale of 1:10,000,000 issued in 6 sheets with an over-all size of 108 by 126 inches. It provides realistic representation of global relationships between the most vital areas of the world. Relief is shown by gradient tints. The same chart may be obtained on a scale of 1:40,000,000, with a size of 31 by 27 inches. This chart may be obtained from the Coast and Geodetic Survey, Department of Commerce.

The Army Map Service has produced a *Wall Map of the World* on a scale of 1:11,000,000. This is a Mercator projection issued in 9 sheets with an over-all size of 9 by 12 feet. Relief is indicated by contours at 1,000, 2,000, 6,000, and 10,000 feet, augmented by altitude tints.

Selected Maps and Charts of Antarctica, an annotated list of maps of south polar regions published since 1945, compiled by Richard W. Stephenson, 1959 (193 pages), is available from the Map Division, Reference Department, Library of Congress.

Maps of Foreign Areas

Mapping and map-making activities of the federal government increased rapidly during World War II. The demand for maps of foreign areas for a variety of uses brought into being a number of federal agencies to meet these specialized needs and to provide for the continuing demand. Primary producers of foreign maps are the Naval Oceanographic Office of the Navy Department, the Army Map Service, and the Aeronautical Chart and Information Center of the United States Air Force.

CHAPTER SEVENTEEN

TECHNICAL AND OTHER
DEPARTMENT PUBLICATIONS

THE PRECEDING CHAPTERS have described publications which
deal with legislation, the courts, administrative action, and certain well-defined types of executive publications. There re-
mains to be considered the great mass of publications which are
issued by the executive branch of the government and which do
not fall within any of the groups heretofore discussed.

It may appear inconsistent that so little space is devoted to a
group that includes so large a number of publications of importance, but the only alternative is a voluminous cataloging of
publications in many diverse fields.

The difficulty of covering this field in a general work like the
present one is illustrated by the fact that statistical publications
of the government have been described in a volume of over 500
pages published in 1925,[1] and while many of the series described are still being published, there have been new developments that must be taken into account. Statistical reports
are more easily described than publications in any other group,
because as a rule they are issued in continuous or periodic
chronological series, each of which has defined characteristics.
The scientific and informative publications of the government
cover almost every field, and it is manifest therefore that a
chapter devoted to this subject must be confined to a broad
discussion and can indicate only in the most general way how

[1] Laurence F. Schmeckebier, *The Statistical Work of the National Government*, Institute for Government Research.

441

the student may avail himself of the great mass of valuable material. Beginning in 1965, a long-needed attempt at bibliographical control of government-sponsored research was started with the publication of *Government-wide Index to Federal Research and Development Reports* by the Clearinghouse for Federal Scientific and Technical Information, which in 1964 had taken over the functions of the Office of Technical Services.

Technical Reports and Translations

Since World War II the federal government has greatly increased its scientific and technical activities and directly or indirectly is supporting much of the scientific research and development being carried on in the United States. This has been a matter of growing concern to some private publishers, with some fears voiced that the federal government might dominate the scientific publishing field. However, most government agencies have encouraged federal scientists to publish reports in nongovernment scientific and technical journals.

Several agencies are sponsoring translation series of scientific reports originating in foreign countries. Among these agencies are the Atomic Energy Commission, Cold Regions Research and Engineering Laboratory, Department of the Air Force, Joint Publications Research Service, National Aeronautics and Space Administration, National Science Foundation, and the Naval Research Laboratory.

Translations are listed in the *Monthly Catalog*. Miss Mary Elizabeth Poole has prepared an *Index to Readex Microprint Edition of Joint Publication Research Service Reports* for the Readex Microprint Corporation of New York. This covers the period from 1958 to the end of 1963. Translations were published in *U. S. Government Research Reports* until January 1959, when the Office of Technical Services began the publication of *Technical Translations*. This publication was arranged by 22 major subject fields and indexed by author, journal, and report number. It ceased publication in 1967. Beginning in

1968, all United States government-sponsored technical translations have been announced in the Department of Commerce clearinghouse journal, *U. S. Government Research and Development Reports,* and also included in the index of this publication.

The Group as a Whole

The departmental publications here discussed include results of original research, compilations of data already published in another form, and publications describing the work and activities of the government agencies.

The publications in this field include many noteworthy and valuable contributions in almost every branch of the physical and social sciences. In scope they vary from popular articles to technical treatises, and in size they range from pamphlets to large volumes.

If the field is approached by way of the subject matter, a listing would include almost every field of scientific inquiry and human interest. It would comprise subjects of interest to the specialist in every branch of science, to the workers in diverse fields of industry, to the traveler, to the teacher, to the engineer, to the manufacturer, to the merchant, to the housewife, and to the general seeker after knowledge for its own sake. One classification of the research activities of the government is as follows:[2]

Field 1. AERONAUTICS. Includes the following groups: Aerodynamics, Aeronautics, Aircraft, Aircraft Flight Control and Instrumentation, Air Facilities.

Field 2. AGRICULTURE. Includes the following groups: Agricultural Chemistry; Agricultural Economics, Agricultural Engineering, Agronomy and Horticulture, Animal Husbandry, Forestry.

Field 3. ASTRONOMY AND ASTROPHYSICS. Includes the following groups: Astronomy, Astrophysics, Celestial Mechanics.

Field 4. ATMOSPHERIC SCIENCES. Includes the following groups: Atmospheric Physics, Meteorology.

[2] Taken from *U. S. Government Research and Development Reports,* February 10, 1968.

444   GOVERNMENT PUBLICATIONS

Field 5. BEHAVIORAL AND SOCIAL SCIENCES. Includes the following groups: Administration and Management; Documentation and Information Technology; Economics; History, Law, and Political Science; Human Factors Engineering; Humanities; Linguistics; Man-machine Relations; Personnel Selection, Training, and Evaluation; Psychology (Individual and Group Behavior); Sociology.

Field 6. BIOLOGICAL AND MEDICAL SCIENCES. Includes the following groups: Biochemistry; Bioengineering; Biology; Bionics; Clinical Medicine; Environmental Biology; Escape, Rescue, and Survival; Food, Hygiene, and Sanitation; Industrial (Occupational) Medicine; Life Support; Medical and Hospital Equipment; Microbiology; Personnel Selection and Maintenance (Medical); Pharmacology; Physiology; Protective Equipment; Radiobiology; Stress Physiology; Toxicology; Weapon Effects.

Field 7. CHEMISTRY. Includes the following groups: Chemical Engineering, Inorganic Chemistry, Organic Chemistry, Physical Chemistry, Radio and Radiation Chemistry.

Field 8. EARTH SCIENCES AND OCEANOGRAPHY. Includes the following groups: Biological Oceanography; Cartography; Dynamic Oceanography; Geochemistry; Geodesy; Geography; Geology and Mineralogy; Hydrology and Limnology; Mining Engineering; Physical Oceanography; Seismology; Snow, Ice, and Permafrost; Soil Mechanics; Terrestrial Magnetism.

Field 9. ELECTRONICS AND ELECTRICAL ENGINEERING. Includes the following groups: Components, Computers, Electronic and Electrical Engineering, Information Theory, Subsystems, and Telemetry.

Field 10. ENERGY CONVERSION (Non-propulsive). Includes the following groups: Conversion Techniques, Power Sources, Energy Storage.

Field 11. MATERIALS. Includes the following groups: Adhesives and Seals; Ceramics, Refractories, and Glasses; Coatings, Colorants, and Finishes; Composite Materials; Fibers and Textiles; Metallurgy and Metallography; Miscellaneous Materials; Oils, Lubricants, and Hydraulic Fluids; Plastics; Rubbers; Solvents, Cleaners, and Abrasives; Wood and Paper Products.

Field 12. MATHEMATICAL SCIENCES. Includes the following groups: Mathematics and Statistics, Operations Research.

Field 13. MECHANICAL, INDUSTRIAL, CIVIL, AND MARINE ENGINEERING. Includes the following groups: Air Conditioning, Heating, Lighting, and Ventilating; Civil Engineering; Construction Equipment, Materials, and Supplies; Containers and Packaging; Couplings, Fittings, Fasteners, and Joints; Ground

Transportation Equipment; Hydraulic and Pneumatic Equipment; Industrial Processes; Machinery and Tools; Marine Engineering; Pumps, Filters, Pipes, Fittings, Tubing, and Valves; Safety Engineering; Structural Engineering.

Field 14. METHODS AND EQUIPMENT. Includes the following groups: Cost Effectiveness; Laboratories, Test Facilities, and Test Equipment; Recording Devices; Reliability; Reprography.

Field 15. MILITARY SCIENCES. Includes the following groups: Antisubmarine Warfare; Chemical, Biological, and Radiological Warfare; Defense; Intelligence; Logistics; Nuclear Warfare; Operations, Strategy, and Tactics.

Field 16. MISSILE TECHNOLOGY. Includes the following groups: Missile Launching and Ground Support, Missile Trajectories, Missile Warheads and Fuses, Missiles.

Field 17. NAVIGATION, COMMUNICATIONS, DETECTION, AND COUNTERMEASURES. Includes the following groups: Acoustic Detection, Communications, Direction Finding, Electromagnetic and Acoustic Countermeasures, Infrared and Ultraviolet Detection, Magnetic Detection, Navigation and Guidance, Optical Detection, Radar Detection, Seismic Detection.

Field 18. NUCLEAR SCIENCE AND TECHNOLOGY. Includes the following groups: Fusion Devices (Thermonuclear), Isotopes, Nuclear Explosions, Nuclear Instrumentation, Nuclear Power Plants, Radiation Shielding and Protection, Radioactive Wastes and Fission Products, Radioactivity, Reactor Engineering and Operation, Reactor Materials, Reactor Physics, Reactors (Power), Reactors (Non-power), SNAP Technology.

Field 19. ORDNANCE. Includes the following groups: Ammunition, Explosives, and Pyrotechnics; Bombs; Combat Vehicles; Explosions, Ballistics, and Armor; Fire Control and Bombing Systems; Guns; Rockets; Underwater Ordnance.

Field 20. PHYSICS. Includes the following groups: Acoustics; Crystallography; Electricity and Magnetism; Fluid Mechanics; Masers and Lasers; Optics; Particle Accelerators; Particle Physics; Plasma Physics; Quantum Theory, Solid Mechanics; Solid-state Physics; Thermodynamics; Wave Propagation.

Field 21. PROPULSION AND FUELS. Includes the following groups: Air-breathing Engines, Combustion and Ignition, Electric Propulsion, Fuels, Jet and Gas Turbine Engines, Nuclear Propulsion, Reciprocating Engines, Rocket Motors and Engines, Rocket Propellants.

Field 22. SPACE TECHNOLOGY. Includes the following groups: Astronautics, Spacecraft, Spacecraft Trajectories and Reentry, Spacecraft Launch Vehicles and Ground Support.

Over the years there have been excellent books issued which list titles of some of the more important publications of the government. Among these books are *Guide to Reference Books,* by Constance M. Winchell, 8th edition, American Library Association, 1967 (741 pages); *Annotated Bibliography of Bibliographies on Selected Government Publications and Supplementary Guides to the Superintendent of Documents Classification System,* by Alexander C. Body, Edwards Brothers, Inc., Ann Arbor, Michigan, 1967 (181 pages); *A Popular Guide to Government Publications,* by W. Philip Leidy, Columbia University Press, 1968 (367 pages); *Basic Reference Sources,* by Louis Shores, American Library Association, 1954 (378 pages); *United States Government Publications,* by Anne Morris Boyd, 3d edition, revised by Rae Elizabeth Rips, H. W. Wilson Co., 1949 (627 pages); *Subject Guide to United States Government Publications,* by Herbert S. Hirshberg and Carl H. Melinat, American Library Association, 1947 (228 pages).

If the field were approached by publishing units it would be necessary to give a description of the work of practically every government agency, as even the purely administrative units have at times issued publications containing basic data, conclusions derived from facts that have been assembled, or information pertaining to their fields of operation.[3]

A complete knowledge of the work undertaken by each government agency would enable the student to know the units which issue the publications in which he is interested, but few persons have acquired such knowledge. The names of the units do not always indicate the fields of their activity and there are constant changes in the scope of their operations. Moreover, several agencies may have a legitimate interest in the same general field. The Geological Survey, for instance, may be regarded as the primary source for geology. However, the National Museum and the Smithsonian Institution are concerned with all branches of science and have issued publications in this

---

[3] The organization and functions of most of the government agencies are described in the *United States Government Organization Manual,* published by the General Services Administration (see pp. 399–400).

field. The National Park Service issues publications dealing with the natural features of the reservations under its control and such publications include some dealing with geology. But all publications on national parks are not issued by the National Park Service. Material on the parks has been issued by the Geological Survey in the field of geology, by the Public Health Service on sewage and sanitation, and by the Fish and Wildlife Service on fishes. A bulletin on city parks has been issued by the Bureau of Labor Statistics.

Turning to another field we find that while the Public Health Service is a primary publisher in the fields of medicine, hygiene, and sanitation, reports on problems in the field of health or medicine are issued by the Children's Bureau, the Bureau of Labor Statistics, the Bureau of Mines, the Veterans Administration, the Atomic Energy Commission, and the medical departments of the Army, the Navy, and the Air Force. Vital statistics of all kinds are published by the Public Health Service. Articles on medical education are published by the Office of Education.

As illustrations of the inadequacy of the names of organizations in indicating the character of publications, it should be noted that the Geological Survey has for many years issued an important series of reports on surface-water supply, and that prior to the organization of the Bureau of Mines it published reports on fuel testing and prevention of mine accidents.

Examples like the foregoing could be multiplied indefinitely, but the illustrations given are sufficient to indicate that the student in search of information should not restrict his searches to the publications of any one organization unit.

It is manifest, therefore, that no detailed list of a reasonable length can be prepared indicating the specific topics that are treated in government publications, and it is also clear that all publications in a particular general field are not issued by the same organization unit. Moreover, as the result of the development of new units and the consideration of new problems by the older units, a general statement that would be true today would be incorrect if applied to last year or next year.

Fortunately, however, the general catalogs, indexes, and

bibliographies listed in Chapters 2 and 3 will furnish a guide to all issues except the periodicals and the processed material. While the *Monthly Catalog* arrangement is by publishing offices, it has an excellent annual index. In the biennial *Document Catalog* all the publications of a particular office are listed successively under the name of the office, and each publication is also listed under the subject matter and the author. Both of these catalogs are described in detail in Chapter 2.

Most of the department lists and indexes described on pages 37–63 cover only the publications of one bureau or one department, and hence do not give citations to all government publications on a particular topic. The advantages of the special indexes are that they cover longer periods and the indexing is generally in more detail.

Currently, the General Services Administration, which is now in charge of government procurement of general supplies, issues *Federal Specifications, Federal Standards,* and a *Stores Stock Catalog.* The pamphlets included in *Federal Specifications* contain the detailed specifications adopted by the government for use in purchasing the articles enumerated. They are of interest not only to bidders on government contracts but also to purchasers who may want to obtain supplies of an established standard. The *Stores Stock Catalog* describes—in many cases with illustrations—regularly used government supplies stocked by the General Services Administration which may be requisitioned by federal agencies from General Services Administration warehouses.

Writers and editors will be interested in the following publications: *United States Government Printing Office Style Manual,* 1967 (512 pages), and *Suggestions to Authors of the Reports of the United States Geological Survey,* 1958 (255 pages).

Processed Publications

In addition to the periodicals, a great amount of processed material is issued by the departments. This ranges in size from single-page press releases to compilations of several hundred pages. Some are in series; others are independent publications.

Two factors have combined to increase the output of processed publications: (1) the time required for printing, and (2) lack of funds for printing. As the processed work is done on the premises of the several agencies, small jobs, such as press releases, can undoubtedly be finished in less time than if sent to the Government Printing Office. Where speed is an element, the processed publication is an efficient aid to administration. A large part of the processed publications issued by agencies established prior to 1933 is undoubtedly due to the restriction on use of funds for printing. Most of the permanent agencies can spend money for printing only from appropriations made specifically for that purpose, and the amounts of these appropriations have never kept pace with the sums available for research and administrative work. Consequently it has not been possible to print much of the output. But the appropriations for operating expenses have been available for the purchase of processing equipment and supplies and for compensation of typists and machine operators. As a result, the departments have been forced to process a portion of their output.

Some of the processed material now issued is done by the offset printing method in field plants under the control of the Government Printing Office. The various departments and agencies availing themselves of this service must, of course, pay for the work performed from their printing appropriations.

Prior to 1936 current lists of processed issues were not available, as little material of this character was included in the *Monthly Catalog*. An exception was the general list of publications of the Bureau of Mines, which was published at varying intervals. There was, therefore, no general guide until the biennial *Document Catalog* appeared. Some processed material is included in the earlier volumes, but not nearly so much as in the issues beginning with the 71st Congress (1929–31). Since then the amount of processed material included in the *Document Catalog* (up to its discontinuance) and in the *Monthly Catalog* has steadily increased, until at the present time it constitutes over one-third of all publications listed in the *Monthly Catalog*. As the issuing offices do not always make the publications available to the compilers, no doubt some are not cataloged.

Processed material is not to be despised, as much of it is of prime importance. In some cases it is of temporary value only. This is true of many preliminary statistical statements, particularly those of the Bureau of the Census. These preliminary statements give the results for specified areas, or particular branches of the subject, and while all are superseded in the printed reports, a considerable period of time elapses before the final reports are available.

An appreciable number of reports containing statistics, bibliographies, results of research, and accounts of operations are issued in processed form only. For instance in March 1934 the President created the National Recovery Review Board, headed by Clarence Darrow, to report on monopolistic tendencies under the codes of the National Recovery Administration. This board made three reports to the President, which were released in processed form only. Although these reports dealt with matters of great public interest, they have not been printed and are probably available in few libraries. They were not listed in the *Monthly Catalog*, but were entered in the biennial *Document Catalog*, Volume 22.

Press releases are of primary importance to all students of government affairs. The best of them contain official statements of fact, policy, or opinion, and in many cases are indispensable in tracing the development of policies. They include material that could otherwise be obtained only by laborious search through department files, if such files were available to the student.

Press releases have been of increasing importance since March 4, 1933, as after that date the executive agencies of the government developed extensive units devoted solely to reporting and publicizing the activities of the agencies.

CHAPTER EIGHTEEN

PERIODICALS

Most government offices issue periodicals in order to make available to the public short articles or timely information in their respective fields. Some periodicals contain decisions, rules, and regulations issued by government agencies, while others are limited to statistical tabulations. Periodicals are of paramount importance to persons who are concerned with the program and policies of a particular government office. By following the articles in the periodicals, the reader is able to keep in touch with changes in government policy or shifts in emphasis and can evaluate more fully items which appear in the press.

Commercial periodical indexes list some of the articles which appear in government periodicals. The *Monthly Catalog* lists articles if they are reprinted in separate form; this was also the practice in the biennial *Document Catalog*. A survey made by Mary Elizabeth Poole in 1968 covering 109 government periodicals showed that 59 were indexed in some publication and 50 were not carried in any index.

A list of periodicals, both printed and processed, as well as regularly issued statistical statements and releases, can be found in the February issue of the *Monthly Catalog. Price List 36*, issued by the Superintendent of Documents, lists all periodicals and other publications which are sold on a subscription basis by the Government Printing Office.

A comprehensive report on the various regularly issued publications of government agencies, both printed and processed, is contained in Appendix A to *Paperwork Management and*

Printing Facilities in the United States Government, Part II, Publications Management, prepared by the Subcommittee to Study Federal Printing and Paperwork of the Committee on House Administration, House Report 2945, Part II, 84th Congress, 2d session.

Following is a selected list of representative government periodicals. Omitted are periodicals which are primarily concerned with regulations and decisions, publications issued quarterly or less often, and publications issued irregularly.

AGRICULTURE

Agricultural marketing. Issued by the Consumer and Marketing Service, Department of Agriculture. Monthly. Concerns all phases of this agency's work. Of primary interest to persons engaged in marketing farm products.

Agricultural research. Issued by the Agricultural Research Service, Department of Agriculture. Monthly. Lists research projects in livestock management, crops, soils, fruits and vegetables, poultry, and related subjects.

Agricultural situation. Issued by the Statistical Reporting Service. Monthly. Contains statistics about crops, livestock, and prices and brief summaries of economic conditions.

Extension Service review. Issued by the Cooperative Extension Service, Department of Agriculture. Monthly. Includes pertinent information on agriculture extension programs of the United States, 4-H Club work, conservation, home demonstration, community cooperation, and related subjects.

Foreign agriculture. Issued by the Foreign Agricultural Service, Department of Agriculture. Monthly. Gives an insight into agriculture in foreign nations, and a look at the types and extent of American participation in foreign agriculture.

News for farmer cooperatives. Issued by the Farmer Cooperative Service, Department of Agriculture. Monthly. Composed of articles concerned with the operations and management of farmers' cooperatives and with recent developments in outstanding cooperatives in various parts of the country.

Plant disease reporter. Issued by the Agricultural Research Service, Department of Agriculture. Monthly. Carries articles emphasizing new developments in plant pathology.

Soil conservation. Issued by the Soil Conservation Service, Department of Agriculture. Monthly. Contains interesting and informative articles on new developments in the field of soil conservation.

AVIATION

Air university review. Issued by the Aerospace Studies Institute, Maxwell Air Force Base. Bimonthly. Contains articles of a professional nature of interest to members of the Air Force.

The airman. Issued by the United States Air Force. Monthly. Published for the enlightenment and the building of morale of all Air Force personnel. A vivid portrayal of the Air Force verbally and pictorially.

International notams. Issued by the Federal Aviation Administration. Weekly. Provides information necessary to promote air safety.

The MAC flyer. Issued by the Department of the Air Force. Monthly. Contains articles designed to promote greater safety and efficiency in MATS air operations.

Naval aviation news. Issued by the Department of the Navy. Monthly. Presents articles of interest on all phases of Navy and Marine air activity.

United States Army aviation digest. Issued by the Army Aviation School, Fort Rucker, Alabama. Monthly. Provides information of an operational or functional nature concerning safety and aircraft accident prevention, training, maintenance, operations, research and development, aviation medicine, and related data.

BUSINESS, ECONOMICS, AND LABOR

Business service checklist. Issued by the Department of Commerce. Weekly. Contains notice of materials published by the Department of Commerce and defense agencies, and lists news releases, books, pamphlets, reports, and other materials of interest to industry and business.

Economic development. Issued by the Economic Development Administration of the Department of Commerce. Monthly. Provides a means of communication between the Federal government and local governments on economic redevelopment.

Economic indicators. Prepared for the Joint Economic Committee by the Council of Economic Advisers. Monthly. Gives pertinent economic information on prices, wages, production, business activity, purchasing power, credit, money, and federal finance.

Employment and earnings. Issued by the Bureau of Labor Statistics, Department of Labor. Monthly. Presents the most current information available on trends and levels of employment, hours of work, earnings, and labor turnover. Shows developments in particular industries in the states and in local metropolitan areas, and contains the material formerly issued in *Current Population Reports.*

The Employment Service review. Issued by the Employment Service of the Bureau of Employment Security, Department of Labor. Monthly. Contains articles on various phases of employment counseling, interviewing, worker placement, unemployment, claims adjustment, and related subjects.

International commerce. Issued by the Bureau of Foreign Commerce, Department of Commerce. Weekly. Shows trends in overseas commerce, lists trade opportunities, examines exports and imports, and gives other important information concerning foreign trade and commerce.

Labor developments abroad. Issued by the Bureau of Labor Statistics, Department of Labor. Monthly. Presents research information on recent labor developments in foreign countries.

Marketing information guide. Issued by the Department of Commerce. Monthly. Contains annotations of selected current publications and reports in addition to basic information and statistics on marketing and distribution.

Monthly labor review. Issued by the Bureau of Labor Statistics, Department of Labor. Monthly. The medium through which the Labor Department publishes its regular reports on such subjects as trends of employment and pay rolls, hourly and weekly earnings, weekly working hours, collective agreements, industrial accidents, and industrial disputes.

Monthly retail trade report. Issued by the Census Bureau. Monthly. Presents various monthly statistical summaries on trends in retail business in such categories as dollar volumes, percentage changes, and types of businesses and by selected areas.

Survey of current business. Issued by the Office of Business Economics, Department of Commerce. Monthly. Gives information on trends in industry, the business situation, outlook, and other points pertinent to the business world. Weekly supplements give the latest information on indicators of business activity, and the July issue is a national income number which contains up-to-date figures on national income and output.

CONSTRUCTION

Construction review. Issued by the Business and Defense Services Administration, Department of Commerce. Monthly. Brings together under one cover virtually all of the government's current statistics that pertain to construction.

EDUCATION

American education. Issued by the Office of Education. Monthly except July–August and December–January, which are combined issues. Covers preschool to adult education, new research and demonstration projects, major education legislation, school and college bond data, grants, loans, contracts, and fellowships.

FINANCE

Daily statement of Treasury. Issued by the Treasurer of the United States. Daily except Saturdays, Sundays, and holidays. Consists of the daily statement of the United States Treasury and monthly and final statements for the fiscal year of receipts and expenditures of the United States government. Shows cash deposits and withdrawals as they affect the account of the Treasurer of the United States, gives changes in the public debt, shows effect of operations on the public debt, details interfund transactions, and gives figures on the United States Savings Bonds program.

Federal Reserve bulletin. Issued by the Board of Governors of the Federal Reserve System. Monthly. Contains current articles on economics, money, and banking. One section contains statistics dealing with domestic and foreign banking, industrial production indexes, and foreign exchange.

Treasury bulletin. Issued by the Office of the Secretary of the Treasury. Monthly. Gives a synopsis of Treasury activities covering financing operations, budget receipts and expenditures, debt operations, cash income and outgo, internal revenue collections, capital movements, yields of long-term bonds, ownership of federal securities, and other Treasury activities.

FOREIGN RELATIONS

Department of State bulletin. Issued by the Department of State. Weekly. Provides information on the development of foreign relations, operations of the State Department, statements by the President and Secretary of State, regular information on all treaty developments, check lists of pertinent congressional and United Nations documents, and special articles on international affairs.

Department of State news letter. Issued by the Department of State. Monthly. Published to acquaint the Department's officers and employees at home and abroad with developments of interest which may affect operations or personnel.

Foreign policy briefs. Issued by the Public Services Division, Bureau of Public Affairs, Department of State. Biweekly. Contains short, newsworthy comments on various aspects of American international relations. Is issued as an aid to wider public understanding of this nation's foreign policy.

MEDICINE

Index medicus. Issued by the National Library of Medicine, Department of Health, Education, and Welfare. Monthly. The first issue of this index was January 1960. It replaces the *Current List of Medical Literature*, which was discontinued with the December 1959 issue.

Journal of the National Cancer Institute. Issued by the National Institute of Health. Monthly. Devoted to the publication of original observations and investigations in laboratory and clinical research in cancer.

Public Health reports. Issued by the Public Health Service. Monthly. Contains scientific, technical, administrative, and analytical articles of interest to the public health profession.

MILITARY ESTABLISHMENTS

All hands. Issued by the Bureau of Naval Personnel, Department of the Navy. Monthly. Includes articles of general public interest about the United States Navy and its operations.

Army digest. Issued by the Department of the Army. Monthly. Provides timely and authoritative information on the policies, plans, operations, and technical developments of the Department of the Army and reserve components.

Army research and development. Issued by the Department of the Army. Monthly. Contains articles on Army research and development progress, problem areas, and program planning.

Naval Ships System Command technical news. Issued by the Department of the Navy. Monthly. Articles of interest to naval architects, ship builders, officers, ship repair personnel, and others concerned with building and maintaining vessels and their components.

Navy management review. Issued by the Department of the Navy. Monthly. Articles on advanced management techniques and philosophies in the Navy and Marine Corps.

Sealift magazine. Issued by the Military Sea Transportation Service, Department of the Navy. Monthly. Articles on Military Sea Transportation operations, promotion of safety, military shipping, and military-maritime efficiency and conservation.

Transportation proceedings. Issued by the Department of the Army. Monthly. Provides information on policies, plans, operations, and technical developments in the defense transportation field.

PATENTS

Official gazette of the Patent Office. Issued by the Patent Office. Weekly. Contains the patents, trademarks, and designs issued each week, as well as decisions of the Commissioner of Patents and of the United States courts in patent cases. *Decision Leaflets,* issued weekly, are separate from the *Official Gazette* and contain patent notices, decisions in patent cases, and patent suits. The Trademarks Section of the *Official Gazette* is also issued separately. It contains trademark notices, marks published for opposition, trademark registrations issued, principal register, supplemental register, and list of registrants of trademarks.

PUBLIC ROADS

Public roads (Journal of Highway Research). Issued by the Bureau of Public Roads, Department of Transportation. Bimonthly. Contains articles relating to highway research, engineering, safety on the highways, surfacing, and other areas in this field.

SAFETY

Aerospace maintenance safety. Issued by the Department of the Air Force. Monthly. Articles designed to encourage safety in the operation of aircraft by preventive maintenance.

Aerospace safety. Issued by the Department of the Air Force. Monthly. Articles cover many fields of flight, aircraft engineering, training, and safety measures.

Approach, naval aviation safety review. Issued by the Naval Safety Center, Department of the Navy. Monthly. Articles on the subject of aviation accident prevention.

Safety review. Issued by the Department of the Navy. Monthly. Contains articles whose objective is to provide all levels of management with information encouraging greater effort to accident prevention in the Naval Service.

Safety standards. Issued by the Bureau of Labor Standards, Department of Labor. Bimonthly. Devoted to news and articles on developments in the field of industrial safety.

SCIENCE AND RESEARCH

Ionospheric predictions. Issued by the Institute for Telecommunication Sciences, Environmental Science Services Administration, Department of Commerce. Monthly. Predictions are issued as an aid in determining the best sky-wave frequencies over any transmission path, at any time of day, for average conditions for the month. Issued three months in advance, each issue provides tables of numerical coefficients that define the functions describing the predicted world-wide distribution of foF2 and M(3000)F2 and maps for each even hour of universal time of MUF (Zero)F2 and MUF(4000)F2.

Journal of research of the National Bureau of Standards. Issued by the National Bureau of Standards in three sections. Section A, Physics and Chemistry, bimonthly, presents papers of interest primarily to scientists working in these fields, and covers a broad range of physical and chemical research, with major emphasis on standards of physical measurement, fundamental constants, and properties of matter. Section B, Mathematics and Mathematical Physics, quarterly, presents results in pure and applied mathematics, including mathematical statistics, theory of experiment design, numerical analysis, and short numerical tables; theoretical physics, chemistry, and engineering where emphasis is on the mathematical content or methodology; and logical design, programming, and applications of electronic computers and computer systems. Section C, Engineering and Instrumentation, quarterly, reports results of interest chiefly to the engineer or applied scientist. This section includes many of the new developments in instrumentation resulting from the National Bureau of Standard's work in physical measurement, data processing work in acoustics, applied mechanics, building research, and cryogenic engineering.

Naval research reviews. Issued by the Office of Naval Research, Department of Defense. Monthly. Reports briefly on highlights of technical progress in research by Navy laboratories and contractors and the development of important naval research facilities.

Nuclear science abstracts. Issued by the Division of Technical Information of the Atomic Energy Commission. Semimonthly. Abstracts literature relating to nuclear science and engineering, including materials of the Atomic Energy Commission, other government agencies, universities, and industrial research establishments. An index is issued quarterly.

Radio science. Issued by the Environmental Science Services Administration, Department of Commerce. Monthly. Reports research in radio propagation, communications, and upper atmospheric physics.

Research review. Issued by the Office of Scientific and Technical Information, Office of Aerospace Research, Department of the Air Force. Monthly. Articles concerning Air Force–conducted and Air Force–sponsored research activities.

Scientific information notes. Issued by the National Science Foundation. Bimonthly. Provides a medium for reporting new and improved methods of disseminating scientific information and news of projects, grants, surveys, and cooperative undertakings sponsored by the National Science Foundation and other federal agencies, and by other public and private organizations—domestic, foreign, and international.

Technical news bulletin. Issued by the National Bureau of Standards. Monthly. Contains summaries of current research at the National Bureau of Standards. Articles are brief, with emphasis on the results of research, and are chosen on the basis of their scientific or technologic importance. Lists of all bureau publications issued during the preceding month are given, including research papers, handbooks, Applied Mathematics Series, and miscellaneous publications.

SOCIAL SECURITY

Social Security bulletin. Issued by the Social Security Administration. Monthly. Reports current data on the operations of the Social Security

Administration and the results of research and analysis pertinent to the social security program. An annual statistical supplement is also issued.

Average monthly weather outlook. Issued by the Weather Bureau. Semimonthly. Gives a résumé of average rainfall and temperature for the preceding month and the weather outlook for the following month.

Climatological data, national summary. Issued by the Environmental Science Services Administration. Monthly, with an annual summary. Gives a general summary of weather conditions, condensed climatological summary for the states, climatological data by stations for the states, Pacific Area, and West Indies, degree day along with various climatological charts, river stages and flood data, and upper-air data.

Monthly weather review. Issued by the Environmental Science Services Administration. Monthly. Contains meteorological and climatological data for the United States and adjacent regions, and brief contributions, primarily concerned with synoptic and applied meteorology.

Weekly weather and crop bulletin, national summary. Issued by the Environmental Science Services Administration, Department of Commerce, in cooperation with the Statistical Reporting Service, Department of Agriculture. Gives a synopsis of weather conditions and their effect on crops and farming operations in the United States, and snow and ice conditions during the winter season.

CHAPTER NINETEEN

MICROFORM EDITIONS OF GOVERNMENT PUBLICATIONS

Microform Processes

DEVELOPMENTS IN THE FIELD of photography have produced several methods of photographing pages of books, newspapers, magazines, and other publications in extremely small sizes. Reading these small images is accomplished by means of projectors, viewers, and reading machines, which enlarge and project the pages usually on a ground-glass screen.

The process which was developed first in this field was microfilm. In this process, reduced images of the printed pages are recorded on 16- or 35-millimeter rolls of film. This produces a negative image when the roll of film is developed. From this negative any number of positives can be made for projection. Reading machines provide for placing the film on reels and projecting the enlarged images to a size approximating the original printed page. By turning a crank the reel of film can be moved forward or backward to locate the image of the page desired. As each page is read, the crank advances the film to the next page.

Another form of microform is called the microcard. This process uses positive photographic prints with a large number of pages reduced in size to fit on one card approximately 5 inches by 3 inches. The images of the pages are so reduced that 100 or more pages of an average size will fit on one card. At the top of the card is printed the name of the author and

460

title of the book in a manner similar to a card in the card-index file of a library.

Microprinting is a printing process which utilizes a larger card (approximately 9 by 6 inches) and which also results in reduced positive images of the original printed pages. In both microcards and microprinting, the cards are placed in a reading machine which enlarges and projects the images to the approximate size of the original pages on a ground-glass screen. As a page is completed, the machine provides a means for moving the card to bring the next page into position on the screen.

Sheet microfilm is another process utilizing a flat sheet of film instead of a roll of film. Page images in reduced form are arranged on the flat sheet in a manner similar to the microcard and microprint. Microfiche is the name given to the most popular form, a sheet approximately 6 by 4 inches.

The advantages of these microphotography processes are numerous. The minute reductions in page size make it possible to store thousands of pages, whole series of publications, on only a small amount of film or a small number of cards. When the original printed copies are in danger of becoming worn out through age or use, a microcopy can be made at relatively small cost, much cheaper than reprinting the document or making a photostat copy.

Microform documents also have their disadvantages. They are certainly more easily stored than they are used. Some filing key is necessary in order to locate desired material. In the case of microfilm this can be a problem of real consequence. Microcards and microprints do have subject or author headings to assist in identification. Browsing and scanning are not easy. They are also unsatisfactory if they contain illustrative material, large maps, charts, tables, etc.

The whole problem of training users in the intricacies of the reading machines is complicated by the fact that the images projected on the screens are not too good. Great improvements have been made in the reading machines, but still further improvements will have to be made before the quality approaches the original document. Where readers have the option of using the printed original or the microform, the present evidence indicates that the choice favors the original on almost every occasion. As a new generation grows up perhaps this situation will be changed, but at present microcopies will apparently be consulted only when the printed document is not available. For this reason, some librarians hesitate to discard printed documents even though they have purchased a microedition. Where storage space is at a premium, the librarian will usually have to dispose of the printed copy where a microcopy is available. Of course, the greatest use of microeditions is where the printed editions were never available to the library.

The Superintendent of Documents has issued instructions to all designated depository libraries permitting the substitution of microform copies for any holdings of United States government publications. The microcopies must be purchased by the depository, as the Superintendent of Documents has no funds available for the purpose of supplying microcopies to depositories. However, libraries which serve as depositories for the Atomic Energy Commission receive nearly all of their collection in microform.

Availability of Microform Government Documents

Documents are available from commercial sources in various microcopy forms. The documents offered are usually long document series, the mass output of an agency and, most inclusive, the microprint edition of the United States government publications published by Readex Microprint Corporation. This microprint edition is issued in two convenient sections: the Depository Publications and the Nondepository Publications. The arrangement of the material in each of these sections is by the entry number under which each publication is listed in the *Monthly Catalog*. This arrangement was chosen because the monthly, annual, and cumulative indexes of the *Monthly Catalog* also serve as an index to the microprint edition. The Readex Microprints for February 1959 were the first to contain press releases.

A number of government libraries will make individual microfilms of any document in their collections not containing copyrighted material. Some libraries contain unpublished government documents which are of particular interest to some researchers.

The addresses of the principal publishers of microform copies of government publications are as follows:

Photoduplication Service, Library of Congress, Washington, D.C. 20540.
National Agricultural Library, Washington, D.C. 20250.
Director, Bureau of the Census, Suitland, Md. 20233.
Bureau of Land Management, Department of the Interior, Washington, D.C. 20240.
Director, National Library of Medicine, Washington, D.C. 20014.
United States National Archives and Records Service, Washington, D.C. 20408.
Clearinghouse for Federal Scientific and Technical Information, Springfield, Va. 22151.
Readex Microprint Corporation, 5 Union Square, New York, N.Y. 10003
University Microfilms, Inc., 300 North Zeeb Road, Ann Arbor, Mich. 48107.
ERIC Document Reproduction Service, The National Cash Register Co., Box 2206, Rockville, Md. 20852.
Lawyers' Co-operative Publishing Co., Rochester, N.Y. 14603.
J. S. Canner & Co., 618 Parker Street, Boston, Mass. 02120.
Godfrey Memorial Library, Middletown, Conn. 06457.
Hoover Institution on War, Revolution, and Peace, Stanford University, Stanford, Calif. 94305.
Microcard Editions, Inc., 901 26th Street, N.W., Washington, D.C. 20037.
Micro Photo Division, Bell and Howell Co., 1700 Shaw Avenue, Cleveland, Ohio 44112.
Princeton Microfilm Corp., P.O. Box 235, Princeton, N.J. 08540
Photographic Service, New York Public Library, Fifth Avenue and 42nd Street, New York, N.Y. 10018.

The volume of government publications available in microform has grown to large proportions and is ever increasing. A complete listing in this chapter is not feasible. Over 400 government documents are listed in *Guide to Microforms in Print, 1967*, edited by Albert James Diaz, Microcard Editions, Inc., Washington, D.C., 1967 (111 pages). The same editor and publisher have issued *Subject Guide to Microforms in Print, 1966–*

67, 1966 (110 pages). Some of the publishers in the list above have issued catalogs which include government documents, and some government agencies have also published lists. *List of National Archives Microfilm Publications,* 1968 (108 pages), has been published by the National Archives and Records Service. The same agency has also issued *Federal Population Censuses 1790–1890,* 1966 (154 pages). *Library of Congress Publications in Print,* 1968 (38 pages), includes microform publications and the sources from which such publications may be obtained.

LIST OF DEPOSITORY LIBRARIES

Libraries that were designated depositories of government publications on July 1, 1968, are listed below:

Alabama

Alexander City—Alexander City State Junior College

Auburn—Auburn University

Birmingham

Birmingham-Southern College

Public Library

Samford University

Enterprise—Enterprise State Junior College

Florence—Florence State College

Gadsden—Public Library

Huntsville—University of Alabama, Huntsville Campus

Jacksonville—Jacksonville State University

Maxwell Air Force Base—Air University Library

Mobile

Public Library

Spring Hill College

University of South Alabama

Montgomery

State Department of Archives and History

Supreme Court Library

Normal—Alabama Agricultural and Mechanical College

St. Bernard—St. Bernard College

Troy—Troy State College

Tuskegee Institute—Hollis Burke Frissell Library

University—University of Alabama

Alaska

Anchorage

Anchorage Community College

Anchorage Methodist University

College—University of Alaska

Juneau—Alaska State Library

Arizona

Flagstaff—Northern Arizona University

Phoenix

Department of Library and Archives

Public Library

Prescott—Prescott College Library

Tempe—Arizona State University

Thatcher—Eastern Arizona Junior College

Tucson—University of Arizona

Yuma—City-County Library

465

Arkansas
  Arkadelphia—Ouachita Baptist
    University
  Batesville—Arkansas College
  Clarksville—College of the
    Ozarks
  College Heights—Arkansas Ag-
    ricultural and Mechanical
    College
  Conway—Hendrix College
  Fayetteville—University of
    Arkansas
  Little Rock
    Arkansas Supreme Court
      Library
    Public Library
  Magnolia—Southern State
    College
  Russellville—Arkansas Polytech-
    nic College
  Searcy—Harding College
  State College—Arkansas State
    University
  Walnut Ridge—Southern Baptist
    College
California
  Anaheim—Public Library
  Arcata—Humboldt State College
  Bakersfield—Kern County
    Library
  Berkeley
    University of California,
      General Library
    University of California, Law
      Library
  Chico—Chico State College
  Claremont—Pomona College
  Culver City—City Library
  Davis—University of California
  Downey—City Library
  Fresno
    County Free Library
    Fresno State College

  Fullerton—California State Col-
    lege at Fullerton
  Gardena—Public Library
  Hayward—California State Col-
    lege at Hayward
  Inglewood—Public Library
  Irvine—University of California
    at Irvine
  La Jolla—University of California,
    San Diego
  Lancaster—Regional Library
  Long Beach
    California State College at
      Long Beach
    Public Library
  Los Angeles
    California State College at
      Los Angeles
    County Law Library
    Loyola University of Los
      Angeles
    Occidental College
    Pepperdine College
    Public Library
    University of California at Los
      Angeles
    University of California,
      School of Law
    University of Southern Cali-
      fornia
  Lynwood—Lynwood Library
  Marysville—Yuba College
  Menlo Park—Department of the
    Interior, Geological Survey
    Library
  Montebello—Montebello Library
  Monterey—Naval Postgraduate
    School
  Monterey Park—Bruggemeyer
    Memorial Library
  Newhall—Newhall Library of
    Los Angeles County

Northridge—San Fernando Valley State College
Oakland
    Mills College
    Public Library
Orange—Public Library
Pasadena
    California Institute of Technology
    Public Library
Pleasant Hill—Contra Costa County Library
Redding—Shasta County Library
Redlands—University of Redlands
Redwood City—Public Library
Reseda—West Valley Regional Branch Library
Richmond—Public Library
Riverside
    Public Library
    University of California at Riverside
Sacramento
    California State Library
    City Library
    County Law Library
    Sacramento State College
San Bernardino—County Free Library
San Diego
    County Library
    Public Library
    San Diego State College
    University of San Diego Law Library
San Francisco
    Mechanics' Institute
    Public Library
    San Francisco State College
    University of San Francisco
San Jose—San Jose State College

San Leandro—San Leandro Community Library Center
Santa Ana—Public Library
Santa Barbara—University of California at Santa Barbara
Santa Clara—University of Santa Clara
Santa Cruz—University of California at Santa Cruz
Santa Rosa—Santa Rosa/Sonoma County Public Library
Stanford—Stanford University
Stockton—Public Library
Thousand Oaks—California Lutheran College
Turlock—Stanislaus State College
Visalia—Tulare County Free Library
Walnut—Mount San Antonio College
West Covina—West Covina Library
Whittier—Whittier College

Canal Zone
    Balboa Heights—Canal Zone Library-Museum

Colorado
    Alamosa—Adams State College
    Boulder—University of Colorado
    Colorado Springs—Colorado College
    Denver
        Colorado State Library
        Department of Interior, Bureau of Reclamation Library
        Public Library
        Regis College
        University of Denver
    Fort Collins—Colorado State University

Golden—Colorado School of
Mines
Greeley—Colorado State College
Gunnison—Western State
College
La Junta—Otero Junior College
Pueblo
McClelland Public Library
Southern Colorado State
College
United States Air Force
Academy—Academy
Library

Connecticut
Bridgeport—Public Library
Danbury—Western Connecticut
State College
Hartford
Connecticut State Library
Public Library
Trinity College Library
Middletown—Wesleyan
University
Mystic—Mystic Seaport Library
New Haven
Southern Connecticut State
College
Yale University
New London
Connecticut College
United States Coast Guard
Academy
Storrs—University of
Connecticut
Thompsonville—Enfield Public
Library
Waterbury—Silas Bronson
Library

Delaware
Dover
Delaware State College
State Law Library in Kent
County

Newark—University of Delaware
Wilmington—Wilmington
Institute

District of Columbia
Bureau of the Budget
Civil Service Commission
Department of Commerce
Department of Health, Educa-
tion, and Welfare
Department of the Interior,
Central Library
Department of the Interior, Geo-
logical Survey Library
Department of Justice
Department of State
Department of State, Law
Library
Department of Transportation,
National Highway Safety
Bureau Library
District of Columbia Public
Library
National Agricultural Library
National War College
Navy Department
Navy Department, Office of
Judge Advocate General
Post Office Department
Treasury Department
Veterans Administration, Medi-
cal and General Reference
Library

Florida
Boca Raton—Florida Atlantic
University
Coral Gables—University of
Miami
Daytona Beach—Volusia County
Public Libraries
De Land—Stetson University
Fort Lauderdale
Nova University
Public Library

Gainesville—University of
Florida
Jacksonville
Haydon Burns Library
Jacksonville University
Lakeland—Public Library
Leesburg—Lake-Sumter Junior
College
Melbourne—Florida Institute of
Technology
Miami
Miami-Dade Junior College
Public Library
Opa Locka—Biscayne College
Orlando—Florida Technological
University
Palatka—St. Johns River Junior
College
Pensacola—University of West
Florida
St. Petersburg—Public Library
Tallahassee
Florida Agricultural and Me-
chanical University
Florida State Library
Florida State University
Tampa
Public Library
University of South Florida
University of Tampa
Winter Park—Rollins College

Georgia
Albany—Public Library
Americus—Georgia Southwestern
College
Athens—University of Georgia
Atlanta
Atlanta University
Emory University
Emory University, School of
Law
Georgia Institute of
Technology

Georgia State Library
Public Library
Augusta—Augusta College
Brunswick—Public Library
Carrollton—West Georgia
College
Dahlonega—North Georgia
College
Gainesville—Chestatee Regional
Library
Macon—Mercer University
Marietta—Kennesaw Junior
College
Milledgeville—Georgia College
at Milledgeville
Savannah—Savannah Public and
Chatham-Effingham-Liberty
Regional Library
Statesboro—Georgia Southern
College
Valdosta—Valdosta State College

Guam
Agana—Nieves M. Flores Memorial Library

Hawaii
Hilo—University of Hawaii
Honolulu
Chaminade College of
Honolulu
Hawaii Medical Library
Hawaii State Library
Municipal Reference Library
University of Hawaii
University of Hawaii, Com-
munity College System
Library
Laie—Church College of Hawaii
Lihue—Kauai Public Library
Wailuku—Maui Public Library

Idaho
Boise
Boise College
Idaho State Law Library
Public Library

Caldwell—College of Idaho
Moscow—University of Idaho
Pocatello—Idaho State
    University
Rexburg—Ricks College
Illinois
Bloomington—Illinois Wesleyan
    University
Carbondale—Southern Illinois
    University
Carlinville—Blackburn College
Champaign—University of Illinois Law Library
Charleston—Eastern Illinois
    University
Chicago
    Chicago State College
    Field Museum of Natural
        History Library
    John Crerar Library
    Loyola University
    Newberry Library
    Northeastern Illinois State
        College
    Public Library
    University of Chicago
    University of Chicago, Law
        Library
    University of Illinois, Chicago
        Circle Campus
Decatur—Public Library
De Kalb—Northern Illinois
    University
Edwardsville—Southern Illinois
    University
Elsah—Principia College
Evanston—Northwestern
    University
Freeport—Public Library
Galesburg—Public Library
Jacksonville—MacMurray
    College

Kankakee—Olivet Nazarene
    College
Lake Forest—Lake Forest
    College
Lebanon—McKendree College
Lisle—St. Procopius College
Lockport—Lewis College of
    Science and Technology
Macomb—Western Illinois
    University
Monmouth—Monmouth College
Normal—Illinois State University
Oak Park—Public Library
Peoria
    Bradley University
    Public Library
River Forest—Rosary College
Rock Island—Public Library
Rockford—Public Library
Springfield—Illinois State
    Library
Urbana—University of Illinois
Wheaton—Wheaton College
Woodstock—Public Library
Indiana
Anderson—Anderson College
Bloomington—Indiana University
Crawfordsville—Wabash College
Evansville—Public Library
Fort Wayne
    Indiana-Purdue Universities,
        Regional Campus
    Public Library
Gary
    Indiana University, Northwest
        Campus
    Public Library
Greencastle—De Pauw
    University
Hammond—Public Library
Hanover—Hanover College
Huntington—Huntington College

Indianapolis
  Butler University
  Indiana State Library
  Indiana University, Law
    Library
  Public Library
Jeffersonville—Indiana University, Southeastern Campus
Lafayette—Purdue University
Muncie
  Ball State University
  Public Library
Notre Dame—University of
  Notre Dame
Rensselaer—St. Joseph's College
Richmond
  Earlham College
  Morrison-Reeves Library
South Bend—Indiana University,
  South Bend-Mishawaka
  Campus
Terre Haute—Indiana State
  University
Valparaiso—Valparaiso
  University

Iowa
  Ames—Iowa State University
  Cedar Falls—University of
    Northern Iowa
  Council Bluffs—Public Library
  Denison—Midwestern College
  Des Moines
    Drake University
    Iowa State Traveling Library
    Public Library
  Dubuque
    Loras College
    Public Library
  Fairfield—Parsons College
  Grinnell—Grinnell College
  Iowa City—University of Iowa
  Lamoni—Graceland College
  Mount Vernon—Cornell College

Sioux City—Public Library
Kansas
  Atchison—St. Benedict's College
  Baldwin City—Baker University
  Colby—Colby Community Junior
    College
  Emporia—Kansas State Teachers
    College
  Hays—Fort Hays Kansas State
    College
  Hutchinson—Public Library
  Lawrence—University of Kansas
  Manhattan—Kansas State
    University
  Pittsburg—Kansas State College
    of Pittsburg
  Salina—Kansas Wesleyan
    University
  Topeka
    Kansas State Historical Society Library
    State Libraries of Kansas
  Wichita—Wichita State
    University
Kentucky
  Ashland—Public Library
  Barbourville—Union College
  Bowling Green—Western Kentucky University
  Danville—Centre College
  Frankfort
    Kentucky Department of
      Libraries
    State Law Library
  Lexington—University of
    Kentucky
  Louisville
    Public Library
    University of Louisville
  Morehead—Morehead State
    University
  Murray—Murray State
    University

Owensboro—Kentucky Wesleyan
College
Pikeville—Pikeville College
Richmond—Eastern Kentucky
University
Louisiana
Baton Rouge
Louisiana State University
Louisiana State University,
Law Library
Southern University
Hammond—Southeastern
Louisiana
Lafayette—University of South-
western Louisiana
Lake Charles—McNeese State
College
Monroe—Northeast Louisiana
State College
Natchitoches—Northwestern
State College of
Louisiana
New Orleans
Isaac Delgado College
Law Library of Louisiana
Louisiana State University in
New Orleans
Loyola University
Public Library
Southern University in New
Orleans
Tulane University
Ruston—Louisiana Polytechnic
Institute
Shreveport
Louisiana State University at
Shreveport
Shreve Memorial Library
Thibodaux—Francis T. Nicholls
State College
Maine
Augusta—Maine State Library
Bangor—Public Library
Brunswick—Bowdoin College

Lewiston—Bates College
Orono—University of Maine
Portland
Public Library
University of Maine Law
Library
Springvale—Nasson College
Waterville—Colby College
Maryland
Annapolis
Maryland State Library
United States Naval Academy
Baltimore
Enoch Pratt Free Library
Johns Hopkins University
Morgan State College
Bel Air—Harford Junior College
Bethesda—Montgomery County
Department of Public
Libraries
Chestertown—Washington
College
College Park—University of
Maryland
Frostburg—Frostburg State
College
Germantown—Atomic Energy
Commission
Salisbury—Salisbury State
College
Towson—Goucher College
Westminster—Western Maryland
College
Massachusetts
Amherst
Amherst College
University of Massachusetts
Boston
Boston Athenaeum
Boston College
Northeastern University
Public Library
State Library of Massa-
chusetts

Brookline—Public Library
Cambridge
  Harvard College
  Massachusetts Institute of
    Technology
Lowell—Lowell Technological
  Institute
Lynn—Public Library
Medford—Tufts University
New Bedford—Public Library
North Dartmouth—Southeastern
  Massachusetts Technological
  Institute
North Easton—Stonehill College
Springfield—City Library
Waltham—Brandeis University
Wellesley—Wellesley College
Wenham—Gordon College
Williamstown—Williams College
Worcester
  American Antiquarian Society
  Public Library

Michigan
Albion—Albion College
Allendale—Grand Valley State
  College
Alma—Alma College
Ann Arbor—University of
  Michigan
Battle Creek—Willard Library
Benton Harbor—Public Library
Bloomfield Hills—Cranbrook
  Institute of Science
Dearborn—Henry Ford Commu-
  nity College
Detroit
  Marygrove College
  Mercy College of Detroit
  Public Library
  University of Detroit
  Wayne County Public Library
  Wayne State University
East Lansing—Michigan State
  University

Escanaba—Michigan State
  Library
Farmington—Oakland Commu-
  nity College
Flint
  Charles Stewart Mott Library
  Public Library
Grand Rapids
  Knollcrest Calvin Library
  Public Library
Houghton—Michigan Techno-
  logical University
Jackson—Public Library
Kalamazoo
  Kalamazoo Library System
  Western Michigan University
Lansing—Michigan State Library
Livonia—Schoolcraft College
Marquette—Northern Michigan
  University
Mt. Clemens—Macomb County
  Library
Mt. Pleasant—Central Michigan
  University
Muskegon—Hackley Public
  Library
Petoskey—North Central Mich-
  igan College
Port Huron—Saint Clair County
  Library System
Rochester—Oakland University
Saginaw—Hoyt Public Library
Traverse City—Northwestern
  Michigan College
University Center—Delta College
Ypsilanti—Eastern Michigan
  University

Minnesota
Bemidji—Bemidji State College
Collegeville—St. John's
  University
Duluth—Public Library
Mankato—Mankato State College

Minneapolis
Public Library
University of Minnesota
Moorhead—Moorhead State
College
Morris—University of Minnesota
Northfield
Carleton College
St. Olaf College
St. Cloud—St. Cloud State
College
St. Paul
Minnesota Historical Society
Minnesota State Law Library
Public Library
Saint Peter—Gustavus Adolphus
College
Stillwater—Public Library
Willmar—Kandiyohi County-
Wilmar Library

Mississippi
Columbus—Mississippi State
College for Women
Hattiesburg—University of
Southern Mississippi
Jackson
Jackson State College
Millsaps College
Mississippi Library
Commission
Mississippi State Law
Library
State College—Mississippi State
University
University
University of Mississippi
University of Mississippi,
School of Law

Missouri
Cape Girardeau—Southeast Mis-
souri State College
Columbia—University of
Missouri
Fayette—Central Methodist
College

Fulton—Westminster College
Hannibal—Public Library
Jefferson City
Lincoln University
Missouri State Library
Missouri Supreme Court
Library
Joplin—Missouri Southern State
College
Kansas City
Public Library
Rockhurst College
University of Missouri at
Kansas City
Kirksville—Northeast Missouri
State Teachers College
Liberty—William Jewell College
Rolla—University of Missouri at
Rolla
St. Joseph—Public Library
St. Louis
Public Library
St. Louis University Law
Library
St. Louis University
University of Missouri at St.
Louis
Washington University
Springfield
Drury College
Southwest Missouri State
College
Warrensburg—Central Missouri
State College

Montana
Billings—Eastern Montana Col-
lege Library
Bozeman—Montana State
University
Butte—Montana College of Min-
eral Science and Technology
Helena
Montana Historical Society
Montana State Library

Missoula—University of Montana
Library
Nebraska
Blair—Dana College
Crete—Doane College
Fremont—Midland Lutheran
College
Kearney—Kearney State College
Lincoln
Nebraska State Library
University of Nebraska
Omaha
Creighton University
Public Library
University of Omaha
Scottsbluff—Public Library
Nevada
Carson City—Nevada State
Library
Las Vegas—Nevada Southern
University
Reno—University of Nevada
New Hampshire
Concord—New Hampshire State
Library
Durham—University of New
Hampshire
Hanover—Dartmouth College
Henniker—New England College
Manchester
City Library
St. Anselm's College
New Jersey
Atlantic City—Public Library
Bayonne—Public Library
Bloomfield—Public Library
Bridgeton—Cumberland County
Library
Camden—Rutgers Library in
South Jersey
Convent Station—College of St.
Elizabeth
East Orange—Public Library
Elizabeth—Public Library

Freehold—Monmouth County
Library
Glassboro—Glassboro State
College
Hackensack—Johnson Free Public Library
Irvington—Public Library
Jersey City
Jersey City State College
Public Library
Madison—Drew University
Mount Holly—Burlington
County Library
New Brunswick
Public Library
Rutgers University
Newark
Public Library
Rutgers—The State University
Passaic—Public Library
Princeton—Princeton University
Rutherford—Fairleigh Dickinson
University
South Orange—Seton Hall
University
Teaneck—Fairleigh Dickinson
University, Teaneck
Campus
Toms River—Ocean County
College
Trenton
New Jersey State Library
Public Library
Upper Montclair—Montclair
State College
West Long Branch—Monmouth
College
West New York—Public Library
Woodbridge—Public Library
New Mexico
Albuquerque—University of New
Mexico
Las Cruces—New Mexico State
University

Las Vegas—New Mexico High-
lands University
Portales—Eastern New Mexico
University
Sante Fe
New Mexico State Library
Supreme Court Law Library
New York
Albany
New York State Library
State University of New York
at Albany
Binghamton—State University of
New York at Binghamton
Brockport—State University of
New York
Bronx—Hunter College at Bronx
Brooklyn
Brooklyn College
Polytechnic Institute of
Brooklyn
Pratt Institute
Public Library
State University of New York,
Downstate Medical Center
Buffalo
Buffalo and Erie County
Public Library
State University of New York
at Buffalo
Canton—St. Lawrence University
Corning—Corning Community
College
Cortland—State University of
New York, College at
Cortland
Elmira—Elmira College
Farmingdale—State University of
New York at Farmingdale
Flushing—Queens College
Garden City
Adelphi University
Nassau Library System

Genessee—State University
College
Greenvale—C. W. Post College
Hamilton—Colgate University
Hempstead—Hofstra University
Huntington—Public Library
Ithaca
Cornell University
New York State Colleges of
Agriculture and Home
Economics
Jamaica
Queens Borough Public
Library
St. John's University
Kings Point—United States Mer-
chant Marine Academy
Mount Vernon—Public Library
New Paltz—State University
College
New York City
City University of New York
College of Insurance
Columbia University
Cooper Union
Fordham University
New York Law Institute
Public Library (Astor
Branch)
Public Library (Lenox
Branch)
New York University
State University of New York,
Maritime College
Newburgh—Free Library
Oakdale—Adelphi Suffolk
College
Oneonta—State University
College
Oswego—State University
College
Plattsburgh—State University
College

Potsdam
  Clarkson College of
    Technology
  State University College
Poughkeepsie—Vassar College
Rochester
  Public Library
  University of Rochester
St. Bonaventure—St. Bona-
  venture College
Saratoga Springs—Skidmore
  College
Schenectady—Union College
Staten Island (Grymes Hill)—
  Wagner College
Stony Brook—State University
  of New York
Syracuse—Syracuse University
Troy—Public Library
Utica—Public Library
West Point—United States
  Military Academy
Yonkers—Public Library

North Carolina
Asheville—Asheville-Biltmore
  College
Boone—Appalachian State
  University
Buies Creek—Campbell College
Chapel Hill—University of
  North Carolina
Charlotte
  Public Library
  Queens College
  University of North Carolina
    at Charlotte
Cullowhee—Western Carolina
  University
Davidson—Davidson College
Durham—Duke University
Greensboro
  North Carolina Agricultural

  and Technical State
    University
  University of North Carolina
    at Greensboro
Greenville—East Carolina
  University
Mars Hill—Mars Hill College
Murfreesboro—Chowan College
Pembroke—Pembroke State
  College
Raleigh
  North Carolina State
  North Carolina State
    University
Salisbury—Catawba College
Wilmington—Wilmington
  College
Wilson—Atlantic Christian
  College
Winston-Salem
  Public Library
  Wake Forest University

North Dakota
Bismarck
  North Dakota State Histori-
    cal Society
  North Dakota State Law
    Library
  Public Library
Fargo
  North Dakota State
    University
  Public Library
Grand Forks—University of
  North Dakota
Minot—Minot State College
Richardton—Assumption College
Valley City—State College

Ohio
Ada—Ohio Northern University
Akron
  Public Library
  University of Akron

Alliance—Mount Union College
Ashland—Ashland College
Athens—Ohio University
Bluffton—Bluffton College
Bowling Green—Bowling Green
State University
Chillicothe—Ohio University at
Chillicothe
Cincinnati
Public Library
University of Cincinnati
Cleveland
Case Western Reserve
University
Cleveland State University
John Carroll University
Public Library
Columbus
Capital University
Ohio State Library
Ohio State University
Public Library
Dayton
Public Library
Wright State University
Delaware—Ohio Wesleyan
University
Elyria—Public Library
Gambier—Kenyon College
Granville—Denison University
Hiram—Hiram College
Kent—Kent State University
Marietta—Marietta College
New Concord—Muskingum
College
Oberlin—Oberlin College
Oxford—Miami University
Portsmouth—Public Library
Rio Grande—Rio Grande College
Springfield—Warder Public
Library
Steubenville—Public Library
Tiffin—Heidelberg College

Toledo
Toledo Public Library
University of Toledo Library
Van Wert—Brumback Library
of Van Wert County
Westerville—Otterbein College,
Centennial Library
Wooster—College of Wooster,
the Andrews Library
Youngstown—Public Library of
Youngstown and Mahoning
County
Oklahoma
Ada—East Central State College
Alva—Northwestern State
College
Bartlesville—Bureau of Mines,
Petroleum Research Center
Durant—Southeastern State
College
Edmond—Central State College
Enid—Public Library
Langston—Langston University
Norman—University of
Oklahoma
Oklahoma City
Oklahoma City University
Oklahoma Department of
Libraries
Shawnee—Oklahoma Baptist
University
Stillwater—Oklahoma State
University
Tahlequah—Northeastern State
College
Tulsa
City-County Library
Commission
University of Tulsa
Weatherford—Southwestern
State College
Oregon
Ashland—Southern Oregon
College

Corvallis—Oregon State
University
Eugene—University of Oregon
Forest Grove—Pacific University
La Grande—Eastern Oregon
College
McMinnville—Linfield
College
Monmouth—Oregon College of
Education
Portland
Department of the Interior,
Bonneville Power
Administration
Lewis and Clark College
Library Association of
Portland
Portland State College
Reed College
Salem—Oregon State
Pennsylvania
Allentown—Muhlenberg
College
Bethlehem—Lehigh University
Bradford—Carnegie Public
Library
Carlisle—Dickinson College
Cheyney—Cheyney State
College
Collegeville—Ursinus College
East Stroudsburg—East Strouds-
burg State College
Erie—Public Library
Greenville—Thiel College
Harrisburg—Pennsylvania State
Library
Haverford—Haverford College
Hazleton—Public Library
Indiana—Indiana University of
Pennsylvania
Johnstown—Cambria Public
Library
Lancaster—Franklin and
Marshall College

Lewisburg—Bucknell University
Mansfield—Mansfield State
College
Meadville—Allegheny College
Millersville—Millersville State
College
New Castle—Public Library
Newton—Bucks County Com-
munity College
Philadelphia
Drexel Institute of
Technology
Free Library of Philadelphia
Temple University
University of Pennsylvania
Pittsburgh
Bureau of Mines, Pittsburgh
Research Center
Carnegie Library of
Pittsburgh
Carnegie Library of Pitts-
burgh, Allegheny Branch
University of Pittsburgh
Pottsville—Public Library
Reading—Public Library
Scranton—Public Library
Slippery Rock—Slippery Rock
State College
Swarthmore—Swarthmore
College
University Park—Pennsylvania
State University
Villanova—Villanova University
Warren—Public Library
Washington—Washington and
Jefferson College
Waynesburg—Waynesburg
College
West Chester—West Chester
State College
Wilkes-Barre—King's College
Williamsport—James V. Brown
Library
York—York Junior College

Puerto Rico
Mayaguez—University of Puerto Rico
Ponce—Catholic University of Puerto Rico
Rio Piedras—University of Puerto Rico
Rhode Island
Kingston—University of Rhode Island
Newport—Naval War College
Providence
  Brown University
  Public Library
  Rhode Island College
  Rhode Island State Library
Warwick—Public Library
Westerly—Public Library
South Carolina
Charleston
  Baptist College of Charleston
  College of Charleston
  The Citadel
Clemson—Clemson University
Columbia
  Columbia College
  South Carolina State Library
  University of South Carolina
Due West—Erskine College
Florence—County Library
Greenville
  County Library
  Furman University
Greenwood—Lander College
Orangeburg—South Carolina State College
Rock Hill—Winthrop College
Spartanburg—Public Library
South Dakota
Aberdeen—Northern State College
Brookings—South Dakota State University

Rapid City
  Public Library
  South Dakota School of Mines and Technology
Sioux Falls—Public Library
Spearfish—Black Hills State College
Vermillion—University of South Dakota
Yankton—Yankton College
Tennessee
Chattanooga—Public Library
Clarksville—Austin Peay State University
Jackson—Lambuth College
Jefferson City—Carson-Newman College
Johnson City—East Tennessee State University
Knoxville—University of Tennessee
Martin—University of Tennessee at Martin
Memphis
  Cossitt Reference Library
  Memphis State University
Murfreesboro—Middle Tennessee State University
Nashville
  Fisk University
  Joint University Libraries
  Public Library
  Tennessee State Library and Archives
Sewanee—University of the South
Texas
Abilene—Hardin-Simmons University
Arlington—University of Texas at Arlington
Austin
  Texas State Library

University of Texas
University of Texas, Lyndon
B. Johnson Institute of Public Service
University of Texas, School
of Law
Beaumont—Lamar State College
of Technology
Brownwood—Howard Payne
College
Canyon—West Texas State
University
College Station—Texas Agricultural and Mechanical
University
Commerce—East Texas State
University
Corsicana—Navarro Junior
College
Dallas
Bishop College
Dallas Baptist College
Public Library
Southern Methodist University
Denton—North Texas State
University
Edinburg—Pan American
College
El Paso
Public Library
University of Texas at El
Paso
Fort Worth
Public Library
Texas Christian University
Galveston—Rosenberg Library
Houston
Public Library
Rice University
University of Houston
Huntsville—Sam Houston State
College

Kingsville—Texas Arts and Industries University
Longview—Public Library
Lubbock—Texas Technological
College
Marshall—Wiley College
Nacogdoches—Stephen F. Austin State College
Plainview—Wayland Baptist
College
San Angelo—Angelo State
College
San Antonio
Public Library
St. Mary's University
Trinity University
San Marcos—Southwest Texas
State College
Sherman—Austin College
Texarkana—Texarkana College
Waco—Baylor University
Wichita Falls—Midwestern
University
Utah
Cedar City—College of Southern
Utah
Ephraim—Snow College
Logan—Utah State University
Ogden—Weber State College
Provo—Brigham Young
University
Salt Lake City
University of Utah
University of Utah, Law
Library
Utah State Library
Commission
Vermont
Burlington—University of
Vermont
Johnson—Johnson State College
Middlebury—Middlebury
College

Montpelier—Vermont State
Library
Northfield—Norwich University
Putney—Windham College
Virgin Islands
Charlotte Amalie—St. Thomas
Public Library
Virginia
Blacksburg—Virginia Polytechnic Institute
Bridgewater—Bridgewater
College
Charlottesville
University of Virginia
University of Virginia Law Library
Emory—Emory and Henry College
Fairfax—George Mason College
Fredericksburg—Mary Washington College
Hampden-Sydney—Hampden-Sydney College
Hollins College—Hollins College
Lexington
Virginia Military Institute
Washington and Lee University
Norfolk
Armed Forces Staff College
Old Dominion College
Public Library
Petersburg—Virginia State College
Quantico—Marine Corps Schools
Richmond
University of Richmond
Virginia State Library
Roanoke—Public Library
Salem—Roanoke College
Williamsburg—William   and
Mary College

Washington
Bellingham—Western Washington State College
Cheney—Eastern Washington
State College
Ellensburg—Central Washington State College
Everett—Public Library
Olympia—Washington State Library
Port Angeles—Public Library
Pullman—Washington State University
Seattle
Public Library
University of Washington
Spokane—Public Library
Tacoma
Public Library
University of Puget Sound
Vancouver—Fort Vancouver Regional Library
Walla Walla—Whitman College
West Virginia
Athens—Concord College
Charleston
Public Library
West Virginia Department of
Archives and History
Elkins—Davis and Elkins College
Fairmont—Fairmont State College
Glenville—Glenville State
College
Huntington—Marshall University
Institute—West Virginia State
College
Morgantown—West Virginia University
Salem—Salem College
Weirton—Public College

Wisconsin
  Appleton—Lawrence University
  Beloit—Beloit College
  Eau Claire—Wisconsin State University
  Fond du Lac—Public Library
  Green Bay—University of Wisconsin at Green Bay
  La Crosse
    Public Library
    Wisconsin State University
  Madison
    Department of Public Instruction, Division for Library Services
    Public Library
    State Historical Society Library
    University of Wisconsin
    Wisconsin State Library
  Milwaukee
    Milwaukee County Law Library
    Public Library
    Mount Mary College
    Oklahoma Neighborhood Library

  University of Wisconsin—Milwaukee
  Oshkosh—Wisconsin State University
  Platteville—Wisconsin State University
  Racine—Public Library
  River Falls—Wisconsin State University
  Stevens Point—Wisconsin State University
  Superior
    Public Library
    Wisconsin State University
  Waukesha—Public Library
  Whitewater—Wisconsin State University

Wyoming
  Casper—Natrona County Public Library
  Cheyenne—Wyoming State Library
  Laramie—University of Wyoming
  Powell—Northwest Community College
  Sheridan—Sheridan College

INDEX

485